DEPARTMENT OF HEALTH AND SOCIAL SECURITY

A refuge for
Battered women

A study of the rôle of a women's centre

London: Her Majesty's Stationery Office

HER MAJESTY'S STATIONERY OFFICE

Government Bookshops

49 High Holborn, London WC1V 6HB
13a Castle Street, Edinburgh EH2 3AR
41 The Hayes, Cardiff CF1 1JW
Brazennose Street, Manchester M60 8AS
Southey House, Wine Street, Bristol BS1 2BQ
258 Broad Street, Birmingham B1 2HE
80 Chichester Street, Belfast BT1 4JY

Government Publications are also available through booksellers

ISBN 0 11 320350 0

Contents

Summary

The project described in this report was carried out for the Department of Health and Social Security between January and December 1976. It is concerned with the Canterbury Women's Centre, from its opening in November 1975 to November 1976.

The aim of the study was, first, to monitor the setting up and development of the Centre and, secondly, to evaluate the assistance it offered to the women who stayed there.

The study was carried out by a combination of a variant of participant observation and of more formal interviewing. Twenty-five of the women who stayed at the Centre, and nine of the women who set the Centre up, were interviewed. These interviews provided detailed information. The report also presents outline information on all the women who stayed at the refuge while the study was going on.

The Canterbury Women's Centre was set up according to principles which are similar to those adopted by many Women's Aid refuges. These principles include: the encouragement of self-help and mutual support among the women living in the Centre; the sharing of power among all those concerned with the Centre; and the open door policy.

Forty-two of the women had no children with them, either because they were childless or because their children were elsewhere. Some were single women, and the existence of the Centre revealed the extent of the problem of single homeless women in the area.

The needs of battered women, whether with or without children, were summarized under four main headings. These were: protection, accommodation, support and advice. The study shows that the Centre did cater for many of these needs.

The Centre was used by women from all over Kent, and not just by those from the immediate area. This has implications for the housing difficulties of the women; three different housing 'routes' which they are likely to take are outlined.

Before coming to the Centre the women had sought help from a variety of sources, both informally from family, friends and neighbours, and more formally from agencies. An 'isolated' group of women had not been able to use informal sources of help and so were dependent on formal sources.

Social workers, the police, doctors and solicitors were most frequently approached for help, but many women felt that they had not received the help they needed. This often seemed to be because the woman's own perception of her problem differed from that of the person whom she was consulting.

The women valued the protection and accommodation which the Centre offered and the support of the other women. Many of them were confused by the ideas of self-help and of power sharing, but it seemed as though these principles did in practice enable some women to regain their self-confidence and self-reliance. Most of the women experienced feelings of personal change during their time at the Centre.

The group of people who set up the Centre were highly motivated. They provided a solution which was in general appropriate to the problem, and which involved a relatively small financial burden to the community. Such a group would best be assisted by making available suitable accommodation for the refuge, and by respecting the autonomy and motivating principles of the group itself.

Acknowledgements

This research was financed by the Department of Health and Social Security and I should like to acknowledge their help.

Many people at the University of Kent have shown interest in the study, and I am grateful for their help. I must also thank all those who helped me at the National Women's Aid Federation, at Chiswick Women's Aid, and at the Canterbury offices of the Kent Area Health Authority, the Kent Social Services, the Kent Police and the Citizen's Advice Bureau.

I feel grateful to Joan Denning and Barbara Holland, who helped with typing, and to Pat Parkinson, who not only did a lot of typing, but who gave me encouragement when I needed it most.

My husband, Ray, has helped me in very many ways, not least in discussing with me most aspects of this report. However, my warmest thanks must go to all at the Canterbury Women's Centre, for their help and support and for all that they have taught me during the past year.

Chapter 1
Introduction

1.1 The initiative for this research came originally from the Department of Health and Social Security. In 1975 the Department was concerned both about the problem of marital violence and about the lack of research which had been undertaken on the subject. Applications for research were invited and I submitted a proposal which I entitled 'The rôle of a Women's Centre in assisting wives with violent husbands'. It was agreed that the study should be an exploratory one in the first instance and should focus on the Canterbury Women's Centre and the women who came to it.

1.2 At the time I put in my proposal the Women's Centre was one week old. The building in which it was housed had been occupied as a squat by the group which set it up, there was considerable local antagonism to the project, and it was not clear how many women would want to use the Centre.

1.3 In the circumstances it seemed realistic to suggest that the study should be run for one year only, and that the direction which the work should take should be reassessed at the end of the time. My other commitments were such that I proposed to spend one-quarter of my time on the study. As the work progressed it became clear that it could, in fact, best be carried out by someone who was working part-time; for example, in order to obtain the sample of twenty-five women it was necessary for the interviewer to be calling regularly at the refuge over a period of nearly five months in order to be there when the women were available to be interviewed. This report represents, therefore, one year's part-time work.

1.4 The study which was undertaken was to be exploratory and it must be emphasized that any conclusions presented here are tentative. Nevertheless, this report does describe what is, I think, the first empirical study which has been done of a women's refuge and of the people who use it and who run it.

1.5 As soon as I began work on the study it became clear that my original proposal was based on certain assumptions which would have to be modified in the light of experience. In my title I had used the words 'wives with violent husbands' but the women who came to the refuge included

1

many who had been beaten-up by the men with whom they were cohabiting and some who were attacked by their ex-husbands. For this reason I have altered the title on this report from that on the original proposal.

1.6 I had also assumed that the new Women's Centre would have a traditional authority structure with an organizing committee, and I had suggested that one focus of the research would be on the relationship between the organizers of the Centre and the representatives of other, more established, statutory and voluntary bodies. However, as the work progressed I became more and more interested in the organizational and normative framework of the refuge itself. It seemed that what was significant was what was happening *within* the Centre; relationships with other bodies were relatively unimportant, and, indeed, it was impossible to understand these relationships unless one understood the Centre itself. Accordingly, I spent a lot of time talking to the people who set the Centre up and participating in the many discussions which took place. It has not been possible to work through the implications of all the data which I gathered. All relevant factual material is presented in this report, but it will take longer to work through all the many ideas which the study has stimulated.

1.7 The project has been successful in many ways. The organization which was the subject of the study has proved to be of great interest and significance. A group of women who have experienced violent relationships have been interviewed once, and, since their present whereabouts is in most cases known to the researcher, would be likely to be available for further interviews.

1.8 The success of the exploratory study has led to the suggestion that a follow-up study should be undertaken which would build on what has been achieved already. The proposal for this was sent to the Department of Health and Social Security in December 1976 and is entitled 'Coping responses to inter-sex violence: a longitudinal study of women who have sought help from a refuge'. The value of follow-up work on specific areas is referred to at various points in this report, and it would seem that a most valuable opportunity exists here to develop some understanding of the problems of these women and their children, not just at one point in time, but over a longer time and in a wider context. Interviewing the woman at the refuge and again after she has left it, will make it possible to attempt some evaluation of the usefulness of the refuge to herself and her children, as well as setting the 'event' of her stay there in the context of her problem or problems.

Chapter 2

The Canterbury Women's Centre

2.1 The Women's Centre was opened on November 3rd 1975, when a group of women squatted in Errol House and announced that they had opened "a women's refuge and support centre". To most people in Canterbury their action was a complete surprise. But to those who set up the Centre it was the logical outcome of many months of frustrated effort to set up just such a place.

2.2 Most of the members of this original group were also members of a radical women's group at the University of Kent, which had approached the Canterbury City Council with a request for accommodation in which to set up a Women's Centre. This request was turned down. Jo, who was a member of this group, described the feelings which prompted the squat in Errol House: "We had all been involved before for two years or so, and had been talking to people about the need for a Women's Centre, which definitely wasn't only just for battered wives ... we hoped to be able to get women coming to a place, talking to other women, maybe working out some ways to reduce the tension of having kids around you all the time, maybe in terms of a crèche or playgroup, or just somewhere to talk to other women." Tess, another member of this original group, described her dissatisfaction with the more intellectual sort of women's group: "I was a bit put off by it. They weren't out to reach the grassroots problems. They were very much sitting round discussing within their own circle problems and they were not really getting out to the grassroots of the actual people." J.M.P.: "Who do you mean by the actual people?" "The ordinary housewives, who are restricted. They were all university students or ex-university students and I really thought they were just keeping within their own circle and weren't going out. It's very hard to just go out, particularly if you are a student type because they know you are a student type."

2.3 Many of the women in the original group were also members of a squatters' association and this, too, was concerned about doing something for the wider community. As Jo said, "The Squatters' Group was looking for more than just putting people into squats – it was looking at problems in Canterbury, homelessness problems, and was trying to find out ways in

3

which the Squatters' Group could expand itself, take on larger projects or something."

2.4 The original group, then, was motivated mainly by ideas about the position of women in society and by a desire to break out of the isolation of their life as students at the university. Experience of squatting gave them a way of putting their ideas into practice. The house they chose was ideally suited for the purpose. It was a large old house in the centre of the city and two doors away from the Social Services office. At the time, it was in the hands of the Official Receiver; its previous owner had bought it to use for offices but had not been allowed to do so because it was a listed building and had a preservation order on it. On the ground floor of the house were two communal rooms, an office, a kitchen, and some large outhouses which were at different times used for meetings, the playgroup, jumble sales and the storage of furniture. One other ground floor room was used as a bedroom, as well as eight rooms on the first and second floors.

2.5 An early publicity sheet proclaimed "on November 3rd the doors were opened to all women 24 hours a day, and Canterbury Women's Centre, refuge, and support centre, was now a fact – no longer just an idea in our heads". But what sort of an idea had it been? What sort of a fact was it to become? The members of the original group admitted afterwards that their ideas about what the Centre should be had been very unclear. As Di said, "We didn't discuss it enough – this was one of the mistakes that we didn't . . . we should have had a bit more organization, a bit more planning, in the first place. We all of us thought we knew vaguely what we wanted from the Women's Centre – we had all these phrases like self-help – in actual fact, we didn't discuss it properly. We just went ahead and did it."

2.6 Extracts from a publicity handout of February 1976 give some outline of the ideas of the women who set up the refuge. (Key concepts italicised by J.M.P.) "The most important principle behind the running of a refuge is one of *self-help*. Most women on arrival are totally lacking in self-confidence and by entering the community here, by taking responsibility with the other women here for the day-to-day running of the house it helps them to regain their self-confidence and does not allow them to sink back into another form of dependence. . . . The voluntary workers here are busy, co-ordinating, writing letters, fund raising, playing with the children, decorating, giving advice and help where possible and lending a sympathetic ear. Between themselves and with the women at the centre there is a *mutual relationship of support*. Although it is often the voluntary workers who do give advice and help, it is often the case that the best

4

person to understand the problems of a battered woman is another battered woman; and, here again, there is this mutual relationship of support. . . . It is essential that a woman can see that her problem here is no longer hers alone – but that it is shared in the refuge and in refuges up and down the country. This is dependent upon the friendship, trust and informal caring that is established and worked for in each refuge – it cannot come from any relationship of authority or hierarchy. For this reason there can be *no one 'in charge'*; there can be no warden. . . . Finally, and very importantly, is to stress that here at Stour Street we operate an *Open Door Policy* . . . which means that we turn no woman away. This is because there are very few crisis centres for women and until that situation is changed we must continue with this policy. Also, it is very true to say that, since we believe that it is all the women who are here who are helping themselves, it is a case of the more the merrier . . . and although it may make a few difficulties being overcrowded, what woman will say to another woman on the doorstep, 'No, You Can't Come In.' "

2.7 This statement sets out the key principles by which the Women's Centre was to attempt to run – by self-help, mutual support, power sharing, and the open door policy. Later in this report, the women's perception of, and attitudes to, these principles will be described and discussed. At this point it should perhaps be stressed that it seemed as though the overriding norm was that the norms themselves should be flexible. That is to say, it was stressed that decisions about how the Women's Centre should be run could be made by all those who, by their work at the Centre or by their need of the Centre, were involved in its everyday life. No committee or other formal organization was set up lest it have the effect of excluding anyone who would like to be included. Anyone who wanted to be involved could become so by taking part.

2.8 One effect of the organizational framework, or lack of framework, was the great importance of meetings in the life of the Centre. At one time there were three meetings every week. One of these was for the women in the house to arrange the day-to-day life of the house and bring disputes into the open; one was for more general discussion about such topics as abortion, contraception, equal rights and Social Security; and the third was for all those concerned with raising money and negotiating to get a long-term home for the Centre. Anyone who was interested could go to any of these meetings. Two small children living in the refuge were heard playing mothers and fathers: "Come to bed now", said one, "You've got to hurry to bed tonight." "Why?" asked the child who was playing the role of the baby. "Because there's a meeting tonight and I've got to go."

5

Local reactions to the opening of the Centre

2.9 Reactions were varied and illuminating, and it is worth mentioning how they differed. On the one hand, a very large number of *individuals* offered their support to the new venture though, as we shall see, many of them misunderstood the nature of what they were supporting. However, media publicity about 'battered wives' had done its work and people gave furniture, bedding, clothes, toys, a Christmas tree, a turkey, and a great deal of other help; more help was offered, in fact, than the workers could cope with at the time, particularly as they were still not sure what it was that they had set up, though they were more sure about *how* it should be set up. Many individuals contributed money towards the costs of running the house and towards the eventual aim of buying a house; most of these were small donations, though one cold winter morning an old man knocked at the door, handed in a bundle of a hundred one pound notes and walked away without leaving his name.

2.10 Secondly, it was striking how very little support was offered to the Women's Centre by *organizations* in Canterbury. Members of organizations would offer their individual support, but would explain that their organization could not support something which involved squatting. Many organizations were reluctant to support a new organization with no clear authority structure, and hesitated to give money when there was no official 'treasurer' to give it to. My field notes of 23rd January describe the visit of the representative of one women's organization. "Her committee had asked her to visit the refuge and report back as to whether it should receive financial support. She sat through the meeting with a doubtful expression on her face and, after the meeting, confided her doubts to me. She had three main objections. One was that so many people were living on Social Security rather than 'standing on their own feet'. Her second objection was that 'it all seems a bit chaotic' and she made various suggestions about who was 'really' in charge. Her third objection was to the offer of help and advice by unqualified people, and she asked 'Why not turn to the Samaritans – after all, they are trained to give advice?' " That is to say, her attitudes to what she saw were based on concepts of hierarchy and of professionalism, and she felt confused by the rejection of the authority patterns to which she was accustomed. No help came from that organization, though individual members gave their support. It seemed as though organizations found it hard to accept and support such an apparently ill-defined organization, though individuals could respond to and accept individuals. Thus it was a long time before the Social Services 'officially' acknowledged their new neighbour, though individual social

6

workers had been sending their clients there since the Women's Centre opened.

2.11 Thirdly, however, a lot of support came from organizations *outside* Canterbury, and in particular from Ashford. This support got off to a good start when one women's group organized a social evening where the chief entertainment was a male stripper, and raised £250. Many other organizations gave generous financial support and it is mainly from Ashford that the £2,500 at present in the Women's Centre deposit account has come. Sympathizers in Ashford did not seem so concerned, as were people in Canterbury, that the refuge was in a squat, that there was no formal committee, and that no-one was 'in charge'; but then it is harder to ignore deviance when it is on one's own doorstep.

Significant words

2.12 In Canterbury, one of the problems was that, from the very beginning, people who were outside the Women's Centre found it so difficult to understand what was being attempted inside it; indeed, often their lack of understanding was such that they did not even understand that they did not understand. Some of this confusion arose out of, and is expressed in, the key words of the Women's Centre. There are always some words which carry a burden of ideological significance over and above their overt meaning; they can express value judgements, political positions, allegiances or non-allegiances. Thus 'Derry' and 'Londonderry' tell us something about the political position of someone using either term; and the use of the term 'Women's Lib.' discriminates the outsider from the insider in the 'Women's Liberation Movement'. The tendency for words to acquire these extra functions seems to be greater at times when values are in the process of changing and when conflicts exist but are not fully spelt out.

2.13 Thus, it must be stressed that it was impossible to understand what was going on at the Canterbury Women's Centre without understanding the significance of certain key words and phrases.

2.14 *The 'Women's Centre'* was the phrase used to describe the whole enterprise by those who set it up. They did *not* at first call it the refuge. As Jo said, "We didn't want to define it, that was very important to us. We didn't want to define what we were going to set up because we did not know exactly what the people, what the women of Canterbury, wanted. So we thought we should basically provide a place for people to come and meet and develop from there. But then, everyone seemed to want a battered wives refuge. We hoped that if we had a Women's Centre there as well

7

women could discuss their problems and feel that it was not just them and their inadequacies that made them battered, and maybe they would come to the realization that they don't have to accept everything that comes to them and that they can actually take control of their own lives."

2.15 At the beginning it was planned that the Women's Centre should provide not just a refuge and a meeting place, but advice and support, and such services as pregnancy testing and abortion counselling. As Rosa, another member of the original group, said, "I didn't see it primarily as a refuge. I saw it as a socialist feminist centre, for self-help, abortion counselling, and things like that, showing films, somewhere to base campaigns, and also a place for discussion groups on education and things like that." As the year went on the 'refuge' aspect of the enterprise became more and more dominant and the other activities either never got off the ground or ceased to be important. However, the phrase 'the Women's Centre' continues to be used and continues to carry the implication that the refuge is something more than just accommodation.

2.16 The 'Women in the house'

This is the phrase used to describe those who come for shelter at the refuge. They are not known as battered 'wives', 'clients', 'residents' nor by any other term which might seem to categorize or stigmatize them. It is for this reason that I have put inverted commas round the term 'battered wives' up to this point and it is for the same reason that I shall cease to use it from now on. Many of the women are not 'wives' but, as we shall see, may be cohabitees or even ex-wives; and the word 'battered' also seems inappropriate.

2.17 Some women are appallingly injured; they suffer broken bones, knife wounds, and severe bruising; some are hit over the head with furniture, some are thrown downstairs, and one had a nail hammered into her foot. But some women suffer in other ways and may have no bruises to show for it. One of the women who has stayed longest at the refuge, putting up with what are clearly for her extremely difficult circumstances, has never said what it was that drove her from her home; all she has said is that she has not been physically battered; but her need of the refuge is clearly great.

2.18 A key norm is that it is for the woman herself to define in what ways she has been injured and in what ways she can be helped; she may have been mentally or physically battered or both; she may not want to say in what ways her marriage has become intolerable to her; it is for her to define herself as needing the refuge. The implication of this is that there must be no labelling, and in particular no derogatory labelling, of the women who come to the refuge. At the Chiswick refuge the women who come are known as the 'mothers', a word which would seem to emphasize one particular characteristic, and which is rejected by most refuges in favour of the word 'women'.

2.19 The significance of this norm was brought home to me when within a short space of time I attended two conferences. The first was the 'Kent Cares' conference, organized by the Kent Social Services Department in September 1976. After several sessions a lone voice from the hall wondered aloud why there were no clients at the conference. "There is no reason", it was suggested, "why some physically handicapped, or perhaps some blind people, could not have been here." But there were none; not even clean, intelligent clients had been invited to join in the discussion about the care which they were to receive. Two months later I attended the conference of the National Women's Aid Federation at Bradford. Not only were the 'clients' at this conference, but they had an equal right to speak and vote. Many refuges hired mini-buses to travel to the conference and anyone from the refuge who wanted to go was able to do so. As each group arrived, with its sleeping bags and its rucksacks and its tired children, it was impossible to tell who was a 'helper' and who had asked for help.

2.20 'The workers', 'the helpers', 'the support group'
This was the word which caused the most embarrassment and confusion, thus reflecting perhaps the embarrassment and confusion felt about the rôle of those who set up and who organized the refuge. For a long time no word could be found for this group at Canterbury, by those who comprised the group. Outsiders expected to find a committee, someone in charge who could be seen to be organizing the venture. The women arrived at the refuge expecting to find a warden or an organizer, and were often puzzled to find that, not only was there no-one in charge, but there was nobody whose job it was to tell them that there was no-one in charge. The questionnaire which was used in the study reflects this confusion, by using the words which the women themselves used, and asking about their feelings about "the girls, the helpers, the ones who organize things".

2.21 The problem of finding a name for this group seems to be the result of a key value which was held by most members of the group which set up the refuge. This was expressed in the phrase, "We all need the refuge." In other words, a deliberate attempt was being made to break down the distinction between the helpers and the helped, by spelling out the universal need for help. Thus when Lucy, one of the original group who set up the refuge, was asked, "Do you think it would be better if there was just one person in charge?" she replied, "No, I think it would be much better if the women learned to fend for themselves, actually took the responsibility. Otherwise everyone is playing their stereotyped rôles – irresponsible women/irresponsible rulers. They should be living together in an amicable way organizing their life without some figure who says 'yes' and 'no' to going out, or whatever." Asked the same question, Jo replied, "We didn't want to have a committee because we felt that a committee would alienate some of the women who came if they thought it was run by a committee. I think they were a bit surprised that there wasn't a warden or something there, and then they accepted that there wasn't a committee and then accepted that there were these different people who weren't, sort of, 'battered wives', but who were there trying to make things as easy as possible for them."

2.22 It must be understood, of course, that these significant words carry not only their explicit and implicit meanings, but also meanings related to hopes and aspirations. They express not only what people thought was happening, but also what people hoped was happening, or would be happening. That is to say, for example, that while people outside the refuge might take for granted the distinction between 'the battered wives' and the 'committee', and people inside the refuge might aim to do away with the distinction altogether, what actually happened was different from either, as will be described later in this report.

2.23 These significant words represented important values and aspirations and it is impossible to understand either the institution or the people without understanding their words. If a norm is described as being the expression of a value, then the dominant value was that any distinction between helpers and helped was essentially artificial; this value was expressed in the series of norms about self-help, mutual support and power sharing. Though there was always some discrepancy between theory and practice, it was significant that some of the 'women' lobbied councillors on behalf of the refuge, raised money for the refuge by running a market stall, formulated 'rules' and pinned them up on the wall, and participated in decisions both large and small; while, on the other hand, some of the 'workers' needed the refuge as much as any of the women, and most of those involved gained support from it at some time or other in the course of the year.

Chapter 3
The methodology of the study

3.1 The research was carried out by a combination of two techniques; first, by a variant of participant observation, and secondly, by a series of more formal interviews using two relatively structured questionnaires. My own rôle might best be described as that of participant-as-observer. This has been summarized as a rôle in which "an observer develops relationships with informants through time, and where he is apt to spend more time and energy participating than observing. At times he observes formally, as in scheduled interview situations; and at other times he observes informally – when attending parties, for example. During early stages of his stay in the community, informants may be somewhat uneasy about him both in formal and informal situations, but their uneasiness is likely to disappear when they learn to trust him and he them" (Gold in McCall and Simmons 1969). My own commitment to, and participation in, the work of the refuge began before I started doing the research study and continues now (December 1976).

3.2 I have been aware of the problem of over-identification with the refuge and with those who live and work there. At times I felt acutely the strains of participating in the work of getting the refuge going, while at the same time observing myself participating in the work. However, my public identification with the refuge did have an advantage in that people outside the refuge tended to talk to me about what they perceived to be going on there. I was very much aware, however, that to some people I spoke of the workers at the refuge as 'them', while to others I would use the word 'us'; thus to some I found myself saying "They are being evicted and they haven't found anywhere else to go", while to others I would say "We are being evicted – do you know of anywhere we could go?"

3.3 In general, I think it could be said that, in relation to the world outside the refuge, I played what could be described as a legitimating rôle, providing a link between the refuge and the more established organizations and more respectable people in the community, and in this I feel that I was of real value to the refuge.

3.4 At the same time, I was aware of some special problems related to the research topic I had undertaken. Women's refuges have been sensitive to the dangers of being 'used' by outsiders; for this reason, most have refused access to male researchers, and have viewed with suspicion any outside observers who do not seem to be sympathetic to what they are trying to do. At the National Women's Aid Federation conference, someone said that "research isn't simply writing academic material – it's for the benefit of the women in the houses". John Greve has written perceptively about the rôle of the researcher in the community (Jones and Mayo 1975). He discusses the obligations people who do research have towards those who supply the information upon which the research is based, particularly in situations in which those who supply the information are poor, deprived, inarticulate or of low status. He writes of the importance of introducing "measures designed to raise the status of people-as-research-objects in the research situation and, simultaneously, to achieve their real participation in the research process" (p. 167). The stress placed upon participation within the refuge made me sensitive to the possibilities of involving both workers and women in the work which I was trying to do; I feel that their contribution gave an added relevance to my enquiries.

3.5 The rôle of all researchers has also been critically appraised by the National Women's Aid Federation who have attacked the idea of research as a 'neutral' activity, and have stressed that research not only reflects the value positions of those who did it, but can also be used to justify the value judgements of those who use it. In saying this, the National Women's Aid Federation is making explicit truths which relate to all empirical research work. Much research, and most 'policy recommendations' contain value judgements, and it is important that these should be made explicit.

3.6 The problem of bias in sociological research has been much discussed. On the one hand, it is suggested that researchers should strive to be neutral, and objective in their search for the truth, while, on the other hand, it is argued that it is impossible to do research that is uncontaminated by personal sympathies, and that what the 'truth' is depends on whose viewpoint one takes. Personally, I have attempted to follow the recommendation that "We take sides as our personal and political commitments dictate, use our theoretical and technical resources to avoid distortions introduced into our work, limit our conclusions carefully, recognize the hierarchy of credibility for what it is, and field as best we can the accusations and doubts that will surely be our fate" (Becker 1970: 134).

12

3.7 The study, then, was carried out by a combination of a variant of participant observation and of more formal interviewing. During the year I attended at least fifty formal meetings and other members of the group became accustomed to my taking notes during such meetings.

3.8 I carried out formal interviews with twenty-five women, using the Questionnaire which will be found in Appendix 1. These interviews were carried out between 1st February 1976 and 11th June 1976. During this time I attempted to interview all the women who both stayed at the refuge for four or more days *and* had children. Twenty-nine women fell into this category during this time, and of these I interviewed twenty-five, one of whom did not have her children with her at the time. These interviews were tape-recorded and the answers were transferred to the questionnaire forms for analysis.

3.9 I had no outright refusals among the four women whom I failed to interview and who fell into the category which I have described. I simply did not contact them before they left the refuge. One problem which I encountered was that the women themselves often did not know what they would be doing in the near future – a woman would promise to be available to be interviewed the next day, but by the next day her husband might have called and persuaded her to return home.

3.10 I have also interviewed the nine workers who were most involved in the refuge from the beginning and who seemed to me to be the most powerful and active members of the group which 'ran' the refuge during its first year. Some women's refuges now have one or two paid workers, as well as a number of voluntary workers. At Canterbury, however, all those involved gave their time voluntarily and no-one was paid for their work at the refuge. The interviews with the workers were carried out in September and October 1976, and were fortunately timed in that, shortly after this, the conflicts within the group came to a crisis point. These interviews were carried out in a less structured way than were the interviews with the women, but I did work through a series of topics in each interview, as can be seen from the Interviewer's Checklist in Appendix 2. These interviews were tape-recorded, and they were transcribed verbatim for analysis.

3.11 All those who were interviewed have been given pseudonyms and some personal details have been altered in order to preserve anonymity. It might seem that, when any individual woman is mentioned in the report, some indication should be given of whether she was a 'worker' or a 'battered wife'. I would suggest that the fact of not at once knowing 'who' any particular woman is may give an imaginative insight into the experience of being involved in the place. However, for those who would find such classification useful, a list of all the pseudonyms is given in Appendix 3, and is divided into 'women' and 'workers'. It is perhaps significant that one woman was interviewed twice, first, upon her arrival at the refuge as a 'battered wife', and secondly, some months later, as one of the organizers. She has been given a different pseudonym for each role in order to protect her anonymity.

3.12 These nine workers were, of course, only a small proportion of the total population of people who helped the refuge in some way during the year, just as the twenty-five women I interviewed were only a proportion of the total population of 130 women who stayed at the refuge from 20th November 1975 to 20th November 1976, the year during which I did my study. I hesitate to use the term 'sample' to describe the groups of women and workers which I interviewed; they might better be described as 'informants' were it not that others were also informants, or as 'interviewees' were this not so clumsy. So I have described the two groups who were interviewed as 'samples' in order to distinguish them from those who were not interviewed, but must stress that these are in no way statistical samples in the strict sense: it is just a convenient word to describe the women who were interviewed.

3.13 Similarly, I have made no attempts to analyse the data which I collected in any statistical way. With such small total numbers, and with a self-selected total population, it seemed meaningless to construct any great statistical structures. The strengths of the study lie rather in the richness and complexity of the material and in the developing and continuing relationships with key respondents which would not have been possible using more traditional sample survey methods.

3.14 This study is not concerned with the *causes* of violence within intimate relationships. It would seem extremely difficult to unravel the psychodynamics of any one marital relationship even if one knew both points of view, and with only the woman's point of view it becomes impossible. As Gelles says, "The categorization of intra-family violence depends on whose norms and whose perspectives one takes" (1972). A useful discussion of the current state of research on battered women has been produced by Elizabeth Wilson (1976), who points out how much of the work which has been done approaches the problem from the point of view of the psychology of the individual. For example, the questionnaire which Gayford (1975) used at the Chiswick refuge puts considerable emphasis on the woman's sexual history and on the masochistic and sadistic elements in her sexual relationships.

3.15 Wilson emphasizes the value of discussing the problem within the framework of discussion about the family as a social institution. This approach has been adopted by several other researchers (Steinmetz and Strauss 1974). Goode (1973) sees the family as a power system based on force, in which the dominance of the male is the result of his greater economic power and greater prestige outside the family. It is argued that violence is more prevalent in families where the husband does not possess the *achieved* skills and status upon which his *ascribed* status as head of the household is based. Thus a husband will fall back on violence as a way of maintaining his dominance at a time when he feels threatened. This perspective has been developed by Jalna Hanmer, who has traced the relationship between Women's Aid and the Women's Liberation Movement (1976). She points out the extent to which the problem of battered women arises out of the unequal relationships between men and women, both in the family and in society, as expressed in terms of income, access to housing, and in the degree of protection afforded by the law.

3.16 No reliable evidence is available about the amount of violence which exists within marriage in general. All the work which has been done depends on samples which are biased to one degree or another, either because the women in the sample sought help from a refuge (Gayford 1975) or because the family came to the notice of a social work agency (Moore 1974, Dobash and Dobash 1974), or because the women came forward in answer to an appeal (Marsden and Owens 1975), or because the couple were seeking a divorce (Steinmetz and Straus 1974). The most useful study from this point of view is that by Gelles, who investigated violence in families who had sought help from the police and from a private social work agency, and who used as a control group the next-door neighbours of these families. He found that, while more violence was reported in families who were known to the police or to the social work agency, there was still an appreciable amount of violence reported in the families of their neighbours. Gelles points out, however, that the stigma attached to violence within the family must lead to the under-reporting of the extent of family violence; the family is still seen as being 'naturally' harmonious, with violence being the result of individual pathology. He suggests that a model based on conflict theory would prove more useful in understanding marital violence.

15

3.17 Much very useful evidence was presented to the Select Committee on Violence in Marriage, and the Committee's Report provides the best account of the problem as it exists in Britain today (1975). However, the Report does stress "the remarkable paucity of information about domestic violence" (p. xxiii), and the recommendations urge that more research should be undertaken. It was within the context of the Select Committee's recommendations that the work described in this report was undertaken, and it is hoped that the findings reported here will make a contribution to our understanding of the problem of marital violence.

Chapter 4

The women in the house

Outline information on the 130 women who stayed at the refuge during the year

4.1 Information on all the women who stayed at the refuge was collected by the workers, who noted down the following information about each woman soon after her arrival: the date of her arrival, her name, the number of children with her, her home town, the address of her next-of-kin, and the means by which she knew of the refuge. When she left, the date of her leaving was usually added to the record, together with anything that was known about her destination. However, many women simply took their children and disappeared, so this part of the record is incomplete. On the basis of these records it is possible to get a general picture of the women who used the refuge, a picture which will be filled out in greater detail by the information which was gathered from the twenty-five women who were interviewed. The 130 women in the total population were those who stayed at the refuge between 20th November 1975, shortly after it had opened, and 20th November 1976, shortly before the refuge was evicted from its first home and moved to a village some miles from Canterbury.

4.2 Table 1 shows the total number of visits each woman who stayed at the house made to the refuge. It can be seen that, while most paid only one visit, a sizeable minority of 18% paid two or more visits to the refuge. Among this group are many who seem to use the refuge, not in order to escape permanently from their unsatisfactory relationship, but in order that the relationship should continue, though they might need help through bad times. As Joy said, "I've thought of getting divorced, but what it is, I think we just get on top of one another, after a while. Have a break and then I can go back and carry on as usual."

4.3 However, Table 1 must be considered along with Table 2, which shows the length of time each woman stayed at the refuge, taking all her visits together if she made more than one visit. Those who made three or more visits usually fell into the middle categories as far as the length of their stay was concerned. Thus one could suggest dividing the women into three broad categories. A first group only made one visit to the refuge, which

17

lasted only a short time – the 56% who stayed for less than eleven days. There was a second group who stayed for up to three months and which includes most of those who made several visits, and a small third group who needed the refuge for more than three months.

4.4 The second and third of these three categories will be discussed using the more detailed information gained from the interviews. At this stage some comment on the first group, none of whom was interviewed, seems necessary. This large number of women who stayed for only a few days was a source of considerable concern to the workers at the refuge, and

TABLE 1 **Total number of visits made by women to the refuge**

No. of visits	All women staying at refuge		Women in sample
	%	No.	No.
1	82	106	15
2	13	17	6
3	3	4	2
4 or more	2	3	2
TOTALS	100	130	25

TABLE 2 **Length of time women stayed at the refuge – total of visits**

Length of stay	All women staying at refuge		Women in sample
	%	No.	No.
3 days or less	35	46	0
4–10 days	21	27	0
11–30 days	22	29	10
More than 30 days but less than 3 months	15	19	7
More than 3 months but less than 6 months	4	5	5
Over 6 months	3	4	3
TOTALS	100	130	25

18

many different explanations were put forward to explain why they did not stay for longer. Tess saw this as one of the failures of the refuge and said, "You've really got to question why they go back. Some go back because they can't stand the conditions; some go back because when they get here they think, 'Oh, well, I'd better go and try and sort it out. It's better than being here on my own.' . . . I think we fail when we get overcrowded, because we book them in, give them a cup of tea and talk to them as long as we possibly can and then we've got another one come in and we dole them out to someone else." Some went back because they could not stand life at the refuge, whether because of the overcrowding, or because it seemed to them so disorganized, or because of the poor physical state of a house which had not been lived in for years.

4.5 Some, it has been suggested, went back because they did not really 'need' the refuge. But this suggestion has many implications. Many of those who stayed found life at the refuge hard and difficult, and, as we shall see, some were forced to go back when they did not want to because of the day-to-day hardships of living so closely with so many people from so many different backgrounds. If a refuge were deliberately made 'hard' to deter those who did not really 'need' it, many of those who did need it would suffer more at a time when they need all the support they can get.

Children

4.6 Table 3 shows the number of children who stayed at the refuge, a total of 200 in the year. Some women came more than once and brought different numbers of children on different visits; the number counted is the

TABLE 3   **Number of children with the women when they stayed at the refuge**

	All women staying at the refuge		Women in sample
	%	No.	No.
No children	32	42	1
1 child	25	32	7
2 children	16	21	8
3 children	16	21	5
4 or more children	11	14	4
TOTALS	100	130	25

largest number each woman ever brought with her. Many women (six out of the twenty-five who were interviewed) had other children whom they never brought to the refuge. Some of these had been sent to stay with grandparents, some were in care, some stayed with their father. Many of the women, including some of those in the category of 'no children', were pregnant at the time of their visit: many women suggested that their pregnancy seemed to trigger off attacks of violent behaviour in the men with whom they were living.

4.7 Accommodation at the refuge was arranged so that the woman and her children slept in the same room. When the refuge was very crowded, two families might have to share a room, but a large family was usually able to have a room of its own. Each woman was responsible for the care of her own children and would do their washing and cook for them when the kitchen equipment was not being used by other women. For several months, and throughout the time of the interviewing, a playgroup was organized every afternoon by some of the workers; this was for the pre-school children. Arrangements were made for all older children to attend school as soon as possible after their arrival at the refuge.

Housing

4.8 Table 4 shows the usual places of residence of the women. Where a woman had spent a length of time away from her usual home, for example at another refuge, or staying with relations, this place was not counted as her usual place of residence. The table shows that, while 19% of the women came from Canterbury itself, and 13% from the area immediately round the city, more than half the women (53%) came from other parts of Kent. These women came from towns such as Dover, Faversham, Chatham, Maidstone, Deal and Margate, with a greater number from Ashford than from any other town. Many women commented that they would not have felt safe going to a refuge in the town in which they usually lived and that they preferred to seek shelter where their husband would not know where to find them. Yet they did not want to go too far because they needed to keep in touch with family and friends, and wanted to be able to get in touch with their husbands if they chose to do so.

4.9 This table underlines the point that refuges should be seen as serving not just their immediate neighbourhood, but the wider area for a radius of perhaps thirty miles. Even if there is a nearby refuge, a woman may not want to go to it and run the risk of her husband finding her there and assaulting her again: the Canterbury Women's Centre suffered several broken windows as a result of the visits of irate husbands. Some women

TABLE 4 Usual places of residence of the women

	All women staying in refuge		Women in sample
	%	No.	No.
Canterbury	19	24	3
Rest of Canterbury City* (excluding Canterbury)	13	17	3
Rest of Kent (excluding Canterbury City)	53	69	12
London	5	7	5
Rest of Britain (excluding Kent and London)	9	12	2
Not known	1	1	0
TOTALS	100	130	25

* Canterbury City is the local government administrative area based on Canterbury. It includes Whitstable, Herne Bay and the old Bridge-Blean rural district.

who came to the refuge asked to be transferred to other refuges in order to feel more secure, and some of the women who came to Canterbury from other refuges did so for this reason.

4.10 However, Table 4 also illustrates one cause of the housing problems experienced by so many battered women. Women arriving at the Canterbury Women's Centre had to be told that, unless they came from the local area, Canterbury City (which also includes Whitstable, Herne Bay and a number of villages), they would not be accepted on to the Canterbury City housing list. However, many of the 68% who came from other areas lost their rights to be re-housed in their own home area by moving out of it. A woman will leave the area in which she is living because she is afraid of the man with whom she is living; she is forced to go back because no other area will accept responsibility for housing her and her children.

4.11 Much evidence on the housing problems of battered women has already been convincingly presented elsewhere, in the Select Committee Report (1975), in the National Women's Aid Federation Report *Battered Women are Homeless* (1976), and in the Shelter Housing Action Committee Report on *Violence in Marriage* (1976). These reports deal with the problems women face in becoming defined as technically homeless, in being accepted on to local authority housing lists, in getting tenancies transferred from the man's to the woman's name, and in being granted the exchange of council properties from one area to another. Experience from the Canterbury survey confirms the need to implement the recommendations made in these reports.

Homeless single women in the refuge

4.12 There was some criticism of the number of women without children who stayed at the refuge. The women themselves, if they had children, found the presence of women without children unsettling. It was frustrating for them to see the much greater freedom such women enjoyed. However, it was always agreed that childless women who had been the victims of violence should be admitted.

4.13 There was a certain number, however, of women without children who came to the refuge who were simply homeless. These women tended to be disruptive in the refuge in that they suffered none of the traumas of the battered women. They would, for example, answer the door without first checking to see who was outside, or even go out leaving the front door unlocked. The early policy of the refuge had been that any woman in need should be admitted and that it should be up to her to decide that she needed the shelter of the refuge. However, as time went on homeless women became less welcome. Petra felt that this was one of the failures and said, "It doesn't make it run very well as a house, as a shelter, with a lot of single women flitting in and out. The common bond of fear which everyone has, that they are all escaping from a bad marriage or something, isn't there where there are just a lot of single women looking for somewhere cheap to stay. I think we are going to have to say fairly soon, that while we still take in women with children who need to come and of course any woman who is battered or uptight about something, we can't take just ordinary women who are on the doss."

4.14 The organizers of the refuge were in something of a dilemma here. Of the forty-two women without children who stayed at the refuge, ten were referred to the refuge by the police and nine were referred by the Social Services. (Table 5 shows the main referring agencies.) From this it seems as though the police and the Social Services, at least, were seeing the refuge partly as a short-term solution to the problem of homelessness in the area. One policeman said in an interview that "it is useful as a place to send penniless homeless women". Yet when the refuge moved to its

22

TABLE 5   **Agencies referring women to the refuge**

	All women staying in refuge		Women in sample
	%	No.	No.
Social services	28	37	8
Police	13	17	1
Samaritans	12	16	4
C.A.B.	4	5	0
Other refuges	12	15	6
Women told of refuge by other people or agencies	31	40	6
TOTALS	100	130	25

present home, a house made available by the Canterbury City Housing Department, it was specifically laid down that no single homeless women should be admitted. This seems to be an example of inconsistency in local policies which may provide a welcome flexibility but can certainly create problems as well.

4.15 The problem of homelessness complicates the problem of defining need for refuge accommodation. I found little evidence that women were presenting themselves as battered when this was not so, simply in order to gain access. This was probably because of the Women's Centre policy of accepting any woman who herself felt she was in need. A rigorous selection policy, only allowing 'genuine' cases into the refuge, would seem likely to lead to more homeless women presenting themselves as battered, at any rate in areas where housing is in short supply.

4.16 Canterbury has a serious shortage of the sort of accommodation for which single homeless women are searching. The town itself has a resident population of rather over 33,000 but has a large student population as well, so that in 1976 it was estimated that 2,590 students were also seeking accommodation (Canterbury Community Guild Report 1976). Not all of these students found accommodation in the town and had to live in surrounding towns and villages, but most of them would have liked to have lived in Canterbury itself, and the resulting pressure on cheap, privately-rented accommodation was great. The City Council waiting list for November 1976 also reflected this shortage in that, out of a live list of

23

530 households, 151 of the applications came from single people. There is a hostel for single homeless men at Sittingbourne and the Cyrenians run a hostel for men in Canterbury; however, there is no equivalent accommodation for single homeless women in all Kent.

4.17 Against this background the pressure on the refuge to take in such women can be understood, though this is not a problem that other refuges seemed to have experienced in the same degree. By providing accommodation the refuge attracted those who needed *only* accommodation, and so it became harder for those who needed more than just accommodation to stay there and get the help they needed. Offering a solution and limiting it to one problem only, when it is also a solution to a second problem, would seem likely to alter the label on the second problem. The existence of a refuge can show up the existence of a problem of homelessness among single women, but since the two groups have rather different needs it seems preferable that they should be provided for differently. Battered women are homeless, but they have needs for protection, and for support and advice, which are not shared to the same extent by women who are not battered.

Chapter 5

The women in the sample

5.1 Formal interviewing of the women who came to the refuge began on 1st February 1976 after a short series of pilot interviews. As it turned out, the following four months were good months in which to do the interviewing. At the beginning the refuge had been very unsettled, as the workers strove to get the electricity, water and gas turned on, and as furniture and bedding were being collected. However, by February the house had become more comfortable. On the other hand, the first enthusiasm of the workers had not yet evaporated; many of them were still involved and the Centre was running as nearly according to the ideals by which it had been set up as it ever would. Later in the year conflicts among the workers, general lessening of enthusiasm, and the growing threat of eviction were to make the Centre a more troubled place. Thus it seemed as though the months from February to June saw the Women's Centre at its most typical.

5.2 Tables 1, 2, 3, 4 and 5 show how the women who were interviewed compared with the total population of women. It did not seem appropriate to turn such small totals into percentages, so they are given as numbers and can be compared with the numbers of the total population as given in the adjacent columns.

5.3 It can be seen that the sample contained a higher proportion of women who made several visits, and who stayed longer. It is possible that the experience of being interviewed itself gave a greater feeling of belonging at the refuge – certainly I had a closer relationship with the women whom I interviewed and, of course, I continued to see them in the following months. It seems more likely, however, that the more settled nature of the refuge during this time made women feel that they could endure the long wait until they could find other accommodation.

5.4 Another difference between the sample and the total is the larger proportion of women who were referred from other refuges. The reason for this is that this was the time when the refuge in Chiswick was particularly overcrowded and was under the threat of legal action for overcrowding. When the situation in Chiswick became too difficult women would be found places at other refuges and some of them came to Canterbury.

The ages of the women in the sample

5.5 Table 6 shows that while the women ranged in age from nineteen to forty-six, more were in their late twenties than in any other age group. This seems to reflect a pattern found among women who leave the home because of violence; the two most characteristic stages in the life-cycle for a woman to leave are either the stage when the children begin to notice how their father is treating their mother, or when the children have left home and she feels free to do as she wants. The tragic effect of the endurance of this latter category of women is that by this time her sons may have

TABLE 6   Age of woman at time of interview

Under 20	1
20–24	6
25–29	9
30–34	3
35–39	3
40+	3
TOTAL	25

internalized the image of the aggressive, bullying male, and will go on to play the same rôle in their own families. However, more of the women in the sample fell into the first category. As Debbie said, "They are better since we have been here. There is no worry on themselves [*sic*]. When he is hitting me this one is always saying, 'Daddy, please don't hit Mummy – leave her, leave her.' And he will start kicking her too, and telling her who is she to tell him to stop what he is doing. When she grow up and see this happening all the time, maybe it will put her off marriage. Maybe she will think that is how all men are." Many other women commented that it was when their children began to 'notice' that they decided to do something about changing the situation.

Socio-economic status

5.6 Tables showing the occupations of the women, and of their fathers and of the man who battered them could have been presented here; however, the information did not seem to warrant it in the case of such a small

26

sample. Most of the women were not in paid employment because they had dependent children, though some had been forced to take on such work as night nursing or night shifts in factories, because of the inadequacy of the housekeeping money they were given. When they arrived at the refuge most claimed Social Security benefits, and some commented that they were better off than they had been when they had been dependent on their husbands.

5.7 All occupations were classified, with the help of the Registrar General's classification, into the two broad categories of 'manual' and 'non-manual'. The most recent occupations of seventeen of the women were classified as manual and eight as non-manual, this latter group including a wages clerk, a laboratory technician, an assistant in a children's home and a computer programmer. Of their fathers, sixteen were classified as manual and eight as non-manual, and one woman had lost touch with her father. The non-manual fathers included a manager of a caravan site and a scrap metal merchant; the owner of a farm in Nigeria was also included in this category. Of the men who battered the women in the sample, twenty-two fell into the manual category, but it is perhaps more significant that eight were unemployed at the time the woman left home. The information on occupation does not seem very useful, but there is perhaps some support for the thesis that battered women tend to be higher in socio-economic status than are the men who batter them.

5.8 Tables 7 and 8 should be taken together and will do much to dispel any quick generalisations about the 'battered wife'. They show that a quarter of the women (six out of twenty-five) were not battered by their husbands, and that two were being attacked by their ex-husbands; these two experienced some of the worst attacks and were frustrated by the

TABLE 7 **Marital status before coming to refuge**

	No.
Never married	2
Divorced	2
Still married to first husband and living with him	11
Still married to first husband but living apart	4
Living with second husband	5
Living with third husband	1
TOTAL	25

27

TABLE 8   Relationship of the woman to the man referred to
in the above table

	No.
Husband	17
Man with whom she was living	6
Ex-husband	2
TOTAL	25

seeming impossibility of getting rid of their attackers. The six women who
were attacked by the men with whom they were living often experienced
additional difficulties with housing; if the accommodation was in the
man's name it was impossible for the woman to establish a right to live
there, while if the accommodation was in her name she seemed to find it
hard to make him go away and stop bothering her. She did not have the
protection which the law gives to the married woman's right to live in the
matrimonial home. In five cases the woman was battered by her second
husband, and in one case by her third. It seems as though some of these
women are either very unfortunate, or are not very perceptive about
picking a husband with whom they will be able to live happily.

Marital problems

5.9 This study was specifically not concerned with the causes of marital
violence. However, it has been hypothesized that this is a problem which
frequently co-exists with other problems, though it seems unclear whether
these other problems are more accurately seen as 'causes' of the violence,
as 'enablers' which allow violent feelings to be expressed, as 'symptoms'
with the violence of some deeper malaise, or as unrelated to the violence.
In order to come to any conclusion about these different analyses of
marital violence it would be necessary to have a larger sample and to
follow the women over a longer period of time.

5.10 However, Table 9 does show the extent to which physical violence
was accompanied by other conditions which the woman defined as
problematic for her. It can be seen that all the women except one (see
para. 2.14) experienced physical violence, though for some this was less
distressing than other unsatisfactory aspects of their married life. Many
women found that they often did not have enough money, and were
unable to earn for themselves because of their dependent children. This
was particularly a problem where the man was out of work or where he

spent a lot on drinking or gambling; drinking, in particular, seemed to be associated with violent behaviour in men who were said to be peaceable when sober, and the report produced by the Bedfordshire Police showed what a large proportion of violent attacks took place during the night, presumably when the pubs had recently shut. (*Report on acts of domestic violence committed in the County between 1st February and 31st July 1976.*) Paula's story is typical of many: "I was just going to sleep when he came in, drunk again. It were half past eleven. He dragged me out of bed.

TABLE 9   **Problematic characteristics of the man with whom the woman was involved before she came to the refuge and whose behaviour caused her to leave home**

	No. of times mentioned
Physically violent towards her	24
Often in difficulties with money	20
Often drunk	12
Frequently out of work	10
Demands that woman be submissive	9
Gambles excessively	3
Engages in criminal activities	3
Involved with other women	3

'Get down the f—ing stairs and get me summat to eat, you f—ing whore', he says. So I went downstairs and put something on the cooker. Then he came downstairs and started on me again. He got me bent over the clothes horse so I couldn't move. And he got me round the neck with one hand, squeezing as hard as he could, and just knocking into me with his fist with the other hand, so that my head kept knocking on the wall. And he just kept hitting me and hitting me and I was screaming and screaming."

5.11 Paula's husband has another characteristic common to many men who are violent towards their wives, or the women with whom they live. This is his demand that his wife be submissive towards him, a demand which in some cases reaches absurd proportions. Jane described how "he wanted me to be totally his and do exactly as he said. And in the end I had to act as a fool. It annoyed him if I came back with anything; he used to make me do things which I would never do for anybody. He would say,

'Go and get me the pillow because I want to rest my back on it'. And I would say, 'You've got two hands and two feet, do it yourself'. And he would say, 'I could make you', and I would say, 'You can't'. And then it would start. He would punch me and punch me, and I would stand up, and he would continuously punch me, until I would think, 'This is a waste of time, I'd better do it'. So in the end if he asked me to get a pillow I'd get up and get a pillow. And he thought, because I did it as quick as he could get the words out of his mouth, that I was his underdog, and that was how he liked it. And after she was born it was hell. He'd think he had me then. I used to do everything he said. He didn't have a reason and he just kept on and on."

5.12 Many of the women I interviewed described how their husbands would attempt to dominate and subdue them – would ask them to cook meals in the middle of the night, or fly into a rage because they spoke to the milkman, or forbid family or friends to call at the house. One husband habitually took the handle off the gas meter so that she couldn't cook; another flew into a temper because he thought she was in the house when she was actually in the garden bringing in the nappies. Some of these men had suffered from mental illness and it may be that their behaviour could be attributed to this. However, in many cases it seemed as though the real dispute was over the nature of the marital relationship. Many of the men seemed to expect to dominate, and sought trivial ways in which to humiliate so that their dominance should be in no doubt.

Housing situation

5.13 Tables 10, 11 and 12 have to be taken together in order to build up a picture of what was known about the housing situation of the women in the sample. The category described as 'Set up new home on her own or with new partner' needs further definition, since it includes some women who were rehoused, one who married and now lives in army quarters, and two women who are living in the 'half-way houses' which are rented by the Women's Centre. These houses were made available by the Social Services of the Kent County Council in November 1976 and are to be used for women who have been accepted on to local authority housing lists but have not yet been found accommodation. The workers at the refuge hope that living in these half-way houses will help women to get used to living without the day-to-day support of the refuge, and will save them from living for long periods of time in the crowded and strainful atmosphere of the refuge. A follow-up study would enable some evaluation to be made of the place of such housing in the provision for battered women.

TABLE 10 Type of housing in which she was living before coming to the refuge

Owner occupied	5
Rented from Council	10
Privately rented	8
Squat	1
Army quarters	1
TOTAL	25

TABLE 11 Ownership or tenancy of house in which she was living

In man's name	12
In woman's name	4
In both names	6
DK or DNA	3
TOTAL	25

TABLE 12 Destination after leaving the refuge

	1. Her plan for future at time of interview	2. Actual destination after leaving refuge
Return to previous home, obtain custody of children and divorce	5	4
Return to previous home and to living with husband (or, in two cases, boy friend)	3	8
Return to previous, own, home	2	2
Set up new home* on her own or with new partner	12	8
Don't know	3	1
Still at refuge	–	2
TOTALS	25	25

*Second stage housing defined as new home since those living there have been accepted on to council housing lists.

5.14 Table 12 illustrates what appear to be the three main housing 'routes' followed by the women, though again, follow-up work would be needed in order to confirm the categorization by finding out what happened to each woman in the long term; her 'destination after leaving the refuge' may not be the destination which she would regard as a permanent solution to her problems, whether those problems be defined as housing or as marital problems.

5.15 First, there are those women who obtain custody of the children and the right to return to live in the matrimonial home, either by getting a divorce or a separation. A woman in this category has two main problems. Her first is to evict her husband from the matrimonial home. This involves both legal and, in the case of local authority housing, administrative processes. These processes usually take about six months, though it is possible for them to be completed in a much shorter time. Speed seems very necessary since the experience of living for many months in a refuge can be very strainful both for the woman and for her children.

5.16 The second problem of a woman in this category is that of keeping her husband out of the matrimonial home. Some women described how they were afraid that their husbands would be so enraged by what had been done to them they would continue to attack them after the divorce proceedings were complete, and the experience of the two women in the sample who were in this position shows that these fears were not entirely fanciful. It should be possible for local authority tenants who have been battered to have their tenancies transferred to houses away from their home area. Many women expressed the fear that they would never be safe until their whereabouts was unknown to their husbands. This is an illustration of the way in which one problem (in this case a policing problem) can manifest itself as another problem (in this case an accommodation problem). If the first problem could be solved the second would disappear. This is particularly clear in the case of a woman who lived in a house which she rents in her own name and where she lives by herself. If she is driven from her house by the violence of her ex-husband or her ex-lover, she may have nowhere else to go. She cannot be re-housed because she already has a house; she simply want to be able to live in it. Thus, what is in reality a police problem appears as a housing problem.

5.17 The second main housing 'route' is followed by those women who return to their previous home and to the man with whom they were previously living. Eight women in the sample did this, though, as Table 12 shows, only three had planned to do this when they were interviewed at the refuge. Information from the workers at the refuge would suggest that many of the women in this category return home voluntarily in the hope that the relationship may improve. Some later return to the refuge again, and it would seem that the availability of a refuge can enable some marriages to continue. Certainly women who make several visits to a refuge, returning home between visits, should not be seen as being less in need of the refuge than other groups.

5.18 Other women, however, return home involuntarily, either because they can see no alternative or because any alternative would take so long to become available that they could not endure living in the refuge for so long. It seems as though the chief difference between women in this category and women who succeed in setting up homes of their own is their ability to adjust to living in the refuge. The existence of this group of women underlines the importance of speed in completing legal proceedings and in arranging the transfer of tenancies.

5.19 The third housing 'route' is followed by those women who succeed in doing what half the women in the sample wanted to do, that is, to set up a new home of their own with their children. Some women, though none in the sample, go to living-in domestic jobs. There is clearly a danger of women taking such jobs simply in order to get accommodation, but for some this can provide a long-term solution. Some refuges welcome offers of such jobs, which they can make known to women living in the house.

5.20 Those women in the sample who set up new homes were those who were re-housed by local authorities. It is important that workers in refuges should be able to advise women about their housing position in order that women who could be defined as homeless, and rehoused on those grounds, do not neglect to apply to their local authority. Most local authorities now recognize that a woman who has been forced to leave her home because of the violence of her husband is homeless, but a woman who has left her own area and gone to a refuge in another local authority area may find that neither area accepts responsibility for re-housing her. There would seem to be an urgent need for co-operation between local authorities on this issue.*

* The research described here was carried out before the Housing (Homeless Persons) Act came into force on 1st December 1977. This Act lays on housing authorities the duty to provide accommodation for homeless people who have priority needs and includes battered women with children among those who qualify for such help. Women from other areas must be provided with accommodation while enquiries are undertaken about their position.

5.21 The refuge played a crucial rôle in helping battered women to solve their housing problems. It could give them temporary accommodation, protection, and advice about the legal and administrative processes which they would have to initiate. However, in those cases in which there were long delays in these processes the stress of living in the refuge could mean that women returned to their previous homes and previous partner when they had not planned to do so. Half-way houses would seem to offer one solution to the problem of legal and administrative delays; however, efforts should also be made to cut down such delays when a battered woman and her children are concerned.

Chapter 6

Previous attempts to seek help from other individuals and agencies

6.1 A large part of the interview with each woman was concerned with her experiences before deciding to come to the refuge, and in particular with her attempts to get help from both formal and informal sources. It is hypothesized that analysis of her feelings about these previous experiences may not only throw light on the adequacy of the agencies to which a woman turned for help, but may also enable some evaluation to be made about the nature of the help which she hoped she would receive at the refuge.

6.2 Nineteen of the women had made previous attempts to leave the men who were battering them, and many of these had made several such attempts. Some returned home when the house where they were staying proved too small to hold so many people, or when their violent partner began to threaten those who had taken them in. Some simply became homesick, and many had hoped that it might be possible to 'make a new start' with their marriage.

6.3 All of the women had asked for help from, or had confided their troubles to, someone else. The majority had sought help from both informal sources (their parents, brothers and sisters, friends and neighbours were included in this category), and from formal sources (their doctor, the police, the Social Services, solicitors, Marriage Guidance Council, the Samaritans and so on). In the interview each woman was asked whether each of the different potential helpers had known of her difficulties, if so, whether they offered any help and, if they were said to have offered help, whether it had been useful. That is to say, the focus was on *the woman's own perception of her problem*. By looking at how she perceived the help she was offered, we may come to some understanding of how she perceived her problem.

6.4 This subject is one of great complexity, in that we are concerned with what actually happened and with what was perceived as happening, in a situation in which both the women and the person she consulted probably held very different and unspecified expectations about what was likely to happen. Mayer and Timms (1970) have written sensitively about the complexities of the client/worker interaction in the case of social workers, and many people, notably Cartwright (1967) and Stimson and Webb (1975) have discussed the relationship between doctors and their patients. All stress the problems of analysing these relationships. However, it seems worth attempting the analysis since, as Robert Holman has said, "The few research projects directly interviewing clients and presenting their expressed needs, often reveal perspectives underestimated by agencies. For instance, unsupported mothers complain of the crushing demands of finding enough money, accommodation and adequate day care for their children. They not only feel that social agencies underestimate these aspects, but they are also critical of the kind of help they do offer" (Holman, Lafitte, Spencer and Wilson 1970, 193). Another hazard which must be borne in mind in this, as in any social survey which lays stress on what people say as opposed to what they do, is the possibility of lying. At least one of my respondents told me an outright lie when she claimed never to have seen a social worker, but later turned out to be the subject of a particularly fat file in her borough Social Services department. One can only hope that seeing the women over a period of time and in a relaxed setting would minimize the likelihood of such falsification.

6.5 The results of the series of questions on this topic are presented in numerical form in Table 13 and are summarized in percentage form in Table 14. In Table 13 the answer 'No' to the first question includes those for whom the coding should, strictly speaking, be 'does not apply'; that is, those whose parents are both dead or who had no siblings are included in this category. In Table 14 the percentages were arrived at by taking as 100% the number of women who answered 'Yes' in column 1 of Table 13. The combined totals of those who did not offer help ('No' in column 2) or whose help was not useful ('No' in column 3) was then calculated as a percentage of the first total.

6.6 Most of the women had sought help from formal and informal sources. However, eight women, or a third of the sample, seemed more *isolated* than the rest. These women did not seem able to use informal sources, either because all their family were abroad or because they had quarrelled with them, or because they did not expect to meet with understanding. This 'isolated' group was therefore very dependent on the help which could be given by the formal helping agencies, and this meant that they had a very much less flexible set of 'coping responses' when they did experience problems. It would be interesting to be able to follow these women and find out whether their lack of informal sources of support affected their attitude to the support the refuge offered them. The sample

36

TABLE 13   Sources of help which might have been available to the woman

	1. Were they aware of her difficulties?		2. If they were aware, did they offer help?		3. If help offered, was that useful?		
	No	Yes	No	Yes	Yes	Quite	No
Parents	7	18	5	13	5	6	2
Siblings	8	17	8	9	7	2	0
Friends	13	12	2	10	7	0	3
Neighbours	7	18	9	9	5	4	0
Doctor	10	15	0	15	6	2	7
Police	9	16	6	10	2	4	4
Social worker	4	21	2	19	9	2	8
Solicitor	10	15	1	14	12	2	0
Marriage Guidance	19	6	1	5	2	1	2
Samaritans	18	7	0	7	5	0	2

TABLE 14   Percentages of women who felt they had received 'no help'

39% received no help from their parents ⎤
47% ,,   ,,   ,,   ,,   ,, siblings   ⎬ All of whom were said to be aware of the difficulties
42% ,,   ,,   ,,   ,,   ,, friends   ⎥
50% ,,   ,,   ,,   ,,   ,, neighbours ⎦

47% received no help from their doctor ⎤
63% ,,   ,,   ,,   ,, the police   ⎬ All of whom having been consulted about the difficulties
48% ,,   ,,   ,,   ,, social workers   ⎥
7%   ,,   ,,   ,,   ,, their solicitor ⎦

was too small and the time scale too limited to be able to say anything very definite about the composition of this 'isolated' group. However, it seemed to include more than a random number of women who either were immigrants or were married to immigrants, or who had a long history of finding it hard to cope generally. Here again, further research would be valuable and might produce more substantive conclusions.

Help from family, friends and neighbours

6.7 Apart from the eight 'isolated' women, most of the women turned first for help to their parents and siblings, their friends and neighbours. Mayer and Timms comment on the tendency "to look upon help-seeking as though it were a choice of either seeking professional assistance or going without help *of any kind*. Such a view entirely overlooks the rôle played by friends and relatives in the problem-coping process. . . . In our view, it is useful to place informal *and* professional methods of coping under the same conceptual umbrella and to look upon them as alternative ways of dealing with difficulties" (Mayer and Timms 1970, 37). Many of the women spoke warmly of the help they had received and appeared to have a realistic awareness of what help they might expect and of why it was not given them when it was not given.

6.8 The three main types of help which the women received from these sources were, first, sympathy and emotional support, secondly, short-term accommodation, and thirdly, money. In some cases sympathy was not forthcoming as in the case of Mandy's parents who simply told her, "You've made your bed and you must lie on it". But more often the woman's family would urge her to leave the man and would fail to understand why she continued to stay with him.

6.9 Many women commented, however, that while sympathy was welcome, what they were really in need of was information, protection and longer-term accommodation. Some relatives simply did not have room to have another family to stay, though many had had the woman and her children in the past. These visits were often strainful – Judy described how her sister "got pissed off with having us; I always felt we were a burden to her" – and sometimes frightening. Judy could not go to stay with her mother because "he's a big bloke, he's menacing, and she's very scared of him." When Jackie fled from the persistent attacks of her ex-husband she sent her older daughter to stay with her mother at the other end of England and went with her younger child to stay with a friend. However, her mother was pursued by obscene and threatening phone calls, and, "He was pestering my friend so much – we had the police to her house, protecting her. He said he was going to kill her and the children if she didn't tell him where I was."

6.10 There was some confusion between the category of 'friends' and that of 'neighbour' and the totals here are not very precise. Neighbours who were not friends, however, came in for more criticism than any other group in this category, mainly for being aware of what was going on and doing nothing about it. Gay said of her neighbour in Herne Bay, "They're refined, nice people – they don't want to be involved." Beth described how "They knock at the door and say 'Cut the row' but they don't care if you're dead." And Jane described how her husband would "hit me all day, like first thing in the morning, in the middle, there was no limit. Any time you like, with the windows open and people outside cleaning their cars. And if I said to him 'Keep your voice down' he'd open the windows more and say 'I'd like to see them helping you'. And they didn't do anything."

6.11 An immense amount of help was received by the women from their informal helpers; however, in the end it was not enough, or they would not have had to turn to the refuge. It may be that many battered women receive enough help in the community for them to be able to avoid seeking professional help of any kind: we simply do not know whether this is so or not. Before coming to the refuge, however, most of the women had turned to professional helping agencies to try to get the help which had proved beyond the resources of their family and friends.

Help from doctors

6.12 Many women turn to their doctor for help and, indeed, if she is to prosecute for assault, get an injunction to stop the man molesting her, or apply for a divorce or separation using the violence as evidence, a woman will need a medical certificate to support her case.

6.13 Nine of the women had visited the doctor during the previous year but had not mentioned the violence they were suffering. Some of them explained that on visits to the surgery they had passed off bruises and cuts by describing how they had "walked into the wardrobe" or "fallen down the stairs". Amy consulted her doctor about her persistent headaches, but did not say that the cause was the way her husband hit her about the head. Sally was ashamed – "You'd never expect a battered wife to be in Broadstairs with all the old people. When the doctor saw my bruises he said 'How did you get them?', and I said, 'I fell over', and he said, 'Are you sure?', and I said, 'Yeah'. I was embarrassed. It made me feel in the wrong."

6.14 Of the fifteen who had consulted their doctor about their violent marriages, seven found that they received 'help' which was of no help to them. Alexa said that her doctor had lectured her. "He said that I should help him. He said that my husband was sicker than I was and that it was up to me to help him." Nicola's doctor had told her to see that her husband got psychiatric treatment but she had been too frightened to be able to tell him this.

6.15 Many women described how their doctors had offered nothing but tranquillizers; Jane was one of these; she said, "He wasn't sympathetic at all. Actually I wasn't looking for sympathy. I was wondering if he could advise me of anywhere to go. And he just sort of said, 'Take these tranquillizers and you'll be alright'. I said to him, 'I've come for help. I don't know who to go to but I read in many magazines that people go to their doctors.' And he asked me what was wrong, and I said, 'I'm feeling very depressed and I'm having a lot of problems with my husband and I would like some advice', and he just wrote the prescription out and said, 'Well, take these and you'll be alright'. He said something like he hasn't got the time or he's not paid to do what the Social Services should do. So I said, 'Who are the Social Services?', and all he said was, 'Go to the Town Hall'. I sat down for two weeks and I thought – going to the Town Hall seems silly."

6.16 Table 14 shows that 47% of those who had told their doctor about their problems felt that they received no help. One might ask what help doctors could have given. Yet some *were* perceived as being helpful and these were, on the whole, those who considered the problem first and foremost as a marital problem. These doctors were perceived as going to the roots of the problem instead of simply being concerned with the exterior symptoms; they were also perceived as understanding the patient's own point of view. Doctors who persisted in treating only the medical aspects, and offering only medical solutions, were more likely to be perceived as being unhelpful.

6.17 The evidence presented here confirms the recommendation of the Select Committee (Report on Violence in Marriage 1975, xvi) that "it is not, in our view, sufficient for doctors just to treat physical injuries and dispense tranquillizers. We recommend that medical schools and nursing colleges should also give special attention to the social dynamics of family life, and to the medical (both physical and psychiatric) correlates of marital disharmony."

Help from the police
6.18 Table 14 shows that there was more dissatisfaction with the police than with any other of the official agencies to which the women turned. Sixty-three per cent of those who called in the police felt that they had

40

received no help from them. This figure underestimates the dissatisfaction with the police since, of the nine women who did not call in the police, six had considered doing so but had decided it would not be worth it. Joy said, "My mum called them in when I was a child and they just said, 'It's a family dispute – there's nothing we can do'. So I didn't think it worth it." Karen said, 'I'd heard of other people who had broken arms, broken noses, blood everywhere, and the police hadn't been interested. So I never bothered."

6.19 There seems to be a great disparity between the attitudes of those who call upon the police for help and of the police themselves. Some Senior Police Officers suggested that the police had adequate powers to deal with domestic violence under the 1861 Offences Against the Person Act. Their policy was to recommend to their officers to spend as little time as possible in the house when they were called to a domestic incident; and one officer said, "People who are married and want to have a go at each other – let them get on with it; that's my attitude." He was grateful to have the refuge as a place to which homeless people could be sent and as a place where 'missing persons' could be conveniently contacted; however, he criticized it on the grounds that "It makes it easier for people who want to opt out of their family responsibilities to go somewhere at someone else's expense".

6.20 This attitude seemed similar to that expressed to the Select Committee on Violence in Marriage by the Association of Chief Police Officers. In their evidence it was stated that "Whilst such problems take up considerable police time during, say, twelve months, in the majority of cases the role of the police is a negative one. We are, after all, dealing with persons 'bound in marriage', and it is important, for a host of reasons, to maintain the unity of the spouses" (p. 366). Later in this same evidence it was said that "The Police are concerned with the enforcement of the Law" (p. 369) and this was also the attitude of the Chief Superintendent in Canterbury, who emphasized how few women do eventually press charges against the men who assault them and how much police time is wasted in consequence.

6.21 Yet women continue to turn to the police for protection against assault. Often, indeed, the police are the only people to whom they can turn when the assault occurs, as it usually does, outside office hours (Bedfordshire Police Report 1976). Only two out of the twenty-five women in the sample felt they had really been helped and these two had been taken to the refuge by the police.

41

6.22 The comments of the other women indicate the degree of the disparity between their expectations of the police and their actual experience. Lena, talking of the police, said, "They wouldn't do *a thing*. They just said, 'It's a matrimonial affair and we don't need to get involved in it.' I said, 'The house is mine, will you remove him?' They said, 'We can't do that either. All you can do is lock the door on the inside, and then if he forces an entry we can arrest him then.' And I thought, 'Well, if he forces an entry, by the time you get up here I'll be dead.' So I wouldn't do it. I was too frightened to do it. So that was the only advice I got from them. No help."

6.23 Clare called the police in to protect her from her violent and alcoholic husband. She said, "I rung them up and asked if I could have police protection to get in to get a few things. They came up and they said, 'You know we're not allowed to get involved.' So I said, 'Does that mean I've got to go in there on my own?' and he said 'Yes', so I said, 'Well, I can't go in there, it's no good', so he said, 'Well, we'll knock on the door and just ask if you can go in, but I'm afraid we can't come in with you.' So they knocked on the door, and when he (her husband) saw the police there he said to him, 'I could smash your face in.' And the policeman said to me 'Come on, hurry up, hurry up, because we're not allowed to stop.' So they gave me two minutes to get some things, and I just snatched up some things that was airing in front of the fire, and they was after me all the time, 'Hurry up, hurry up'."

6.24 Judy accepted the police definition of their rôle as being limited to carrying out the law. "There's nothing they can do except arrest or not arrest. They can't get in the house. They shouted through, 'Mr. Jones, we want to see your wife.' And he shouted, 'Fuck off, this is my house.' It was the time after he hurt me seriously." (She had spent eight days in hospital because of bruised kidneys.) "And I'd made a vow then that I would stand no more. If he ever bashed me up again like that, that would be it. And this particular night he'd just pulled a lump of my hair out, and thrown me on the floor and kicked me. So I went down to the police station and tried to press charges. And if I could have done I would have done. But they said I wasn't grievously harmed. They said, 'You should have come the time before.' "

6.25 There is much police criticism of the women who take out charges against men who have assaulted them and then drop the charges later. Of the 288 domestic acts of violence which were recorded in the Bedfordshire Report, 36% led to court proceedings and 17% of these complaints were withdrawn before the case came before the court, that is, in eighteen out of the 288 cases, charges were withdrawn after having been made. It may be that police awareness of the possibility of the woman withdrawing makes them sceptical of taking up such cases. Karen said, "So I went down to the police station and I said, 'I'd like to press charges against my husband for assault.' And the policeman just said, 'You don't look to me like you've been assaulted.' Oh, I was in such a state and it annoyed me so much. And I said, 'But I've been to the doctor, and I've been to the solicitor and this is what they advised me to do.' I couldn't drink for twenty-four hours, it was awful, and I could barely eat for three days. My throat was so swollen. But nobody seemed interested in doing anything about it. I had to push all the time." Since the man involved was in fact her ex-husband, there was no question in this case of 'maintaining the unity of the spouses'. Eventually, Karen did manage to get the case to court and the man was fined; however, her dissatisfaction with the police assistance was considerable.

6.26 It seems as though there is a disparity between the assumption of the police that their rôle is to enforce the law, and the assumption of the women that the police can be asked for protection from assault. A refuge can play an important rôle in simply protecting battered women from assault, but many women would prefer to stay in their own homes if better protection could be afforded them there.

Help from social workers

6.27 Women in the sample turned to social workers for help more than to any other individual or agency; in eighteen cases the woman's parents were aware of her problems, while in twenty-one cases a social worker had been involved. However, in nearly half these cases (48%) the woman did not feel that she had been helped. Reading through the interview transcripts it seemed as though there was a degree of confusion, both among the women as to the sort of help they could expect, and among the social workers about the sort of help which would be most appropriate. Many women would have been helped by being given a clearer idea of what help the social worker could and could not give.

6.28 The women who felt that they had been helped had often been given the information which they required at the time. This might be information about such questions as getting a tenancy transferred or arranging a divorce, or it might be information about the refuge. If this information was seen as being relevant and realistic then the social worker was perceived as being helpful. The other type of help which was particularly valued was friendly support by the social worker over a period of time. Karen described how her social worker came every week for six months. When asked what sort of help she gave, Karen replied, "She helped us to talk to each other and helped us to bring out what we were feeling. Because we just couldn't do it on our own. I found her a great help. I used to look forward to her coming, to talk to her, because she was the only person around who seemed to understand. I couldn't talk to my mother or my sister like I talked to her."

6.29 However, this sort of relationship can be impossible in the case of the woman with a very jealous and demanding husband. Sally's social worker suggested that she should go to the mother-and-baby club, but the man with whom she was living would not allow her to go. She said, "Every time the Welfare Visitor came round he was always in the other room. He used to threaten me before anybody came (because he always used to look out of the window); he used to say, 'Keep your mouth shut or you'll get that.' And I had to tell a pack of lies to bloody everybody."

6.30 The women who were dissatisfied were often those who had been given what they regarded as inappropriate or unrealistic information, information which may have been correct but which did not relate to their situation. Jane said, "I went to the Town Hall and I spoke to the social worker and they said, 'It's your flat – you can easily get him out. Get an injunction.' And I said, 'Yes, I could do all this, but what about when everybody's gone? What about in the night? He'll wait. He's not stupid. He'll walk straight out when the police come and act like nothing's going on. He'll speak to them as though I'm the idiot. Wait two days and he'll be ringing me, threatening me, until he thinks it's all clear, and then just come and get me. What do I do then?' 'Well, you call the police.' That's ridiculous. I've been holding the phone, trying to dial the number, and he's bent my fingers back and hit me and broken the phone. The engineers are fed up because they know our house so well. If we have a row he just pulls it out."

6.31 Some women were confused by what they perceived as the wilful withholding of information. When Nicola was asked about social workers she said, "They're not much good really. He just kept saying, 'What do you think you should do? What do you think you should do?' I needed him to give *me* ideas, not just keep saying what do you want to do. I came for help, not for blooming . . . oh, dear. . . ."

6.32 It might be relevant to look at attitudes to the help received from social workers in the light of attitudes to the help received from solicitors and from marriage guidance counsellors. There was a high degree of satisfaction with solicitors, but it seems likely that this reflects a realistic appraisal of what a solicitor could offer. A woman would go to a solicitor to have a separation or a divorce arranged, and when this was put in motion for her she would feel that she had been helped. However, she would go to a marriage counsellor to have her marriage problem solved and was almost always disappointed both in the methods used and the results achieved. Women went to social workers in the hope that their many problems would be eased, and were disappointed, not necessarily because the social worker was inadequate, but because their expectations had been unrealistic.

6.33 It may be worth quoting at some length from the interview with Jackie, who was being severely beaten up by her ex-husband. Her comments sum up much of the criticism of social workers and introduce the question of the help she received at the refuge. Her emphasis on self-help is interesting. She said:

6.34 "Social workers – I don't think they are very qualified at all to deal with this sort of thing. They often say the wrong things. There's only one person that can help you and that's yourself. I've been to all these people and there's nobody can help you. Really, these social workers, they don't know what they're talking about. It's a good job – like Citizens' Advice too – it's a good job. It must be lovely to sit and listen to new things every day.

"The social worker came to see me and he said it was because I came from a broken home – because my parents were divorced. He said that it usually runs in families. I couldn't help laughing because my parents got divorced two years ago after being married for thirty years. And then he started suggesting that it was sexual and that women enjoyed being beaten. As soon as he started on about that I moved away, I sort of moved the chair away. The only practical advice he could give me was that he could get me a warrant to go home to me mother's in Leeds. That wasn't practical at all – I'm a woman, not a runaway teenager. I've got a home and a family! You can't run home to your mother.

"The only people that's helped me are the women that have suffered themselves. And the way they've helped is not by giving me advice – but by me listening to exactly the same things that I've gone through. And funnily enough, you can laugh about it then. You hear the other women talking, and they say the same things that you thought that only you suffered and only your husband said to you. It seems funny because you thought it was just said and thought up specially for you, and yet you hear the women repeat the same things."

Conclusion

6.35 The last two sections of this report have been concerned with building up a picture of the needs of battered women, as revealed in the twenty-five interviews. If a woman has been injured her first need will be for medical treatment. Her longer-term needs can be summed up under four main headings:

1. protection
2. accommodation
3. support
4. advice

The advice which she needs may be concerned with Social Security payments, with her housing situation, with the care and education of her children, with the future of her relationship with the man with whom she was living, and with the different legal proceedings which she might want to put in motion. Not all women will experience all four needs but most of those interviewed experienced more than one of them and some had an urgent need for help under all four headings.

6.36 It is important to stress the subjective element in this problem. What is intolerable in one relationship may be acceptable in another. This was illustrated in the women's accounts of their attempts to seek help from different agencies, where those helpers who looked at the problem from the woman's own point of view were likely to be perceived as being more helpful. In some cases the battering was not seen by the woman as being the most unsatisfactory aspect of the relationship, but was used as evidence of the breakdown of the relationship and of the need for help. Many of the women had put up with ill-treatment for many years, and it was not the battering itself but another aspect of the situation, such as the children becoming aware of their parents' antagonism, which finally made the woman leave home.

6.37 Against this background, the final section of the report will consider the women's experience of the refuge and the extent to which they were able to find there the help they needed.

46

Chapter 7
The Canterbury Women's Centre
How the women experienced the refuge

7.1 At the time when the women were being interviewed the Centre was still being run by the group of people who originally set it up, and the dominant norms were still those of self-help, mutual support and power-sharing (see 2.6). This original group was made up of postgraduate and undergraduate students, some of whom intermitted from their university courses in order to be able to work at the Centre, and a number of young married women. The core members of the group worked full time at the Centre and a wide range of people gave different sorts of support. Two social workers and the health visitor for the area were often in the house, and many other social workers called to visit their clients.

7.2 However, it was the members of this small and highly committed core group who were most influential, and whose ideas and energy made the Centre function as it did. At an early stage the group formed itself into Canterbury Women's Aid and became affiliated to the National Women's Aid Federation, recognizing that the Five Aims of the N.W.A.F. expressed also the aims of the Canterbury Women's Centre. This is not the place in which to discuss the internal struggles of the core group, though the rich data which is available would provide the basis for an interesting case study. However, a brief account must be given of the changes which were taking place in the running of the refuge while the women were being interviewed.

7.3 Part of the interview with each of the workers was concerned with the ideals which led her to work at the Centre, and with her concept of how those ideals could best be put into practice. As the year went on, some members of the core group of workers became increasingly dissatisfied with the way in which the original ideas were being implemented; they began to spend less and less time there, and had less and less power. This meant that other members became more powerful, and so the dominant norms of the Centre gradually altered. Preliminary analysis of the interviews with the workers shows that those who became dissatisfied were those for whom ideas about the position of women in society were a strong motivating force; they were also those who believed most strongly that jobs, information and power could be shared among all those who were involved at the Centre, whether they were women or workers. By contrast, those members of the core group who maintained their commitment, and who gained in power, were those for whom the desire to help battered women as a specific group was a strong motivating force. They were also those who were more sceptical about the possibility of running the Centre without some degree of division of labour and some sort of hierarchy of authority.

7.4 This has been a brief summary of a long and complicated process of change. However, a brief summary seems all that is necessary at this stage since the interviewing of the battered women mainly took place during the time when all the core workers were still actively involved in the daily life of the Centre. Only towards the end of the time of the interviewing did things begin to change. This was clearly seen in the answers to the question, "Do you sometimes think it would be better if there were one person in charge here?" Most of the women accepted the assumption implicit in the question that no one person was in charge; however, the last six or seven women, who were interviewed in May and June, were increasingly likely to look surprised and to answer, "But I thought so-and-so and so-and-so were in charge." Another significant question was the one which asked, "And cleaning and tidying, how is that arranged?" The women who were interviewed in February would answer that everybody shared in the work and did what cleaning and tidying seemed to them to be necessary; the women who were interviewed in March and April said the same, but often added that it would be better if there were a rota so that the work would be shared more fairly; the women who were interviewed in May and June answered by describing the rota which one of the women had devised.

7.5 However, by and large, the women who were interviewed were living in a refuge which was run according to its founding principles. There was no 'warden' or other clear authority figure; there was no management committee; decisions were taken at meetings which anyone was free to attend; and the only fixed rules were that no men were allowed beyond the office, the children had to be in bed by 8.30, and no woman in need should ever be turned away. For each woman, her first experience of the Centre was being welcomed in and given a cup of tea; she would then be shown where she was to sleep, perhaps by one of the workers or perhaps by one of the other women living in the house (it would not be clear to her into which category the person came). In the following days she would find out by trial and error what the norms of the house were; she would be given help if she asked for it, and left in peace if it seemed that that was what she would prefer.

The help offered by the refuge

7.6 What did the women feel about the experience of living in the refuge? How much was the refuge relevant to the needs which led them to come there, needs, that is, for protection, accommodation, support and advice? How much did being at the refuge make them more able to cope when they left it? The full answers to some of these questions would require follow-up interviews which would, hopefully, make possible some evaluation of the use of the refuge to the woman and her children. This present study could only cover the women's experiences of the refuge as they saw it while they were still living there; their answers would probably have been different had they been interviewed after they left. However, they appeared to speak frankly, in that criticism came as readily as appreciation, and I did not feel that I was being identified with the 'organizers', the 'committee' or with whatever word was used to describe the elusive authority figures.

7.7 Certainly the women appreciated the *protection* which the refuge offered them. Stress was always laid on the importance of keeping the front door locked and any other potential entrances well barred. Callers might be asked to shout their names through the door before they would be allowed in, and women were warned of the dangers of giving away information to telephone callers. Many of the women said what Ann said, "I love hearing that front door shut, especially when it slams; it makes you feel safe; it shuts you off from the outside world and I think that's good." When she was asked what she liked best about the refuge, Clare said, "I've got peace, that's my main thing I've got at the moment. I'm a lot more settled now than I am in my own house because I've got peace of mind."

7.8 Many of the workers spoke gratefully of the prompt assistance which the Canterbury police had given to the house on several occasions. The police themselves said that the Women's Centre caused them less trouble than many private houses in the town, but it was reassuring to all those living in the refuge to know that any appeal for police help was always responded to quickly.

7.9 Many women said that the best thing for them about the refuge was simply that it was there, providing *accommodation* for themselves and their children when they needed it. One woman described it as "a port in a storm", another called it "a haven", and for a third the best thing was "not being turned away". Beth wept as she described her feelings when she arrived at the refuge: "You feel rejected; you're thrown out of your house; you don't know what's going to happen; you're trying to get

49

yourself organized; you're thinking of your kids; everything's going through your mind at the same time really. So when I arrived I was just thankful that there was somewhere to come. It was the feeling that you wasn't going to be shoved out – that nothing was too much trouble – a queer feeling but a nice feeling. You wasn't in the way; you wasn't a bother. They made you a cup of tea. You was welcomed."

7.10 Most of the women supported the idea of the open door policy, even though they knew it was responsible for the crowded conditions of the house. They were very aware of the feeling of having nowhere to go and answered questions about the open door policy by describing the feelings of women who might have to be turned away, were a limit to be imposed. As Beth said, "You can't turn someone away. People have to have somewhere to go. It's not very nice being lost and lonely in the world. Its muddly here, but it's somewhere to come home to." The women were very aware of the problems following from such crowded living conditions, but most were reluctant to see any limit on numbers so long as there are so few refuges that a woman who is turned away might have nowhere else to go.

7.11 A third aspect of the refuge which many women liked was the *support and companionship* which they found there. Particularly for women who had lived with very jealous and possessive men, this might be their first opportunity for years to find friendship outside the home. Jane described her favourite time of the day "in the evening when all the women get together and we have a good laugh, because I haven't had a good laugh for a long time. And they tell their stories. It comforts you without them knowing. I feel comfort to know I'm not the only person that's been beaten about for really utterly nothing." Mandy had been rejected by her family and had been beaten up while living with her husband in homeless family accommodation; she said, "The best thing is to get people like us together so that we can help each other to come out of our shells, to know that each other is not the only one that is like it and has got to live on their own with babies on Social Security. Get them all together and say, look, we're all in the same boat, we've all got to help each other, and in one big house you can do it." Paula paid tribute to the success of the attempt to break down the divisions between helpers and helped when she was asked how she felt about 'the girls, the helpers': "They're OK. They don't class you as a battered wife. They class you as a friend. Sit down and have a chat, you know. Have a laugh. . . . The thing I like best is the way we live as one family. It's not like going into prison – rules and regulations and specific times for doing this and that. You just live each day as you want to live it. If you want to go out you go out. If you want to come in you come in. It's more like a home than being home, because here you can sit down and not worry who's coming home after the pubs shut."

7.12 Some of the women liked what they regarded as the *homeliness* of the refuge, by which they meant that the lack of rules and the general dilapidation of the house saved them from worrying, for instance, about any damage their children might do. Ann thought back to when she first arrived and said, "I didn't dream that there was such a place easy run sort of way, not hospital or 'dormitoryfied', as I presumed it would be. I didn't expect it to be like one dirty great big home." When Kay was asked what she liked best about the place she said, "It's free and easy. It seems like a home. There's no hassle with anything – you can do what you like after being cooped up with stinkers of men." But she revealed one of the crucial contradictions when, in the following question, she was asked, "If you were starting up a refuge, how would you arrange it?" She replied, "It would be very well organized – people for specific jobs to run the place properly. Here, there's just a big committee and they all sit arguing about the same thing. If they all had something particular to do then something might get done. I'd like a specific job to do each day. There should be a rota, and someone should make sure the jobs get done each day." This basic contradiction between wanting freedom for oneself, but not liking the consequences of other people having the same freedom, will be discussed later, since it is crucial to the women's experience of the refuge.

7.13 Among the many aspects of living in the refuge which the women disliked, *the physical conditions* of life there were most often the subject of adverse criticism. Women disliked the mess and the dirt, the unwashed dishes which cluttered up the kitchen, and the dirty nappies in the bathroom. They criticized the way in which some women evaded their share of the work, and hated the bickering and quarrelling which this gave rise to. They found it hard to live with women whose standards were so different from their own, and hard to live with so many children. The house itself, with its peeling wallpaper and leaking roof, came in for some criticism, and some women did not seem to be aware that they were living in a house that had been occupied as a squat. All these criticisms were sometimes summed up by the specific suggestion that there should be more rules – rules about the cleaning, the use of the kitchen, the washing-up and the behaviour of the children. Lena said, "When you've got so many women, one wants to wash, one wants the iron, another wants to cook, somebody else wants to have their meal. If you don't time it, don't space it properly, you've got chaos. It's OK for these young girls, living a communal life, but everybody isn't thinking the way they're thinking. Women my age with three kids can't live like a hippy and muck in – it's just not me. I like privacy, and I like to know if I leave something in a set place it's going to be there when I come back."

7.14 Other women criticized the *lack of information* and, more particularly, the way in which they were given advice and information. They did not understand the idea that women who had lived in the refuge for longer might be able to help those who had newly arrived, and the anti-authoritarian ideology worked against this idea being explained to new-comers. Many women were confused because there did not seem to be anyone in charge who would tell them what they ought to do. When a woman arrived at the refuge she was entered in the register; an appointment would be made for her with the local Social Security office, and her children would be found places in local schools. If she wanted to see a solicitor an appointment would be made for her. After that it was usually up to her to decide what she wanted to do and to ask for whatever help she needed.

7.15 This point may be made best by juxtaposing a comment made by one of the workers with another made by one of the women who stayed in the house. Di was one of the original group who squatted in Errol House; she said, "I would say that we don't need anyone in charge because everybody who comes here is part of the house. When a woman comes she doesn't know what is going on – but there are the women who have been there longer. I just cannot accept this thing of having just one person or two knowing and doing everything, because this is defeating most things. The women are either going to move back into their old houses or some-where new, so they have got to take responsibility from the time they leave home, although it is hard, very hard. Maybe they just want a rest, but I don't think it should be allowed."

7.16 Jackie described her experience thus: "When I arrived I did expect someone to come and talk to me or maybe give me some advice. I thought that would be what would happen instead of just getting up and living. I did think someone would come and see me and sort out my problems. Or say – go here and go there. . . .

"The first day Jo phoned up the Social Security and made an appointment for me; but that's the only arrangement that's been made. I've been here three weeks and I still don't know who's in charge, or runs it, or what. Polly's here . . . I don't know what Tess does. . . . I think sometimes you need someone who's in charge. Not to lay down the law, but someone that you could ask for advice. Say you come back off the phone and your husband has said that he's going to kill you or he's smashed up your house. And all the women say, 'Oh, what are you going to do – what are you going to do?' and I haven't got a clue what I'm going to do. I would just like to go and ask somebody else, 'What should I do?' "

(Question) "Do you think they'd be able to tell you what you should do?"

(Jackie) "No, they couldn't. I never met anyone yet who could tell me what to do. The only person that I've spoken to that's done anything constructive is the solicitor who got me the divorce. He just knew what he was talking about."

Self-help and power sharing – in practice

7.18 It was clear that some women did grasp the idea of self-help, and understood that they could contribute to the work of the refuge and to the care of more recently arrived women. Some of them ran a stall at the market and raised money for Canterbury Women's Aid; some helped to organize jumble sales and made and sold cakes; others sold raffle tickets and lobbied councillors and participated vigorously in meetings. Moira said, "If a window gets broken, any of us that could put in a pane of glass would get a pane of glass and put it in. This place is supposed to be run by women for women."

7.19 Table 15 shows that twenty of the women definitely felt they had changed during their stay at the refuge. When they described how they had changed, most described changes which they appeared to regard as being for the better. Ann said, "I've got more confidence in myself. If I went down to the solicitor's I would come back and say, 'I've been down to the solicitor's on me own' and I would pat myself on the head. But now I do it and don't stop to look back. Just take it in my stride more." Many women described how they felt younger and more self-confident, more independent and more determined. Jackie said, "I feel my own self is coming out more. At home I was brainwashed – I had to watch what I said all the time." Lil described the changes she observed in the women: "When they first come in they are not up to it. I think they are entitled to ask us to make decisions for them in those first two or three days. And then it's just a matter of just gradually building up their lives again. Once we've made their first appointment for their Social Security or their solicitor, then it's up to them to make the next appointment. And gradually they expect less of you. Instead of coming into the office and saying, 'Could you just phone Social Security for me?', they just say, 'I'm going to phone Social Security, they're buggering me about.' I think it very foolish to give too much help."

53

TABLE 15 **Feelings of personal change while at the refuge**

Woman felt she had changed for the better	14
Woman felt she had changed for the worse	6
Woman felt she has not changed	3
Not sure	2
TOTAL	25

7.20 Those women who felt they had changed for the worse still described how they had become 'harder' or 'tougher' and Judy, who was perhaps the most critical of all the women, and who hated the time she spent in the refuge, commented "it does make women more independent because there is so little support".

7.21 It was also clear that the women did see the meetings as a forum at which disputes could be decided. The series of questions about how different problems would be resolved were usually answered with references to meetings. It was significant that when the core group of workers split into two factions, each of which wrote and circulated a paper to put its point of view, the women living in the house at the time also wrote and circulated a paper, though the chief point of the paper was that they felt they needed to be organized and supported. All three papers were discussed at a meeting.

7.22 However, as Table 16 shows, a majority of the women would have liked there to be someone in charge; as we have seen, whether they felt there *was* someone in charge or not might vary. It was thought that someone in charge would supervise the housework and make sure that everyone did her share. Whether this would in fact have met with approval is less certain, since those women who had stayed in other, more organized refuges often criticized what they perceived as disciplinarian and authoritarian organizers – "It was bloody terrible – that's why I came back here. True enough it was cleaner – but it was horrible. They just come in and they look down on you all the time. They were a toffee-nosed lot." There was also a demand for someone who would give more authoritative advice. "It should be warm and friendly, with someone in charge with a lot of information, who is good at giving advice but not ramming it down your throat."

7.23 Those who preferred that there should be no-one in charge emphasized the advantages of equality. Ann said, "I don't think you need a warden – someone doling out pills, to me that is a warden. It's got to be

TABLE 16   **Replies to question "Do you sometimes think it would be better if there was one person in charge here?"**

No – assumption in answer that no-one was in charge	6
Yes – it would be better, assumption in answer that no-one is in charge	10
Yes – it is better, assumption in answer that someone is in charge	6
Not sure	3
TOTAL	25

a person they class as a friend, like Hilary; they'll sit in the front room and they'll have a laugh and a talk with her, and they are stunned when they find out she is a social worker. That puts a barrier. If they don't know about that barrier until they have made a relationship, OK, she's not a social worker, she's Hilary." Paula, who was one of the earliest arrivals, spoke of an even earlier arrival: "Coming from somebody in authority it's like rules and regulations – but coming from Kay it's just like everyday things: you just settle into your own place." Sally described what many women seemed to want: "No, I don't think there should be anybody in charge. I think they should have somebody coming round who's got some legal advice, the legal side, the medical side, there should be a family doctor we could all go to. But as it says outside, this is an institution run by women for women, therefore there should be a completely equal say for everybody."

7.24 Though some of the women felt that more information should have been available at the refuge, the Divisional Director of Social Services felt that the needs of the women for information had been well contained by the voluntary workers in the refuge. Though her office was next door to the refuge she did not feel that its existence had placed an undue burden on her staff. Partly this was because, anticipating such difficulties, a meeting between the social workers of the area had agreed that each woman who was referred to the refuge would continue to be the responsibility of the social worker who had referred her there. On the whole the workers at the refuge felt that the social workers in the area had been helpful and supportive, and they particularly welcomed the continuing support which some individual social workers gave to individual clients.

7.25 There was much dissatisfaction with the contacts which the women had with Social Security offices, and the workers in the refuge were continually giving information to the women about the system of payments. Some women who had been at the refuge for longer than others also became able to give advice about how much Social Security benefit any one woman was entitled to. The local office was criticized for keeping women waiting for long periods of time, for failing to explain why payments were not made, for not sending out payments on time, and above all, for making mistakes in the amounts sent. Tess said, "The DHSS treat the women very badly. The way they muck them around. They expect a woman with a couple of kids to starve for a couple of days while they get through their paper work. And they make so many mistakes. And it's also messing them about – saying to a woman, 'Your Giro will be there in the morning'. And then you find that they haven't even sent it out when she goes up there the next morning to find out why it hasn't come. They've been a bit better lately; I think they are beginning to realize that we work fairly efficiently and that we are not trying to 'do' them, but that we expect that every woman should get what she is entitled to. We explain to each woman what she is entitled to and tell her to tell them. And since we have been doing that we have had far less hassles." Problems of this sort inevitably arise when a new kind of accommodation is set up; before both sides have had time to appreciate each other's difficulties and to work out new arrangements. Meetings have since taken place between the Centre and the Local Social Security office and the difficulties seem to be less frequent. Many battered women arrive at the refuge with nothing but the clothes which they and their children are wearing; they are completely dependent on the Social Security benefits to which they are entitled. Information about those benefits thus becomes a priority for them, and, if the local office cannot or will not help them, information about their entitlements will have to be available within the refuge.

7.26 There was also dissatisfaction with the medical care that was available to the women. No one practice in Canterbury was responsible for the women and children at the refuge. In theory, each practice in the town was supposed to care for one family at the refuge at any one time. What actually happened was that each new arrival would make a visit to each practice, would be refused at each, and would eventually be allotted to one practice by the Family Practitioner Committee at Maidstone. Tess described how "They have to traipse the streets and go to every doctor . . . it's a hell of a long walk for them. They said there had been a meeting of all the GPs in the town who were going to take an equal amount, but they haven't done it. They just won't do it. So we have to write to Maidstone with a card sending the information and they allocate. I think it's a pity we haven't got a doctor for this place. Ideally someone who could just come in like a member of the support group. That would be really good."

7.27 There seems to have been some misunderstanding about medical care, since the Community Physician for the area was confident that the women staying at the refuge would have been taken on as temporary patients by any doctor in the town. It seems likely that the women were not aware that they ought to ask to be taken on as temporary visitors and asked instead to become registered permanently with the doctors whom they approached. Since every doctor in Canterbury at the time had a full list of patients, each woman was refused and so had to apply to the Family Practitioner Committee to be allotted to a doctor. In addition, the doctors may not have been aware when a woman left the refuge, and so continued to refuse to take on new patients on the grounds that they were already responsible for one family living in the refuge, even though that family had left.

7.28 The medical authorities were also concerned about the health hazard which the refuge presented. To some extent this was a product of the state of the building in which the refuge was housed. It had not been lived in for many years and was damp and dilapidated; the piping was made of lade and the Health Visitor had to warn the women not to use the water which had stood in the pipes during the night. However, in part, the problem was associated with the principle of self-help and with the lack of supervision. Because it was left largely to the women living in the house to set their own standards of cleanliness, the house was cleaner and tidier at some times than at others, depending on the standards of the women who were living there at the time. Conditions would deteriorate, until an angry meeting would be called, a new set of rules would be drawn up, and suddenly the house would become much cleaner. The norm that the refuge was the temporary home of those women and children who were living there made the workers unwilling to intervene and to suggest that standards should be different.

7.29 The medical example illuminates particularly clearly the advantages and disadvantages of the way in which the refuge was run. On the one hand the lack of supervision meant that the house could become dirty and squalid, and that women whose standards were higher than those of the majority found it especially difficult to live there. On the other hand the lack of supervision meant that the women did assume responsibility for themselves and their children in a way that they might not have done had they been allowed to become more dependent; they did take it upon themselves to help other women and to criticize others who did not seem to be doing their share of the work; and many of them *did* feel that they had become more capable, more determined and more self-reliant during their stay at the refuge.

Chapter 8

Conclusion

8.1 In some respects this report describes a situation which is now in the past. In November 1976 the Canterbury Women's Centre was evicted from its first home. It moved to a house made available by the Canterbury City Housing Department, and situated in a village a few miles from the city. It is hoped that in the future the Women's Centre will be able to buy a house in the city, and Canterbury Women's Aid is having discussions with a housing association with this aim in mind.

8.2 During its first year the running costs of the Centre were met from payments made by the women staying there, out of their Social Security benefits. No other financial help was given to the Centre, though it must have effected a considerable saving on the costs of bed and breakfast accommodation or on the costs of taking children into care. £2,500 has been raised by voluntary donations and this is intended either for a deposit on a house, or for renovation of a house bought with the help of a housing association. In November 1976, the present home of the Women's Centre and the two half-way houses were rented to Canterbury Women's Aid by the local authority. The provision of *suitable accommodation* seems to be the chief need of a group such as this, and the running costs of the refuge should be able to be met out of the rent allowances made to the women as part of their Social Security benefit. It seems important that there should be liaison between the local Social Security office and the refuge to determine the level of the rent allowances.

8.3 The move to the new house showed up the changes which had been taking place gradually over the previous few months. Some of the original workers had become more and more disillusioned and this was the point at which they ceased to be involved. It seems as though the Centre is gradually becoming more formally organized; both power and information are being concentrated in fewer hands; and in general there seems to be a greater degree of differentiation between helpers and helped. It has not been possible in the time available to work through all the material which has been gathered on the processes of change within the institution. However, a follow-up study would make a useful comparison between the group of women who experienced a more self-managed refuge with a future group who seem likely to experience a more established and organized refuge.

8.4 This study has not been concerned with the nature of the battering which the women had experienced. The approach has been through the woman's own perception of her problems. It was felt that any attempt to evaluate the severity of the battering or to make any objective measurement of violence would be contrary to this approach, and indeed would present extreme difficulties. The study started from the assumption that the woman had experienced marital stress so severe that she had felt she had no alternative but to leave home, and it was concerned with her coping responses to this situation.

8.5 The problem of marital violence is so intractable because it has such wide implications. A woman who defines herself as battered is likely to have not one, but many different problems; her needs will be many, and have been summed up in this report under four headings – protection, accommodation, support and advice. Many different departments may be involved in helping her and her children, and the problems she brings to a refuge may be single or many.

8.6 Thus it is important to stress that a refuge should be seen as *multi-functional*, offering different help to different women, and different help to the same woman at different times during her stay. It was of great importance to the women that they should be able to stay in the refuge for as long as they felt they needed to stay there; they valued the feeling of security this gave. On the other hand many found the refuge stressful, and it would seem important that women should be helped to find a more permanent solution to their difficulties as quickly as possible.

8.7 The principles according to which the refuge was run did seem helpful to many women once they understood them; they gained from being encouraged to help each other and participate in the running of the house. However, there are three points which should be made.

8.8 First, it is necessary to explain to women coming to the refuge the principles by which it is run. Many women waited for days for someone 'in charge' to appear, and their confusion and distress over leaving home were compounded by this further confusion.

8.9 Secondly, it was clear that a self-managed refuge can be very stressful for those whose standards differ from the living standards of the majority in the house. Many women would have liked an authority figure who would have imposed their own standards on the other women, though it seems likely that such an authority figure would have evoked antagonism from other women. No one refuge can be liked by every woman who stays there.

8.10 Thirdly, the self-managed refuge can become extremely squalid, so much so that it deters too many women and is a health risk to those who are there. There would seem to be a need for some minimum standards to be enforced, without taking away too much autonomy from the women in the house.

8.11 All this implies a very high degree of commitment and skill on the part of the workers. In the first few months of the Canterbury Women's Centre most of the workers were in the Centre every day, and the distinctions between them and the women were often unclear. Partly, this was because many of the workers did indeed *need* the refuge themselves. Some needed it in order to escape from unsatisfactory home lives; others needed it as a tangible expression of ideas about which they cared deeply, or as a way of expressing their commitment to certain principles.

8.12 The high degree of motivation of the workers meant that they did not welcome outside interference. They did not see the Women's Centre as just another Social Service; nor did they see themselves as just ordinary voluntary workers. They were motivated by ideas about the position of women in society, about the nature of family life, and about the position of women within marriage; this ideological basis for their work 'fitted' with the problems which the women brought to the refuge. When the women approached other professional helpers, such as doctors, the police or social workers, their problems seemed to become fragmented. By contrast, the refuge provided a wider set of solutions, and the workers offered more appropriate explanations than did other sources of help.

Chapter 9

Policy recommendations

1. A refuge should be seen as serving a wider area than its immediate neighbourhood. Women should not lose their rights to be rehoused in their own home area because they are living temporarily in a refuge in another area. (4.8 to 4.11)

2. Battered women, with or without children, should be allowed to stay in the refuge for as long as they choose. However, single women without children who have not been battered should be encouraged to find other accommodation. A large demand from such women should be seen as indicating a need for hostel accommodation for this group in the area. (4.12 to 4.17)

3. Decisions about the housing needs of battered women should be treated as urgent. (5.14 to 5.21)

4. Women who have been battered should be given priority if they request the transfer of a local authority tenancy to another area. (5.16)

5. There should be greater concern about the need for speed in carrying out legal proceedings on behalf of women who have been battered. (5.14 to 5.21)

6. The rôle of the police in intervening in domestic disputes is a difficult one, but in many cases they could do more to protect the victims of domestic violence. (6.18 to 6.26)

7. The medical needs of a refuge could best be met by making it the responsibility of one sympathetic practice. (7.26 to 7.28)

8. Refuges should be housed in accommodation which is large enough. If the house becomes overcrowded, women may have to be sent to other refuges, but it should be possible for any woman in urgent need to be taken in temporarily. (7.10)

61

9. Ideally, refuge accommodation should be large enough to have space for a playgroup, meetings, advice-giving sessions, fund-raising activities and other functions. A refuge is more than just accommodation. (Section 2 and Section 7)

10. Local Social Security offices should consider sympathetically the costs of running the refuge when coming to a decision about the rent allowances paid to women staying there, bearing in mind that if the refuge were not available much heavier costs might have to be incurred, though these costs would be borne by other departments. 7.25 and 8.2)

11. Half-way houses are a valuable addition to refuge accommodation, particularly when legal and administrative proceedings are prolonged. (5.13)

12. The self-help principle is relevant to the needs of battered women. It can best be fostered by providing accommodation and by respecting the autonomy of the group in its use of the accommodation. (Sections 7 and 8)

University of Kent at Canterbury
Centre for Research in the Social Sciences

Questionnaire

University of Kent at Canterbury
Centre for Research in the Social Sciences

The Role of a Women's Centre in Assisting Wives
with Violent Husbands

Questionnaire

Family background

1. Where were you born?
2. What year were you born? Age now.
3. Are your parents still alive – Father?
4.   – Mother?
5. Are they still married?
6. (If divorced or if one is dead) have they, or has he or she married again?
7. What is/was your father's job?
8. Where are they living now – Father?
9.   – Mother?
10. How often have you seen them during the past year? – Father?
11.   – Mother?
12. Do you have any sisters or brothers? For each one, could you tell me:

	13. What sex?	14. Where does he/she live?	15. How often have you seen him/her during the past year?
i.			
ii.			
iii.			
iv.			
v.			
vi.			

Education and employment

16. How old were you when you left school?
17. Did you pass any exams before you left?
18. And after you left school – did you
    get any qualifications?
19. What was your first full-time job?
20. Have you had a paid job within the
    last 12 months?
21. What job was it?
22. How many hours per week was it?

Marital history   1.   2.

23. Have you at any time been married?
    (If no, go to Q.33. If yes, continue)
24. What year did you get married?
25. How old were you then?
26. How old was he?
27. Are you still married to him?
    (If no, go to Q.30. If yes, ask Q.28 and 29)
28. What is his job now?
29. Were you living with him before you came here?
30. When did your marriage end?
31. Are you divorced?
32. Did you marry again?
    (If no, go to Q.33. If yes, go back to Q.24)
33. Do you have a regular boyfriend that you live with?
34. What is his job?
35. Were you living with him before you came here?
36. (If she didn't come straight to Centre from
    marital home)
    Could you tell me with whom you stayed
    and how long you were there between leaving
    him and coming here?
37. So where was your home before
    you came here?
38. How long have you lived in that house?
39. Is it a rented house (council or private)
    or do you own it?

Marital history (continued)

40. Is the house in your husband's name, or
    yours, or in both your names.

41. Do you have any children?
    (If she has children) Please tell me about each one in turn, whether
    it is a boy or a girl and how old it is and where it is living now.

	42. Sex	43. Age	44. With Mother	45. If not with Mother, where living now	46. With whom
a.					
b.					
c.					
d.					
e.					
f.					

Marital difficulties (Rest of questionnaire refers to most recent spouse)

47. Now what about the incident which made you decide to come here.
    Could you tell me what happened? What brought things to a head
    do you think?

    (Try to find out:

    who did it

    what did they do – damage caused

    date and time of incident

    cause as perceived by respondent

    whether there were any witnesses.)

48. (If physical violence is mentioned)
    When did he first hit you?

Marital difficulties (continued)

49. So how long has that been going on?

50. (If other marital troubles are mentioned)
When did things start to go wrong?

51. And have you had other troubles – such as, for example:

    money troubles?

    housing problems?

    other disagreements, about drinking or
    gambling, for example?

52. Have you ever left him before?

53. How many times have you left him?

54. How long was the longest time you
were away like that?

55. Where did you go that time?

56. Why did you go back to him that time?

57. Did you want to go back to him?

Sources of help

When we are in trouble, there are a number of different people and organizations which we could ask for help. I'm going to mention some of them. For each one I'd like to know whether you ever thought of going to them about the problems you've been telling me of.

58. For example, what about your *parents* or mother/father.
Did they/she/he know about your difficulties?

    If *No* (a) Why wouldn't you want to tell them?

    If *Yes* (b) Did they give you any help or advice?

    (c) Was that advice/help useful?

59. And your *brothers and sisters* (if any).
Did any of them know about your difficulties?

    If *No* (a) Why wouldn't you want to tell them?

    If *Yes* (Obtain answers about *one* which seemed most helpful)

    (b) Did he/she give you any help or advice?

    (c) Was that help/advice useful?

67

Sources of help (continued)

60. Did any other *relatives* of *yours or your husband's* know about your difficulties?

    If *No* (a) Why wouldn't you want to go to them?

    If *Yes* (b) Did they give you any help or advice?

            (c) Was that help/advice useful?

61. Did any of your *friends* or your *husband's friends* know about your difficulties?

    If *No* (a) Why wouldn't you want to go to them?

    If *Yes* (b) Did they give you any help or advice?

            (c) Was that help/advice useful?

62. Did any of your *neighbours* know?

    If *No* (a) Why wouldn't you want to go to them?

    If *Yes* (b) Did they give you any help or advice?

            (c) Was that help/advice useful?

63. Another person that people sometimes go to about these sorts of difficulties is their Doctor.

    Did you think of going to your *Doctor* for help?

    If *No* (a) Have you seen your Doctor during the past year?

            (b) Why wouldn't you want to ask him/her for help?

    If *Yes* (c) What happened when you talked to him/her?

            (d) Did he/she give you any help or advice?

            (e) Was that help/advice useful?

64. Did you ever think of going to the **Police**?

    If *No* (a) Why wouldn't you want to go to them?

    If *Yes* (b) Did they give you any help or advice?

            (c) Was that help/advice useful?

65. Have you been in contact with the *Social Workers* about your troubles?

    If *No* (a) Have you met any social workers during the past year?

            (b) Why wouldn't you want to go to them?

    If *Yes* (c) Did they give you any help or advice?

            (d) Was that help/advice useful?

68

Sources of help (continued)

66. Have you ever been to a *Solicitor*?
    If *No* (a) Why was that?
    If *Yes* (b) Did he/she give you any help or advice?
         (c) Was that help/advice useful?

67. What about *Marriage Guidance* – did you think of going to them?
    If *No* (a) Why wouldn't you want to go to them?
    If *Yes* (b) Did they give you any help or advice?
         (c) Was that help/advice useful?

68. Is there *anyone else* (prompt for church leaders, NSPCC,
    Samaritans, Citizens' Advice Bureau)
    (For each one mentioned)
    (b) Did they give you any help/advice?
    (c) Was that help/advice useful?

Present situation

69. When did you come here?

70. How did you know about this Centre?

71. How did you get here? (transport method)

72. Have you got any money coming in at present?

73. Where from? (source of income)

74. (If receiving Supplementary Benefit)
    (a) Were they helpful?
    (b) Did they give you any advice?
    (c) Was that advice useful?

75. Do you hope you'll soon be getting money
    from any other source?

76. What sorts of things have you got to decide about while you are here?

77. So what do you think you'll do next?
    (Try to find out her plans, if any, with regard to her marriage,
    housing, children, source of income, etc.)

78. So how long do you think you'll stay here?

The refuge

I'd like you now to think back to the first time you came into the refuge . . . when you first arrived.

79. What did you notice first?

80. Who told you where you were to sleep and how things are done here?

81. What were your first feelings about the other women here?

82. And how about the girls, the helpers, the ones who help to organize it, how did you feel about them?

83. What did you expect to happen, which didn't happen?

84. Can you remember how your children felt? (Prompt) Did you have to comfort them a lot?

    If *Yes* What was it that was upsetting them?

85. How many people sleep in your room?

    How do you feel about being so crowded?

86. Do you feel you have changed since you've been here?

87. How do you feel, for example, about what the place looks like?

88. How do you feel now about the other women living here?

    Do they get on quite well together do you think?

89. And how do you feel about the girls and the helpers?

90. How do your children feel about being here now?

Now I want to ask you some questions about the arrangements here – about how you do things.

91. How do you arrange about cooking, for instance?

    Do you think that way of doing it could be improved?

92. And cleaning and tidying, how is that arranged?

    Any improvements there?

93. And what about the children – are there any rules for them?

    about quietness at bedtimes, for example.

    Do you think there should be any other rules for the children?

94. What are the arrangements about men coming in here?

    Do you think that is right?

70

95. Are there people living here now who are not really battered women?

    Do you think any woman who needs accommodation should be allowed to live here, or should the refuge be only for battered women?

96. What would happen if the house got very crowded?

    Are there limits on the number of people who can live here?

    Do you think that is right?

97. Do you think in general there should be:
    More rules?   if *Yes* in what areas?
    About the same amount of rules?
    Fewer rules?   if *Yes* in what areas?

98. Do you sometimes think it would be better if there were one person in charge here?

I'm going to ask you about some problems which might arise here. I'd like to know how you think they would be sorted out.

99. If someone's child was a real nuisance, and upset the other children, what do you think would happen?
     Do you think that is what ought to happen?

100. If one of the women habitually left the kitchen in a mess, didn't do her share of the cleaning, what would happen about that?
     Do you think that is what ought to happen?

101. If you found that someone was stealing your things or money, what would happen about that?
     Do you think that is what ought to happen?

102. If there was a serious disagreement between the women who are living here and the girls, what do you think would happen?
     Do you think this is what ought to happen?

103. If there was a serious quarrel between the women living here, suppose it came to violence even – what do you think would happen about that?
     Do you think that is what ought to happen?

The refuge (continued)

104. If one of the women had a man in her room at night and this was discovered, what do you think would happen?

    Do you think that is what ought to happen?

105. Under what circumstances do you think someone might be asked to leave the refuge before they wanted to go?

106. And finally, could you tell me what you like best about this place.

107. If you were starting up a refuge somewhere else, what sort of place would you look for and how would you arrange it differently from this one?

Departure Information

108. Date of leaving Centre

109. Total length of stay

110. *Where did she go when she left?*

    Place

    Ownership of house she went to live in

    Did she go with anyone?

111. Other comments:

APPENDIX 2

University of Kent at Canterbury
Centre for Research in the Social Sciences

Investigator's Checklist

The beginning of the Canterbury Women's Centre

1. When does the story of the Canterbury Women's Centre begin for you?

2. How did you get involved?

3. When was the first time you heard of the idea of having a Women's Centre in Canterbury? Who did the idea come from as far as you were concerned?

4. Who did you talk to at that time about the Women's Centre?

5. At that time, what did you think the Women's Centre should be like? What sorts of activities did you think should go on there?

6. Did any of the people you have mentioned have different ideas from yours?

7. Were you involved in the original squat in Errol House? (if yes) Tell me about that – what did you do? Who else was involved at that time?

8. Did you go to the meeting at the Sydney Cooper Centre? (if yes) What happened at that meeting? What were your feelings about it?

9. So if we go back, say, to November/December 1975, how much would you say you were going to the Women's Centre then? What were you doing?

10. At that time, what did you think the Women's Centre should be like? What sorts of activities did you think should go on there?

11. At that time, did any of the people involved have different ideas from yours? (if yes) What did they think?

12. At that time, what was your *occupation*?
    (if in employment) – what job was it?
    – how many hours per week?

    (if in education) – what course was it?
    – in what institution?
    – which year were you then?

    (if neither) – were you working at home?
    – unemployed?
    – or other.

13. Where were you living at the time?

14. How long had you lived in that house?

15. Was it rented? Did you own it? Were you squatting?

74

Commitment to the Women's Centre

16. What do you think made you get involved with the refuge in the first place? What made you go on being involved?

I'm going to make various suggestions; I'd like you to tell me, for each one of these suggestions, whether it was important for you in maintaining your involvement.

	Important	Quite important	Not important
How important?			

17. Ideas about women's position in society.

18. Ideas about changing society – political ideas.

19. Desire to help battered women as a specific group.

20. Desire to provide alternatives to conventional family life.

21. Other motives.

22. Do you feel you've changed since becoming involved with the Women's Centre?   (if yes) In what ways?

23. Do you feel the people working with you have changed? (if yes) In what ways?

24. Do you feel the women change when they come to the Centre? (if yes) In what ways?

25. Do you think more positive efforts should be made to change them, to alter their ideas about things?

(if yes) How should this be done?

Family background

30. Where were you born?
31. What year were you born?   Age now?
32. Are your parents still alive – mother?
                                          – father?
33. Are they still married?
34. What do they think about your work for the Centre?
35. What are their jobs now (or what were their last jobs) – mother?
36.   – father?

Family background (continued)

37. Do you have any brothers or sisters?

38. (if yes) What do they think of your work for the Centre?

39. How do you feel you get on with your family?

40. In what ways do you feel your family has influenced you?

Education and employment

41. What sort of secondary school did you go to?

42. Did you pass any exams before you left?

43. How old were you when you left school?

44. Was there anyone who particularly influenced you during your last years at school? Friend, teacher, other?
    (if yes) In what ways did they influence you?

45. When you left school, what did you do then?

    Record to October 1975

    Year   Nature of job, or   Where were you living?
                    education course

46. Was there anyone who particularly influenced you during the 4 or 5 years after you left school?
    (if yes) What was their relationship to you? In what ways did they influence you?

47. Since you left school, have you been a member of any societies or organizations, or have you taken part in any campaigns or movements?
    (if yes) Did you take any leading part, or special responsibility?
    (prompt for interest groups, pressure groups, women's groups, political organizations)

48. Do you regard yourself as a member of the Women's Movement?

49. (if yes) What do you mean by the Women's Movement?

50. Which of these organizations/societies/movements which you have described seem relevant to the work you do at the Women's Centre? In what way?

51. Have you had other experiences which seem relevant to the work you do at the Women's Centre?
    (if yes) In what way?

76

Marriage and children

52. Have you at any time been married?
    (if no, go on to Q.62. If yes, continue)
53. What year did you get married?
54. How old were you then?
55. How old was he?
56. Are you still married to him?
    (if no, go to Q.58. If yes, Q.57 and then Q.61)
57. What is his job now?
58. When did your marriage end?
59. Are you divorced?
60. Did you marry again?
    (if no, continue. If yes, go to Q.53)
61. Do you feel that marriage has changed you?
    (if yes) In what areas of your life has it changed you?
62. Have you ever had any children?
    (if yes, continue. If no, go to Q.70)
63. Please tell me about each one in turn – how old is it?
    Is it a girl or boy? Is it living with you?
64. How do you feel your attitudes have changed since you have had children?

The Women's Centre now

70. How do you feel it has changed since it was set up?
71. What do you see as its successes?
72. Its failures?
73. There are quite a lot of people who used to be involved who have stopped coming. Why do you think they have stopped coming?
74. How much do you feel the Women's Centre has had to compromise with forces outside it? What sorts of compromises?
75. Do you think people should ever be asked to leave?
    (if yes) For what reasons?
76. Should women living at the Centre be able to decide to throw people out?
77. What about single women – should they be allowed to stay at the Centre? What about if they are not battered?
78. What would you like to see the Centre like in a year's time?

Contact with other agencies

I'd like to know if you have had any contact with any of the agencies I am going to mention – contact, that is, on behalf of the Women's Centre. If you have, I'd like you to tell me what happened when you were in contact with them, and whether that was helpful.

80. The Police.

81. The Social Services.

82. Social Security.

83. Housing Department.

84. Health Services – doctors/hospital/health visitors.

85. Solicitors.

86. Schools.

87. Any other voluntary organizations.

List of pseudonyms used for those who were interviewed

Sample of 25 women	9 workers
Alexa	Di
Alison	Jo
Amy	Lil
Ann	Lucy
Beth	Nan
Clare	Petra
Debbie	Polly
Gay	Rosa
Gloria	Tess
Jackie	
Jane	
Joy	
Judy	
Karen	
Kay	
Lena	
Mandy	
Moira	
Nancy	
Nicola	
Paula	
Ruth	
Sally	
Sarah	
Tina	

References

Abrams, P., and McCulloch, A. (1976). *Communes, Sociology and Society*, Cambridge University Press.

Bailey, R., and Brake, M. (1975). *Radical Social Work*, Arnold.

Becker, H. S. (1970). *Sociological Work*, Allen Lane, Penguin Press.

Bedfordshire Police (1976). *Report on Acts of Violence Committed in the County*.

Borland, M. (1976). *Violence in the Family*, Manchester University Press.

Calouste Gulbenkian Foundation (1973). *Current Issues in Community Work*, Routledge and Kegan Paul.

Canterbury Community Guild (1976). Report – *Living in Canterbury*.

Cartwright, A. (1967). *Patients and their Doctors*, Routledge and Kegan Paul.

Dobash, R. E., and Dobash, R. (1974). '*Violence between men and women in a family setting*', presented at the VIII World Congress of Sociology in Toronto.

Dobson, A. (20th Aug. 1975). 'What makes a wife batterer?', *Community Care*.

Department of Health and Social Security (1976). *Observations on the Report from the Select Committee on Violence in Marriage*, HMSO.

Gayford, J. J. (1975). 'Wife battering: a preliminary survey of 100 cases', *British Medical Journal*, Vol. 1.

Gelles, R. J. (1972). *The Violent Home*, Sage.

Goode, W. J. (1973). *Explorations in Social Theory*, Oxford University Press.

Hanmer, J. (Sept. 1976). *Women's Aid and the Women's Liberation Movement in Britain*, Paper presented to the British Association.

Holman, R., Lafitte, F., Spencer, K., and Wilson, H. (1970). *Socially Deprived Families in Britain*, National Council of Social Service.

Jones, D., and Mayo, M. (eds) (1975). *Community Work Two*, Routledge and Kegan Paul.

Jones, K. (ed) (1974). *Yearbook of Social Policy in Britain*.

Kanter, R. M. (1972). *Commitment and Community*, Harvard University Press.

Lipsky, M. (1970). *Protest in City Politics*, Rand McNalty, Chicago.

80

Manis, J. G. (1976). *Analysing Social Problems*, Praeger Publishers, New York.

Marsden, D. (1968). *Mothers Alone: Poverty and the Father-less Family*, Allen Lane, Penguin Press.

Marsden, D., and Owens, D. (8th May 1975). 'Jekyll and Hyde Marriages', *New Society*.

Mayer, J. E., and Timms, N. (1970). *The Client Speaks*, Routledge and Kegan Paul.

McCall, G., and Simmons, J. L. (1969). *Issues in Participant Observation*, Addison-Wesley, Reading, Massachusetts.

McQuaig, D. (25th July 1974). 'Preliminary Report on Battered Wives in Scotland', *Social Worker*.

Moore, J. (1974). *Yo-Yo Children: a Study of 23 Violent Matrimonial Cases*, National Society for the Prevention of Cruelty to Children.

National Women's Aid Federation (1976). *Battered Women are Homeless*, N.W.A.F.

Pizzey, E. (1974). *Scream Quietly or the Neighbours Will Hear*, Penguin.

Punch, M. (September 1974). 'The Sociology of the Anti-institution', *British Journal of Sociology*.

Select Committee Report (1975). *Violence in Marriage*, H.C.553.11.

Shelter Housing Action Group (1976). *Violence in Marriage*, S.H.A.C.

Steinmetz, S., and Strauss, M. (1974). *Violence in the Family*, Dodd, New York.

Stimpson, G. V., and Webb, B. (1975). *Going to see the Doctor*, Routledge and Kegan Paul.

Tomlin, C. (May 1974). 'Refuge for Battered Women' in *Health and Social Services Journal*.

Wilson, E. (1976). *The Existing Research into Battered Women*, National Women's Aid Federation.

Wilson, J. (1973). *Introduction to Social Movements*, Basic Books, New York.

Wright Mills, C. (1959). *The Sociological Imagination*, Oxford University Press.

Printed in England for Her Majesty's Stationery Office
by Staples Printers Rochester Limited at The Stanhope Press.

Dd. 595829 K20 1/78

Medical Ethics and
Medical Law

A Symbiotic Relationship

José Miola

·H A R T·
PUBLISHING

OXFORD AND PORTLAND, OREGON
2007

Published in North America (US and Canada) by
Hart Publishing
c/o International Specialized Book Services
920 NE 58th Avenue, Suite 300
Portland, OR 97213-3786
USA
Tel: +1 503 287 3093 or toll-free: (1) 800 944 6190
Fax: +1 503 280 8832
E-mail: orders@isbs.com
Website: www.isbs.com

Hart Publishing, 16C Worcester Place, OX1 2JW
Telephone: +44 (0)1865 517530 Fax: +44 (0)1865 510710
E-mail: mail@hartpub.co.uk
Website: http://www.hartpub.co.uk

British Library Cataloguing in Publication Data
Data Available

ISBN: 978-1-84113- 508-3 (paperback)

Typeset by Columns Design Ltd, Reading
Printed and bound in Great Britain by
TJ International Ltd, Padstow, Cornwall

Este livro é dedicado a memória da minha vó, Maria da Lourdes Pelizari, e do João Ramalho.

Acknowledgements

This book is loosely based on my PhD thesis, although little of it remains, and thus the list of people that I need and want to thank begins with that. First, I would like to thank Margot Brazier, who was inspirational as a supervisor during my PhD, and continues to be so as a friend now. The examiners of my thesis, Professors John Harris and Katherine O'Donovan, also made several helpful comments to me that nudged me in the direction that this book has eventually taken. The book has benefited greatly from their wisdom, as it has from my conversations with Professor Jonathan Montgomery.

Drs Mark Bell and Sara Fovargue read and commented on drafts of chapters. Sara has looked at so many different versions and drafts that I asked her permission to say that any errors were her, rather than my, responsibility – sadly she declined this kind offer on my part, and it appears that they must remain my own. Again, the book has benefited hugely from their expertise – thank you, both of you. Richard Hart has been brilliant, extremely patient and invariably supportive. I would like to take this opportunity to thank him for all of that. Mel Hamill and everyone at Hart have also been fantastic. I would also like to thank the copy editor, Julian Roskams, who did a great job.

Finally, I am of course indebted to my parents Ueber and Maria, whose love, support (and money!) enabled me to go to university, do the PhD and become an academic. This book would have been impossible without them and, ideally, it would have been dedicated to them. Equally, Tania Rowlett has had to put up with me and this project for some time now. Her love, support and understanding also deserve recognition.

Some parts of Chapter 2 were used in an article published in the *Cambridge Quarterly of Healthcare Ethics* (J Miola, 'The Need for Informed Consent: Lessons from the Ancient Greeks' (2006) 15(2) *Cambridge Quarterly of Healthcare Ethics* 152). They are reproduced with the kind permission of Cambridge University Press. Some parts of Chapters 2, 3 and 5 were used in an article published in *Medical Law International* (J Miola, 'Medical Law and Medical Ethics – Complementary or Corrosive?' (2004) 6(3) *Medical Law International* 251. They are reproduced with the kind permission of AB Academic Publishers.

José Miola
February 2007

Symbiosis

Symbiosis has been defined as 'the living together of two dissimilar organisms' and 'a relationship between two people in which each person is dependent upon and receives reinforcement, whether beneficial or detrimental, from the other' (www.dictionary.com). This is the definition adopted by this book.

Contents

Table of Cases and Statutes

Statutes

1

Introduction

I. Setting the Scene

IN THE LAST half century, medical ethics has undergone a renaissance. Never before has there been so much written on the subject as there is now. A multitude of ethical theories and perspectives provide a plethora of discourse emanating from a wide variety of sources. Indeed, medical ethics is no longer the sole preserve of doctors, as lawyers, philosophers, theologians, economists, sociologists and others all provide it with the benefit of their wisdom and expertise. But can this increase in the volume and variety of sources be said to have improved medical ethics? Is more necessarily better? In this book, I argue that the medical ethics renaissance and the consequent rise in volume of discourse has not made medical ethics more effective but, rather, has allowed the various discourses to cancel each other out, leaving a regulatory vacuum to be filled by the conscience of the individual medical practitioner. Furthermore the law, which would be expected to step into such a vacuum and restore regulatory order, has misunderstood the nature of contemporary medical ethics and thus exacerbates rather than resolves the problem. The process by which this has occurred – cultural flaws combining with excessive professional autonomy leading to a fragmentation of and failure in regulation – had already been identified as having occurred at the Bristol Royal Infirmary, in a clinical setting, in 2001, and I argue that it is the same with regard to medical ethics. The relationship between medical law and medical ethics can therefore be seen as symbiotic, in the sense that the two are dependent upon each other. However, I will demonstrate that it is not mutually beneficial but instead detrimental to both parties.

II. The Bristol Inquiry Report

In 2001 the inquiry chaired by Professor Ian Kennedy published its report into the events at Bristol Royal Infirmary (BRI) between 1984 and 1995.[1] What

---

[1] *Learning From Bristol: The Report of the Public Inquiry into Children's Heart Surgery at the Bristol Royal Infirmary 1984–1995* (Cm 5207, 2001).

Kennedy referred to as the 'story' of Bristol is undoubtedly steeped in tragedy. In essence, the Inquiry found that individual and organisational failings, combined with what it defined as a 'club culture' at the BRI, severely affected the quality of paediatric cardiac surgery at the hospital. This led to a large discrepancy in mortality rates between Bristol and other centres. The Inquiry observed that, from 1988 to 1994, the mortality rate at Bristol was double the national average in five of the seven years and that mortality rates fell in the country as a whole over that period. It concluded that this discrepancy could not be explained by 'statistical variation or any systematic bias' in the collated data.[2] Furthermore, many more infants were left with brain damage. Almost as concerning was the fact that the hospital was found to have routinely been less than honest with the children's parents regarding the chances of success of the surgery.[3] Regulation had clearly failed to monitor medical behaviour. The Inquiry's report identified that these failures were allowed to occur as a result of a process, the first part of which was what the Inquiry termed the existence of 'cultural flaws' inherent in the medical profession, which manifested themselves as 'excessive paternalism, lack of respect for patients and their rights to make decisions about their care'.[4] Patients were 'discourage[d] from asking questions', and were given 'only limited access to information'.[5] Worryingly, the Inquiry found that these flaws were 'evident in all parts of the NHS', and thus not just at BRI.[6]

Given that the culture of medical professionals during the 1980s and 1990s was identified as being antiquated and flawed, it was important that a system of regulation existed to mitigate the excesses of individuals or groups. This, how-ever, was not in evidence; rather, the next step of the process was that doctors at Bristol benefited from excessive professional autonomy. Early on in its report, the Inquiry noted that 'the prevailing wisdom was that policy-makers and managers should keep out of matters involving professional judgment'.[7] However, the managers were not dissatisfied with this state of affairs:

> [Chief Executive of the Trust] Dr Roylance's view was that it was his role to recognise and go along with the culture of consultants, which he characterized as being grounded in clinical freedom. He saw it as his role to free them to do their job. He told the Inquiry that he was not in the business of 'herding cats'. Clinicians at the bedside were to make decisions and *it was not for management to interfere*.[8]

Almost inevitably, those inside the autonomous clique developed a club culture which 'fostered a sense of "them and us"'.[9] Consequently, a person or category of

---

[2] *Ibid* 241.
[3] *Ibid* chs 12 and 17.
[4] *Ibid* 268.
[5] *Ibid* 268.
[6] *Ibid* 268.
[7] *Ibid* 74.
[8] *Ibid* 201. Emphasis added.
[9] *Ibid* 169.

persons either belonged to the club or they were 'excluded'.[10] In this way, a sense of belonging inculcated into doctors extended only to that professional group.[11] In the light of this, it is easy to see how, within a 'them and us' culture, a situation developed where the notion of 'professional autonomy ... expressed in the form of "clinical freedom"' created boundaries.[12] Involvement from those outside the boundaries was discouraged and marginalised. Moreover, this finding was made with specific reference to the General Medical Council (GMC), and the involvement of laypersons with medical bodies in general was not seen as being accepted by medical professionals: 'healthcare professionals in the NHS have increasingly tended to regard public involvement as at best a token, not to be taken too seriously, and at worst troublesome, challenging well-laid plans, and raising what are perceived to be awkward questions'.[13] The problem at Bristol was thus that those inside the club reinforced each other's opinions rather than challenged them. This led to an insular and largely autonomous group becoming almost untouchable within the BRI. As the Inquiry recognised, this state of affairs was not limited to Bristol but was prevalent throughout the medical profession. It is surely here that a self-regulating profession such as the medical profession should be seen to become involved in order to control medical behaviour. Indeed, the GMC has a statutory mandate under the Medical Act 1983 to discipline doctors and remove their registration to practice if it sees fit. Yet the Inquiry found that GMC guidelines were being ignored.[14] The culture at Bristol was inimical to that sought by the GMC, yet nothing was done. Again, regulation can only be seen to have failed at BRI, as the doctors essentially did as they pleased.

The third step of the process was that the boundaries created by Bristol's club culture inevitably led to a fragmentation of the various different bodies. The Inquiry noted that the NHS was marked by the 'coexistence of competing cultures';[15] moreover:

> [t]his is very much the case within the NHS, where the cultures, for example, of nursing, medicine and management are so distinct and internally close-knit that the words 'tribe' and 'tribalism' were commonly used by contributors to the Inquiry Seminars on this subject.[16]

This competition between cultures therefore not only encouraged tribalism, but, also, what the Report referred to as 'silos' of responsibility.[17] Each tribe had its own, discrete area of responsibility, not to be encroached upon by others. The

---

[10]   *Ibid* 196.
[11]   *Ibid* 275–6.
[12]   *Ibid* 303.
[13]   *Ibid* 401.
[14]   *Ibid* 295. The attitude reported is inimical to the GMC's ethical guidance.
[15]   *Ibid* 266.
[16]   *Ibid* 266.
[17]   *Ibid* 197.

separation created was 'hard to sustain',[18] and the overall effect of this fragmentation was a lack of co-ordination with respect to standards. Thus the Inquiry found that guidelines 'appear from a variety of bodies giving rise to confusion and uncertainty'.[19] Fragmentation was not limited to the BRI:

> [a]t a national level there was confusion as to who was responsible for monitoring quality of care ... What was lacking was any real system whereby any organisation took responsibility for what a lay person would describe as 'keeping an eye on things'.[20]

It was therefore no surprise that the Report later identified that the monitoring of paediatric cardiac surgery on children under one year of age had 'no clear place in the system, whether locally in Bristol or centrally in the DoH [Department of Health]'.[21] Amazingly, such was the lack of agreed, national standards that the Inquiry found it difficult to assess the standard of care at the BRI. Even as the Report was being written, it noted that 'no such standards exist'.[22] Effectively, therefore, no single group took responsibility for the maintenance of standards, with many believing that it was simply not their role to do so:[23]

> The SRSAG [Supra Regional Services Advisory Group] thought that the health authorities or the Royal College of Surgeons were doing it; the Royal College of Surgeons thought that the SRSAG or the trust were doing it, and so it went on. No one was doing it. We cannot say that the external system for assuring and monitoring the quality of care was inadequate. There was, in truth, no such system.[24]

What was left was a regulatory vacuum that could only be filled by the conscience and attitudes of individual doctors. Given the cultural flaws identified by the Inquiry, this meant that some patients were subjected to behaviour that was not appropriate. The report thus noted that it was 'no longer acceptable for patients, having been treated, as they are now for the most part, as equal partners by their GP, then to go into hospital and be confronted with old-style paternalistic attitudes by some consultants'.[25] The fragmentation of regulation meant that although the volume of guidelines may have risen, they effectively cancelled each other out. Thus, the Inquiry identified 'disadvantages in the appearance of a host of guidelines from different bodies, some, indeed, on the same subject'.[26] In particular, 'healthcare professionals may not know which standards should be followed, or what status or authority the standards have'.[27] Thus,

---

[18] *Ibid* 302.
[19] *Ibid* 17.
[20] *Ibid* 6.
[21] *Ibid* 155.
[22] *Ibid* 180.
[23] See generally ch 11 of the report.
[24] *Ibid* 192.
[25] *Ibid* 285.
[26] *Ibid* 383.
[27] *Ibid* 383.

if patients with a particular condition were to seek to refer to the guidelines which relate to the care of their condition they might find several, aimed at different specialists, emanating from different Royal Colleges and professional associations. Equally, they might also find standards developed by local clinicians, or by the DoH, or possibly by NICE. Or, they might find none at all.[28]

This led to a situation where the Royal Colleges, in particular, were frustrated that they had guidelines but no means of ensuring compliance and, as the British Paediatric Cardiac Association recognised, 'there is at present a vacuum in relation to the enforcement of standards'.[29] The guidelines produced had no *hierarchy* and doctors had no other method for *prioritising between them* or ensuring that the various sources of guidance worked together. One of the central points of the Inquiry's Report was the identification of this and a recommendation that there should be co-ordination of guidance between the different bodies:

> Currently, there are a large number of bodies involved in the activities which together constitute regulation. They include the new Nursing and Midwifery Council, the GMC, the proposed new body which will regulate the professions allied to medicine, the Royal Colleges, the various professional associations, the DoH, health authorities and trusts. Each operates in its own sphere, with, historically, little collaboration or co-operation. The various activities must be brought together and properly co-ordinated. The role of the various bodies must be clearly identified. And all of the bodies should be brought under the overall leadership of one overarching body.[30]

What can therefore be seen from the Bristol Inquiry's Report is a situation where the volume and variety in the sources of guidance, when combined with the autonomy granted to the profession, was a hindrance rather than a help. Paradoxically, the guidance cancelled itself out, leaving less rather than more regulation. Decisions were left to individual doctors and their personal views, as the different sources of guidance presumed that others were regulating medical behaviour. There was little, if any, regulation identified by the Bristol Inquiry Report.

III. The Analogy with Medical Ethics

Although the Inquiry was mainly concerned with technical medical matters, in the sense that the issue was the adequacy of paediatric heart surgery performed there, in this book I argue that the situation identified within the Report is equally applicable to medical ethics and medical law. Thus, the cultural flaws are as prevalent with regard to ethical issues as technical ones. The medical profession, as a self-regulating entity, necessarily demands and receives autonomy in ethical matters. Indeed, s 35 of the Medical Act 1983 provides that:

[28] *Ibid* 383.
[29] *Ibid* 383.
[30] *Ibid* 315.

The powers of the General Council [of the General Medical Council] shall include the power to provide, in such manner as the Council think fit, advice for members of the medical profession on –

(a)   standards of professional conduct;
(b)   standards of professional performance; or
(c)   medical ethics.

The statute thus allows the ethical conduct of medical practitioners to be regulated and controlled by the profession itself. It would thus be presumed that the GMC would be the sole, or at least predominant, source of ethical discourse. As we shall see, this is not the case. Indeed, in another reflection of the situation at Bristol, medical ethics is also fragmented. As I demonstrate in Chapters 2 and 3, there has never been such a high volume of medical ethics discourse. However, this growth has been accompanied by a concurrent increase in the number and variety of its sources. Three different categories of ethical discourse may be identified; with the first being what I call the 'formal' sector. This can only include the GMC, as it is the sole body with a statutory mandate to provide ethical advice to the medical profession. Moreover, it is the only body with the power to discipline errant doctors. The second group is the 'semi-formal' sector of discourse that comprises doctors groups. Led by the British Medical Association (BMA), which is effectively the doctors' trade union, this category also includes other medical groups such as the Royal Colleges. These groups are likely to be influential, particularly within a self-regulating profession with its club culture and silos; however, as they have no disciplinary powers and no statutory mandate, they are a separate category to the GMC. Finally, there is what I refer to as the 'unofficial' sector of ethical discourse. This group comprises all others involved in discussing ethical issues. This discourse emanates from, for example, academics, pressure groups and religious bodies, and contains expertise from a range of disciplines such as law, philosophy, sociology, and economics.

These sectors combine to create a mass of ethical discourse that is just as fragmented as the guidance produced by the bodies referred to in the Bristol Inquiry Report and, as Chapter 3 argues, the influence of the unofficial sector has been the most problematic. This is because it has encouraged and exacerbated fragmentation and a discursive rather than directive approach to medical ethics. Furthermore, there is no method for prioritising or choosing between the different categories of discourse and the consequent lack of regulation highlighted in the Bristol Inquiry Report is thus likely to develop. In this book, I argue that this has already occurred, despite what I call a medical ethics 'renaissance', which is the explosion of interest in and volume of medical ethics discourse in the second half of the 20th century. In Chapter 2 I will consider the lead-up to this renaissance, and examine the historical development of medical ethics. I will look at the ancient Greeks (Hippocrates and Plato), consider the 'dark ages' of

medical ethics, when there were few developments, and then the institutionalisation of the medical profession in the 19th century. The chapter will demonstrate
that, historically, medical ethics has been designed for doctors by doctors.

In Chapter 3 I further argue that the rise in medical technology and the trials
of doctors involved in Nazi medical atrocities had a great impact on medical
ethics rendering the previous, traditionally insular and paternalistic model unacceptable to society. Not only did these factors highlight the naïveté in trusting the
benevolence of human beings as individuals but they also, in a significant break
with the past, encouraged non-doctors to involve themselves in medical ethics.
This renaissance in medical ethics discourse has provided us with a situation
where we have a higher volume of ethical discourse than ever before. Nevertheless, it is also true that medical ethics has never been more confusing. Indeed, the
subject-specific nature of debates and the increasing academisation of the
subject, when combined with the variety of sources of discourse, have fragmented medical ethics to a critical degree.

As a result of the renaissance the unofficial category of ethical discourse
became its most prolific, and this in turn has had consequences. The first is that
some medical professionals have become more and more detached from ethical
discourse. As we shall see, the appropriation of medical ethics from the medical
profession by outsiders has led some doctors to question the relevance of what
medical ethics discourse has become in their eyes. Indeed, it is inevitable that the
more that non-doctors engage in ethical debates, the more those debates will take
place on their terms and using their language. Instead of working in tandem with
the medical profession, the renaissance has succeeded only in alienating parts of
it. Secondly, the fragmentation and academisation of medical ethics discourse
that this caused has made the entire concept one that is difficult to define. Thus,
if someone is asked to find some 'medical ethics', it is likely that they will pause
before actually doing so. There is, quite literally, so much that it can be said to
have cancelled itself out, as one may always find some discourse that refers to
itself as ethics that supports any given view. For example, if a doctor wants to
know whether it is ethically acceptable to give a blood transfusion to a Jehovah's
Witness, she will easily be able to find books and articles, purporting to be
'ethics', that will both support and reject that proposition. A plurality of
opinions, often diametrically opposed, can be found within the unofficial sector
with respect to any and every ethical enquiry. In essence, the question of what to
do with opposing ethical viewpoints is never answered satisfactorily. This leads
directly back, of course, to a perceived lack of relevance of ethical discourse in
dealing with ethical issues in practice.

In this way, then, it can be seen that this definitional problem inherent in
contemporary medical ethics makes it very difficult to actually find its boundaries and its purpose. Put simply, it is difficult to *use* medical ethics if we do not
know what it is and what it is for. Medical ethics as a concept remains amorphous
and little more than a collection of disparate and fragmented discourse from a
wide variety of sources. As a regulatory tool, or the corporate conscience of the

medical profession, it is not up to the job in its current state. In part this is due to the lack of categorisation and assignation of differing roles to the various strands of medical ethics discourse. The word ethics, for example, is vastly overused, and no thought appears to be given to what it means. Indeed, in some cases it is simply used as a synonym for morality – as we shall see, for example, in Chapter 7 with cases at the end of life, and in Chapter 8 in relation to its use by witnesses to the House of Lords Select Committee on Medical Ethics in 1994.[31] They are far from isolated examples, and certainly not what medical ethics is meant to be, a fact recognised by the BMA as far back as 1988.[32]

The consequence is that this high volume of discourse that refers to itself as medical ethics, without categorisation and including an infinite range of opinions, effectively cancels itself out in a manner that is redolent of the consequence of fragmentation at Bristol. Problems will be created if different ethical discourses clash. Thus, if it may be termed ethical both to transfuse a Jehovah's Witness and also not to then something *other than* medical ethics will have to form the basis of the decision. One option is the personal morality of the individual medical practitioner. As Chapters 2 and 3 will argue, Plato and then, tragically, the Nazis proved that such a Hippocratic ideal cannot be relied upon, as not all individuals are inherently good. Another forum for decision-making, however, might be the law. Indeed, there are several reasons why the law might be expected to involve itself in such a scenario, and why it is uniquely able to resolve some of the problems inherent in medical ethics, for several reasons. First, it is well placed to protect the general public from any abuses that the medical profession may propagate. As McLean argues, the law should be like a 'buffer which should be expected to stand between medicalisation and human rights'.[33] Secondly, as a concept it is essentially a regulatory framework, and thus can arbitrate between competing principles, as that is its purpose. Thirdly, and perhaps most importantly, the common law in particular deals with specific 'real life' issues and situations. It is thus an effective outlet for considering the treatment of 'Mrs Jones in Ward 5 at 4.10 in the afternoon', so reinjecting the relevance that contemporary medical ethics lacks.[34]

IV.   Enter the Law

In many ways, the law cannot help but be involved in this area, as many of the medico-legal cases that come before the courts have an inherently ethical content.

---

[31]   *Report of the Select Committee on Medical Ethics* (HL Paper 21-I, 1994).

[32]   See BMA, *Philosophy and Practice of Medical Ethics* (BMA, 1988) (iii), where the words 'legal', 'ethical' and 'moral' are defined and differentiated.

[33]   S McLean, *Old Law, New Medicine: Medical Ethics and Human Rights* (London, Pandora 1999) 2.

[34]   D Callahan, 'Bioethics as a Discipline' in J M Humber and R F Almeder, *Biomedical Ethics and the Law* (New York, Plenum, 1976) 6.

Issues such as consent, the confidential nature of the doctor–patient relationship, and euthanasia are all played out in courtrooms. But how is the concept of medical ethics dealt with by the courts, and how do they envisage their role? Will the law recognise the problems identified in this book and help to resolve them, or will it exacerbate them? The answer to these questions can be arrived at by looking at *how* the courts have conceptualised and utilised medical ethics in the cases before them. In Chapters 4–7 I examine the major cases in four issues in medical law with an inherent ethical content. The designation of ethical content is based on three criteria. First, in all cases there are what may be termed traditional ethical principles involved. Secondly, each issue is the subject of ethical guidance from the medical profession, which thus claims an authority over them. Lastly, in each case the decisions are not strictly medical in nature in the sense that doctors are not uniquely qualified to make them.[35] The cases are considered in chronological order to chart judges' conceptions of, and attitudes towards, medical ethics. They demonstrate that while sometimes acutely aware of medical ethics, and even the medical ethics renaissance, English judges often consider that medical ethics is a matter for the medical profession. In other words, the prefix 'medical' has not yet been removed from ethics in the eyes of a number of judges. At times, medical ethics is seen as nothing more than 'professional etiquette', not to be interfered with. At others, judges will instinctively abrogate decision-making responsibility to medical ethics as soon as they identify the ethical issue in a case.

This does not have to be so for, as McLean argues, 'the law can meet the standards which meet the challenges posed by the present and the future by thinking about the underpinning principles which are timeless and context free'.[36] In other words, judges *could* be the arbiters of competing medical ethical conclusions and principles. It is arguable that, given the fragmentation, they indeed *should* be. In order to do this, however, it is first necessary for the courts to identify and define a conception of medical ethics, and this has so far been lacking. As the chapters demonstrate, some judges may start out reluctant to enter into ethical debate, but their awareness of the ethical context to cases appears to grow, though not in a consistent manner. Paradoxically this can sometimes lead to a lessening of the role given to medical ethics. Nevertheless, in order to assess the courts' treatment of medical ethics as a concept, it is first necessary to consider the extent of judicial deference to the medical profession in English law, and in particular the influence of the decision in *Bolam v Friern Hospital Management Committee*.[37]

---

[35] See I Kennedy, *The Unmasking of Medicine* (London, George Allen & Unwin, 1981) at 78. This point is further considered in Chapter 3 of this book.

[36] S McLean, *Old Law, New Medicine: Medical Ethics and Human Rights* (London, Pandora 1999) 3.

[37] *Bolam v Friern Hospital Management Committee* [1957] 1 WLR 582.

A.   The Influence of *Bolam*

Perhaps the most important and influential case in medical law, *Bolam* is something of an oddity, for several reasons. First, it is a High Court case; it was never appealed, and thus was heard by only one judge – McNair J. Second, the case was decided in 1957 – an age ago in a subject where the law can develop on a monthly basis. Indeed, its enduring influence is something of an anomaly in medical law. Thirdly, the judgment is not even a decision by the judge, but instead a direction to the jury. Thus, the judge did not apply the law to the facts of the case, but only restated them and advised the jury of what law it had to apply to them. Finally, particularly for the purposes of the analysis in this book, *Bolam* is an oddity because it is a case that claims to have little to do with medical ethics. It is, on the whole, a medical negligence case, asking what standard of care a doctor must conform to in order not to be sued for negligence. Nevertheless it is so influential that it casts a shadow over many of the cases considered in Chapters 4–7. For this reason, it is imperative that it is examined here.

The facts of the case are relatively simple. While being treated for depression the plaintiff, John Bolam, was advised to undergo electroconvulsive therapy (ECT). Mr Bolam signed a consent form agreeing to the placing of electrodes on his head and having an electric current administered to his brain. At the time, there were differing views among medical professionals over whether relaxant drugs should be provided before the procedure was carried out. Dr Bastarrechea, the consultant psychiatrist at the hospital, and Dr Allfrey, the senior registrar who administered the treatment, did not believe that they were necessary, and Mr Bolam was thus not provided with them. Unfortunately, he suffered significant injuries in the course of the treatment, including dislocation of both hip joints and fractures of the pelvis on both sides resulting from the femurs being driven through the cups of the pelvis. Mr Bolam claimed that the standard of care provided to him was faulty on two grounds: first, that there was negligence in not warning him that he was not to have relaxant drugs and, second, that there was negligence in not administering those drugs. The issue that McNair J had to explain to the jury was how they could determine whether the doctors had been negligent. In other words, whether the standard of care received by Mr Bolam fell below that which he had a right to expect.

McNair J said that in order to avoid charges of negligence, people had to act in a reasonable manner. If they were professionals, they had to act as a reasonable member of that profession. Thus, an architect must attain the standard of the reasonable architect, the solicitor that of the reasonable solicitor and, needless to say, the doctor that of the reasonable doctor. The problem was how to determine whether this standard had been achieved, and it is here that expert evidence became crucial. This is because, as McNair J explained to the jury, the key was whether the doctor did as other reasonable doctors might have done:

A doctor is not guilty of negligence if he has acted in accordance with a practice accepted as proper by a responsible body of medical men skilled in that particular art … Putting it the other way round, a doctor is not negligent, if he is acting in accordance with such a practice, merely because there is a body of opinion that takes a contrary view.[38]

McNair J also considered the decision in the Scottish case of *Hunter v Hanley*, decided only two years before *Bolam*.[39] In that case the Lord President, Lord Clyde, had constructed the test in a similar way to McNair J., who quoted Lord Clyde stating that:

In the realm of diagnosis and treatment there is ample scope for genuine difference of opinion, and one man clearly is not negligent merely because his conclusion differs from that of other professional men, nor because he has displayed less skill or knowledge than others would have shown. The true test for establishing negligence in diagnosis or treatment on the part of a doctor is whether he has been proved to be guilty of such failure as no doctor of ordinary skill would be guilty of if acting with ordinary care.[40]

Despite the superficial similarities, however, the difference in language between McNair J and that of Lord Clyde's test is more than merely semantic. Indeed, there is a fundamental difference between a requirement that a doctor acts in a 'reasonable' or 'responsible' manner as per the wording in *Bolam* and one that acts in an 'ordinary' manner as per *Hunter*. As Kenneth Norrie has noted, the word reasonable is normative in nature and thus '[a] test of "reasonable care" necessarily carries with it a connotation which allows the court to say what *ought to have been done* in the circumstances'.[41] A standard that demands that a doctor act in an "ordinary" manner, on the other hand, is descriptive in nature, as it asks what *is* done without analysis of the quality of that practice. In particular, the role of the court changes dramatically depending on whether a normative or descriptive test is applied.

A normative assessment of behaviour allows the judge to examine the conduct itself and reach a conclusion on its adequacy. She is able to overrule what might even be the unanimous practice of the profession. Whether the body of opinion is reasonable will depend on the act itself, and the judge's determination of its merits. Conversely, the judge is afforded no such luxury with a descriptive approach to medical conduct. Here, whether the behaviour is ordinary or not will depend not on the behaviour itself, but instead on whether the doctor can find others that would do as she did in the circumstances. If she can provide witnesses to that effect, then she has satisfied the test and her conduct is automatically deemed to reach the required standard of care to make a charge of negligence fail.

---

[38] [1957] 1 WLR 582 at 586.
[39] *Hunter v Hanley* [1955] SLT 213.
[40] *Bolam v Friern Hospital Management Committee* [1957] 1 WLR 582 at 586.
[41] K Norrie, 'Common Practice and the Standard of Care in Medical Negligence' (1985) *Judicial Review* 145 at 148.

In short, if a normative approach is taken, the judge is the ultimate arbiter of medical behaviour. If, on the other hand, the descriptive one is adopted, it is for the medical profession to judge itself. The problem in interpreting the case is that, at various points, McNair J utilised both normative and descriptive language interchangeably. Thus, the body of medical opinion required was at different times described by him as ordinary, reasonable and respectable.[42] It may be argued that McNair J intended for his test to be normative; indeed, the following extract from the judgment suggests that it was being left open to the jury to reject the defendant's experts' body of opinion:

> [I]t is not essential for you to decide which of two practices is the better practice, as long as you accept that what Dr Allfrey did was in accordance with a practice accepted by responsible persons; but *if the result of the evidence is that you are satisfied that this practice is better than the practice spoken of on the other side, then it is really a stronger case.*[43]

However, this was not how the case was to be interpreted for the next 40 years. Rather, the judgment of McNair J was held, not least by the House of Lords, to be a test that was descriptive in nature. The nadir was perhaps reached in 1984 when this point was considered by the House of Lords in *Maynard*.[44] In that case, the trial judge, having evaluated the expert testimony from both sides, found himself impressed by that of the plaintiff's experts, rejected that of the defendants, and accordingly found for the plaintiff. The question for the House of Lords was whether he had the authority to do so. The House held that he did not, with Lord Scarman particularly unequivocal in his judgment:

> I have to say that a judge's 'preference' for one body of distinguished professional opinion to another also professionally distinguished is not sufficient to establish negligence in a practitioner whose actions have received the seal of approval of those whose opinions, *honestly expressed, honestly held,* were not preferred. If this was the real reason for the judge's finding, he erred in law ... For in the realm of diagnosis and treatment, negligence is not established by preferring one respectable body of professional opinion to another. Failure to exercise the *ordinary* skill of a doctor (in the appropriate specialty, if he be a specialist) is necessary.[45]

This suggests that all that was required to defeat a claim in negligence was that the body of opinion gave evidence that could be shown to be *honest*. In this sense, the use of the word ordinary is clearly deliberate. Moreover, the number of doctors needed to qualify as a body was extremely small – in the case of *DeFreitas*

---

[42] This was noted by the court in *M (A Child) v Blackpool Victoria Hospital NHS Trust* [2003] EWHC 1744.

[43] *Bolam v Friern Hospital Management Committee* [1957] 1 WLR 582 at 587–8. Emphasis added.

[44] *Maynard v West Midlands Regional Health Authority* [1984] 1 WLR 635.

[45] [1984] 1 WLR 634 at 639. Emphasis added.

v O'Brien, for example, only five out of 250 neurosurgeons considered the procedure to be safe, yet this was considered a sufficient number to absolve the defendant.[46]

But what has this to do with medical ethics? The answer, and the problem with *Bolam,* was that it became out of control through its interpretation by the courts and, crucially, grew out of context. As Michael Davies noted, the predominant judicial attitude to medical law cases became '[w]hen in doubt *"Bolam*ise"'.[47] Issue after issue saw responsibility abrogated by the courts to the medical profession. When the cases contained ethical rather than technical medical issues, the abrogation was to *medical ethics.* Thus *Bolam,* and its descriptive interpretation, came to dominate medical law in almost all areas. Margot Brazier and I divided the actions of the courts into three categories – overt *Bolamisation,* covert *Bolamisation* and the widening of *Bolam's* sphere of influence.[48] All of these categories took the case outside its intended and proper limits – the exercise by doctors of their technical medical skill. In the following chapters, all three of these categories are represented. Overt *Bolamisation* is clear and easy to explain. Quite simply, the courts have at times extended the *Bolam* principle to include decisions that are not, strictly, medical. An example of this is the law concerning risk disclosure (also known as 'informed consent'), which is considered in Chapter 4. The issue at hand is how much information about a medical procedure a medical practitioner has to give her patient before the latter's consent can be considered to be legally valid. Clearly, this is not a matter of technical medical skill. Nevertheless, for a time in the late 1980s and early 1990s the courts held that the answer to this question was simply a matter of applying the law of negligence, and thus the descriptive interpretation of *Bolam,* which was the interpretation of the time, applied. An example of covert *Bolamisation* can be found in the law relating to the ability of minors to consent to medical treatment. In the case of *Gillick,* the House of Lords never invoked or mentioned *Bolam,* yet they managed to effectively *Bolamise* the issue anyway.[49] A majority of their Lordships held that minors under 16 could receive contraceptive advice and treatment in certain circumstances if they were sufficiently mature. Whether this was so was designated a decision for doctors to make. Thus, if a challenge was to be made to a doctor's decision, it would have to be on the basis that she displayed poor clinical judgement, and any action would have to be in negligence – using *Bolam. Gillick,* and the cases that followed, are considered in Chapter 5.

The final category, the widening of *Bolam's* sphere of influence, applies to the cases considered in Chapters 6 and 7. These chapters consider cases concerning

---

[46] *DeFreitas v O'Brien* [1993] 4 *Medical Law Review* 281. See generally M Brazier and J Miola, 'Bye-Bye *Bolam*: A Medical Litigation Revolution?' (2000) 8 *Medical Law Review* 85.

[47] M Davies, 'The New *Bolam*' Another False Dawn for Medical Negligence?' (1996) 12 *Professional Negligence* 10.

[48] M Brazier and J Miola, 'Bye-Bye *Bolam*: A Medical Litigation Revolution?' (2000) 8 *Medical Law Review* 85 at 90–5.

[49] *Gillick v West Norfolk and Wisbech Area Health Authority* [1985] 3 All ER 402.

the sterilisation of adults with learning disabilities and the withdrawal of life-sustaining medical treatment respectively. In both of these chapters, the courts have grappled with the concept of 'best interests' in order to justify the provision of treatment without the patient's consent. In both sets of cases, which involve decisions which are in no way technical and medical, the House of Lords has held that a patient's best interests are to be defined by using the *Bolam* test. Thus, a procedure would be said to be in a patient's best interests if a responsible body of medical opinion could be found to state that that was the case. In the case of *F v West Berkshire Health Authority*, considered in Chapter 6, the House of Lords specifically rejected the unanimous verdict of the Court of Appeal that *Bolam* was insufficiently stringent a tool to make decisions regarding sterilisations.[50] In the case of *Bland*, considered in Chapter 7, the House decided that whether or not to withdraw life-sustaining treatment from a patient in a persistent vegetative state should be governed by *Bolam* through the same best interests principle.[51]

The *Bolam* test thus became all pervasive. Medical law was saturated by its influence. A consequence of *Bolam* moving away from medical negligence into other areas of medical law was that decision-making responsibility was not just abrogated to the medical profession in issues to do with technical medical skill, but also with regard to *ethical* questions. The themes of all of the cases considered in the four chapters are intrinsically *ethical* rather than *medical* in nature, in terms of the three criteria provided earlier in this chapter. Indeed, 'medical ethics' has been identified as one of the euphemisms used by the courts in order to *Bolamise* decisions (another often used is 'clinical judgement').[52] However, in 1997 *Bolam* was reconsidered by the House of Lords. In *Bolitho*, the House held that the descriptive interpretation was no longer to be used, and that the test would be normative instead.[53] In order to qualify as a responsible or reasonable body of opinion, expert evidence had to be logically defensible.[54] As might be expected, the case was considered to be a watershed and, to this end, it constituted something of a change of culture on the part of the courts.[55] However, *Bolitho* was specifically concerned with medical negligence, and thus did not necessarily change the situation in other areas of medical law. Nevertheless, as we shall see, some of the cases in Chapters 4–7 that were decided after 1997 highlight that the courts were more willing to change their approach to the medical

---

[50]   *F v West Berkshire Health Authority* [1990] 2 AC 1.

[51]   *Airedale NHS Trust v Bland* [1993] 1 All ER 821.

[52]   See M Brazier and J Miola, 'Bye-Bye *Bolam*: A Medical Litigation Revolution?' (2000) 8 *Medical Law Review* 85.

[53]   *Bolitho v City & Hackney Health Authority* [1998] AC 232.

[54]   See M Brazier and J Miola, 'Bye-Bye *Bolam*: A Medical Litigation Revolution?' (2000) 8 *Medical Law Review* 85.

[55]   *Ibid.* See also Lord Woolf, 'Are the Courts Excessively Deferential to the Medical Profession?' (2001) 9 *Medical Law Review* 1.

profession, and to reclaim some of the decision-making power that it had given to doctors. In this way, *Bolitho* can be seen to mark a change in attitude on the part of some judges.

It is important, however, not to overplay the significance of *Bolitho*, for two reasons. First, the aftermath of *Bolitho* hardly represented an opening of the medical negligence floodgates; and the claimant in *Bolitho* itself still lost.[56] Indeed, a standard that requires that an expert prove that their argument has 'logical force' is hardly onerous. Secondly, the House of Lords in *Bolitho* specifically stated that they were excluding risk disclosure from their considerations, and thus it might be presumed to be limited to negligence.[57] Consequently *Bolamisation*, if reversed, would have to occur on an issue by issue, case by case basis. Thus, it is unlikely that the law will develop in the same way in each area. Fundamentally, as shall become apparent, medical dominance has been dented but not eradicated in the *Bolitho* aftermath. Thus, in the cases and scenarios considered, where courts can be seen to have been abrogating responsibility to *medical ethics* when *Bolam* is interpreted descriptively, they have not necessarily reversed that trend since 1997. Thus, each chapter will also consider the ethical guidelines that pertain to it from the formal and semi-formal sectors of discourse. This has been limited to the GMC and the BMA as representatives of the formal and semi-formal sectors of ethical discourse. It is taken as axiomatic that any ethical position may be justified with recourse to the unofficial sector of discourse.

B. The Structure of the Legal Chapters

The four issues that constitute the chapters were chosen because they are the issues that contain at least one House of Lords decision on the topic since 1980. Each chapter begins with that decision, and continues by examining what I consider to be the major cases in that area. The chapters do not profess to be a comprehensive analysis of the case law as only a few cases are considered, and only enough to give a representative idea of how the courts treat medical ethics. They are organised with the cases in chronological order. EU case law is not considered, as I am specifically concerned with how English courts treat the UK medical profession's ethics. The Human Right Act 1998, while important in English law, is tangential to the discussion in the book, and is thus treated as such. The issues, as the descriptions below highlight, each contain an inherent

---

[56]   See A Maclean, 'Beyond *Bolam* and *Bolitho*' (2002) 5 *Medical Law International* 205.

[57]   Lord Browne-Wilkinson held that 'in cases of diagnoses and treatment there are cases where, despite a body of professional opinion sanctioning the defendant's conduct, the defendant can properly be held liable in negligence', then added cryptically, in parentheses, 'I am not here considering questions of disclosure of risks' (*Bolitho v City & Hackney Health Authority* [1998] AC 232 at 243).

ethical content. Thus, as mentioned above, if responsibility is abrogated by the courts to the medical profession, it is abrogated to *medical ethics*.

The first issue, considered in Chapter 4, is risk disclosure and informed consent. It begins with the House of Lords judgment in *Sidaway* in 1985.[58] This was the first time that the House considered a medico-legal case that involved a substantially ethical, rather than technical, question. The plaintiff had suffered paralysis due to a small inherent risk materialising following an elective operation to cure back pain. She had not been warned of this risk and sued, arguing that she should have been. The ethical, as opposed to technical medical, issue was how much information a doctor must provide to a patient before her consent can be said to be 'informed' and therefore valid. The House of Lords, however, was to have trouble in reaching a decision and, indeed, in the end *Sidaway* may best be described as messy. The courts could not seem to decide on which interpretation of *Bolam* to use, and some judges seemed to want to dispense with it altogether. The chapter examines two *Bolamite* cases after *Sidaway*, and a further two that sought to rein back medical dominance, before finishing by considering the recent, important House of Lords decision in *Chester v Afshar*, a judgment that is of significance to the aims of the chapter.[59]

Chapter 5 examines minors' right to consent to and refuse medical treatment. The first case is the House of Lords decision in *Gillick*, decided months after *Sidaway* in 1985.[60] *Gillick* involved a challenge to the legal validity of a Department of Health document that stated that medical practitioners could provide contraceptive advice and treatment to minors under the age of 16 in certain circumstances. Again, the ethical component is clear, involving questions of autonomy and confidentiality. That and subsequent cases concern the question of when a minor becomes a patient in her own right, and when she inherits decision-making authority from her parents. The cases that follow *Gillick* involve the right of minors to refuse treatment, and in these cases a clear view of medical ethics can be seen to have been formed, in particular, by Lord Donaldson. The chapter ends with a discussion of the recent decision in *Axon*, which might be seen as a reprise of the issues in *Gillick*, as the facts are very similar.[61]

The issue in Chapter 6 is that of the sterilisation of people with learning disabilities. It is different to the other chapters in that it contains two House of Lords cases from the outset – *Re B* in 1987 and then *F v West Berkshire Health Authority* two years later. The cases involve requests for the courts to rule on the lawfulness of performing sterilisations on patients with learning disabilities. In all but one case the patients are adults, and in all but one case they are female. The two House of Lords cases are examined, followed by another two cases that emphasise a change in approach that can be identified in the law. Yet again, the

---

[58]   *Sidaway v Board of Governors of Bethlem Royal Hospital* [1985] 1 All ER 643.
[59]   *Chester v Afshar* [2004] UKHL 41.
[60]   *Gillick v West Norfolk and Wisbech Area Health Authority* [1985] 3 All ER 402.
[61]   *R (on the Application of Axon) v Secretary of State for Health* [2006] EWCA 37.

ethical dimension is not hard to identify, particularly since in most cases the sterilisations were non-therapeutic. Although autonomy was not an issue, as the patients were deemed to be incapable of consenting to medical treatment, there were still questions and value judgements surrounding what was best for the patients. Also considered is the sporadic law reform that culminated in the passing of the Mental Capacity Act 2005.

The final topic, discussed in Chapter 7, considers issues at the end of life. It begins with the House of Lords judgment in the well-known case of *Bland*.[62] In terms of the ethical content, the facts of that case in themselves constitute a staple of any medical ethics course. Anthony Bland was injured during the Hillsborough disaster, and was diagnosed as being in a persistent vegetative state. He was fed through a naso-gastric tube, and there was no prospect of any form of recovery. The court was asked to issue a declaration stating that it would be lawful to withdraw the medical care, thus effectively causing his death. Again, *Bolam* was seen as relevant to determining whether treatment could be withdrawn, and the next case examined, *Re G*, demonstrates just how far its influence reached at one time.[63] Thereafter, the cases considered highlight the tension that can arise when patient and doctor disagree. In the case of *Ms B*, the patient wished for her life-sustaining treatment to end, and had her request refused by her doctors, while in *Burke* the patient challenged GMC guidance that stated that his wish to have treatment continued would not be binding on his treatment team.[64] The case of *Pretty* is not included because the legal conflict was between Mrs Pretty and the Attorney-General.[65]

Chapter 8 contains an analysis of three government-commissioned reports on topics with an ethical component. One is chosen from the 1980s, one from the 1990s and one from the 2000s. The Warnock Committee considered human fertilisation and embryology in 1984, and its recommendations were to form the basis of the Human Fertilisation and Embryology Act 1990. The 1994 House of Lords Select Committee was asked to report on euthanasia, while the 2005 Select Committee Report considered Lord Joffe's Assisted Dying for the Terminally Ill Bill. They are considered as it is important to gauge the attitude to medical ethics when law is being drafted rather than applied. Indeed, they might be expected to be more sensitive to medical ethics and its role for two main reasons. First, there was the extra time that they enjoyed to consider the issues. They did not have to reach decisions quickly, and they did not rely on barristers for their evidence. Each report could call whoever it liked, and take as much time as it liked to reach conclusions. Secondly, they were recommending changes to the law and were

---

[62] *Airedale NHS Trust v Bland* [1993] 1 All ER 821. The All England Reports give all of the judgements in the case concurrently, from the High Court to the House of Lords' decision. This section is only concerned with the latter judgement, which begins at p 859.

[63] *Re G* [1995] 2 FCR 46.

[64] *R (on the application of Burke) v General Medical Council* [2004] EWCH 1879 (High Court); *R (Burke) v General Medical Council* [2005] EWCA Civ 1003 (CA).

[65] See *R (on the Application of Pretty) v Director of Public Prosecutions* [2002] 1 AC 800.

thus not constrained by it. The judges in the cases in Chapters 4–7 had to work within an existing legal model and set of rules. The committees in Chapter 8, on the other hand, were asked to recommend what the law *should be.* Consequently, it might be expected that these committees would infuse medical ethics into the law, and vice versa, in order to allow the two to work in tandem. Indeed, any appreciation of the problems identified by the Bristol Inquiry Report and highlighted in this book could lead to solutions being suggested. Nevertheless, only the Warnock Committee Report can be said to show such an appreciation, and place medical ethics and law as separate entities with different, clearly-defined roles. The two House of Lords Select Committees that followed it, however, instinctively abrogated responsibility for the ethical matters that they identified to medical ethics. Indeed, the 1994 committee even mentioned in its report that it might be criticised for being too deferential to the medical profession.[66]

What emerges from Chapters 4–7 is a frequent abrogation of responsibility on the part of the courts in favour of the medical profession and, by extension, its ethics. Moreover, there is a marked confidence displayed by the courts regarding the regulatory function of medical ethics, and its ability to discharge that perceived duty. The chapters therefore also examine the ethical guidance itself in order to ascertain whether that confidence is justified, and to see how the law and medical ethics interact and whether the problems identified by the Bristol Inquiry are indeed replicated. As the above indicates, the courts' treatment of medical ethics, once it identifies it, is inconsistent. Sometimes it leads to a reassertion of the courts' power to take decision-making authority away from medical professionals but, at others, the courts abrogate responsibility to medical ethics. The pattern is the same in Chapter 8, where the first committee kept power from the medical profession, but the later two did not. In my conclusion, I argue that this inconsistent treatment of medical ethics suggests that the courts and committee members have failed to recognise the dangers highlighted by the Bristol Inquiry Report. In this sense, the danger that the fragmentation of discourse would lead to a regulatory vacuum is unrecognised, and thus not prevented. Indeed, it may be argued that the law itself, through its inconsistent approach to medical ethics, has become nothing more than another fragment of discourse, almost indistinguishable from any other. Certainly, it is not the buffer between medicalisation and human rights that Sheila McLean argued that it should be. Consequently, the regulatory vacuum places the decision-making onus on the conscience of the individual medical professional. This is not only totally inimical to the message of Nuremburg but also, ironically, to the aims of the medical ethics renaissance that followed it.

---

[66] *Report of the Select Committee on Medical Ethics* (HL Paper 21-I, 1994) at para 272.

2

Historical Perspectives of Medical Ethics

I. Introduction

There is no profession that comes close to medicine in its concern to inculcate, transmit and keep in constant repair its standards governing the conduct of its members.[1]

While the ethics of medical practice grows ever more complicated due to the inexorable march of medical technology and the multi-disciplined academisation of the subject, media interest has reached previously unparalleled highs, and doctors are under close scrutiny whenever they make an ethical decision. An analysis of the impact of contemporary medical ethics would be incomplete without at least a brief overview of the history of medical ethics. As this chapter and the next show, the medical ethics renaissance has not benefited from its history. In fact, it has been somewhat bedevilled by it. The ancient Greek, Hippocratic model of medical ethics, still considered something of an ideal, is not readily applicable in a contemporary setting. Furthermore, many of the principles in these codes are unacceptable to the vast majority of today's patients and doctors. However, the Greek model has not been given the opportunity to be 'phased out' through history due to the relative paucity in medical ethics debate between the Greeks and the renaissance in the last century. In other words, there is little between the old and the new, and medical ethics can be said to have 'jumped' rather than developed. The pervasive theme of this chapter is that it demonstrates that while medical ethics *has* progressed through history, the doctor-based nature of ethical codes has not changed to any significant degree, and therefore the development of medical ethics has tended to reflect changes in the attitudes of medical practitioners rather than patients or society as a whole.

An overview of the history of medical ethics can aid an understanding of contemporary ethical principles by placing them in the context of their progression. This chapter offers an examination of what I consider to be some of the defining moments in the formation of contemporary medical ethics. While in no way a comprehensive or full history, it considers the major (but by no means all)

---

[1] P Ramsey, *The Patient as Person* (Yale University Press, New Haven, 1970) (ix)

influences on contemporary medical ethics. These are: Ancient Greek ethics, medieval medical ethics and 19th century medical ethics. The next chapter also considers the influence of Nuremburg and what I call the medical ethics renaissance. The inclusion of Greek ethics is due to the importance traditionally attributed to the writings of Hippocrates (especially the Hippocratic Oath), and Plato. The fact that the Greeks are considered to be the 'fathers' of medical ethics means that there is great merit in examining the principles that they espoused and the general approach that they took to the practice of medicine. As with the rest of the chapter, though, the Greeks are examined in a critical context, with Plato being discussed with particular reference to the critique levelled by Thomas Szasz.

The intervening period between the Greeks and the 19th century is considered to be a period when medicine was demeaned as a profession. Medical practitioners ceased to be the educated, respected figures that they were in Greece, and their profession was no longer considered an 'art'. In this historical period there was thus a redefinition of the medical practitioner as little more than a semi-skilled worker. Subsequently, there were two major developments: firstly, the 18th century witnessed the rise of the gentleman physician. Secondly, the 19th century heralded the institutionalisation of medical ethics in Britain through the formation of the GMC and the BMA. This period shaped not only the public perception of medical practitioners, but also gives a valuable insight into how the physicians *themselves* defined their role in society.

II.   Ancient Greek Medical Ethics – The Beginning

The importance of ancient Greek medical ethics originates from the fact that, despite the technological advances of the two millennia since they were first written, their fundamental principles continue to be seen as relevant in modern medicine. Such longevity can be ascribed to their emphasis on mostly non-specific ethical principles which can be adapted to almost any situation. As will be shown later, some of those principles are not considered acceptable in the 20th century,[2] yet some documents, such as the Hippocratic Oath,[3] were embraced by Judeo-Christian cultures and remain to this day intrinsic to any study of medical ethics. Indeed, no body of principles has replaced them as a coherent 'code' to govern medical ethics. This section examines the two major approaches to ethics that emerged from this period.

---

[2] In particular, the Platonic ideal places undue emphasis on a paternalistic approach which is unacceptable in contemporary medicine. See, in particular, F M Cornford (trans) *The Republic of Plato* (New York and London, Oxford University Press, 1945). It is discussed in more detail below.

[3] See W D Smith, *The Hippocratic Tradition* (New York, Cornell University Press, 1979) and L Endelstein, 'The Hippocratic Oath: Text, Translation and Interpretation', in O Temkin and C L Temkin (eds), *Ancient Medicine: Selected Papers of Ludwig Endelstein* (Baltimore, John Hopkins Press, 1967).

A.   Hippocrates

I swear by Apollo the physician, by Æsculapius, Hygeia, and Panacea, and I take to witness all the gods, all the goddesses, to keep according to my ability and my judgement, the following Oath.

'To consider dear to me as my parents him who taught me this art; to live in common with him and if necessary to share my goods with him; to look upon his children as my own brothers, to teach them this art if they so desire without fee or written promise; to impart to my sons and the sons of the master who taught me and the disciples who have enrolled themselves and have agreed to the rules of the profession, but to these alone the precepts and the instruction. I will prescribe regimen for the good of my patients according to my ability and my judgement and never do harm to anyone. To please no one will I prescribe a deadly drug nor give advice which may cause his death. Nor will I give a woman a pessary to procure abortion. But I will preserve the purity of my life and my art. I will not cut for stone, even for patients in whom the disease is manifest; I will leave this operation to be performed by practitioners, specialists in this art. In every house where I come I will enter only for the good of my patients, keeping myself far from all intentional ill-doing and all seduction and especially from the pleasures of love with women or with men, be they free or slaves. All that may come to my knowledge in the exercise of my profession or in daily commerce with men, which ought not to be spread abroad, I will keep secret and will never reveal. If I keep this oath faithfully, may I enjoy my life and practice my art, respected by all men and in all times; but if I swerve from it or violate it, may the reverse be my lot'.

The Hippocratic Oath remains, almost certainly, the most famous medical ethics document, even in the 21st century. No comprehensive book on medical ethics is complete without it, and there have been many written about it in its own right.[4] Its influence is undoubted, even by Pellegrino as recently as 1989:

No Code has been more influential in heightening the moral reflexes of ordinary men. Every subsequent medical code is essentially a footnote to the Hippocratic precepts, which even to this day remain the paradigm of how the good physician should behave... *[But]...the intersections of medicine with contemporary science, technology, social organisation, and changed human values have revealed significant missing dimensions in the ancient ethic.*[5]

Pellegrino's last sentence shows how the Hippocratic Oath's relevance is lessened by the developments of modern medicine. Indeed, its main drawback is that it is pre-technological.[6] Nevertheless, although the Oath can no longer be regarded as

---

[4]   *Ibid.*

[5]   E Pellegrino, 'Toward an Expanded Medical Ethics: The Hippocratic Ethic Revisited' in R Veatch (ed), *Cross Cultural Perspectives in Medical Ethics* (Boston, Jones and Bartlett, 1989) 25–6. Emphasis added.

[6]   'The relevance of the tradition is limited when it comes to problems posed by the interposition of technology between health professionals and people': K Vaux, *Biomedical Ethics- Morality for the New Medicine* (New York, Harper and Row, 1968).

'unchanging absolutes'. Hippocratic norms can still be considered to have influence as 'partial statements of ideals, in need of constant re-evaluation, amplification, and evolution'.[7] Given its pervasive influence, what may be the impact of the Oath?

To answer this question, it is essential to break it down and examine its contents. Immediately striking is the fact that the Hippocratic Oath is in no way concerned with social medicine or ethics:

> There is in the Hippocratic corpus little explicit reference to the responsibilities of medicine as a corporate entity with responsibility for its members and duties to the greater human community. The ethic of the profession as a whole is assured largely by the moral behavior of its individual members. There is no explicit delineation of the corporate responsibility of physicians for one another's ethical behavior. On the whole, the need for maintaining competence is indirectly stated.[8]

As Johnson recognises, there are six basic duties outlined in the Oath: (1) to do no harm, (2) not to assist suicide or administer euthanasia, (3) not to cause abortion, (4) to refer patients for specialist treatment, (5) not to abuse professional relationships (particularly for sexual motives); and (6) to keep the patient's confidences.[9] These principles were adopted after the Christianisation of Europe because of their similarity to the Christian ethics of the time, and thus cannot be considered to be proactive in their influence. Indeed, the Hippocratic corpus was not even recognised and practised by the majority of Hippocrates' colleagues, and was only a 'manifesto by a small group of ancient Greeks'.[10]

So what *is* the Oath? On reading it, what is immediately apparent that it is an amalgamation of situation-oriented ethics and a generalised code of conduct. While the doctor has specific duties (for example, to consider his teacher's offspring his brother) and prohibitions (such as those against abortion and euthanasia), much of the Oath simply consists of statements of general principle.[11] It is these general principles that are considered timeless, and still command respect in the medical profession. The prohibitions of abortion and euthanasia have both been breached by medical practitioners,[12] and the Oath retains authority only in the parts that remain relevant to contemporary medicine. Thus, what survives from the Oath is its *way of thinking* or underlying philosophy. However, this way of thinking does not promote patient autonomy, as modern medicine claims to; rather, the main concern of the Oath is the *health*

---

[7]   E Pellegrino, Toward an Expanded Medical Ethics: The Hippocratic Ethic Revisited in R Veatch (ed), *Cross Cultural Perspectives in Medical Ethics* (Boston, Jones and Bartlett, 1989) 27.

[8]   *Ibid.*

[9]   A Johnson, *Pathways in Medical Ethics* (London, Edward Arnold, 1990) 15.

[10]   *Ibid* 14.

[11]   For example: 'I will use treatment to help the sick according to my ability and judgment, but never with a view to injury and wrongdoing'. The entire Oath can be found, among other places, in M Gelfand, *The Philosophy and Ethics of Medicine* (Edinburgh, E&S Livingstone Ltd, 1968) 107. A discussion of it can be found on pp 108–110.

[12]   See A Johnson, *Pathways in Medical Ethics* (London, Edward Arnold, 1990) 15.

of the patient, without regard to the *wishes* of the patient herself. Autonomy is thus a value not recognised by Hippocrates. Beneficence is effectively the core principle governing the doctor–patient relationship.

Many of the duties outlined by the Oath are clearly non-specific, but cannot be said to place the patient centre stage.[13] Rather, they are designed to safeguard and perpetuate the dignity of the medical profession. It is this demand for respect that betrays the Oath's heavily paternalistic influence. Although it comprises duties for the physician to abide by, it is very vague as to how those duties should be carried out. Thus, although 'the genius of the oath is that it anchors responsibility in the moral power and ability of man and does not concede to any transcendent moral law or moral arbiter',[14] this gives free reign to the physician to do what she thinks is best, relying on the conscience of the individual medical practitioner. This entirely subjective approach is inconsistent with contemporary, post-Nuremberg medical ethics:

> …the notion of the physician as a benevolent and paternalistic figure who decides all for the patient is inconsistent with today's educated public. It is surely incongruous in a democratic society in which the rights of self-determination are being assured by law.[15]

Examples of Hippocratic paternalism unacceptable in modern medicine can be found in *Decorum*, which forms part of the Hippocratic corpus. Firstly, the physician is advised to perform 'all things calmly and adroitly, concealing most things from the patient while you are attending him'.[16] Secondly, the physician is told to treat the patient with solicitude, revealing nothing of her present and future condition.[17] The resulting position of the Hippocratic Oath is difficult to ascertain. On the one hand, it sometimes seems that all other ethical codes are merely 'footnotes' to the Hippocratic ideal; yet on the other hand the Oath is clearly hindered by its antiquity, and its relevance must be expected to decline further as medicine becomes even more dependent on technology. Nonetheless, its decline in relevance has not brought with it a replacement; and there lies the crux: imperfect as it is, the Hippocratic Oath cannot be 'forgotten' until there is something there to take over from it.

---

[13] Indeed, the second paragraph, which is the first statement of principle, concerns the duties owed to the doctor's teacher and his offspring.

[14] K Vaux, *Biomedical Ethics – Morality for the New Medicine* (New York, Harper and Row, 1968) 4.

[15] E Pellegrino, Toward an Expanded Medical Ethics: The Hippocratic Ethic Revisited in R Veatch (ed), *Cross Cultural Perspectives in Medical Ethics* (Boston, Jones and Bartlett, 1989) 27.

[16] W H S Jones, *Hippocrates*, Vol II (Cambridge, Mass., Harvard University Press, 1923) 297.

[17] *Hippocrates* 299.

B.   Plato

The reasons for a discussion of Plato are twofold. Firstly, it demonstrates that Hippocrates had no monopoly on medical ethics discourse in ancient Greece;[18] and, secondly, Plato demonstrates well the distinctions and parallels between the 'old' medical ethics and the 'new'. In order to achieve the latter of these points this section draws heavily on Thomas Szasz's critique of Plato's model of medical ethics. What Szasz shows is the timelessness of Plato's theories and, as a consequence of this, how little medical ethics may have moved on. Furthermore, what Szasz best demonstrates is that the lessons from Plato, tragically brought to life by the Nazis, were ignored. These lessons are that the medical profession should not be allowed exclusively to define its ethics and regulate itself. The reason for this is that undiluted self-regulation of ethics gives the profession the *potential* to disregard the Hippocratic principle (also at the crux of more modern ethical codes) that the doctor should do her best for the patient. Furthermore, an examination of Plato shows us that paternalism does not necessarily lead to beneficence, as the doctor may not have the patient's interests at heart. Plato's approach to medical practice can be found in *The Republic*. In this work, the bulk of the medical ethics commentary is found in Socrates' discussion with Thrasymachus. It is important as it specifically addresses the question of whose agent the expert is. This is of particular significance if we accept the assertion that the medical profession has the potential to be, if it so wishes, a negative and authoritarian influence on society. Before his own involvement, Plato informs us that Socrates had asked Thrasymachus whether it was the business of the physician to earn money or to treat people. The physician replied that the business of a physician worthy of his name was to treat his patients.

Plato, through Socrates, seemingly supports the idea that the physician's role is to prevent and treat illness. Also, he seemingly supports the idea of the doctor as the agent of the patient, when he does not really support this at all. By making the physician the definer not only of his own but also the patient's best interests, Plato actually supports a coercive–collectivistic medical ethic rather than an autonomous–individualistic one. In other words, medicine should operate for the good of society rather than for the benefit of the individual patient. Thus he develops his defence of the physician as an agent of the state:

> [The art of medicine] does not study its own interests, but the needs of the body, just as a groom shows his skill by caring for horses, not for the art of grooming. And so every art seeks, not its own advantage – for it has no deficiencies – but the interest of the subject on which it is exercised.[19]

---

[18]   Indeed, other ancient Greeks engaged in ethical discourse. For example Aristotle also discussed medical ethical issues in his writings.

[19]   FM Cornford (trans), *The Republic of Plato* (New York, Oxford University Press, 1945) at 23.

This argument for benevolent altruism produces the ethical conclusion that Plato was aiming at all along: that there is moral justification for the control of the subordinate by the superior – the patient by the doctor:

> But surely, Thrasymachus, every art has authority and superior power over its subject … So far as the arts are concerned, then, no art ever studies or enjoins the interest of the superior party, but always that of the weaker over which it has authority … So the physician, as such, studies only the patient's interest, not his own. For as we agreed, the business of the physician, in the strict sense, is not to make money for himself, but to exercise his power over the patient's body … And so with government of any kind: no ruler, in so far as he is acting as ruler, will study or enjoin what is for his own interest. All that he says and does will be said and done with a view to what is good and proper for the subject for whom he practices his art.[20]

The remarkable aspect of these arguments from Plato is their relevance in modern times. An important problem of medical ethics, which has existed for millennia, can thus be identified: the physician has a dual allegiance; to himself and to his patient.[21] This is a simple case of rights and duties and, more specifically, competing rights: that of the patient to receive the full attention of the doctor, and that of the doctor to earn a wage. Plato disregards the question of the physician earning a wage as an oblique and, in any case, just by-product of the practice of her art; the capacity of the doctor as a wage-earner is a 'further capacity'[22], due to the fact that 'no form of skill or authority provides for its own benefit'.[23] However, later, Plato does show another side to his arguments, just the potential for danger that Szasz spoke of. His arguments in later sections of *The Republic* implicitly show that the person who makes the decisions about the patient's best interests is not the patient but the doctor:

> Surely, there could be no worse hindrance than this excessive care of the body … Shall we say then, that Asclepius [an older doctor epitomising a less malingering era] recognised this and revealed the art of medicine for the benefit of people of sound constitution who normally led a healthy life, but had contracted some definite ailment? He would rid them of their disorders by means of drugs or the knife and tell them to go on living as usual, so as not to impair their usefulness as citizens. But where the body was diseased through and through, he would not try, by nicely calculated evacuations and doses, to prolong a miserable existence and let his patient beget children who were likely to be as sickly as himself. Treatment, he thought, would be wasted on a man who could not live in his ordinary round of duties and was consequently useless to himself and society.[24]

---

[20] *Ibid* 23–4.
[21] T Szasz, *The Theology of Medicine* (New York, Oxford University Press., 1979) 5. However, it would be unwise to ignore a third allegiance that he does not put forward at this point: that to the state, in the form of public health issues such as finite resources and their allocation.
[22] FM Cornford (trans), *The Republic of Plato* (New York, Oxford University Press, 1945) at 28.
[23] *Ibid.*
[24] *Ibid* 97.

This approach of Plato's makes it necessary to answer two questions about the role of the doctor: do we support or oppose the view that the expert's role should be limited to providing truthful information to the client, so that the client can make her own, informed choice? Do we support or oppose the view that the expert's duty is to decide how the non-experts should live and that he should therefore be provided with the power to impose her policies on those who are so unenlightened as to reject them? The answer to the first question would almost universally be in the affirmative. It is the second question, where the role of the physician is pushed more towards paternalism, that is more controversial. Szasz compared modern medicine's ability to exert social control with that of religion centuries earlier, and if we accept that then it is clear that medicine has, in practice, entered the sphere of the second question. However this reality, when phrased in this way, seems unpalatable. For example, if the state employed priests to ensure the spiritual well-being of society, with the power to force people to worship God, there would rightly be indignant protests about a dictatorial state. Yet what is the difference between that and a society where doctors, in tandem with others employed by the state, can incarcerate a person simply by deeming that person to be insane? Szsaz considers that there is a real danger that this phenomenon of selective treatment will become a reality: 'never before – not just in totalitarian societies but in all societies – has Western medicine been so close to realising this Platonic ideal as today'.[25] Nevertheless, in darker times and regimes, these feelings, nestling just below the surface in the medical profession, have been encouraged to emerge publicly.[26]

Obviously, this leads to the potential for social control highlighted by Szasz, and he provides historical examples of this. For example, in the Middle Ages physicians were prominent in the Inquisition, helping the inquisitors 'ferret out witches by appropriate "diagnostic" examinations and tests'.[27] This 'discipline' of public health culminated in what Rosen referred to as 'medical police' (*medizinal polizei*) in the 17th century to serve the interests of absolutist rulers in Europe:

> This idea of medical police, that is, the creation of a medical policy by government and its implementation through administrative regulation, rapidly achieved popularity. Efforts were made to apply this concept to the major health problems of the period, which reached a high point in the work of Johann Peter Frank (1748–1821) and Franz Anton Mai (1742–1814).[28]

Indeed, the medical police were never intended to help the individual citizen or sick patient; they were designed to 'secure for the monarch and the state increased

[25] *Ibid* 9.
[26] See, for example, the defence of eugenics by the Nobel Prize- winning physiologist Alexis Carrel in his book *Man, The Unknown* (New York, Harper and Row, 1939), especially at pp 299–302 and 318–19.
[27] T Szasz, *The Theology of Medicine* (New York, Oxford University Press, 1979) 12.
[28] G Rosen, *A History of Public Health* (New York, MD Publications, 1958) 161–2.

power and wealth'[29]. As such an increase in power and wealth could only be achieved at the expense of decreased health and freedom for certain citizens, we are left with a conflict or struggle between Platonic and Hippocratic principles, in which the former seems to have prevailed. As Rosen notes, Frank's work clearly shows the triumph of the Platonic principles. Frank considered the health of the people to be the responsibility of the state, but,

> ... as might be expected from a public medical official who spent his entire life in the service of various absolute rulers, great and small, the exposition serves not so much for the instruction of the people, or even the physicians, as for the guidance of officials who are supposed to regulate and supervise for the benefit of society all the spheres of human activity, even the most personal.[30]

For example, one of Frank's proposals was a tax on bachelors – part of the medical police's efforts to increase the population in order to provide more soldiers for the monarch. While contemporary society has not gone this far, Szasz states that it is noticeable that almost every agency employs a physician to look after its own interests (for example, schools, factories, prisons, and immigration authorities). The doctor is left with two choices:

> [He can be] a loyal agent of his employer, serving his employer's interests as the latter defines them, or being a disloyal agent of his employer, serving interests other than his employer's as the physician himself defines them.[31]

Thus, we must ask to whom the doctor owes a duty. The concept of medical ethics is radically metamorphosed from the Hippocratic model if the doctor owes a duty not to her patient, but to something or someone else, such as the state. If this is the case, then there is a danger that the philosophy underlying medical ethics would become less about the protection of the patient, but the implementation of the state's social agenda, and beneficence may not be taken for granted:

> ... the best way of expressing its [society's] interest is through the counsellor-physician, who in effect has a dual responsibility to the individual whom he serves and to the society of which he and she are parts ... we will all certainly be diminished as human beings, if not in great moral peril, if we allow ourselves to accept abortion for what are essentially trivial reasons. On the other hand, we will, I fear, be in equal danger if we don't accept abortion as one means of ensuring that both the quantity and quality of the human race are kept within reasonable limits.[32]

Thus, if the doctor refuses to respect the wishes of her employer, then she will be dismissed from service and another, more amenable practitioner, be found to

---

[29]   G Rosen, 'Cameralism and the Concept of Medical Police' (1953) 27 *Bulletin of the History of Medicine* 42.

[30]   G Rosen, *A History of Public Health*, n 28 at 162.

[31]   T Szasz, *The Theology of Medicine* (New York, Oxford University Press., 1979) 14.

[32]   R S Morison, 'Implications of Prenatal Diagnosis for the Quality of, and Right to, Human Life: Society as a Standard' in B Hilton et al (eds), *Ethical Issues in Human Genetics: Genetic Counselling and the Use of Genetic Knowledge* (New York, Plenum, 1973) 210–11.

take her place. What an examination of Plato highlights is the flaw in the Hippocratic argument. Hippocrates espoused a form of benevolent paternalism, with beneficence at the heart of the model. However, Plato demonstrates how one does not necessarily lead to the other. Rather, for paternalism to be translated into beneficence, the individual medical practitioner has to have the moral integrity to make it so and, as he shows, this is not always the case. Indeed, it is quite simply contrary to all human experience that *all* individuals in any profession are of good conscience.

III.   Between the Greeks and the 19th Century – The 'Dark Ages'

In this historical period medical ethics, like medical practice itself, developed little. The practice of medicine was predominantly performed by monks in monasteries. Due to this, medicine almost ceased to be a profession in itself. Rather, it became something that monks *also did.* There was thus little need for a professional ethic unique to medicine. This is reflected by the relative paucity of literature available documenting the period. In particular, the medieval period of history produced little novel work on medical ethics. This may be attributed to the fact that much of the medical literature in this period originated from the monasteries,[33] and the medical ethics of the time were simply the restatement of Christian principles. In other words, ethical principles 'arise out of man's understanding of the world in which he lives and the role he ought to be playing in it'.[34] This adherence to Christian principles also stifled scientific progress: '[Medicine] in that era made no great contribution to the advancement of the medical profession, [though] it did make a very great contribution to its humanitarian aspect'.[35] This reflects the limited interest that the church had in any issues that did not involve either sex or death – it was simply not within the church's ethical scope to consider such issues as medical paternalism or consent.[36] However, the church also had little inclination to adhere to any notions of patient autonomy. Its self-proclaimed role has been to lead rather than follow. In

---

[33]   The change in the source of medical ethical writings from philosophers in ancient Greece to clerics can be attributed to literacy. Particularly in the middle ages, literacy levels were exceptionally low and the monasteries were one of the very few places where there were scholars who were of sufficient literacy to translate the Greek texts.

[34]   G Scorer, *Moral Values, Law and Religion*, in G Scorer and A Wing (eds), *Decision Making in Medicine* (London, Edward Arnold Publishers Ltd, 1979) at 2.

[35]   M Webb-Peploe, *The Medical Profession*, in G Scorer and A Wing (eds), *Decision Making in Medicine* (London, Edward Arnold Publishers Ltd, 1979) at pp 146–7.

[36]   While consent now does invite commentary, this may still be true today: '[b]y dealing with the controversial rather than the commonplace ... commentary has invited its own marginalisation; doctors can argue that it is mostly irrelevant' (J Montgomery 'Medical Law in the Shadow of Hippocrates' (1989) 52 *MLR* 566, 566). The question of medical practitioners' alienation from medical ethics is discussed later in Chapter 3 below.

this way, it seemed more interested in preserving itself and its faith rather than focusing on patients: '[T]he Church's priority was the eternal salvation of the soul. Hence it was concerned to see that Christian midwives, not Jews or heretics, attended births, where they might, *in extremis*, baptise the new-born and thereby help them to heaven.'[37] It was not until the secularisation of society that medical practice was allowed to progress.[38]

The process of secularisation was a slow one. By the 18th century, the medical ethical model seemed to reflect social change by adhering to the class system rather than a religious one. The physician's role became that of the English gentleman. Possibly the most influential medical ethics document is Thomas Percival's *Medical Ethics*, published in 1803.[39] In this book, the virtues of the English gentleman are paramount. The study of ethics will 'soften your manners, expand your affections, and form you to that propriety and dignity of conduct, which are essential to the character of a gentleman'.[40] Indeed, this change in emphasis can be seen to be the beginnings of social ethics. The class system influenced the profession and operated on two levels. Doctors were, as Percival argued, to behave like, and thus be, English gentlemen, and consequently they should be well paid, such remuneration being commensurate with their social standing. As Percival himself said, the medical profession cannot be upheld 'except as a lucrative one'.[41] The second level, intertwined with this financial issue, is that of how to get the finance. For the first time, doctors had to respond to what the public wanted:

> As Britain became a burgeoning free-market economy, medicine tacitly espoused the principles of Adam Smith, a sort of competitive individualism. In town and country alike, medical professionals were essentially on their own. Success depended on a capacity to satisfy public demand, to be inexpensive, sycophantic, or cut a dash. Medicine in Georgian England was thus demand-led and beholden to its clients.[42]

As Conrad et al note, even Percival advised physicians to do as their paying clients said, while 'denying any such indulgence to charity patients in hospital'.[43] Indeed, Conrad et al are less than enthusiastic about the medical ethics commentary created by Percival and others in that period: 'Such works were not profound philosophical enquiries into the theoretical grounds of the duties of doctors, but rather supplements to the traditional gentlemanly codes of honour that had long

---

[37] L I Conrad, M Neve, V Nutton, R Porter, A Wear, *The Western Medical Tradition 800 BC to AD 1800* (Cambridge, Cambridge University Press, 1995).

[38] Medical Ethics in this period conformed to a Platonic model in its perceptions of its social function. This is discussed in the Plato section above.

[39] C D Leake (ed), *Percival's Medical Ethics* (Baltimore, Williams and Wilkins, 1927 (reprint)).

[40] *Ibid.* See also R Veatch, *Medical Ethics* (Boston, Jones and Bartlett, 1989) 9.

[41] L I Conrad, M Neve, V Nutton, R Porter, A Wear, *The Western Medical Tradition 800 BC to AD 1800* (Cambridge, Cambridge University Press, 1995) 451.

[42] *Ibid* 450.

[43] *Ibid* 446.

dictated the proper behaviour of medical men'.[44] Put another way, Percival simply revived the contention that the doctor's principal ethical approach should remain one of benevolent paternalism. From classical times to the Victorian era little progress was therefore made in the development of medical ethics. Christian morality was simply replaced by the English gentleman's class-ridden view that only those with money should be allowed to make their own decisions. Nevertheless, at least there were the beginnings of a move towards listening to patients, albeit only the ones that had money.

IV. The 19th Century – The Institutionalisation of Medical Ethics

The 19th century saw the formation of both the General Medical Council (GMC) (established by the Medical Act 1858) and the Provincial and Surgical Association in 1832, which became the British Medical Association (BMA) in 1856. The GMC was established as a statutory body empowered by Parliament to govern the training of doctors and the practice of medicine. It is made up of members of the profession and lay members, and, as we have seen, it is authorised by statute to provide advice on ethical matters. Its power comes from its statutory status as a regulatory body, with control over the medical register. It is able to suspend or permanently remove anyone from the register for gross ethical misconduct. In essence, therefore, the GMC can decide who can and who cannot practise medicine. Although it might be assumed that the GMC would be the fount of ethical wisdom, and that its pronouncements would have mandatory status, this has not proved to be the case, as is shown in later chapters of this book.

The aim of the BMA is to promote 'the maintenance of the honour and respectability of medicine by defining those elements that ought ever to characterise a liberal profession'.[45] Its first ethics committee was set up in 1849 and it has published several documents outlining medical ethics. However, the ambit of the first committees (in 1849, 1852 and 1858) was to 'bring the subject of medical ethics before the profession'.[46] In 1902, the BMA's Central Ethics Committee was set up, although it rejected requests to draw up an ethical code until 1949.[47] As the next chapter demonstrates, it is now a prolific publisher of ethical guidance. The stated aim of the BMA is essentially Hippocratic in its pledge to promote the 'honour and respectability of medicine' rather than safeguard the interests of the patient. However, it must be remembered that the BMA is the doctors' trade union, and its role is not to regulate.

---

[44] *Ibid.*
[45] *Medical Ethics Today, Its Practice and Philosophy* (BMA, 1993) (xxv).
[46] *Ibid.*
[47] In 1949 it published *Ethics and Members of the Medical Profession* (BMA, 1949). This booklet was designed to fit in the breast pocket of a doctor's coat, and was only really concerned with relationships between doctors and members of other professions.

The defining characteristic of the establishment of the GMC is that medicine was formally recognised as a self-regulatory profession. Medical ethics belonged, and still belongs, to *medical practitioners*. This was the final phase of the process of secularisation started in the 17th century with the Reformation. Without the constraints of the Church, medical practitioners could make their own decisions. Secularisation also coincided with a vast increase in scientific knowledge and development, and scientists became free to experiment without the constraints of the Church's dogmas. However, the GMC and other providers of medical ethics advice cannot always be present to provide fast ethical advice in an emergency situation:

> … the GMC cannot govern the day-to-day decisions of doctors, and it cannot give instructions for each situation. Doctors cannot telephone the GMC each time they meet a problem; they need to learn to apply guidelines and think the problem through for themselves.[48]

As we shall see in the next chapter, this is reflected in the fact that, until recently, the GMC has not really engaged with its right to provide ethical guidance. Rather, it concentrated on relationships between doctors and other professionals and issues such as advertising. Although the BMA has been far more proactive, it is argued in the next chapter that, until very recently, the institutionalisation of medical ethics has not delivered the regulation in ethical matters that might be expected from a profession that has taken great care to ensure that it governs itself.

V. Conclusion

Medical ethics, through the ages, has not left contemporary society with a model that can be seen to be effective. It is perplexing that, even now, the ancient and flawed Hippocratic Oath (in particular) is still considered something of an inspiration to contemporary doctors, and its mantra of benevolent paternalism has continued to inform ethical models. Nevertheless, history has demonstrated that to keep faith with such a principle can be dangerous. An examination of Plato highlights the fact that the benevolence of a medical professional cannot be taken for granted, yet this lesson, as the next chapter agues, has been largely ignored. Rather, ethical models have continued to have, at their crux, the fact that every individual medical practitioner will be beneficent and of good conscience. However, the 20th century brought about two factors which made change inevitable: Nuremburg and the rise in medical technology.

---

[48] A Johnson, *Pathways in Medical Ethics* (London, Edward Arnold, 1990) 22.

3

The Medical Ethics Renaissance: A Brief Assessment

I. Introduction

That there has been a medical ethics 'renaissance' is undeniable. The growth in medical ethics commentary and debate, and the variety of its sources, has increased almost immeasurably in the last 50 years. Such commentary has more often than not been led from outside the medical profession itself, from such people as lawyers, philosophers and sociologists. In this chapter I first examine some of the *reasons* for the proliferation of medical ethics discourse, then the proliferation itself. I continue by arguing that this proliferation of medical ethics has appropriated the subject from the medical profession, and to a significant extent has alienated doctors.

Purportedly benevolent paternalism informed medical ethics for centuries (although as the discussion of Plato in the last chapter highlights, benevolence cannot be taken for granted), and ethics largely remained the domain of doctors themselves. Modern medical ethics debate, dominated by commentators who are generally not doctors, challenges that tradition. In this way, it can be seen that change has already occurred. But why has it done so, when the principle of benevolent paternalism remained entrenched for millennia? Two reasons can be said to have created, in the last century, an extraordinary era which provided the catalyst needed to bring about change. Firstly, the Nazi 'medical experiments" during the Second World War, culminating in Nuremburg, presented the world with evidence of medical maleficence so shocking that it changed the public's perception of doctors; and, secondly, the inexorable and rapid rise in medical technology has presented society with ethical dilemmas not previously considered. Nuremburg and the rise in medical technology combined to create a climate in which debate surrounding medical ethics issues came to be of concern to non-doctors. Some of the technological experiments aroused the interest of philosophers, while the lowering of trust in doctors encouraged others to examine the area. This increase in outside interest produced a large volume of new literature, particularly from the non-doctors, which constitutes the medical ethics renaissance. However, as I demonstrate, this development has not been unproblematic.

This chapter does not seek to evaluate the new theories on medical ethics. Instead, it highlights several facts: first, that medical ethics commentary now comes from everywhere, not just the medical profession; secondly, that an increase in commentary in medical ethics has occurred, and the resulting appropriation of medical ethics can be seen to originate from it. In between these two factors, the latent dissatisfaction felt by patients with traditional medical ethics came to the fore. Finally, this chapter shows that merely by creating an increase in the volume of debate, it does not logically follow that medical practitioners act more 'ethically'. Rather, the increased volume of writing on medical ethics can actually minimise its impact due to the alienation felt by the medical profession, as well as the nature and source of the commentary. Contemporary medical ethics debate may lose touch with reality by dealing with complex theories that are not practical to use in the real world. Thus, the fragmentation of medical ethics discourse brought about by the renaissance, redolent of that identified at the BRI, can be shown to have created more discourse that is, paradoxically, less effective.

II. Nuremburg and Technology – The Catalysts

'The ethos of modern medicine ... is profoundly shaped by the tradition of Nuremberg'.[1] After the atrocities committed by Nazi doctors during the Third Reich,[2] the medical profession was forced to reappraise its ethics to reflect the revulsion which resulted from the discovery of details of the 'experiments' conducted in the name of medical progress. Indeed, the most sobering thought for the profession was that at Nuremberg it was made clear what medicine had the *potential* to be – and it dispelled once and for all the myth that all medical practitioners were benevolent and beneficent.[3] Further, it was clear that the paternalistic approach promulgated by many leading practitioners would be unacceptable to many in societies which had become sceptical of medicine following such experiments. With secularisation, and thus more freedom of thought for medical practitioners, came a fragmentation of views, and some of these views did little to reassure the public that the medical atrocities of the Nazis 'could not happen here'.[4]

The result was the Nuremberg Code, which firmly established the principle of patient self-determination. The dominant theory which shaped the Code was

---

[1]   Vaux, *Biomedical Ethics- Morality for the New Medicine* (New York, Harper and Row, 1968) 27.

[2]   This occurred mainly in the field of human experimentation. Furthermore, many of the experiments were conducted without any anaesthetic being administered.

[3]   For a more detailed, if slightly vigorous and polemic account of the potentiality argument see T Szasz, *The Theology of Medicine* (New York, Oxford University Press, 1979).

[4]   See once again, for example, the defence of eugenics by the Nobel Prize-winning physiologist Alexis Carrel in his book *Man, The Unknown* (New York, Harper and Row, 1939). The most valuable lesson learnt at Nuremberg was, as Vaux (*Biomedical Ethics- Morality for the New Medicine*, n 1) states 'the reminder . . . [of] . . . the potential evil in man' (p 32).

that of pluralism. As Veatch argues, patient self-determination allows a pluralistic medical ethical approach to reflect an increasingly pluralistic society.[5] Nevertheless, such pluralism inevitably leads to a fragmentation of ethics with a base of universal principles, and this was seen as favourable:

> In a secularized civilization where a plurality of values interplay, it is critical that we search for this constellation of basic morals. This should not be a reduction to 'street morality'. Worse yet, we cannot settle for a least common denominator of shallow 'eclectic' ethics.[6]

In an effort to find such a 'constellation of basic morals', the World Medical Association (WMA) formulated its Declaration of Geneva, which sought to be a modern version of the Hippocratic Oath. However, the WMA also started the trend for subject-specific ethics. In subsequent declarations it dealt with specific subjects, thus introducing subject-specific guidance.[7] Indeed, it ceased to reflect a 'wider picture" of something that could be termed 'medical ethics.'[8] As some authors have noted, such an approach can lead to separate components of medical ethics being philosophically diametrically opposed to each other.[9] Nevertheless, the post-Nuremberg focus seemed to be not to compose a solid, single 'ethic', but to prevent a repeat of the atrocities that had gone on. But was it successful in that aim? While paternalism was officially denounced, and an approach that relied on political philosophy was rejected, medical ethics became confused.[10]

Nuremberg highlights the wider problems caused to medicine by its 20th century phenomenon: that medical practitioners had been seen to have crossed the line between having the *potential* to do inhuman harm to patients and actually being seen to have done so. Indeed, the pluralistic approach opened the door for non-doctors to become interested in, and join, debates surrounding medical ethics issues, as the quest for certainty gave way to the recognition of society's lack of homogeneity.

The effect of Nuremburg was exacerbated by the rise, that century, of medical technology, as scientific developments led to new ethical questions of interest to non-doctors. Indeed, the use of medical technology to exemplify the problems of medical ethics is not controversial,[11] but it is submitted that it is a powerful and self-evident one. Logically, more technology leads to more research, and this in

---

[5] R Veatch, *Medical Ethics* (Boston, Jones and Bartlett, 1989) 16.

[6] Vaux, *Biomedical Ethics – Morality for the New Medicine* (New York, Harper and Row, 1968) 32.

[7] For example the Declaration of Tokyo on doctors and torture and the Declaration of Helsinki on patients and research.

[8] As Johnson, *Pathways in Medical Ethics* (London, Edward Arnold, 1990) notes, '[w]hilst one oath appeared to be sufficient for twenty centuries, at least six have appeared in the last forty years' (p 18).

[9] See R Dworkin, *Life's Dominion* (New York, Vintage Books, 1994) and J Glover, *Causing Death and Saving Lives* (Harmondsworth, Penguin, 1990).

[10] See E Emanuel, *The Ends of Human Life- Medical Ethics in a Liberal Polity* (Cambridge Mass., Harvard University Press, 1991).

[11] For an argument against this see E Emanuel, *The Ends of Human Life- Medical Ethics in a Liberal Polity* (Cambridge Mass, Harvard University Press, 1991).

turn leads to an increase in demand for research subjects (be they human or animal), and raises questions about whether the technology might have gone too far.[12] As Ebert notes:

> Advances in medicine have created ethical dilemmas not previously of concern to moral philosophers. When is a birth control method an abortifacient? When is the foetus viable? What are the ethical issues created by amniocentesis and the resulting ability to diagnose genetic defects *in utero*? How should society view the possibility that the sex of an unborn child can be chosen in advance of artificial insemination with appropriately selected sperm? … These questions are being debated by religious denominations, by philosophers, by lay groups, and even by the courts.[13]

The above quote highlights two points about medical technology: firstly, that the line between a *social* issue, a *medical ethics* issue and a *clinical* issue is a fine one. Secondly, all of the questions posed by the quote have to be answered solely *as a result* of medical technology – again making the difference between the real and the hypothetical. The rise in medical technology also created *new* issues which non-doctors were keen to involve themselves in. However, Ebert further recognises a paradox in that while medical technology creates interest in medical ethics among non-doctors, one of society's first instincts is to 'medicalise' the issues and give responsibility for them to the medical profession:

> Medicine is not only scientific and even effective, but it is also respectable. Even the association of AIDS with homosexuality and drug addiction does not inhibit public discussion. Such openness is to be applauded, but it does not justify making almost every social problem a medical one. Teenage pregnancy is a problem and clearly sex education, instruction in the use of contraceptives and advice about prenatal care are all important, but that does not make teenage pregnancy a medical problem. Teenage pregnancy is primarily a social problem, but a social problem is more difficult to analyze, to talk about, to do something about, so that it becomes easier to make it a medical problem.[14]

In other words, while the new questions posed by medical technology are of concern to non-doctors, who therefore become involved in ethical debate, the medical profession paradoxically claims such issues as its own, and society's instinct is similarly to abrogate responsibility to it. Medicine and the medical profession can be seen to be not only not value-neutral, but, through the medicalisation of societal problems, very much involved in any debates that society finds it hard to talk about. Problems are medicalised because society delegates its responsibility to the medical profession. This, however, is not necessarily a satisfactory solution:

> It is not inherently bad to medicalize social problems, but if the medical approach diverts attention and resources away from an analysis of social issues, it postpones

---

[12]   See generally A Jonsen, *The Birth of Bioethics* (New York, Oxford University Press, 1998).

[13]   R H Ebert, *A Twentieth Century Retrospective*, in E Ginzberg (ed), *Medicine and Society- Clinical Decisions and Societal Values* (Boulder and London, Westview Press, 1987) 15–16.

[14]   *Ibid* 18.

definitive action about these issues. Violence, crime, poverty, and homelessness are all societal problems, and while each may have some medical component, medical science will not solve any of them.[15]

Contemporary medical ethics has had to consider two major problems: the implications of research and the use of research subjects. These have arisen due to the increase in detail brought about by medical technology. With regard to the former problem, medical research has now reached the stage where some breakthroughs in technology can be seen as distasteful or counter-productive. However, technology of this sort increases the cost of medical treatment to the extent that economics is now a major consideration in medical practice and ethics. Indeed, medical technology has arguably gone beyond the 'cure' and now functions also to make life comfortable for humans. Inevitably, this leads to an increase in expectations in the medical profession. However, in tandem with this is the lack of trust created by Nuremburg. Tension arises when the diminishing trust is contrasted with the traditional medical ethics model that is conceived *by* doctors *for* doctors and society's traditional complicity in abrogating responsibility to the medical profession:

> Professional codes, ancient and modern, have customarily been drawn up by the profession. While benevolent in intention, these codes enjoin the physician to do what he deems best for the patient. But no mention is made of the patient's participation in that determination. The physician is assumed to be the patient's moral agent, and no notice is taken of the possibility of a conflict between the physician's and patient's value systems.[16]

The rise of medical technology, therefore, has perhaps led to greater respect for *medicine* as a science or discipline. However, the shadow of Nuremburg had the consequence of lowering society's respect for medical practitioners *themselves*. The issue of trust, crucial in explaining the latter of these points, has also encouraged subject-specificity, and thus a fragmentation of medical ethics debate and commentary. As previously mentioned, one of the consequences of Nuremburg was a determination not to allow the events of the Holocaust to be repeated. To this end, specifics were discussed and acted upon.[17] The rise of technology exacerbated debate on single issues, as medical ethics concentrated on the ethics of the technology rather than those of the doctor; and, of course, all of this led to a rise in the *quantity* of ethical commentary from non-doctors, which became the renaissance.

[15] *Ibid.*
[16] E D Pellegrino and D C Thomasma, *A Philosophical Basis of Medical Practice- Toward a Philosophy and Ethic of the Healing Professions* (New York, Oxford University Press, 1981) 228.
[17] However, perhaps this concentration on research and technology creates its own problems. The last chapter argued that the church was only interested in issues around 'sex and death'. Similarly, the preoccupation after Nuremberg centred on research, while ignoring the 'everyday' doctor-patient relationship.

III.   The Proliferation of Medical Ethics

In this section I examine this rise in the quantity of commentary, and demonstrate that the effect of the proliferation is that *even more* medical ethics debate is created. Much of this increase can be said to come from the non-medical sector of medical ethics discourse. If 50 years ago medical ethics was the preserve of medical practitioners, then today it is anything but. Rather, the 'unofficial' sector has created a body of literature and debate that may well *exclude* medical practitioners.[18] The extent of the proliferation of medical ethics and the domination of the 'unofficial" sector can be demonstrated by reference to the huge volume in discourse now available. The growth of academic debate and literature has been rapid,[19] and there are many academic journals which specialise in medical ethics issues and have little to do with medical practitioners. *Bioethics* is philosophical in nature, as well as the also influential *Journal of Medical Ethics*.[20] Others, such as the *Medical Law Review* and *Medical Law International*, are primarily legal yet also discuss ethical issues. Moreover, the journals mentioned are only the tip of a large iceberg. Indeed, medical ethics can even be said to have entered the mainstream of these subjects. Its issues permeate journals which are not specifically tailored to medical law, or philosophy, and have done so for some time.[21] Furthermore, general medical journals such as the *British Medical Journal* and *The Lancet* frequently publish articles regarding medical ethics. In this way, it

---

[18]   Later sections in this chapter go on to show how contemporary medical ethics debate can alienate doctors from participating in it.

[19]   To give just a taste of some of the books available from selected publishers: Dartmouth have a 'medico-legal' series of books, including over 15 titles on issues such as informed consent (S MacLean, *A Patient's Right to Know: Information Disclosure, the Doctor and the Law* (Aldershot, Ashgate, 1989). Ashgate has a series entitled 'The International Library of Medicine, Ethics and Law'. Oxford University Press publishes books on general medical ethics (W Glannon, *Biomedical Ethics* (Oxford, Oxford University Press, 204)), resource allocation (C Newdick, *Who Should We Treat?* (2nd edn, Oxford, Oxford University Press, 2005)), and the end of life (M Prabst Battin, *Ending Life: Ethics and the Way We Die* (Oxford, Oxford University Press, 2005)). Cambridge University Press publishes books on euthanasia (J Keown, *Euthanasia, Ethics and Public Policy* (Cambridge, Cambridge University Press, 2002)) and general law and ethics (S MacLean and J K Mason, *Legal and Ethical Aspects of Healthcare* (Cambridge, Cambridge University Press, 2003)). Finally, Hart Publishing publishes books on the maternal–foetal conflict (R Scott, *Rights, Duties and the Body: Law and Ethics of the Maternal-Foetal Conflict* (Oxford, Hart, 2002)) and euthanasia (H Biggs, *Euthanasia, Death With Dignity and the Law* (Oxford, Hart, 2001)).

[20]   This was first published in 1974. Another journal which began life in that year is *Ethics in Science and Medicine*.

[21]   To give but one example, Margaret Brazier's 'Patient Autonomy and Consent to Treatment: The Role of the Law' (1987) 7 *Legal Studies* 169 is not only published in a mainstream legal journal unconnected to medical law, but it also considers the debate on informed consent in a way that has an inherent discussion of ethics in sections such as 'Patient Autonomy in Health Care Decision-Making'. This example is chosen to reinforce the point that medical ethics debate in mainstream law journals is not something that is confined to the last two decades. Also in that issue is another article with an inherent medical ethics content: Tan Keng Feng, 'Failure of Medical Advice: Trespass or Negligence?' (1987) 7 *Legal Studies* 149. Medical law and ethics articles are now routinely found in general legal publications. Of course, this is not limited to law journals, and articles on medical ethics appear in, for example, general philosophy journals.

can be seen that the medical ethics renaissance has been instrumental in not only creating new journals specialising in the subject, but also in igniting the interest of more general publications towards medical ethics.

With academics writing articles on medical ethics, it is thus unsurprising that they author books on the subject. Philosophers consider the subject as self-standing, and write textbooks on it,[22] while many medical law textbooks see ethics as an inherent part of the subject, and either incorporate it into the discussions of each topic,[23] or have a self-standing chapter on it.[24] Yet medical ethics debate is not confined only to lawyers and philosophers. Sociologists have an interest, as do many economists (with regard to such issues as resource allocation). Furthermore, discussions of issues with an inherent moral content inevitably encourage the participation of theologians. Inevitably, this encourages the formation of university courses in the subject.

Nevertheless, it is not just academics that form the body of the 'unofficial' sector. Religious groups are interested in debates concerning, for example, death and reproductive choice;[25] and, as we shall see later in this book, pressure groups (many with competing aims) also participate in debates of interest to them, as is particularly evident in the reports discussed in Chapter 8. They contain numerous submissions by such bodies and groups, many of which framed their opinions in terms of being 'ethics'. All of this increase in debate filters down to the public through the media. Print journalism carries many stories concerning medical ethics issues. The radio has programmes such as *The Moral Maze* that frequently highlights issues to do with medical ethics, and the same is true for television's *The Heart of the Matter*. Indeed, it is perhaps indicative of the interest in medical ethics that BBC Television has in the past few years broadcasted a series specifically about a fictional hospital ethicist herself, called *Life Support*.

Whether academics and pressure groups sparked the interest of the media or whether the process occurred the other way around is a moot point, and not of relevance to this chapter. What is undeniable, however, is that all of this has had an impact on the medical profession. As we shall see, formal and semi-formal medical ethics have undergone a similar increase in quantity of ethical advice. But where has the medical ethics renaissance, and the proliferation of ethical discourse, left medical professionals? It can be said to have changed the whole question of where medical ethics comes from, and perhaps formal and semi-formal medical ethics are metamorphosing into a reflection of the unofficial approach. In particular, this can be seen in the way in which it relies on debate rather than explicit guidance. This shift, which is towards subject-specificity and

---

[22] See, for example, J Harris, *The Value of Life: An Introduction to Medical Ethics* (London, Routledge, 1994).

[23] See, for example, J Herring, *Medical Law and Ethics* (Oxford, Oxford University Press, 2006).

[24] See, for example, E Jackson, *Medical Law: Text, Cases and Materials* (Oxford, Oxford University Press, 2006).

[25] Indeed, the Catholic Church has been very active in the debates surrounding such issues as abortion, contraception and euthanasia.

'critical' medical ethics, can be attributed to the increase in the number of non-doctors involved in formulating this guidance. Many non-doctors now form part of the BMA and GMC ethics committees. Of course, different disciplines bring with them different perspectives, and the permeation of the 'unofficial' sector simply cannot have failed to have had an effect on medical practitioners.

This, though, is what the medical ethics renaissance has been all about. The rise in quantity of medical ethics commentary and debate has also had the effect of including a wide variety of different disciplines and perspectives on the subject. These have had something of a 'cross-pollinating' effect on formal and semi-formal medical ethics. Debate leads to more debate (particularly in academia, where *minutiae* of arguments are often the essence of publications), and medical ethics commentary has grown, through the renaissance, until it reached a critical mass that permeated the medical profession. In this way, the medical ethics renaissance can be said to have produced a growth in debate that has threatened to remove the subject from the domain of the medical practitioner. The next section demonstrates how this has been achieved.

IV.   The Appropriation of Medical Ethics

As we shall see, a common theme of the literature deriving from unofficial medical ethics, and in particular one stressed Ian Kennedy, is that the medical practitioner possesses no special skill that makes her the best person to make decisions of an ethical nature. The 'appropriation of medical ethics' is a term that is used here to show that it is this realisation that can be said to have contributed most significantly to the increase in literature and debate on medical ethics today. In fact, the recognition that these ethical decisions are not strictly being entrusted to experts, but to pretenders to expertise, has given a new confidence and legitimacy to non-doctors which has been a crucial and fundamental factor in the medical ethics renaissance and the rise of the unofficial sector of medical ethics. While it may seem obvious to us now, given that recognition has been achieved, the scale of the previous blindness can be demonstrated by Kennedy. The tone of the author, in having to make his point abundantly clear as late as 1981, is telling:

> ... my point is that the scope of the alleged unique competence of the doctor is as wide, as imprecise, as flexible and as inherently evaluative as the meanings given to notions of health and ill health. Doctors make decisions about what is to be done. Some, but only some, of these decisions are matters of technical skill. I submit that the majority of decisions taken by doctors are not technical. They are, instead, moral and ethical. They are decisions about what ought to be done, in light of certain values. Now, this creates a problem. Doctors claim a special, indeed unique, competence in a particular area, the practice of medicine. So medical judgements, medical decisions, are for them and them alone. But, if I am right that it is a fundamental feature of medical practice that doctors are making ethical judgements, it means that ethics, to the extent that they touch on

how doctors choose to practice medicine, are something for them and them alone. This is a surprising and even dangerous notion.[26]

The appropriation of medical ethics, and the birth of the renaissance, can at least in part be attributed to this idea of 'de-medicalising' medical ethics. Kennedy identifies something that, upon close consideration, is all too evident: there are decisions made by medical practitioners that could, and perhaps should, be made by non-doctors. Two simple examples that illustrate this point are the ethically well-documented areas of abortion and cloning. The question of how to clone, and how to abort, are clearly medical decisions. Neither of these could be achieved without the expertise of a medical practitioner or scientist. Nevertheless, it does not follow that any moral, ethical or philosophical questions that arise due to this technology are medical in nature. In other words, the question of *how* to abort or clone must be distinguished, at a fundamental level, from the question of *whether* to abort or clone. The appropriation of medical ethics is concerned with the recognition that in medical ethics the prefix 'medical' may often be superfluous.

Needless to say, events during the Second World War only served to further legitimise the view that medical ethics were not the concern of only medical practitioners. What Nazi doctors did with their 'experiments' was effectively to show that not everything with the prefix 'medical' was automatically morally acceptable. Worst still, these atrocities, committed in the name of scientific progress, coincided with what has been historically the century where the advancement of medical technology has accelerated more than in any other. In other words, at the same time that doctors strove ever more ardently to advance medical knowledge, society in general finally learned that it was possible to question, in some cases, the profession's motives.[27] As a result, laypersons wanted to be involved in the ethical evaluative process. This was how society's recognition of medicalisation came about. The more non-doctors delved into 'medical' ethics, the more the conclusion was reached that doctors were not experts in ethics. In the light of the way in which the Nazi data was collected, it is difficult to find an argument for the exclusion of these groups from the debate.

Members of the unofficial sector of medical ethics discourse now find it difficult to fathom how easily society previously accepted medical ethics in the form that it used to take. The recognition of inappropriate medicalisation has led many to question the paternalist culture within medical ethics. Again, the actions of Nazi doctors can be seen to have had a profound effect on this, and there is now a somewhat incredulous tone regarding some medical attitudes. Willard Gaylin, for example, uses an anecdote to illustrate this point. He writes of an encounter with a senior physician in a medical ward, who felt that medical ethics was certainly not ignored in his ward:

---

[26] I Kennedy, *The Unmasking of Medicine* (London, George Allen & Unwin, 1981) at 78.
[27] See T Szasz, *The Theology of Medicine* (New York, Oxford University Press, 1979).

'[j]ust as I feel that I have the ultimate responsibility for making all medical decisions, I feel that I must bear the ultimate responsibility for making all ethical decisions'. It was said in good faith, and it was not for me to point out to him that there is a fine line between 'assumption of responsibility' and arrogation of power.[28]

This doctor's attitude may be seen as antiquated, yet it is that basic recognition of the physician's lack of expertise that leads to the conclusion that perhaps *non-doctors* should also be involved in medical ethical discourse. Notice again, in the following example, the air of incredulity and the influence of Plato, Szasz and Nuremberg on the opinions of the author:

> If a piece of behavior is defined as immoral by a religious authority, the individual still feels free to accept or reject that definition, particularly in our society, which endows religious or moral leaders with little authority or punitive power ... If, however, you define the very same piece of behavior as 'abnormal' or sick, and if the individual can be convinced of your expertise in matters of health, he will often be forced by fear to abandon that activity. He will in addition not feel forced. He will wish to do that which you wish. The universal terror of illness, operating under the imprimatur of the medical establishment, makes coercion in the traditional sense unnecessary. This is a potent force in behavior control which has not nearly been sufficiently analyzed, evaluated, or supervised.[29]

Furthermore, this has been coupled with a recognition that perhaps 'medical ethics' in the form of codes of conduct or oaths is simply insufficient in these days of technology.[30] Nuremberg showed that the beneficence of medical practitioners (and, as importantly, the non-maleficence) cannot be taken for granted. Again, this has implications. If anything, the point was brought home that the Nazis were not the first to abuse the position of medical practitioners, nor were they to be the last.[31] The rapid technologicalisation of medical practice also impaired, to a large extent, the human relationship between doctor and patient. Specialisation changed that relationship from one between trusted confidants, almost friends, to one between a person labelled as a 'patient', and one as a 'doctor', who have probably never met before. As a consequence of this, the extent to which patients acquiesce to medical hegemony is lowered, because there is not as much of an element of trust in the physician from the outset.

As Strong notes, a more impersonal nature of medical practice meant that 'expertise was displayed rather than proved ... doctors' status was warranted simply by their being there'.[32] MacIntyre goes even further than Strong, for

---

[28]   W Gaylin, 'Foreword', in S Gorovitz, A L Jameton, R Macklin, J M O'Connor, E V Perrin, B P St Clair, S Sherwin, *Moral Problems in Medicine* (London, Prentice Hall Inc., 1976) (xvi).

[29]   *Ibid* (xxi).

[30]   See V Barry, *Moral Aspects of Health Care* (Belmont, California, Wadsworth, 1982) 53–6.

[31]   J Katz, 'Abuse of Human Beings for the Sake of Science', in A Caplan (ed), *When Medicine Went Mad: Bioethics and the Holocaust* (Totowa, New Jersey, Humana Press, 1992) 236–7. The book charts the 'medical experiments' perpetrated by the Nazis, as well as examples of medical atrocities *since* Nuremberg (pp 246–52).

[32]   P M Strong, 'Collegial Authority', in N Abrams and D Buckner (eds), *Medical Ethics: A Clinical Textbook and Reference for the Health Care Professions* (Cambridge, Mass, MIT Press, 1983) 124.

example, arguing that the interaction is now 'stranger to stranger; and the very proper fear and suspicion that we have of strangers extends equally and properly to our encounter with physicians'.[33] In this way there is a realisation of what he calls the 'oddity' of traditional relationships between patients and physicians. Once we do this, 'its oddity is all the more obtrusive because it is so very nearly without parallel in the rest of our social experience'.[34]

Trust in the medical profession has certainly been damaged to a large degree. Nuremburg ensured this. Furthermore, the impersonalisation of medicine since then has had the effect that the doctor we see is not *our* doctor. Rather, she is merely *a* doctor. A logical progression of this is to examine the regulatory framework for their decision-making. In the case of medical oaths and codes, society has found them to be lacking. This is why it has appropriated medical ethics from the medical profession through the growth in volume in discourse and influence of the unofficial sector. Also, non-doctors have finally recognised that medical practitioners are not any more qualified than we are to make ethical decisions. Others sought to fill the vacuum, and thus the medical ethics renaissance occurred.

V.   The Medical Profession's Response to the Appropriation of Medical Ethics

However, if the renaissance has now appropriated medical ethics, then what does that mean for medical professionals? This section argues that the medical profession might well feel 'crowded out' of medical ethics, and that it has come to be seen as something of an irrelevance to the everyday life of medical practitioners. Indeed, theologians, doctors, philosophers, lawyers and everyone else are as capable as each other of disagreement. This fragmentation was recognised as being problematic by Mason and McCall Smith:

> There is a plethora of theories on hand that are designed to help us decide what is morally right ... [M]orality, it seems, is sometimes not so much a maze as a smorgasbord.[35]

The medical profession's disaffection can be seen to arise out of the fact that there is not a foundation in medicine any more. Rather, the roots of some ethical arguments and theories put forward since the medical ethics renaissance are alien to doctors. While it can be said that the medical profession's disaffection with the appropriation of medical ethics has much to do with it being too used to having control over ethical discourse, it is perhaps worthy of note at this point that this was not always so. As the last chapter showed, much of the medical ethics

---

[33]   A MacIntyre, 'Patients as Agents', in S Spicker and H T Englehardt (eds), *Philosophical Medical Ethics: Its Nature and Significance* (Dordrecht, D Reidel Publishing Co, 1977) 207.

[34]   *Ibid* 206.

[35]   J K Mason and R A McCall Smith, *Law and Medical Ethics* (5th edn, London, Butterworths, 1998) 4. The newest edition, published in 2006, does not contain this quote.

commentary and debate used to be founded on religious principles. While this had its drawbacks, at least medical ethics had a base in something. However, the Reformation and the consequent lessening of the Church's influence left a theoretical chasm that the profession itself was best placed to fill. The renaissance in medical ethics debate has sought to reverse this trend while, perhaps confusingly, offering multiple foundations and approaches.

Ian Kennedy notes unsurprisingly that the appropriation of medical ethics has not been regarded in a positive light by medical practitioners. Instead, it can be seen that the emphasis by doctors has traditionally been on the 'medical' rather than the 'ethics'. In other words, medical practitioners claim a unique competence to decide on ethical matters. As with MacIntyre's finding of 'oddity' in the doctor–patient relationship when considered objectively, Kennedy similarly despairs at the notion that a 'medical decision' is defined as one that is, quite simply, made by doctors. As he puts it, '[t]he decision as to what vote to cast in a general election is made by doctors, but that does not make it a medical decision'.[36] But what is or is not a 'medical' decision does not actually matter here. What does is the medical profession's *perception* of such decisions being so. Kennedy continues by considering two cases in US courts with inherent ethical content. Both the *Saikewicz* and the (perhaps better known) *Quinlan* cases involved decisions at the end of life, respectively whether to give a mentally retarded man of 67 years of age chemotherapy to postpone his inevitable death from leukaemia, and whether a doctor is under a duty to continue with 'heroic or pointless' treatment.[37] In both cases the courts decided that the decision was not one for doctors alone. In the former, the Massachusetts Supreme Court decided that it was one for the court, and in the latter the New Jersey Supreme Court agreed, saying that there were such weighty philosophical matters to consider that only the court, as a representative of society's wisdom, could do so.

These decisions, as he documents, were not to be received without comment. The editor of the *New England Journal of Medicine* called the *Saikewicz* case a vote of 'no confidence in the medical profession'.[38] Meanwhile, the President of the Royal Society of Medicine, said that,

> the wise and humane physician, in tune with his patient, will know very well when it is time to withdraw treatment. The decision must be made by, and the responsibility borne by, one doctor who has earned and enjoys the confidence and trust of the patient and his family. We must not allow this to become a committee matter. Still less must a decision of this kind become a matter for the courts of law. We have seen, much publicised in the Karen Ann Quinlan case, what happens when an attempt is made to invoke the legal code, and the spectacle was hardly edifying.[39]

---

[36] I Kennedy, *The Unmasking of Medicine* (London, George Allen & Unwin, 1981) 77.

[37] *Re Quinlan* (1976) 355 A 2d (NJ); *Superintendent of Belcherton State School v Saikewicz* (1977) 370 NE 2d 417

[38] I Kennedy, *The Unmasking of Medicine* (London, George Allen & Unwin, 1981) 84.

[39] *Ibid* 85.

But why is this? The simple answer, which conveys in an explicit manner the message delivered implicitly in each of the above quotes, is that the decision is felt by the medical profession to be a 'medical' one. As Kennedy notes, Reiss wrote in the *Journal of Medical Ethics* about the *Saikewicz* case, '[i]t seems to us that the experienced physician is in a much better position to make such judgments than either the family or a court of law'.[40] Thus when academics, and more specifically non-medical academics, enter into ethical discourse, the veil of technical expertise is lifted, and medical ethics no longer belongs to the medical profession. The consequence of this is a feeling of alienation on behalf of the medical profession. Indeed, there was even resistance to the very idea of teaching medical students medical ethics. As Kennedy notes, the two arguments against ethics training are that there is no room in the curriculum, and that they learn 'on the job'.[41] This reflects a feeling that if medical ethics is not a 'medical' matter any more, then doctors should not concern themselves with it. In other words, the appropriation of medical ethics can perhaps be seen as counter-productive, in the way that non-doctors may have 'academicised' the subject, and lost the interest of those who must actually apply ethical principles.

There is no better illustration of this point than the fictional account conceived by Gillon, himself a doctor and a moral philosopher, of an argument that a medical practitioner might give against philosophical medical ethics:

> There is something wrong with medical education if it has to go in for all this discussion and argument about medical ethics. (In my day) we learnt about medical ethics by learning to become good doctors, in all senses of good. We had had, I hope, good moral education, starting well before we came to medical school, at home, at church, and at school. Our consciences had been formed early on, and when we got to medical school the process continued. We learnt what was done and what was not done, mostly from the example of our teachers ... At the heart of our medical education was an emphasis on character development, on personal integrity, on obeying our consciences – in short, on being a good chap. We never heard about utilitarianism and deontological theories of ethics or even about the virtues; we just learned what was appropriate in which circumstances.[42]

Gillon argues that it could easily have been a quote from a doctor, and I assume that he is correct when he does so. Moreover, I would argue that this attitude is as prevalent today as it was at the time Gillon manufactured the quote in 1986. The prevailing feeling would appear to be one of the *irrelevance* of medical ethics to medical practice and practitioners. One reason for this may be its academisation. In other words, the old system of learning medical ethics by 'osmosis' at least had the advantage of being rooted in the actual *application* of ethical principles. Academic (or philosophical) medical ethics, on the other hand, can easily be

---

[40]   *Ibid* 84.
[41]   *Ibid* 96. This has changed, as the GMC now stipulates that medical ethics must be a part of the undergraduate curriculum.
[42]   R Gillon, *Philosophical Medical Ethics* (Chichester, John Wiley & Sons, 1986) 29.

perceived (rightly or wrongly), as being fundamentally theoretical, and thus of no relevance to 'real life'. Callahan emphasises this problem in an insightful way when he states that,

> the ethicist may be quite correct in his in his theoretical analysis – perhaps utilitarianism is, say, the largest philosophical issue at stake in many ethical dilemmas. Yet he will be quite clearly wrong if he does not recognize that the issue in particular cases – Mrs Jones in Ward 5 at 4.10 in the afternoon – must and will involve far more than utilitarian theory.[43]

The medical ethics renaissance can only be of practical use if the non-medical discourse is ingested by doctors, either directly or indirectly. This, in turn, can only occur if a partnership is established with the medical profession. But, as mentioned above, this has not been forthcoming. Chapman's brutal assessment in 1984 that the medical profession and others involved in ethical commentary and debate 'have as yet only fragments of language in common' can only lead to one outcome: the dislocation of medical ethics from the medical profession.[44] He gives a quote from Ian Thompson that in Britain the 'reaction of the medical profession to most contemporary philosophy is contemptuous for its pedantic irrelevance', and the picture is one of conflict, not co-operation.[45]

VI.　Applying Contemporary Medical Ethics

Previous sections of this chapter have shown that the dominant tradition of benevolent paternalism in medical ethics has confronted serious challenges in the last half century. The growth of literature and debate on medical ethics resulted in non-doctors, to a significant extent, appropriating medical ethics, and this has caused the medical ethics renaissance. It is far too simplistic to attribute it simply to an increase in interest in ethics by philosophers and others or the public, or to say that the only thing that it represents is a proliferation in medical ethics commentary and debate. Indeed, a more plausible factor is that inherent in the medical ethics renaissance is the notion that there was something wrong, and ideas about how these problems could be resolved.

The fundamental 'problem' with medical ethics may simply be attributed to the historical generality of medical ethics, ethical principles and codes. While it is true that no medical ethical code or theory can possibly foresee every possible situation that doctors may find themselves in, the generality of the codes was seen

---

[43]　D Callahan, 'Bioethics as a Discipline' in J M Humber and R F Almeder, *Biomedical Ethics and the Law* (New York, Plenum, 1976) 6. To put this point another way, Callahan also recounted an anecdote about a critic of his seminars about the difference between act and rule utilitarianism. The critic argues that 'philosophers do nothing but make technical distinctions and split verbal hairs; and all that stuff about different kinds of utilitarianism is too abstract to be of any use' (p 2).

[44]　C B Chapman, *Physicians, Law, and Ethics* (New York, New York University Press, 1984) 133.

[45]　*Ibid.*

as having a fundamental flaw. As Gillon notes, medical ethics has traditionally, as a result, placed much emphasis on the 'conscience' of the individual medical practitioner to interpret a principle.[46] In this way, disagreements are inevitable and irresolvable:

> [I]f Dr A's conscience tells him to transfuse a Jehovah's Witness regardless of her own views and Dr B's conscience tells him not to transfuse such a patient, where stands medical ethics? Which position is right and why? Are both right? Why? Is no resolution or even attempt at resolution possible or desirable?[47]

Needless to say, the events that led to Nuremberg will have put the 'conscience' of the medical practitioner in a new and disturbing focus. Thus one purpose of the medical ethics renaissance can be seen to be the construction of a system of medical ethics that does not contain this flaw. For this reason did 'critical' medical ethics emerge. This can be defined as 'the analytic activity in which the concepts, assumptions, beliefs, attitudes, emotions, reasons, and arguments underlying medicomoral decision-making are examined critically'.[48] Put another way, the medical ethics renaissance sought to introduce *normativity* into medical ethics. Normativity means that the emphasis is on what ought to be done rather than on what is done. Thus it can be distinguished from descriptive ethics and metaethics.[49] Of course, a logical consequence of normative analysis, particularly when designed to address the question of generality within ethical commentary, is that of subject specificity. As argued in the last chapter, this does not solve the perceived problem so much as creating one at the opposite end of the spectrum. Indeed, it does not promote agreement or categorise discourse. It is thus arguable that there is now an 'ethics overkill', in breadth and (more importantly) *depth*, in that medical ethics books and articles concentrate not on ethical theories, or theories related to one subject, but to issues *within* subjects relating to ethics.[50]

For this reason, some authors have attempted to steer a middle ground by concentrating on *coherent* theories that straddle the spectrum of medical ethics. Medical ethics debate thus becomes a tool for decision-making.[51] As Harris argues, we must assess our beliefs and values by 'testing them to destruction'.[52] But does this achieve its aims? Does it help Mrs Jones in Ward 5 at 4.10 in the afternoon? This chapter, and Chapter 2, have argued that it does not. One reason

---

[46] R Gillon, *Philosophical Medical Ethics* (Chichester, John Wiley & Sons, 1986) 30.

[47] *Ibid* 31.

[48] *Ibid* 2.

[49] These are more traditional methods of ethical discourse, but are not considered here as they are not really important for the purposes of this section. For definitions see T Beauchamp and J Childress, *Principles of Biomedical Ethics* (4th edn, New York, Oxford University Press, 1994).

[50] See Callahan D, 'Bioethics as a Discipline' in Humber J M and Almeder R F, *Biomedical Ethics and the Law* (New York, Plenum Press, 1979) at 2, and R Veatch, *A Theory of Medical Ethics* (New York, Basic Books Inc., 1981) 4–5.

[51] See Kennedy, *The Unmasking of Medicine* (London, George Allen & Unwin, 1981) 123, T Beauchamp and J Childress, *Principles of Biomedical Ethics* (4th edn, New York, Oxford University Press, 1994) 12, V Barry, *Moral Aspects of Health Care* (Belmont, California, Wadsworth, 1982) (ix).

[52] J Harris, *The Value of Life: An Introduction to Medical Ethics* (London, Routledge, 1994) at 5.

for this is the plurality of views inherent in contemporary society. Some authors have argued that medical ethics needed a rethink when society became secular and plural, and thus ceased to hold, in any way, what can be termed universal values.[53] To return to the example given by Gillon, if Dr A and Dr B still disagree about whether to give a Jehovah's Witness a blood transfusion, critical medical ethics, no matter how coherent, does not help. Put simply, if patients and doctors have diametrically opposed views, then so do ethicists. Elsewhere in this book there are countless examples of opposing viewpoints, each appearing under the heading of 'ethics', which means that no consensual decision is ever possible. As MacIntyre notes, where 'everyone had hoped to move towards a constructive resolution of ... disagreements, instead they find themselves merely restating them'.[54] The fragmentation created by the renaissance, redolent of that at BRI, meant that the higher volume of discourse created less agreement than before.

If contemporary medical ethics does not provide answers, then that is a situation that may be rectified through categorising the different sectors of ethical discourse. The hierarchy created would allow different opinions to be ranked, with unofficial writing at the bottom, semi-formal ethics above it, and the formal sector at the top. In this way, doctors and patients would not be faced with a situation, such as that described by Gillon, where ethical questions are essentially irresolvable. Indeed, categorisation of discourse would serve as an antidote to fragmentation. However, this has not occurred. Rather, what has happened is that the formal and semi-formal sectors of ethical discourse have adopted the approach of the unofficial sector, while claiming to be directive. As we shall see, for different reasons the approaches of the GMC and BMA do not provide the ethical blanket that they pretend to. This has resulted in a regulatory vacuum in medical ethics that, as we shall see in later chapters, the conscience of individual medical practitioners has had to fill, which runs contrary to the lessons of, among others, Plato and Nuremburg.

As the only body with a statutory right to provide the medical profession with ethical advice and treatment, it might be expected that the GMC's guidance would be confident and directive in nature. As I demonstrate in Chapter 4, sometimes this is the case; at others, however, it is not, as Chapter 5 shows. Indeed, the GMC's attitude in its own guidance has altered dramatically over the past decade. Before 1995, its core guidance, known as the 'Blue Book', took virtually no account of ethical debates – it seemed that the renaissance had passed it by. Thus in the final version, published in December 1993, the chapter

---

[53]   See in S Spicker and H T Englehardt (eds), *Philosophical Medical Ethics: Its Nature and Significance* (Dordrecht, D Reidel Publishing Co, 1977) 5.

[54]   A MacIntyre, 'Patients as Agents', in S Spicker and H T Englehardt (eds), *Philosophical Medical Ethics: Its Nature and Significance* (Dordrecht, D Reidel Publishing Co, 1977) 207.

on ethics was concerned with confidentiality, advertising and the relationship between doctors and the pharmaceutical industry.[55]

In 1995, it published the first edition of its new text, *Good Medical Practice*, a 15-page booklet. This document was tentative regarding how it should be used. The introductory paragraph on the inside of the cover stated that the document 'sets out the basic principles of good practice. *It is guidance. It is not a set of rules,* nor is it exhaustive'.[56] It went on to note that the GMC published further booklets on advertising, confidentiality and the ethical problems surrounding HIV and AIDS.[57] By the time of the second edition in 1998, this had changed, and the first page now contained a warning, stating that '[i]f serious problems arise which call your registration into question, these are the standards against which you will be judged'.[58] A further revision in 2001 warned starkly that '[s]erious or persistent failures to meet the standards in this booklet may put your registration at risk'.[59] The latest version of the guidance, published in November 2006, combines the two approaches:

> The guidance that follows describes what is expected of all doctors registered with the GMC. It is your responsibility to be familiar with Good Medical Practice and to follow the guidance it contains. *It is guidance, not a statutory code, so you must use your judgement to apply the principles* to the various situations you will face as a doctor, whether or not you routinely see patients. You must be prepared to explain and justify your decisions and actions.
>
> In Good Medical Practice the terms 'you must' and 'you should' are used in the following ways:
>
> — 'You must' is used for an overriding duty or principle.
> — 'You should' is used when we are providing an explanation of how you will meet the overriding duty.
> — 'You should' is also used where the duty or principle will not apply in all situations or circumstances, or where there are factors outside your control that affect whether or how you can comply with the guidance.
>
> *Serious or persistent failure to follow this guidance will put your registration at risk.*[60]

The problem with the GMC guidance, however, lies in its non-specific nature. The 2006 version of *Good Medical Practice* comprises only 40 pages, and it does not have any more specific, detailed guidance available for two of the four subject areas considered in Chapters 4–7. Despite claiming to be directive, the GMC document is ultimately just a statement of general principles.

---

[55] GMC, *Professional Conduct and Discipline – Fitness to Practice* (GMC, 1993). See Part 3, paras 66–122.
[56] GMC, *Good Medical Practice* (GMC, 1995) 1.
[57] *Ibid.*
[58] GMC, *Good Medical Practice* (GMC, 1998) 1.
[59] GMC, *Good Medical Practice* (GMC, 2001) 1.
[60] GMC, *Good Medical Practice* (GMC, 2006) 5.

Guidance that is of more use to doctors with a specific problem has tradition-ally emanated from the BMA. Indeed its major source of guidance, *Medical Ethics Today*, currently stands at over 800 pages.[61] Yet, as late as 1993, even the advice from the BMA was markedly different. In 1980, the Association published *The Handbook of Medical Ethics*, a book of fewer than 100 pages. Readers today would hardly recognise the format of the document, as it resembled the GMC in its emphasis on relationships with allied professions, the state and the media. The section on 'ethical dilemmas', for example, comprised only eight pages.[62] The section on euthanasia was less than a page long, and essentially described the difference between voluntary, compulsory, active and passive euthanasia. The extent of the critique is best summed up by the final sentence of the section: '[d]octors vary in their approach to passive euthanasia but the profession condemns legalised active voluntary euthanasia'.[63] Indeed, the book was not meant to be a comprehensive encyclopaedia of guidance but instead, as the foreword stated, the BMA hoped that the book would help to 'stimulate debate'.[64]

After three reprints of the handbook in the mid-1980s, the BMA revised its approach and in 1988 published its guidance under a new title: *The Philosophy and Practice of Medical Ethics*.[65] Similar in size to the *Handbook*, but slightly longer at over 130 pages, this book more closely resembled what we are now used to, with chapters on 'philosophical and religious influences on medical ethics', 'autonomy and paternalism', 'confidentiality' and 'consent' amongst others con-cerning 'gifts and hospitality' and 'the doctor and the media'. What was notable about the book, however, was the change in emphasis towards direction rather than debate. Thus, for the first time, the distinction between law, ethics and morals was identified:

> [T]he reader must constantly bear in mind this necessary and implicit distinction between 'Legal' – which is relatively easily determined by reference to statute, 'Ethical' – which is a more difficult assessment of what is currently acceptable and proper to the group of which the reader is a part, and 'Moral' – which requires the reader to view the problem in relation to and authority which the reader accepts personally, even in opposition to other members of the same profession.[66]

The book's self-professed approach was to identify the arguments and counterar-guments which led to 'universally accepted ethical principles'.[67] In accordance with the definitions above, these should be followed as they reflected the corporate ethos of the medical profession. There was a recognition that the book might not answer all queries, but a confidence that 'even if doctors cannot find

---

[61]   BMA, *Medical Ethics Today: The BMA's Handbook of Ethics and Law* (2nd edn, BMA, 2004).
[62]   BMA, *The Handbook of Medical Ethics* (BMA, 1980). See pp 27–35.
[63]   *Ibid* 31.
[64]   *Ibid* 5.
[65]   BMA, *The Philosophy and Practice of Medical Ethics* (BMA, 1988).
[66]   *Ibid* (iii).
[67]   *Ibid*.

answers to specific problems, they can work out answers to ethical problems for themselves' by applying the principles in the book.[68]

A further change of approach occurred in 1993. In response to criticism of the 1988 book as 'failing to provide simple and readily accessible "answers"',[69] the BMA published a larger book that was meant to be much more comprehensive, and thus comprised over 350 pages. Once again there was a warning, though in this case less explicit, that any approach to ethics must rest 'upon some form of reasoned analysis which should be articulated and open to scrutiny'.[70] However, this was somewhat mitigated when the book stated that the BMA had no statutory or disciplinary powers itself while the GMC did, and that its guidance should therefore be seen as a companion to the GMC's.[71] The relationship between the two bodies had, it continued, 'permitted a more flexible system [of regulation] which is capable of responding to change'.[72] The sudden emphasis on flexibility was maintained at the end of the introductory chapter of the book, where it was noted that doctors 'are not a homogenous group', and that it hoped that 'the benefit gained from the exploration of different viewpoints will be evident and will fuel further debate'.[73] The BMA's approach in the 1993 book can therefore be seen to be contradictory. On the one hand, it sought to be directive, while at the same time deferring to the GMC, and promoting debate and flexibility.

The trend for the growth in the size of the guidance with each new edition continued when, in 2004, the BMA introduced what is still the current guidance.[74] As mentioned above, this 800-page book lacks nothing in comprehensiveness, but reflects the 1993 book's contradictory signals. In its introductory chapter, it recognises much that has been argued in this book so far: that medical ethics was traditionally written by doctors for doctors, that it espoused paternalism, and that it changed due to an increase in technologicalisation and Nuremburg.[75] This has led to the rejection of what it terms 'traditional medical ethics', and the adoption of 'analytical medical ethics', which it defines as 'the critical process through which substantive ethical aims are justified (or criticised) in the light of argument and counterargument'.[76] It further states that this should inform traditional medical ethics.

I would argue, however, that this process represents a shift on the part of the semi-formal sector towards the methodology of the unofficial sector of discourse. Indeed, in its conclusion to that chapter, the book outlines that its aim 'is to help health professionals to engage in the practice of analytical medical ethics in order

---

[68]   *Ibid* (iii)–(iv).
[69]   BMA, *Medical Ethics Today: Its Practice and Philosophy* (BMA, 1993) (xxv).
[70]   *Ibid* (xxiv).
[71]   *Ibid* (xxvi).
[72]   *Ibid*.
[73]   *Ibid* (xxvii).
[74]   BMA, *Medical Ethics Today: The BMA's Handbook of Ethics and Law* (2nd edn, BMA, 2004).
[75]   *Ibid* 4.
[76]   *Ibid* 4–5.

to promote and facilitate the ethical practice of medicine'.[77] A table is provided on p 8 of *Medical Ethics Today* that demonstrates how ethical dilemmas should be resolved:

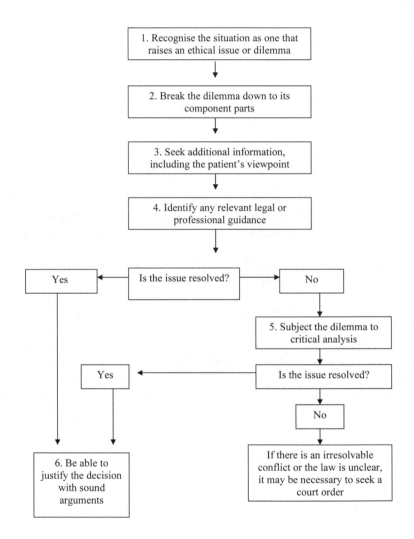

In a more detailed exposition of point 4 of the table, the book provides a hierarchy of discourse that the doctor should take into account. First, the law, then any GMC guidance, and finally the BMA, Royal Colleges and other

[77]   *Ibid* 21.

organisations such as the Department of Health or the Human Fertilisation and Embryology Act.[78] However, this relies on the bodies mentioned having directive guidance that is detailed enough to resolve the issue at the heart of the dilemma. As we shall see in Chapters 4–7, this is not always the case. Thus we shall see the law abrogating responsibility to the medical profession and its ethics, and the GMC and BMA guidance effectively restate the law. Indeed, in all but one of the issues examined in those chapters decisions are left to the individual practitioner's discretion, if not totally then at least partly. Like at BRI, the BMA guidance presumes that others are regulating the profession and its behaviour. The BMA's analytical approach necessarily guides rather than directs, and relies on the good conscience of the individual medical practitioner. Indeed, in such situations the table guides the doctor towards her conscience by asking her to subject the dilemma to 'critical analysis'. The BMA advises, under this heading, that the doctor should consult the treatment team to gather information, then 'the information needs to be analysed to consider the competing interests and to reach the most appropriate solution'.[79]

What is clear from the approaches outlined above is that the recent trend has been to recognise that ethical guidance must have teeth (the GMC), and that categories of ethical discourse need to be ascertained and placed into a hierarchy (the BMA). At the same time, however, 'flexibility' is sought. This can only be seen as contradictory and, as we shall see in Chapters 4–7, does not always work in real life.

VII.   Conclusion

It has been argued in this chapter that society was, and perhaps still is, dissatisfied with medical ethics. One of the causes of this was the perceived generality of ethical codes. But have we gone too far the other way? There is certainly the possibility that there is now *too much* ethics. Moreover, it is important to note the sense of alienation that medical practitioners feel when confronted with contemporary medical ethics. In this way, it can be seen that the medical ethics renaissance has not perfected medical ethics, and on an applied level it cannot be said even to have improved it. Rather, it can be argued that it has served only to marginalise the very people who make applied ethics a possibility. Indeed, if ethics are to be used then, as a prerequisite, practitioners have to be exposed to ethics; and then they have to understand them and how to use them. For medical practitioners, this translates into learning medical ethics at medical school, and then seeing what they have learnt as valuable and applicable.

However, this book has sought to demonstrate, so far, that in this sense doctors are in a difficult position. They cannot be expected to learn ethics and apply

[78]   *Ibid* 10.
[79]   *Ibid* 11.

principles coherently if medical ethics is not coherent itself. Furthermore, this problem is exacerbated if medical practitioners are increasingly marginalised and alienated from medical ethics discourse. The danger is that the confusion and alienation caused by the medical ethics renaissance may translate into medical ethics being seen as irrelevant to doctors, and thus to Mrs Jones on Ward 5 at 4.10 in the afternoon. Analytical medical ethics, with its concentration on minutiae of arguments and debate rather than direction, increases the danger of this occurring.

Contemporary medical ethics can therefore be seen as an amorphous, incoherent and fragmented collection of discourse rather than a structured 'corporate conscience' for the medical profession. In part, this is due to the understandable proliferation of discourse since The Second World War, and also to the medical profession's response to that. However, in another sense problems can be seen to emanate from the very success of the unofficial sector of discourse. It has infused itself into the fabric of the formal and semi-formal sectors, and has brought with it the difficulties inherent in their own sector such as academisation, subject specificity and a predilection for debate rather than guidance. Indeed, their response has been to move towards the methodology of the unofficial sector and encourage analysis and reflection rather than firm direction.

Yet, despite 'failing', medical ethics remains a powerful force. The traditional strength of the medical profession in the United Kingdom, combined with the sheer volume of ethical discourse, ensures that medical ethics is likely to exert influence over other concepts such as the law. Moreover, we shall see that the law's conception of medical ethics – that it is a regulatory tool – makes it even more tempting for the law to abrogate responsibility to it. As we have seen, such an abrogation would effectively involve leaving decisions, ultimately, to a fragmented concept that would encourage the doctor, in some cases, to utilise her own conscience as the decision-making tool. After Nuremburg, this is not seen as acceptable, and it is inimical to what the medical ethics renaissance sought to achieve. The three factors in the Bristol process – cultural flaws, excessive professional autonomy and the consequent fragmentation – can be seen to be present, and only the law has the ability to restore order. The following chapters will examine whether the law has risen to the challenge and regulated, or given in to the temptation to allow the medical profession and its ethics to make non-technical decisions and, if so, whether the ethics justify the confidence placed in them.

4

Risk Disclosure/'Informed Consent'

I. Introduction

In this chapter I examine the issue of risk disclosure, often referred to as informed consent, and how it has been treated by the courts. It begins by looking at the decision in *Sidaway* v *Bethlem Royal Hospital Governors* before examining five subsequent cases.[1] This issue is of significance for two reasons. First, because by the time that *Sidaway* was decided in 1985 it might have been expected that the medical ethics renaissance would have started to have had an effect on the courts. Secondly, and perhaps crucially, *Sidaway* was the first time that the House of Lords dealt with a non-negligence case, and the issue was, in substance if not in form, more concerned with ethics than technical medical practice. In the cases considered here, the key legal issue is consent and, as Kennedy shows, there exists a context that stretches beyond medical practice:

> Is [the issue of consent] ... the great bulwark of 'patients' rights'? Is it a necessary nuisance granted as a concession to modish thinking? Is it simply a figment of some lawyer's (or – awful word – medical ethicist's) imagination which practitioners know is meaningless in practice? Is it just part of the rhetoric of 'patient power' sent to try doctors' patience and challenge their authority?[2]

In the light of this, the question is whether the issues go beyond a mere question of whether the doctor was negligent in each of the cases[3] to whether the doctor concerned infringed the patients' ethical right to self-determination. I thus consider whether the ethical context to the issue of risk disclosure was recognised by the judges in the cases and, if so, how it was then treated. In addition, in this and the next three chapters I shall examine the development of the ethical guidance from the General Medical Council (GMC) and the British Medical

---

[1] [1985] 1 All ER 643; *Blyth v Bloomsbury Health Authority* [1993] 4 Med LR 151; *Gold v Haringey Health Authority* [1988] QB 481; *Smith v Tunbridge Wells Health Authority* [1994] 5 *Medical Law Reports* 334; *Pearce v United Bristol Healthcare NHS Trust* [1999] PIQR 53; *Chester v Afshar* [2004] UKHL 41.

[2] I Kennedy, 'Consent to Treatment: The Capable Person' in C Dyer (ed), *'Doctors, Patients and the Law* (Oxford, Blackwell, 1992) 44.

[3] The word 'negligence' is used here as a legal term of art.

Association (BMA) as examples of the formal and semi-formal discourse. As mentioned in Chapter 1, the GMC is chosen as it is the only member of the formal sector; the BMA as it is the most influential member of the semi-formal sector (as virtually all doctors will be members). From this analysis, it shall be possible to see whether the law and the ethics act in tandem, or whether they conflict.

II.   *Sidaway* – From Radicalism to Conservatism

A.   The Facts

Mrs Sidaway brought an action to recover damages for personal injury sustained at the Maudsley Hospital as a result of a neuro-surgical operation in October 1974. The crux of her submissions was that she was not informed of certain specific risks inherent in the operation that would have resulted in her refusal to consent to the procedure had she been informed of them. It was common ground between all the neuro-surgeons who gave evidence that the operation involved specific risks of injury beyond those inherent in all operations under general anaesthesia.[4] These specific injuries were damage to a nerve root in the area, and damage to the spinal cord by direct contact or some interference. The risk of either sort of damage was calculated at between one and two per cent. Although slight in terms of probability the potential injury, should it occur, was acute, including the possibility of partial paralysis. Mrs Sidaway brought her action because an injury did occur and she was not warned of these risks. She argued that she was legally entitled to such a warning, despite the fact that she had not asked about that outcome. The case thus concerned the provision of unsought information. It is clear that the fundamental issue was a patient's right to decide for herself what she will and will not allow herself to be subjected to. *Sidaway* can thus be considered a 'classic' risk disclosure/informed consent scenario.

B.   The Decision

The law before *Sidaway* contained apparently simple concepts that had proved difficult to define. Before a doctor could lawfully perform any clinical procedure on a competent patient, she first needed to have consented to it and, in order for that consent to be valid, the patient had to have been informed of the relevant risks associated with the procedure, so that she might arrive at an informed choice regarding whether or not to consent.[5] It was and remains settled law that,

---

[4]   *Sidaway v Bethlem Royal Hospital Governors* [1985] 1 All ER 643 at 647.
[5]   See *Chatterton v Gerson* [1981] QB 432.

should a doctor provide an inadequate disclosure of the risks involved in a procedure, albeit in good faith, then any redress should be in negligence rather than trespass to the person as the consent remains valid even though inadequate.[6] A doctor, in order to provide an adequate warning about risks, must disclose to the patient all material risks. The crucial question in *Sidaway* and several of the other cases examined here, and the source of the legal difficulties, lay in the question of *how* a risk was defined as material, and thus necessary to disclose if the patient's consent was to be considered informed and thus autonomous.

Any discussion of *Sidaway* must begin with a recognition that there are three clearly identifiable and differing strands to the judgment that cannot be reconciled, despite all five judges rejecting Mrs Sidaway's claim. As Kennedy notes, Lord Diplock opted for a 'decidedly conservative' view of the law, Lord Bridge (with whom Lord Keith concurred) and Lord Templeman for 'what may be described as a middle way' and Lord Scarman for a 'radical shift' in the law'.[7] While all of the judges rejected Mrs Sidaway's claim, the judgments vary radically in terms of their treatment of medical dominance; thus, each will be considered in turn.

i. Lord Diplock

Kennedy is correct in describing the judgment of Lord Diplock as 'conservative'. If anything, it is an understatement. Not only did his Lordship not join in any of the creativity engaged in by the other judges, he also refused to recognise any ethical content at all in the facts before him. Indeed, he stated starkly his belief that the case was merely a 'naked question of legal principle'.[8] On this basis, he considered the disclosure of risk to be a part of medical practice just like any other, and the doctor's duty to a patient as a single organism:

> This general duty is not subject to dissection into a number of component parts to which different criteria of what satisfy the duty of care apply, such as diagnosis, treatment and advice (including warning of any risks of something going wrong however skilfully the treatment advised is carried out) ... In modern medicine and surgery such dissection of the various things a doctor has to do in the exercise of his whole duty of care owed to his patient is neither legally meaningful nor medically practicable.[9]

This separation is critical to the question of how much medical dominance exists within the judgment. The effect of defining the doctor's duty as a single entity is exacerbated by the fact that the courts were, at the time, in the middle of their most *Bolamite* phase. Thus, once risk disclosure was perceived as just another

---

[6] *Ibid.* This is as long as the patient is informed in broad terms of the nature and purpose of the procedure.

[7] I Kennedy, 'Consent to Treatment: The Capable Person' in C Dyer (ed), *'Doctors, Patients and the Law* (Oxford, Blackwell, 1992) 65.

[8] *Sidaway v Bethlem Royal Hospital Governors* [1985] 1 All ER 643 at 657.

[9] [1985] 1 All ER 643 at 658.

area of medical practice, the law effectively lost any of the powers of oversight that it might have had. Indeed, the House of Lords decisions in *Maynard* and *Whitehouse v Jordan* had just established that a charge of negligence would fail so long as 'honest' expert evidence was provided for the defendant.[10] The danger of this approach had been recognised by Sir John Donaldson MR in the Court of Appeal in *Sidaway*, who was adamant that the courts must retain some control over the issue of risk disclosure:

> The definition of the duty of care is a matter for the law and the courts. They cannot stand idly by if the profession, by an excess of paternalism, denies their patients a real choice. In a word, the law will not permit the medical profession to play God.[11]

Lord Diplock's approach in *Sidaway* can be criticised as leaving open the door to medical dominance with respect to the law and over patients, as the law would be unable to protect them from medical paternalism. This, however, did not seem to unduly concern him, and there are several instances in the judgment where he came close to openly sanctioning such paternalism. For example, he said that the issue before him concerned a question of,

> how to conduct a bilateral discussion with the patient in terms best calculated not to scare her off from undergoing an operation which … [the doctor] is satisfied that it is in her interests to undergo despite such risks as may be entailed.[12]

On another occasion he noted that,

> [t]he only effect that mention of risks can have on the patient's mind, if it has any at all, can be in the direction of deterring the patient from undergoing the treatment which in the expert opinion of the doctor it is in the patient's interest to undergo.[13]

What is striking about these quotes is not just the advocacy of paternalism, but also the idea that the patient's 'interests' are best decided by the doctor and not the patient. In the light of this, it is not surprising that his judgment was met with disapproval from some commentators at that time:

> The virtual rejection of patient autonomy must be blamed on the *Sidaway* judgement. Their Lordships' notion of patient autonomy seems to regard autonomy as properly respected once the patient has chosen to entrust himself to his doctors for treatment and has had explained to him the general nature of what is to be done. *Explanations of risks and side-effects are required only when doctors consider such explanations to be in the patients' interest.*[14]

---

[10]   *Maynard v West Midlands Regional Health Authority* [1985] 1 All ER 635; *Whitehouse v Jordan* [1981] 1 All ER 267. See *Maynard* [1985] 1 All ER 635 at 639

[11]   *Sidaway v Board of Governors of Bethlem Royal Hospital* [1984] 1 All ER 1018 (CA) at 1028.

[12]   *Sidaway v Bethlem Royal Hospital Governors* [1985] 1 All ER 643 at 656.

[13]   [1985] 1 All ER 643 at 659.

[14]   M Brazier, *Medicine, Patients and the Law* (Harmondsworth, Penguin, 1992) 87–8, emphasis added. Although this criticism is aimed at all of the judges, the highlighted sentence is a criticism of the common practice requirement of the *Bolam* test which Lord Diplock was alone in the House of Lords in accepting unconditionally. See also I Kennedy, *Patients, Doctors and Human Rights, in Treat*

While criticism has centred on Lord Diplock's unquestioning application of the *Bolam* test, his Lordship appeared unapologetic regarding its use, believing that only through *Bolam* could medical practice continue in its state of progression:

> [*Bolam's*] value is that it brings up to date and re-expresses in the light of modern conditions in which the art of medicine is now practised an ancient rule of common law. Those members of the public who seek medical or surgical aid would be badly served by the adoption of any legal principle that would confine the doctor to some long-established, well-tried method of treatment only, although its past record of success may be small, if he wanted to be confident that he would not run the risk of being held liable in negligence simply because he tried some more modern treatment, and by some unavoidable mischance it failed to heal but did some harm to the patient.[15]

It is thus difficult to conceive of a more conservative judgment (although, as we shall see later in this chapter, not impossible), in terms of both tone and content. However, it must be remembered that the case concerned the provision of *unsought* information. Lord Diplock was clear in his view that should the patient question the doctor about the risks the doctor would '[n]o doubt ... tell him whatever the patient wanted to know'.[16] Nevertheless, it is a judgment that abrogates almost all decision-making responsibility to the medical profession, leaving the law as a mere 'rubber stamp'. What is also clear in the judgment is how little regard his Lordship has for the patient's right to self-determination. Paradoxically, however, the effect of his judgment is to abrogate responsibility for these issues to *medical ethics*, as the issues involved were ethical rather than medical in nature. The contrast with the approach of the other judges, Lord Scarman in particular, cannot be more marked.

ii. Lords Bridge and Templeman

Lords Bridge and Templeman (Lord Keith concurring with the judgment of Lord Bridge) adopted what was essentially a centre ground between the conservatism of Lord Diplock and the radicalism that we shall see from Lord Scarman. They decided that the *Bolam* test did apply, but with one caveat: that, especially for Lord Bridge, it was for the law, not the medical profession, to decide the standard of care, and therefore the courts would have the power to declare the medical profession's common practices unreasonable (and therefore negligent) if they so chose. For example, Lord Bridge clearly stated that courts *could* choose between

---

Me Right: Essays in Medical Law and Ethics (Oxford, Clarendon Press, 1988) where Kennedy calls the use of the *Bolam* test in the field of the information given to patients 'palpably indefensible ... It is quite beyond my comprehension how it can still be regarded as relevant to the law in this most important area of human rights' (p 392).

[15] *Sidaway v Bethlem Royal Hospital Governors* [1985] 1 All ER 643 at 657.
[16] [1985] 1 All ER 643 at 659.

medical schools of thought, thus establishing a *best* common practice.[17] Meanwhile, Lord Templeman was more concerned with the fact that the patient had the opportunity to ask questions and that, in their absence, the doctor could assume that the patient was content to trust the practitioner's clinical judgment in assessing the risks involved in the procedure.[18]

Lord Bridge approached the issues in the case by recognising the logical force of the North American doctrine of informed consent, were the materiality of a risk was determined with reference not to the 'reasonable doctor' but to the 'prudent patient', since 'the patient's right to make his own decision must at all costs be safeguarded against the kind of medical paternalism which assumes that "doctor knows best".'[19] This was achieved by defining a material risk not as one that a reasonable doctor would disclose, but instead as one that the prudent patient would wish to be told about. Nevertheless, he found that the test was impractical in its application for three reasons. First, it gave 'insufficient weight to the realities of the doctor–patient relationship'.[20] His Lordship saw the disclosure of information as, primarily, a clinical decision, the objective being to volunteer to the patient the 'significant factors necessary to enable the patient to make an informed decision whether to undergo the treatment'.[21] This should be achieved by avoiding giving the patient so much information that remote risks may assume undue prominence in the mind of the patient, thus making it more likely that they will refuse the treatment. Secondly, Lord Bridge could not conceive of any logic in denying the court medical evidence with respect to medical opinion regarding the practice of disclosure of risks. Finally, the objective test was 'so imprecise as to be almost meaningless',[22] as it was left to individual judges.

Lord Bridge thus concluded that the degree of disclosure necessary to enable the patient to make a rational choice about whether to undergo treatment was a matter for clinical judgement. However, he also held that it was open to the courts to find that, despite being common practice, certain medical behaviour could 'in certain circumstances' be so obviously necessary to an informed choice that no reasonable doctor could make it.[23] This was because, despite having defined the issue as primarily clinical, he did recognise some distinction between risk disclosure and diagnosis and treatment.

Lord Templeman adopted a similar approach with respect to the use of *Bolam*, holding that a court might find that a risk was material despite medical evidence on behalf of the defence to the contrary. However, he framed his argument differently: the responsibility to ask questions and become better informed would

---

[17] [1985] 1 All ER 643 at 663.
[18] [1985] 1 All ER 643 at 664.
[19] [1985] 1 All ER 643 at 662. He relied on the Canadian case of *Reibl v Hughes* (1980) 114 DLR (3d) 1 and the American decision in *Canterbury v Spence* (1972) 464 F 2d 772.
[20] *Sidaway v Bethlem Royal Hospital Governors* [1985] 1 All ER 643 at 662.
[21] [1985] 1 All ER 643 at 662.
[22] [1985] 1 All ER 643 at 662.
[23] [1985] 1 All ER 643 at 663.

rest with patients. For his Lordship, a patient required only enough information to enable her to make a 'balanced judgement' in deciding whether or not to submit to the treatment,[24] and the onus thus shifted to the patient to question the doctor, rather than the latter being obliged to volunteer information:

> In my opinion a simple and general explanation of the nature of the operation should have been sufficient to alert Mrs Sidaway to the fact that a major operation was to be performed and to the possibility that something might go wrong at or near the site of the spinal cord or the site of the nerve root causing serious injury.[25]

In this way, less emphasis was placed on the doctor as the gatekeeper of the patient's autonomy, and the patient had to fulfil this role herself. However, this approach somewhat eroded any notion that the principle of self-determination was being prioritised:

> I do not subscribe to the theory that the patient is entitled to know everything or to the theory that the doctor is entitled to decide everything. The relationship between doctor and patient is contractual in origin, the doctor performing services in consideration for fees payable by the patient. The doctor, *obedient to the high standards set by the medical profession*, impliedly contracts to act at all times in the best interests of the patient … An obligation to give a patient all the information available to the doctor *would often be inconsistent with the doctor's contractual obligation to have regard for the patient's best interests*. Some information might confuse, other information might alarm a particular patient.[26]

The doctor should therefore tell the patient what and how much information her medical training and experience informed her that she should disclose; but the patient retained the final right to make a balanced judgment about whether to undergo treatment, having been given the information that the doctor chose to disclose. How the patient was to do this without all of the information was not explained. The quote makes it clear that, according to Lord Templeman, the medical practitioner owed allegiance to *the standards set by the profession*, and the level of disclosure of information should not be so great as to go against the patient's best interests. In other words, informing the patient of risks should not encourage the patient to refuse consent. At this point one is reminded that 'doctor knows best'; after all, a patient may not be able to make a balanced judgment 'if provided with too much information and is made aware of possibilities which he is not capable of assessing because of his lack of medical training, his prejudices or his personality'.[27]

---

[24]   [1985] 1 All ER 643 at 664.
[25]   [1985] 1 All ER 643 at 664.
[26]   [1985] 1 All ER 643 at 665. Emphasis added.
[27]   [1985] 1 All ER 643 at 666. It seems that this also applied, in the Court of Appeal, without prejudice to the doctor, when the patient is a fully qualified nurse who asks questions and is still not given all the information; see *Blyth v Bloomsbury Health Authority* [1993] 4 Med LR 151. However, as she asked questions, the doctor should have been found negligent had this middle road enunciated by Lords Bridge and Templeman been followed.

The judgments of Lords Bridge and Templeman may be described as '*Bolam* with a twist'. They interpreted *Bolam* as *Bolitho* was to do, but this was because they saw the issue of risk disclosure as primarily, but not exclusively, one for the clinical judgement of the doctor. There is reference to the principle of self-determination in both judgments, but they did not see it as one which could only be overridden in extreme cases. Indeed, it appears that this principle operates *subject* to the best interests of the patients, as defined by the medical profession. Decisions were left to medical ethics openly, albeit with some judicial oversight, as their Lordships recognised that the issue was not strictly medical. Indeed, it is noticeable that, as discussed below, Lord Templeman displayed confidence in medical ethics to provide the 'high standards of the profession' that would be the base for regulating medical behaviour.

iii.   Lord Scarman

For Lord Scarman, the materiality or otherwise of a risk was not to be found by looking to the medical profession. Rather, the key principle was the right to self-determination of patients, with everything else flowing from that. He rejected the test for the materiality of risk used by the other judges in the House – that a risk was material if it is one that the reasonable doctor would disclose. For his Lordship, the principle of autonomy *should* be given primacy over medical opinion regarding what was best for the patient. His approach was thus to be inimical to any notion of medical dominance. Lord Scarman refuted the expert witnesses' argument that 'the extent of the warning is a matter for medical judgment with special importance attached to the doctor's assessment of his patient'.[28] This rejection is at the core of Lord Scarman's judgment, and allowed him to assert the dominance of the *court* over the medical profession. He asked rhetorically: 'Does the law seek guidance in medical opinion or does it lay down a rule which doctors must follow whatever may be the views of the profession?'[29] Once he had determined that it was the latter, he held that the 'reasonable doctor' test, and particularly the amount of control it gave the medical profession under Lord Diplock's interpretation of it, could not be reconciled with the principle of self-determination. For Lord Scarman, this was the primary purpose of the law, and a 'basic human right':[30]

> Responsible medical judgment may, indeed, provide the law with an acceptable standard in determining whether a doctor in diagnosis or treatment has complied with his duty ... [but it] would be a strange conclusion if the courts should be led to conclude that our law, which undoubtedly recognises a right in the patient to decide whether he will accept or reject the treatment proposed, should permit the doctors to

---

[28]   *Sidaway v Bethlem Royal Hospital Governors* [1985] 1 All ER 643 at 648.
[29]   [1985] 1 All ER 643 at 646.
[30]   [1985] 1 All ER 643 at 649.

determine whether and in what circumstances a duty arises requiring the doctor to warn his patient of the risks inherent in the treatment which he proposes.[31]

In order to give primacy to this basic right, therefore, Lord Scarman made a clear distinction between diagnosis, treatment and the provision of information, one that Lord Diplock had rejected, and Lords Bridge and Templeman had only partially accepted. Providing information, according to Lord Scarman, was distinct as a non-technical element of medical practice, and thus the *Bolam* test should not apply. Because of this, he saw no reason not to import the transatlantic prudent patient test, also known as the doctrine of informed consent. The shift in focus involved in this is significant, and formed the crux of Lord Scarman's judgment. The medical profession and its ethics should not dictate to the patient what was of material importance to the patient's body; rather, it was for the patient to dictate to the medical profession what was and was not acceptable. The law's role would thus be to prioritise the autonomy of patients. In effect, his Lordship began with the premiss that the principle of self-determination was paramount and then asked how the law could best protect it. His judgment was concerned with removing medical dominance and replacing it with the principle of self-determination:

> The [medical] profession, it is said, should not be judge in its own cause; or, less emotively but more correctly, the courts should not allow medical opinion as to what is best for the patient to override the patient's right to decide for himself whether he will submit to the treatment offered him.[32]

Lord Scarman's judgment is essentially the polar opposite of that of Lord Diplock.[33] Where the latter abrogated complete responsibility to the medical profession, Lord Scarman took the principle of self-determination as his starting point and demedicalised that which Lord Diplock had medicalised. The difference may be explained by the fact that Lord Scarman, unlike Lord Diplock, recognised the ethical content of the concept of risk disclosure. Ironically, his full recognition of the ethical principles in the case led him to reject medical ethics as the decision-making model.

C. Medical Ethics

One point that becomes clear from a reading of the case is that the identification of an ethical context to a case by judges does not necessarily mean that medical ethics are engaged with. In *Sidaway*, for example, all of the judges – even Lord

---

[31] [1985] 1 All ER 643 at 649.
[32] [1985] 1 All ER 643 at 649–50.
[33] This is particularly the case if we ignore the 'therapeutic privilege' given to doctors under the prudent patient test, and adopted by Lord Scarman. This states that a doctor may withhold disclosure of a material risk if she believes the patient would be harmed by hearing it. For an examination of this see I Kennedy and A Grubb, *Medical Law* (3rd edn, London, Butterworths, 2000) 701–4.

Diplock – identified the ethical principle of self-determination at some point.[34] To a greater or lesser extent, this principle was to influence all the judgments in the case. It comes as a surprise, then, that the word 'ethics' or its derivatives appeared only once in the whole judgment, when it was referred to by Lord Scarman. When it did appear, it was mentioned almost in passing:

> Ideally, the court should ask itself whether in the particular circumstances the risk was such that this particular patient would think it significant if he was told it existed. I would think that, as a matter of ethics, this is the test of the doctor's duty.[35]

Lord Scarman noted that such a test would not be workable in law and that the 'prudent patient' approach that he supported was the 'next best thing' to the 'Utopia' that he preferred.[36] The quote's 'ideal', however, is a requirement that goes further in the protection of autonomy than even Lord Scarman's judgment, which only demanded that the doctor disclose risks that the reasonable patient would wish to be told of. Indeed, what is interesting is that he saw this as the *ethical* rather than the *legal* duty – thus presuming the former to be a more onerous standard than the latter. The legal impracticality of ascertaining what an individual patient would wish to know did not extend to medical ethics. Rather, the medical profession should aim to achieve this 'gold standard', with the law only interjecting if the doctor fell a long way short of the Utopian ideal. In this way, then, it is possible to identify a gap between what his Lordship may have seen as the ethical standard, and what he identified as the legal standard. A doctor whose conduct falls below the former, but above the latter, may then only logically be censured by the medical profession itself. Unfortunately, Lord Scarman did not expand on if or when he might expect that this would occur.

With respect to the other approaches, the difference between them in their view of medical ethics was, although superficially significant, merely one of degree. While Lords Bridge and Templeman considered the issue before them as only *primarily* one of clinical judgement, for Lord Diplock there was no distinction to be made between diagnosis, treatment, and the provision of information about risks. As shown above, he saw the case as a naked question of legal principle. In both cases the decision was essentially abrogated to the medical profession. However, within the middle way of Lords Bridge and Templeman the ultimate decision-making authority lay with the courts, albeit somewhat reluctantly:

> I am of the opinion that the judge might in certain circumstances come to the conclusion that disclosure of a particular risk was so obviously necessary to an informed choice on the part of the patient that no reasonably prudent medical man could fail to make it.[37]

---

[34] *Sidaway v Bethlem Royal Hospital Governors* [1985] 1 All ER 643 at 659.
[35] [1985] 1 All ER 643 at 654.
[36] [1985] 1 All ER 643 at 654.
[37] [1985] 1 All ER 643 at 663.

In denying the distinction between the technical and non-technical aspects of medical treatment, Lord Diplock ensured that what are ultimately non-medical decisions would be made by the medical profession *and its ethics* with minimal legal input. Interestingly, however, the only passing reference to medical ethics as a concept or construct, as opposed to the ethical *principle* of self determination, in any of the judgments was made by Lord Templeman. As highlighted earlier, his Lordship held that the doctor '*obedient to the high standards set by the medical profession*, impliedly contracts to act at all times in the best interests of the patient'.[38] The confidence displayed in medical ethics by Lord Templeman can be seen to be high, despite his insistence that the courts would retain oversight. While his Lordship at least referred to the nature of medical ethics, however fleetingly, while retaining a modicum of legal control, Lord Diplock fully abrogated responsibility to the doctors and showed no signs of reflecting on what this might mean. The paradox, which becomes more evident as a pattern in the later cases in this chapter, is that the more weight that is given by the judges to the ethical principles, the less they trust medical ethics to protect them.

III. *Blyth, Gold* and the *Sidaway* Aftermath – Ethics Ignored

Following the decision in *Sidaway*, the Court of Appeal heard two cases in which identical approaches to medical law and ethics were adopted.[39] In both cases the court not only refused to recognise the ethical content, but also moved further away from the principle of autonomy than even the judgment of Lord Diplock in *Sidaway*. The paradox identified in the last section is similarly evident in these cases, but in reverse. In this section, the ethical decision with regard to how much information is to be given to patients is left wholly and without question or thought to medical ethics. This is because, ironically, the lack of recognition of the ethical content to the case led the court to abrogate responsibility to the medical profession and, since the issues *were* ethical rather than technical in nature, that meant that decisions were left to the medical profession's ethics. *Blyth* revolved around whether the duty of care extended to having to fully answer the patient's questions rather than the provision of unsought information in *Sidaway*. In *Gold*, the issue was whether the duty of care remained the same with respect to non-therapeutic procedures.

---

[38] [1985] 1 All ER 643 at 665. Emphasis added.
[39] *Blyth v Bloomsbury Health Authority* [1993] 4 Med LR 151; *Gold v Haringey Health Authority* [1988] QB 481.

A.   The Facts

The facts of *Blyth* highlight the issues. Mrs Blyth had previously used a combined contraceptive pill containing oestrogen and progesterone, which had caused her considerable side effects. After she became pregnant, it was discovered that Mrs Blyth had insufficient immunity to rubella. It was too late in the pregnancy to vaccinate her without risking the foetus, but it was necessary to do so after the birth to protect her and the baby from the disease. As the vaccine could cause adverse symptoms to the foetus should she become pregnant within three months, it was decided that she should be administered Depo-Provera, a progesterone-only contraceptive. It was thought that this would eliminate the adverse side effects of the combined pill. Unfortunately, Mrs Blyth suffered side effects and contended that, despite her specific questioning with respect to them, she was not provided with accurate information. Furthermore, she alleged that no attempt was made to obtain the answers to her questions before giving erroneous reassurances. In terms of the principle of self-determination, it might be expected that the use of the *Bolam* test would be seen as overly restrictive and incompatible with respect for the patient. Indeed, even Lord Diplock in *Sidaway*, as we have seen, asserted the right of the patient to have specific questions answered in a full and truthful manner. As we shall see, however, the Court of Appeal not only used *Bolam*, but it also ignored Lord Diplock's proviso concerning specific enquiries. It thus managed to frame a judgment even more conservative than that of Lord Diplock in *Sidaway*.

The facts of *Gold* are more straightforward, but also highlight the issues. Mrs Gold had decided that she did not wish to have any more children and was advised by a consultant obstetrician to undergo a sterilisation operation. She consented to the procedure, which was properly performed, but it was not successful and she became pregnant. She alleged two things: first, that she should have been warned of the risk of failure; and, secondly, that she was not informed of an alternative method of achieving the same result – that her husband could have a vasectomy (a less invasive procedure with a better chance of success). At first instance, it was found that *Sidaway* could be distinguished as it applied only to therapeutic procedures. The appeal centred on whether this was so. Just as in *Blyth*, it might be expected that the principle of self-determination might be prioritised by the courts, particularly given the fact that the procedure was non-therapeutic. Again, however, it was ignored.

B.   The Decisions

Kerr and Neill LJJ provided substantive judgments in *Blyth*, with the third judge, Balcombe LJ, agreeing. In two judgments which contain much consideration of the facts, and much less content in relation to the legal principles of the case, their Lordships appeared to believe that the law on the matter was clear, and thus did not require close examination. For Kerr LJ, the case was a simple question of medical negligence, just as any question of diagnosis and treatment:

> The question of what a plaintiff should be told in answer to a general enquiry cannot be divorced from the *Bolam* test, any more than when no such enquiry is made ... Any medical evidence directed to what would be the proper answer in the light of responsible medical opinion and practice – that is to say, the *Bolam* test – must in my view equally be placed in the balance in cases where the patient makes some enquiry, in order to decide whether the response was negligent or not. In that connection, ... I would ... draw attention to the speech of Lord Templeman [in *Sidaway*] ... which suggests to me that the *Bolam* test is all-pervasive in this context. Indeed I am not convinced that the *Bolam* test is irrelevant even in relation to the question of what answers are properly to be given to specific enquiries.[40]

Thus *Bolam* should apply, even when specific questions were asked and the patient was thus seeking information in order to exercise her autonomy. In this, he was supported by Neill LJ, who held that:

> I do not understand that in the decision of the House of Lords in *Sidaway* ... in the passages to which my Lord has already drawn attention, either Lord Diplock or Lord Bridge were laying down any rule of law to the effect that where questions are asked by a patient, or doubts are expressed, a doctor is under an obligation to put the patient in possession of all the information on the subject which may have been available in the files of a consultant, who may have made a special study of the subject. The amount of information to be given must depend upon the circumstances, and as a general proposition it is governed by what is called the *Bolam* test.[41]

Leaving aside the point that, as we have seen, their Lordships made exactly the declarations denied here, the problem with this is that such a view can only exist as long as it is accepted that the provision of information about risks is a purely clinical judgement. However, since the issue *was* intrinsically ethical rather than technical, the abrogation of responsibility left the decision to *medical ethics*, despite their being no mention of the word or recognition that the decisions made involved no technical medical skill. This line of reasoning was to be continued two months later by the Court of Appeal in *Gold*.[42] Lloyd LJ was unequivocal in his rejection of any idea that the *Bolam* test did not apply equally to non-therapeutic procedures and he based his opinion on two factors:

> In the first place the line between therapeutic and non-therapeutic medicine is elusive. A plastic surgeon carrying out a skin graft is presumably engaged in therapeutic surgery but what if he is carrying out a facelift, or some other cosmetic operation? ... In the second place, a distinction between advice given in a therapeutic context and advice given in a non-therapeutic context would be a departure from the principle on which the *Bolam* test is itself grounded. *The principle does not depend on the context in which*

---

[40]   [1993] 4 Med LR 151 at 157.
[41]   [1993] 4 Med LR 151 at 160.
[42]   *Gold v Haringey Health Authority* [1988] QB 481.

any act is performed, or any advice given. It depends on a man professing skill or competence in a field beyond that possessed by the man on the Clapham omnibus. If the giving of contraceptive advice required no special skill, then I could see an argument that the *Bolam* test should not apply. But that was not, and could not have been, suggested. *The fact (if it be the fact) that giving contraceptive advice involves a different sort of skill and competence from carrying out a surgical operation does not mean that the Bolam test ceases to be applicable.* It is clear from Lord Diplock's speech in *Sidaway* that a doctor's duty of care in relation to diagnosis, treatment and advice, whether the doctor be a specialist or general practitioner, is not to be dissected into its component parts.[43]

As can be seen from the above quote Lloyd LJ did not just fail to recognise the ethical context to the case, he actively defined the provision of information about risks as a practice that required technical, medical skill, and thus concluded that *Bolam* should apply. It was merely defined, as the second italicised portion demonstrates, as a *different* sort of skill – though no less intrinsically medical in nature. Stephen Brown LJ adopted a similar approach. In an extremely short judgment, he noted only that *Bolam* and *Sidaway* applied, and that any distinction between therapeutic and non-therapeutic treatment was 'wholly unwarranted and artificial'.[44] Once again, though, any ethical dimension remained either unidentified or ignored. Indeed, the lack of difference between therapeutic and non-therapeutic procedures could only be maintained as long as the focus was on the doctor rather than the patient. This was again achieved through the questionable assertion that risk disclosure was a facet of medical practice like any other, involving just as much technical medical expertise as diagnosis and treatment. The fallacy of this argument was recognised by Lord Scarman in *Sidaway* and the other jurisdictions around the world that he cited.

These two judgments demonstrate that the instinctive reaction of the Court of Appeal to the decision in *Sidaway* was to be even more restrictive with respect to the patient's right to self-determination than even Lord Diplock was in that case, as at least he recognised that patients asking questions should be given truthful and full answers. The full *Bolam*isation of risk disclosure is to be regretted, and shows the judiciary's treatment of medico-legal issues in the worse possible light. In doing so, not only did the courts abrogate all responsibility to the medical profession, they also medicalised a non-technical decision. Indeed, the principle of self-determination is not only an ethical concept. Rather, as we have seen, it was legally recognised and protected by the majority in *Sidaway* and before, which makes the abrogation of responsibility to the medical profession and its ethics all the more perplexing. Its erosion could not last.

---

[43]   [1988] QB 481 at 489. Emphasis added.
[44]   [1988] QB 481 at 492.

C. Medical Ethics

It is difficult to examine something that is not there, and medical ethics played no part at all in either of the Court of Appeal judgments. The decision in *Blyth* is all the more unfortunate because the ethical aspects recognised by all of the judges in *Sidaway* were never identified, and thus not discussed. Whether Mrs Blyth had, or should have had, a right to be informed of the potential side effects of Depo-Provera, for example, were never considered. In this sense, no notion of her right to self-determination entered into the judicial equation of the case. Instead of that there was an assumption that the doctor should have acted in the manner that other doctors might have done. If the medical practitioner complied with that requirement, then her actions would be reasonable. As we have seen in the previous section, even Lord Diplock in *Sidaway* had noted that he had the 'right to decide whether any particular thing' was done to his body.[45] Moreover, he was unequivocal in his view that he was referring to volunteered information. It is to be regretted that the Court of Appeal did not recognise this.

The situation is the same in *Gold*. Mrs Gold's potential right to decide what happened to her body was not just sidelined but totally ignored as an issue. Again, the ethical point to be made about the cases is that the issue of risk disclosure was fully medicalised and defined as a matter of technical medical skill. Ironically, as mentioned above, the failure to recognise the ethical component to the case meant that the court effectively abrogated responsibility to *medical ethics*, as it is what governs the practice of ethical issues by medical practitioners. Thus, only some two years after the decision of the House of Lords in *Sidaway*, the ethical dimension identified by all the judges was swept away on a tide of *Bolam*-mania. Medical ethics was not being recognised – much less engaged with, and the 'fundamental human right' of Lord Scarman's in *Sidaway* did not even merit a mention in the Court of Appeal cases, paradoxically giving all the more power to medical ethics.

IV. *Smith* and *Pearce* – Rediscovering the Ethical Context

The conservatism of the Court of Appeal was, thankfully, addressed a few years later. This section demonstrates how the ethical context to risk disclosure cases was rediscovered by the judiciary, paving the way for a reconsideration of the role of medical ethics. Two cases are analysed, *Smith v Tunbridge Wells* and *Pearce v*

---

[45] He held that '[n]o doubt if the patient manifested this attitude by means of questioning, the doctor would tell him whatever it was the patient wanted to know': *Sidaway v Bethlem Royal Hospital Governors* [1985] 1 All ER 643 at 659.

United Bristol Healthcare NHS Trust;[46] and the more 'pro-patient' approach advocated may be even more surprising considering that they concerned the provision of therapeutic procedures.

A.   The Facts

In *Smith*, the plaintiff was a 28-year-old man, who was married and had two children. He suffered from a rectal prolapse, and his consultant advised him to undergo surgery, an ivalon sponge rectopexy. This procedure was normally only carried out on women, because they have a wider pelvis. There was a slight inherent danger in the surgery that nerve damage might occur, and that this could result in impotence. Mr Smith was not informed of this risk and, although the operation was carried out competently and the rectum was restored to its correct place, he suffered impotence and bladder malfunction. In *Pearce*, the plaintiff was pregnant with her sixth child. Already two weeks beyond her due date, and yet to give birth, Mrs Pearce went to see her consultant. Distressed, she strongly expressed her desire to be induced. The consultant, however, thought it was better to allow nature to take its course and he explained that it would be risky to induce the birth, and that Mrs Pearce would take longer to recover if she had a caesarean section. She accepted this advice, but a few days later the foetus died *in utero*.

In both cases the risk was small and the procedure was therapeutic in nature. It might thus be expected that the plaintiffs would lose their cases and that the courts might not prioritise the principle of self-determination or 'punish' doctors for doing what they thought was best for their patients. In fact, not only was autonomy prioritised, but Mr Smith won *despite* the defendants providing expert evidence that other doctors would also not have advised of the specific risks at that time. For Mrs Pearce, the chance (0.1–0.2 per cent) of the risk materialising was deemed too small to be significant, but that does not lessen the impact of the judgment on the law.

B.   The Decisions

What is important about *Smith*, for the purposes of this section, is not the fact that the judge followed the 'middle way' judgment of Lord Bridge in *Sidaway*. Nor is it that he only reluctantly used *Bolam* at all.[47] Rather, the case is important because, for the first time in a case since *Sidaway*, the judge, Morland J,

---

[46]   *Smith v Tunbridge Wells Health Authority* [1994] 5 *Medical Law Review* 334; *Pearce v United Bristol Healthcare NHS Trust* [1999] PIQR 53.

[47]   Extensive quotes are given from the High Court of Australia case of *Rogers v Whittaker* [1993] 4 *Medical Law Review* 78. A landmark case in that country, it rejected *Bolam* in this context, replacing it with a slightly modified version of the transatlantic 'prudent patient' test. This was that a risk is to be

recognised the inherent ethical content in the case before him. Indeed, it is significant that all of the quotes provided in *Smith* from *Sidaway*, with the exception of one quote from Lord Diplock at the beginning of the judgments (which nevertheless mentioned that specific questions should be answered fully), emphasised the right of the patient to make her own decision. For example, Morland J quoted Lord Bridge as saying that 'a conscious adult patient of sound mind is entitled to decide for himself whether or not he will submit to a particular course of treatment'.[48] He was further quoted as saying that the purpose of disclosing risks was to 'assist a particular patient to make a rational choice'.[49] Lord Templeman's judgment was also considered and a lengthy quote provided, which included the following:

> The patient is free to decide whether or not to submit to treatment recommended by the doctor and therefore the doctor impliedly contracts to provide information which is adequate to enable the patient to reach a balanced judgment, subject always to the doctor's own obligation to say and do nothing which the doctor is satisfied will be harmful to the patient ... A patient may make an unbalanced judgment if he is deprived of adequate information.[50]

The importance of this last sentence was emphasised by Morland J, and he concluded that a doctor,

> should use language, simple but not misleading, which the doctor perceives ... will be understood by the patient so that the patient can make an informed decision as to whether or not to consent to the recommended surgery or treatment.[51]

He held that it was open to a court to decide that a body of medical opinion was neither reasonable nor responsible, and thus find for the plaintiff. In other words, the middle way of Lords Bridge and Templeman in *Sidaway* was adopted. Yet the importance of *Smith* for the purposes of this chapter lies in the fact that the ethical dimension in risk disclosure was rediscovered. The purpose of categorising risks as material or immaterial was to enhance patient autonomy by ensuring that they received sufficient information to be allowed to arrive at their own informed choice. This was an aspect of risk disclosure that had been disregarded by the two Court of Appeal cases considered previously, and its recognition can be seen as a marked change of emphasis from doctor to patient.

In *Pearce*, Lord Woolf MR, with whom Roch and Mummery LJJ concurred, delivered a judgment which was almost identical in tone and similar in substance to that of Morland J in *Smith*. Once again the middle way approach in *Sidaway* was adopted, though perhaps with slightly different reasoning, and many of the

considered material if the reasonable patient would have wanted to be told of it, or the doctor knew, or ought to have known, that that particular patient would attach significance to it.

[48] *Smith v Tunbridge Wells Health Authority* [1994] 5 *Medical Law Review* 334 at 336.

[49] [1994] 5 *Medical Law Review* 334 at 336.

[50] [1994] 5 *Medical Law Review* 334 at 337.

[51] [1994] 5 *Medical Law Review* 334 at 339.

same quotes from *Sidaway* were used as justifications. Lord Woolf was as clear as Morland J in emphasising the idea that the law was designed to allow the patient to make her own decision:

> In a case where it is being alleged that a plaintiff has been deprived of the opportunity to make a proper decision as to what course he or she should take in relation to treatment, it seems to me to be the law … that if there is a significant risk … then in the normal course it is the responsibility of a doctor to inform the patient of that significant risk, if the information is needed so that the patient can determine for him or herself as to what course he or she should adopt.[52]

The ethical dimension of the issue was thus not only identified but engaged with. *Pearce* shifted the focus of the law even further from the doctor to the patient, even though the court ultimately found for the defendants. Nevertheless, it is sufficient to say that it continued the move towards recognition that risk disclosure is an ethical rather than technical procedure. After *Sidaway*, then, two different approaches can be seemed to have developed. First, in *Gold* and *Blyth*, the ethical aspect to informed consent was totally ignored, only to be re-engaged with later in *Smith* and *Pearce*. One would have to be adopted, and the other rejected.

C. Medical Ethics

Although ethical principles were recognised in both *Smith* and *Pearce*, there is no real consideration of medical ethics as a concept. Rather, self-determination was treated by the judges as a legal construct which they, instead of the medical profession, should maintain control of. The paradox is evident – the court recognised the ethical content, but then removed control from the medical profession and its ethics. What is interesting, however, is the tone of the judgments. Both Morland J and Lord Woolf identified the principle of self-determination then, in upholding it, sought to protect the patient from the medical profession. It would seem that ethical principles were being reclaimed by the law, at the expense of medical ethics. This is perhaps not surprising for we have, so far, seen no involvement from any sources of medical ethics discourse in any of the cases above. This, however, was to change.

V. *Chester v Afshar* – The Primacy of Principle[53]

The two approaches identified in the previous sections could not coexist because they were so fundamentally inimical to each other. In 2005 the House of Lords

---

[52]　*Pearce v United Bristol Healthcare NHS Trust* [1999] PIQR 53 at 59.
[53]　*Chester v Afshar* [2004] UKHL 41.

had the opportunity to choose between the two competing positions, and chose the approach that was more sensitive to ethical issues espoused by *Smith* and *Pearce*. Indeed, it was to go even further than even those cases did.

A. The Facts

Ms Chester was a journalist who had suffered from lower back pain for some years. It had been treated by a rheumatologist during that time. In 1994 she underwent an MRI scan which showed that her spinal discs had degenerated and she was referred to a consultant neurosurgeon, Mr Afshar. He said that she needed surgery to remove three discs and, despite her reluctance, Ms Chester consented to the surgery, which was performed three days later. As a result of the surgery Ms Chester suffered nerve damage, which resulted in motor and sensory damage. She claimed that she was not warned of this risk, a warning which it was agreed by the parties should have been given. However, with admirable honesty, she admitted that had she been informed of the risk she may not have consented to the operation at that time, but could not say with certainty that she would not subsequently have consented to the operation at all, having considered the issue. Rather, she would have taken extra time to consult with others and explore alternative treatments. Thus in technical legal terms she would fail the 'but for' test for causation, as she could not demonstrate that the breach of duty (the failure to warn) *caused* the harm. The question for the House of Lords was whether it would be possible to relax the rules of causation to allow Ms Chester to recover damages. By a majority of three to two, their Lordships decided that it was. The divisions within the House, in general terms, can be categorised into those who accepted the primacy of the ethical principle of self-determination against those who rejected this notion. It is perhaps more fruitful to first consider the dissenting judgments, of Lords Bingham and Hoffman.

B. The Decision

i. Lords Bingham and Hoffman – Naked Questions of Legal Principle Revisited?

Despite his finding against Ms Chester, the ethical element to the issue was not lost on Lord Bingham. The first thing that he noted, after recounting the facts of the case, was that the doctor had a duty to warn patients of risks inherent in treatment. The reason for this was to 'enable adult patients of sound mind to make for themselves decisions intimately affecting their own lives and bodies'.[54] However, as Ms Chester was likely to have consented to the operation at a later date, warning her of the risk would not have made any difference to whether she

---

[54] [2004] UKHL 41 at para 5.

submitted to the procedure, nor to the level and nature of the risks inherent in it. In that sense, the breach could not be said to have caused damage. To reach this conclusion, Lord Bingham had to view the situation from the point of view of the defendant doctor, Mr Afshar, and emphasise not what was fair to Ms Chester, but to him:

> A defendant is bound to compensate the claimant for the damage which his or her negligence has caused the claimant. But the corollaries are also true: a claimant is not entitled to be compensated, and *a defendant is not bound to compensate the claimant, for damage not caused by the negligence complained of.* The patient's right to be appropriately warned is an important right, which few doctors in the current legal and social climate would consciously or deliberately violate. I do not for my part think that the law should seek to reinforce that right by providing for the payment of potentially very large damages by a defendant whose violation of that right is not shown to have worsened the physical condition of the claimant.[55]

It is of note that Lord Bingham cited the 'legal and social climate' preventing the violation of the patient's rights, but not the ethical one. The ethical component was therefore identified but not engaged with. This approach is inimical to the original proposition that the right of the patient to be fully informed, in order to make her own decision, was paramount. This argument is given further force when, as we shall see, full engagement with medical ethics was undertaken by the majority of their Lordships. In this way Lord Bingham paid 'lip-service' to the ethical issue, but did not actually prioritise it.

Lord Hoffman adopted a similar line of reasoning but, if anything, he was even less tolerant of the ethical underpinnings of the case. At the start of his judgment, he outlined the purpose of the law, which was not overwhelming in its prioritisation of autonomy: 'to give … [the patient] the opportunity to avoid or reduce that risk'.[56] For him, the damage was defined in terms of the strictly legal physical aspect, and not the loss of dignity caused by the absence of an autonomous choice being made. In essence, she was seeking compensation for the lack of adherence to the ethical principle of autonomy rather than any physical damage caused. He was thus unwilling to engage with the ethical element of the case. While he recognised that Ms Chester had suffered some damage of a non-physical sort, his Lordship rejected the idea that the law should be modified in order to compensate her for this:

> The argument for such a rule is that it vindicates the patient's right to choose for herself. Even though the failure to warn did not cause the patient any damage, it was an affront to her personality and leaves her feeling aggrieved. I can see that there might be

[55]   [2004] UKHL 41 at para 9. Emphasis added.
[56]   [2004] UKHL 41 at para 28.

a case for a *modest* solatium in such cases. But … the cost of litigation over such cases would make the law of torts an unsuitable vehicle for distributing the modest compensation which might be payable.[57]

The price for loss of dignity or autonomy, therefore, was not overly important to him. It appeared to be a slightly insignificant inconvenience which was not to be taken too seriously. It might be argued that, particularly in the light of her honesty about whether she would have decided to undertake the operation had she been warned of the risk, that it is precisely the affront to Ms Chester's dignity and autonomy that she litigated to gain compensation for in the first place. She was *not* suing due to the physical damage suffered by her body, but for the loss of her ability to make an autonomous choice. Lords Hoffman and Bingham were in the minority in rejecting this argument.

ii. The Majority View – Ethics Engaged

The paucity of the engagement with medical ethics and its principles provided by Lords Hoffman and Bingham was starkly highlighted by the views of the majority. Indeed, the consideration and primacy given to autonomy by Lords Steyn, Hope and Walker eclipse the judgments in *Smith* and *Pearce*, and perhaps even that of Lord Scarman in *Sidaway*. The contrast between the views of the majority and those of the minority are fundamental. The crux of Lord Steyn's judgment was a desire to ensure that the purpose of the law was adhered to. Thus, he identified the philosophical underpinnings of the law, and then reached a conclusion that would support it. His first task was to identify the principle from which he would construct his judgment:

> The starting point is that every individual of adult years and sound mind has a right to decide what may or may not be done with his or her body. Individuals have a right to make important medical decisions affecting their lives for themselves: they have the right to make decisions which doctors regard as ill advised. Surgery performed without the informed consent of the patient is unlawful.[58]

This was achieved through the doctrine of informed consent, with the arbiters of what constituted this being the courts, and he held that in modern law 'paternalism no longer rules'.[59] Having identified the ethical issue, Lord Steyn examined the nature of the rights that he had highlighted. He emphasised the fact that informed consent ensured that due respect was given to the patient's autonomy and dignity, and believed that these concepts should be defined.[60] To do this, he

---

57 [2004] UKHL 41 at paras 33–4. Emphasis added.
58 [2004] UKHL 41 at para 14.
59 [2004] UKHL 41 at para 16.
60 [2004] UKHL 41 at para 18.

utilised unofficial medical ethics, providing a quotation from a book by Professor Ronald Dworkin.[61] While long, it is worth reproducing in its entirety, as Lord Steyn did:

> The most plausible [account] emphasizes the integrity rather than the welfare of the choosing agent; the value of autonomy, on this view, derives from the capacity it protects: the capacity to express one's own character-values, commitments, convictions, and critical as well as experiential interests-in the life one leads. Recognizing an individual right of autonomy makes self-creation possible. It allows each of us to be responsible for shaping our lives according to our own coherent or incoherent-but, in any case, distinctive-personality. It allows us to lead our own lives rather than be led along them, so that each of us can be, to the extent a scheme of rights can make this possible, what we have made of ourselves. We allow someone to choose death over radical amputation or a blood transfusion, if that is his informed wish, because we acknowledge his right to a life structured by his own values.[62]

The problem for the court was that, as the minority of the House had noted, English law would not allow the ethical principles identified and examined by Lord Steyn to be given primacy. Rather, Lord Steyn would have to choose between the ethics and settled law. The High Court of Australia had considered a similar case six years previously in *Chappel v Hart*.[63] In that case, the Australian court did just what Lord Steyn was to do – it modified the legal rules in order to protect the dignity and autonomy of the patient. Lord Steyn cited several authors, all academic lawyers, who approved of the Australian court's approach, again highlighting the fact that patients had a right to make their own decisions.[64] In accepting the view expressed in *Chappel*, and the academic commentary in England that followed it, Lord Steyn was openly, and unequivocally, prioritising the *philosophy behind the law* above its substantive rules. The basis for this was the importance of the ethical aspect. He therefore held that '[the] right to autonomy and dignity can and ought to be vindicated'.[65] His concluding comments contained a final engagement with medical ethics, this time from the semi-formal sector of discourse, noting that his decision should come as no surprise as it reflected the 'fundamental importance of a surgeon's duty to warn a patient in

---

[61] R Dworkin, *Life's Dominion: An Argument About Abortion and Euthanasia* (New York, Knopf, 1993).

[62] *Chester v Afshar* [2004] UKHL 41 at para 18.

[63] *Chappel v Hart* (1998) 195 CLR 232.

[64] See *Chester v Afshar* [2004] UKHL 41 at paras 21–2. They are: Cane 'A Warning about Causation' (1999) 115 *LQR* 21; Grubb 'Clinical Negligence: Informed Consent and Causation' (2002) 10 *Medical Law Review* 322; Honor 'Medical non-disclosure, causation and risk: *Chappel v Hart*' (1999) 7 *Torts Law Journal* 1; Jones, 'But for' causation in actions for non-disclosure of risk' (2002) 18 *Professional Negligence* 192; Stapleton 'Cause-in-Fact and the Scope of Liability for Consequences' (2003) 119 *LQR* 388; Stauch, 'Taking the Consequences for Failure to Warn of Medical Risks' (2000) 63 *MLR* 261).

[65] *Chester v Afshar* [2004] UKHL 41 at para 24.

general terms of significant risks: Royal College of Surgeons: *Good Medical Practice* (2002) ch 4, guidelines on consent.'[66]

The judgment of Lord Walker was similar in substance. Like Lord Steyn he considered that all the judges in *Sidaway* had recognised that the concept of informed consent existed to protect a basic human right on the part of the patient. Moreover, 'during the twenty years which have elapsed since *Sidaway* the importance of personal autonomy have been more and more widely recognised'.[67] Once again, the basis of his conclusions were formed not by the substantive law, but rather by a desire to see the law fit in with the guiding principle that he identified. Indeed, he noted that if he were not to find for Ms Chester, 'the surgeon's important duty would in many cases be drained of its content'.[68] Just as for Lord Steyn, this was enough to convince Lord Walker that Ms Chester should be compensated for the loss of autonomy that she had suffered.

Similarly, Lord Hope identified the protection of the autonomy of the patient as the primary purpose of the law, and he held that all of the speeches in *Sidaway* supported this. Nevertheless, he was more forceful in his acceptance of this than the other judges in the case. Rather than arguing that he was proposing a minor amendment to the law, as the others had, Lord Hope held that if the autonomy of patients was to be considered paramount, the issue of causation could consequently only be seen as irrelevant:

> Thus the right to make the final decision and the duty of the doctor to inform the patient if the treatment may have special disadvantages or dangers go hand in hand. In this case there is no dispute that Mr Afshar owed a duty to Miss Chester to inform her of the risks that were inherent in the proposed surgery, including the risk of paralysis. The duty was owed to her so that she could make her own decision as to whether or not she should undergo the particular course of surgery which he was proposing to carry out. *That was the scope of the duty, the existence of which gave effect to her right to be informed before she consented to it. It was unaffected in its scope by the response which Miss Chester would have given had she been told of these risks.*[69]

Thus the duty to inform, which was based on the principle of autonomy, was *in itself* a form of damage if it was not adhered to. In the light of this, Ms Chester was not required to show that she would have consented to the operation, and the concept of causation became irrelevant. The law must, he said, ensure that there is a remedy for patients whose right to choose had not been respected,[70] and in order to justify this support was sought from legal academia. He quoted from an influential article by Michael Jones, which argued that *Sidaway* had created an

---

[66]   [2004] UKHL 41 at para 27.
[67]   [2004] UKHL 41 at para 92.
[68]   [2004] UKHL 41 at para 101.
[69]   [2004] UKHL 41 at para 55. Emphasis added.
[70]   [2004] UKHL 41 at para 56.

imbalance of power in the doctor–patient relationship in favour of the doctor,[71] and, moreover, that this imbalance should not be allowed to continue:

> Part of the imbalance between doctor and patient is due to the patient's lack of information, and, on one view, it is the function of the law to redress the imbalance by providing patients with the 'right' to be given that information, or perhaps more accurately imposing a duty on doctors to provide it. There are some within the medical profession who appear to resent the notion that informed consent is part and parcel of 'patient rights'-a patient with rights is a lawsuit waiting to happen. On the other hand, a patient with no rights is a citizen who is stripped of his or her individuality and autonomy, as well as her clothes, as soon as she walks into the surgery or the hospital.[72]

Of course, as with this issue generally, in addressing these questions he raised more. Of particular interest to this section, and this book generally, is one such query: if there was such a duty, should it be left to the law to enforce it or should the medical profession, through its ethics, also play a part? Lord Steyn had touched on the subject by noting that the Royal College of Surgeons' guidelines were consistent with the framing of the duty to disclose as he defined it.[73] Lord Hope, however, was more explicit. He noted that Jones had argued that while the law could not be said to play a direct role in the design of rules for doctors, it could have a 'powerful symbolic and galvanising role', which was its particular advantage.[74] Thus:

> [t]he message that he was seeking to convey was that, while the case law provided little guidance to doctors and even less comfort to patients, litigation on informed consent could provide a stimulus to the broader debate about the nature of the doctor–patient relationship. *The 'happy ending' of his title would be found if the iterative process between case law and professional guidance were to lead to the creation of a more substantive 'right' to truly informed consent for patients.*[75]

As with so much of the case analysis in this chapter, it is something of an exercise in supposition to divine what his Lordship meant by the italicised portion of the quote. I would suggest that Lord Hope was opining that, in creating and upholding legal rules, medical ethics would have no alternative but to follow the law, and that this would then provide the stimulus of which he spoke. In this way, medical ethics and medical law were seen as separate yet conjoined – for where the latter goes the former must inevitably follow. Such an interpretation is consistent with that imputed to the judgment of Lord Steyn, when he appeared to argue that the law should guide the medical profession's institutions, which should in turn guide individual medical practitioners.

---

[71] M Jones, 'Informed Consent and Other Fairy Stories' (1999) 7 *Medical Law Review* 103.

[72] (1999) 7 *Medical Law Review* 103 at 129, quoted by Lord Hope in *Chester v Afshar* [2004] UKHL 41 at para 58.

[73] *Chester v Afshar* [2004] UKHL 41 at para 27.

[74] [2004] UKHL 41 at para 58.

[75] [2004] UKHL 41 at para 58. Emphasis added.

C. Medical Ethics

The decision in *Chester* highlighted two things; first, that differences of opinion remained concerning what approach to take in these cases when considering medical ethics. For Lords Bingham and Hoffman, the emphasis was on the doctor rather than the patient. While the issue was not medicalised as in *Blyth* and *Gold*, what is apparent is that the ethical principle of self-determination was not given primacy over the legal rule. In this regard, Ms Chester's case had to fail. For the majority, however, this was not the case and the contrast could not be more pronounced. For Lords Steyn, Hope and Walker, the strength of the ethical principle was sufficient to cause them to support a change in the law. However, this change further eroded medical control, and even the legal issue of causation could be seen to be of secondary concern when compared to a patient's right to make her own decision. The approach of their Lordships was most reflective of that of Lord Scarman in *Sidaway*.

The second point of interest is that, for the first time, we can see medical ethics interacting with the law, and vice versa. Lord Steyn, for example, clearly not only identified the ethical aspects of the case before him, but also engaged with and prioritised them. This process was repeated on both philosophical and professional levels and this can be seen in the way in which he considered unofficial and semi-formal medical ethics. Nonetheless, it is important that he utilised the different categories of ethical discourse in different ways. With the unofficial sector, Lord Steyn allowed himself to be informed by its opinions, and then made his own decision. The semi-formal discourse, on the other hand, is the reference point for the medical profession rather than the court. Lord Steyn appeared to suggest that the law and the Royal College guidelines were merely a reflection of each other. He did not elaborate on whether the law should guide the Royal Colleges, or whether the Royal Colleges should inform the law, but the fact that he only mentioned the guidelines as a postscript suggests that his approach was more likely to be the former. However, the use of the Royal College's guidelines, rather than those of the GMC, BMA or any other group in the formal and semi-formal sectors of discourse, suggest that his Lordship was not so much engaging with medical ethics, but with ethical principles – which is not the same thing. It is also notable and perplexing that the GMC guidance was not utilised because, as I demonstrate below, it is considered authoritative and influential in this area. Nevertheless, it is the closest that we will come to the law defragmenting medical ethics through categorisation, and for that reason his Lordship is to be commended.

VI. Ethical Guidance

Ethical guidance should provide the standard for the medical profession to follow, and it may be argued that the GMC, as the formal sector of discourse, should set the tone by emphasising and explaining the importance of the ethical issues under consideration. This section therefore examines how the medical profession, through its ethics, views the different issues. For this reason, only the formal and semi-formal sectors of ethical discourse are considered, as they are most likely to influence the medical profession as a corporate entity. The first place that a doctor might be expected to look for advice on information disclosure is the formal sector of discourse, the GMC. The earliest mention by them of the need for consent was in 1995, after the decisions in *Sidaway*, *Blyth*, *Gold* and *Smith*, when the Blue Book was replaced by the first edition of *Good Medical Practice*. The new document stated that '[s]uccessful relationships between doctors and patients depend on trust'.[76] Among the bullet points that followed that statement were duties to 'listen to patients and respect their views'; 'give patients the information they ask for or need about their condition, its treatment and prognosis'; and to 'given information to patients in a way that they understand'.[77] While the guidance alluded to risk disclosure, it certainly cannot be said to have defined what risks had to be disclosed, although it did ask doctors to give patients the information that they requested, in contrast to the legal duty imposed by the Court of Appeal in *Blyth*.

The second edition of *Good Medical Practice* in 1998 slightly increased the scope of the doctor's duty. The fundamental issue remained trust, and the same bullet points appeared, but with the addition of a further duty to 'be satisfied that, wherever possible, the patient has understood what is proposed, and consents to it, before you provide treatment or investigate a patient's condition'.[78] A footnote informed the doctor that further guidance on this issue would be published in 1999. A third edition was published in 2001, after the further guidance, and was thus able to take it into account. It recognised consent as a fundamental part of medical practice, and referred readers to the more detailed document:

> You must respect the right of patients to be fully involved in decisions about their care. Wherever possible, you must be satisfied, before you provide treatment or investigate a patient's condition, that the patient has understood what is proposed and why, any significant risks or side effects associated with it, and has given consent. You must follow the guidance in *Seeking Patients' Consent: The Ethical Considerations*.[79]

A similar approach is taken in the latest edition of *Good Medical Practice* that came into effect in November 2006. It states that:

> You must be satisfied that you have consent or other valid authority before you undertake any examination or investigation, provide treatment or involve patients in teaching or research. Usually this will involve providing information to patients in a

---

[76]   GMC, *Good Medical Practice* (GMC, 1995), at para 12.
[77]   *Ibid.*
[78]   GMC, *Good Medical Practice* (Edition, GMC, 1998), at para 12.
[79]   GMC, *Good Medical Practice* (Edition, GMC, 2001), at para 17.

way they can understand, before asking for their consent. You must follow the guidance in *Seeking Patients' Consent: The Ethical Considerations*.[80]

In both the 2001 and 2006 versions of the guidance, the duty to ensure that the patient understands the information and to answer her questions is included in sections on good communication.[81] In both cases, further discussion is left to the detailed document, the first paragraph of which outlines why consent is important.[82] The key principle that it identifies is again the concept of trust:

> Successful relationships between doctors and patients depend on trust. To establish that trust you must respect patients' autonomy – their right to decide whether or not to undergo any medical intervention even where a refusal may result in harm to themselves or in their own death. Patients must be given sufficient information, in a way that they can understand, to enable them to exercise their right to make informed decisions about their care.[83]

The principle of autonomy is thus perhaps not an end in itself but, rather, a means to an end. The guidance later states that informed consent by the patient provides an 'agreed framework within which the doctor can respond effectively to the individual needs of the patient'.[84] Furthermore, patients who have make their own decisions 'are more likely to co-operate fully with the agreed management of their condition'. In some respects, then, the GMC's commitment to the principle of autonomy may appear less than wholehearted. This argument gains weight when it is considered that the 'right' to self-determination identified in the first paragraph of the guidance is not described as an ethical right but, instead, as legal in nature:

> This right is protected in law, and you are expected to be aware of the legal principles set by relevant case law in this area. Existing case law gives a guide to what can be considered minimum requirements of good practice in seeking informed consent from patients.[85]

In this way, it might be presumed that the priority for the GMC is not so much the right to autonomy itself, but rather the *effects* of autonomy, such as increased compliance. It is worth noting, however, that despite the less than committed language the recommendations in the guidance themselves are ultimately extremely stringent. Thus, for example, doctors are told that 'patients may need more information to make an informed decision … about an investigation for a condition which … could have serious implications for the patient's employment, social or personal life'.[86] Doctors must also strive to 'find out about

---

[80] GMC, *Good Medical Practice* (Edition, GMC, 2006), at para 36.
[81] See GMC (2001) at para 21, and GMC (2006) at para 22.
[82] GMC, *Seeking Patients' Consent: The Ethical Considerations* (GMC, 1998).
[83] *Ibid* para 1.
[84] *Ibid* para 3.
[85] *Ibid* para 2.
[86] *Ibid* para 4.

patients' individual needs and priorities ... [as] beliefs, culture, occupation or other factors may have a bearing on the information they need in order to reach an informed decision'.[87] These prescriptions effectively require the doctor to divulge any information to the patient that *that individual* would wish to be informed of – a standard that is both extremely high and respectful of the patient's autonomy. Moreover, the guidance thus goes beyond the common law in terms of what information a doctor must give a patient before consent can be valid, resembling the Antipodean test rather than the traditional English 'risk disclosure', and going further than the transatlantic 'informed consent" model.

There is no doubt that the GMC guidance is the definitive document concerning informed consent. Thus, when the BMA Working Party on consent issued its report, it specifically mentioned the GMC document, and noted that, of the various Royal Colleges that had issued documents in the area, some had also used the GMC guidance as the basis.[88] The BMA stated that 'members of the medical profession are bound' by the 'detailed' guidance provided by the GMC.[89] In the light of this, it is no surprise that the toolkit effectively restated the GMC's position. This is evident in the 'card' in the toolkit regarding the provision of information, over half of which merely repeated the GMC guidance.[90] However, three years after the report of the BMA's Working Party on Consent, it was to update its major publication: *Medical Ethics Today*.[91] The book repeats the conflation between law and ethics, but continues by going beyond the law, separating the legal and ethical requirements:

> The purpose of consent is not, of course, purely to protect doctors from legal challenge. Seeking consent is a moral requirement, and the BMA believes that respect for others and their rights lies at the heart of this issue. Society emphasises the value and dignity of the individual. Competent adults have both an ethical and legal right to self-determination and to respect for their autonomy.[92]

The duties are not only separate, but also different in nature. Referring to the decision in *Sidaway*, the BMA states that 'there was a general reliance amongst the judges on the approach that had been taken in the earlier case of *Bolam*'.[93] However, it then adds that 'Lord Scarman's reasoning ... is held by many to encapsulate the true ethical position. It was not shared by the other judges at the time, but was later adopted by the Court of Appeal'.[94] A footnote at the end of that quote cites *Pearce* as the Court of Appeal case using Lord Scarman's

---

[87]   *Ibid* para 6.

[88]   BMA, *Report of the Consent Working Party: Incorporating Consent Toolkit* (BMA, 2001).

[89]   *Ibid*. It can be downloaded at: www.bma.org.uk/ap.nsf/Content/Reportoftheconsentworking party.

[90]   The toolkit, updated in February 2003, can be downloaded from the BMA website, at www.bma.org.uk/ap.nsf/Content/consenttk2.

[91]   BMA, *Medical Ethics Today: The BMA's Handbook of Ethics and Law* (BMA, 2004).

[92]   *Ibid* 71.

[93]   *Ibid* 78.

[94]   *Ibid* 79.

approach. What is clear is that what is legally required and what is ethically acceptable might be different, as the ethical position predated the legal move towards that approach. Indeed, the BMA's guidance, historically, can be seen to follow this approach. Thus in its 1980 *Handbook* the BMA stated that consent was valid 'when freely given if the patient understands the nature and consequences of what is proposed'.[95] Furthermore, '[t]he onus is always on the doctor ... to see that an adequate explanation is given'.[96]

By 1988, the BMA had raised the bar. After recognising that the court in *Sidaway* had held that the amount of information to give a patient was a clinical judgment, the guidance rejected that approach as not sufficiently stringent, arguing that '[i]t is important to remember that a doctor's legal obligations are much less than his moral obligations. *The legal minimum is not necessarily ethical*.[97] Similarly, the 1993 document, which came after *Blyth* and *Gold* but before *Smith*, was explicit in its emphasis on the right of the patient to choose. Thus, '[i]n the BMA's view, respect for others and their rights lies at the heart of the issue of consent'.[98] In a reflection of the 1988 *Handbook*, the 1993 guidance noted that the patient should receive all the information that she 'needs or desires', and rejected the use of *Bolam* in determining how much information to provide.[99] It stated that '[g]ood practice ... is not interchangeable with the legal minimum' and, as the 2004 book was to do, noted that the judgment of Lord Scarman in *Sidaway* was the 'true ethical position'.[100]

Thus both the GMC and the BMA guidance can be seen to set standards that are explicitly and deliberately more onerous than those prescribed by law. The content of the BMA's document mirrors the GMC in its belief that individual patients should be informed of risks that they themselves might wish to be told of. This goes beyond the prudent patient test espoused by Lord Scarman in *Sidaway*, and at every turn the guidance can be seen to be ahead of the law in its protection of patient autonomy. With regard to risk disclosure, medical ethics can thus only be seen as more exacting than the law. That is not the case in the next chapter.

VII. Conclusion

If the medical ethics are currently more exacting than the law, then it is clear that the law is moving towards them, in the direction of greater respect for autonomy. This is exemplified by the decision of the House of Lords in *Chester*, which, it must be remembered, did not involve the question of defining whether a risk is

---

[95]   BMA, *Handbook of Medical Ethics* (BMA, 1980) 12.
[96]   *Ibid.*
[97]   BMA, *Philosophy and Practice of Medical Ethics* (BMA, 1988) 30. Emphasis added.
[98]   BMA, *Medical Ethics Today: Its Practice and Philosophy* (BMA, 1993) 7.
[99]   *Ibid* 10.
[100]   *Ibid.*

material, although the law has been moving in that direction since *Smith*. Nevertheless, it still has some way to go to match the ethical standards set by the GMC and BMA. It is also clear that something of a paradox can be identified in the case law. This is because, without exception, the more that the ethical content of a case is identified and engaged with, the less the judges are prepared to actually leave control to the medical profession and its own ethics. In *Sidaway*, for example, Lord Diplock did not really engage with the ethical content, and considered risk disclosure a clinical judgement in the same way as diagnosis and treatment. Thus, he abrogated responsibility to the medical profession and its ethics. Lords Bridge and Templeman saw the issue as primarily one of clinical judgement, and thus gave the majority of the control to the medical profession. Only Lord Scarman gave primacy to the ethical component, and took as much control from the medical profession as any judge could have been expected to in 1985, when *Bolam* was at its height.

The cases that may be considered to form the nadir of this chapter, *Gold* and *Blyth*, did not engage with medical ethics and its principles at all. Indeed, they refused to acknowledge the existence of an ethical element in the cases. Yet the Court of Appeal, in both cases, went further than even Lord Diplock in *Sidaway* with respect to giving the medical profession control of the issue. This trend was reversed in *Smith* and *Pearce*, where a concern for the ethical issues re-emerged and led the judges to wrest decision-making power from clinicians. However, it is only really in *Chester* that the ethical principle was afforded the prominence that it deserves, and the GMC and BMA give it. The majority there not only recognised and engaged with the ethical content, it based its decision on it. If the majority of their Lordships had not given priority to the ethical principles, then Ms Chester would have lost her case. The importance of this should not be understated, as it finally heralds the effective arrival into English law of Lord Scarman's approach, or even perhaps that of the Australian courts.

Nevertheless, while ethical principles are identified and engaged with, medical ethics, in the sense examined in previous chapters, remains on the periphery of the courts' considerations. While there is a belated interaction with semi-formal and unofficial medical ethics in *Chester*, there is insufficient structure to that meeting; judges simply use ethical discourse for their own ends. There was no reference made at all to the formal sector of ethical discourse; and there seemed to be little in the way of a critique or understanding of how medical law and medical ethics should or could interact. I would argue that the majority in *Chester* considered semi-formal medical ethics to be a filter between the law and individual doctors, making an understanding of the former accessible to the latter. Nevertheless, the lack of reference to GMC guidance is all the more perplexing given its comprehensive and influential nature. Indeed, as will be seen in the following chapters, the judges in the cases examined here are not alone in recognising ethical principles, but not the wider picture of medical ethics as a concept. If they are to abrogate responsibility to medical ethics, they should at least know to what they are abrogating responsibility.

Yet if medical ethics may be considered a gold standard that goes beyond a legal minimum, then the minimum is catching up.[101] As the law moves closer and closer to a prudent patient test, it is important that the ethics do not stand still. After all, ethics that are more stringent than the law makes sense, while the opposite is potentially disastrous for the medical profession and its patients. Indeed if medical ethics are less stringent than the law, the new-found willingness of the judiciary to recognise and protect ethical principles will make it increasingly redundant as a regulatory tool, and the paradox identified should become ever more common. Yet this is an area in which medical law and ethics interact well with each other, with comprehensive and authoritative guidance from the formal sector being more demanding than the law. It thus represents a gold standard, to the law's minimum. While fragmentation is still evident, this dampens its effects. As the next chapter demonstrates, that is not a universal situation.

---

[101] Certainly it is the view of the BMA that this is the case. See BMA, *Report of the Consent Working Party: Incorporating Consent Toolkit* (BMA, 2001) 8.

5

Consent, Control and Minors – Gillick and Beyond

I. Introduction

In this chapter I consider four cases in the area of adolescent autonomy and confidentiality, two issues that are inextricably linked because any granting of decision-making power to minors may involve keeping medical information about the minor from her parents.[1] The first case, Gillick, is a prime example of this, and concerns whether a minor under 16 years of age may consent to contraceptive advice and treatment and, if so, whether she has the right to information about that treatment being kept confidential from her parents. In the two subsequent cases, Re R and Re W, I explore the Court of Appeal's response to Gillick and, in particular, the question of whether minors who can consent to treatment have a concurrent right to refuse it. Finally, the recent decision in Axon is considered. This case has similar facts to Gillick and provides an opportunity to review how, if at all, the law has developed in the two decades between the cases.

Among the ethical issues raised in these cases is whether minors should be treated as competent patients in their own right. Ethical principles and questions such as the concept of personhood and what it means to be competent are thus relevant. There is now a consensus that a minor patient should be involved, as much as possible, in making her own healthcare decisions,[2] but does this respect for autonomy extend to refusals of consent? If so, does this continue even when a majority of people would consider the minor's decision to be unwise? Additionally, there are issues surrounding the right to confidentiality regarding health care

---

[1] *Gillick v West Norfolk and Wisbech Area Health Authority* [1985] 3 All ER 402; *Re R (A Minor) (Wardship: Consent to Treatment)* [1991] 4 All ER 177; *Re W (A Minor) (Medical Treatment: Court's Jurisdiction)* [1992] 4 All ER 627; *R (on the Application of Axon) v Secretary of State for Health* [2006] EWCA 37.

[2] See, for example, the United Nations: *Convention on the Rights of the Child* (General Assembly Resolution 44/25, 1989).

information. This raises questions as to what constitutes 'confidential' information and when, if ever, such information may be divulged without the consent of the patient.

II. *Gillick* – A Tale of Two Views

A. The Facts

The facts of *Gillick* explain why the case caused so much controversy and also highlight a number of ethical questions for consideration. In 1980 the then Department of Health and Social Security (DHSS), now the Department of Health, revised its guidance on family planning services for young people, and stated that in 'exceptional circumstances' a doctor could lawfully prescribe contraception for a girl under 16 years of age without informing her parents or obtaining their consent.[3] The section of the guidance in dispute provided not only information about how the doctor should act, but also the justification for the position adopted:

> Clinic sessions should be available for people of all ages, but it may be helpful to make separate, less formal arrangements for young people. The staff should be experienced in dealing with young people and their problems. There is widespread concern about counselling and treatment for children under 16. Special care is needed not to undermine parental responsibility and family stability. The Department would therefore hope that in any case where a doctor or other professional worker is approached by a person under the age of 16 for advice in these matters, the doctor, or other professional, will always seek to persuade the child to involve the parent or guardian (or other person in loco parentis) at the earliest stage of consultation, and will proceed from the assumption that it would be most unusual to provide advice about contraception without parental consent. It is, however, widely accepted that consultations between doctors and patients are confidential and the Department recognises the importance which doctors and patients attach to this principle. It is a principle which applies also to the other professions concerned. To abandon this principle for children under 16 might cause some not to seek professional advice at all. They could then be exposed to the immediate risks of pregnancy and of sexually-transmitted diseases, as well as other long-term physical, psychological and emotional consequences which are equally a threat to stable family life. This would apply particularly to young people whose parents are, for example, unconcerned, entirely unresponsive, or grossly disturbed. Some of these young people are away from their parents and in the care of local authorities or voluntary organisations standing in loco parentis. The Department realises that in such exceptional cases the nature of any counselling must be a matter for

---

[3] Health Service Circular (interim series)(HSC (15) 32), cited in *Gillick v West Norfolk and Wisbech Area Health Authority* [1985] 3 All ER 402 at 405–6.

the doctor or other professional worker concerned and that the decision whether or not to prescribe contraception must be for the clinical judgement of a doctor.[4]

Mrs Gillick, a mother of five daughters under 16, objected to this part of the guidance and sought, first, a court declaration that it was unlawful and, secondly, an undertaking that her consent would be sought before any such prescription was made to one of her daughters.

B. The Decision

The House of Lords decided the case in favour of the health authority by a majority of three to two. Lords Fraser and Scarman provided substantial judgments in favour of the health authority, while Lord Bridge's was shorter and concentrated on the public law aspects of the case. For that reason, it is not considered below. These judges found that if the minor was deemed to have sufficient understanding and maturity to make the decision, known as having '*Gillick* competence', then she could make her own healthcare choices. Meanwhile, Lords Templeman and Brandon dissented and found for Mrs Gillick, but for different reasons. Interestingly, while Mrs Gillick lost at first instance and in the House of Lords, she won unanimously in the Court of Appeal. In a numerical sense, then, a majority of the judges that heard the case found for her.

i. The Majority – Delegating to Medical Ethics

The judgment of Lord Fraser is reminiscent of that of Lord Diplock in *Sidaway*, discussed in Chapter 4 of this book, in that it concentrated on the application of the law to the existing facts of the case, minimised the ethical dilemmas raised by it, and abrogated any decision to the medical profession (and thus its ethics) rather than maintaining control via the law. He thus defined the issue as one of clinical judgement and began his judgment by stating that the question in the case was one that the courts should not involve themselves in, thus medicalising the issue from the outset:

> If the advice had been contained in a legal document there might well have been room for argument as to its exact effect, but, in my view, it is perfectly clear that it would convey to any doctor or other person who read it that the decision whether or not to prescribe contraception for a girl under 16 was in the last resort a matter for the clinical judgement of the doctor, even if the girl's parents had not been informed that she had consulted the doctor, and even if they had expressed disapproval of contraception being prescribed for her.[5]

---

[4] *Ibid.*
[5] *Gillick v West Norfolk and Wisbech Area Health Authority* [1985] 3 All ER 402, per Lord Fraser at p 406.

Once medicalised in this way, the decision was necessarily seen as one for the doctor, making Mrs Gillick's case likely to be rejected. This view was strengthened when Lord Fraser considered various statutory provisions and concluded that 'Parliament regarded advice and treatment on contraception and the supply of appliances for contraception as essentially medical matters'.[6] However, his Lord-ship then appeared to cast doubt on what he had defined as the intention of Parliament by stating that the issues being discussed 'also raise moral and social questions on which many people feel deeply, and in that respect they differ from ordinary medical advice and treatment'.[7] Needless to say, this was more welcomed by Mrs Gillick than Lord Fraser's preceding comments.

The decision on providing treatment and advice had to be taken on some basis, and the principle identified by Lord Fraser as being most important was the welfare of the child. His Lordship noted that parents could no longer be considered to have absolute authority over their children, and said that once this was considered, the 'solution to the problem ... can no longer be found by referring to rigid parental rights';[8] rather, it would depend on a 'judgement as to what is best for the welfare of a particular child'.[9] The question would then be just *who* would be charged with making this judgement. While accepting that in the 'overwhelming majority' of cases the best judges of welfare would be the parents, he held that 'there may be circumstances in which the doctor is a better judge ... than her parents'.[10] After considering that in some situations abstinence was not a realistic option, Lord Fraser stated that it must be desirable for doctors to be able to provide contraceptive advice and treatment in certain cases. Thus, '[t]he only practical course is ... to entrust the doctor with a discretion to act in accordance with his view of what is best in the interests of the girl who is his patient'.[11] In this way, Lord Fraser justified the medicalisation of the issue. Indeed, he recognised that the questions he was dealing with were not intrinsically medical in nature, and he sought to defend his decision in the light of this fact:

> The medical profession have in modern times come to be entrusted with very wide discretionary powers going beyond the strict limits of clinical judgment and, in my opinion, there is nothing strange about entrusting them with this further responsibility which they alone are in a position to discharge satisfactorily.[12]

He considered that doctors would use this power sparingly and that such behaviour would be the exception rather than the rule. Moreover, he entrusted medical ethics to ensure that this was the case. As we shall see later in this chapter, the confidence displayed in medical ethics in this area may have been misplaced.

---

6   [1985] 3 All ER 402 at 407.
7   [1985] 3 All ER 402 at 407.
8   [1985] 3 All ER 402 at 412.
9   [1985] 3 All ER 402 at 412.
10   [1985] 3 All ER 402 at 412.
11   [1985] 3 All ER 402 at 413.
12   [1985] 3 All ER 402 at 413.

Nevertheless, what is clear from Lord Fraser's judgment is that medical law and medical ethics were considered to be two different animals. The latter was a matter for the medical profession, and he was consequently reluctant to involve himself in it. Thus, once the issue had been medicalised, it became a matter for the medical profession rather than the law. This was the case even though, by his Lordship's own admission, the issue at hand was not within the spectrum of medical expertise. In this sense, then, the issue became one to be decided by medical ethics.

Lord Scarman's judgment most clearly highlights the delineation between the legal and ethical issues. After briefly examining the procedural points of the case, he considered the contentious paragraph of the DHSS's guidance, and said that the question to be answered was: what did the text actually mean? It is here that he first highlighted the fact that he viewed the guidance to be something other than legal in nature. Indeed, having identified that it was vague as to when the 'exceptional' circumstances that would allow the doctor to provide treatment would arise, Lord Scarman counselled caution with respect to the interpretation of the paragraph: 'The House must be careful not to construe the guidance as though it was statute or even to analyse it in the way appropriate to a judgment'.[13] Having noted the non-legal status of the guidance, he defined it as medical in nature. Thus, '[t]he question to be asked is: what would a doctor understand to be the guidance offered to him?'[14] The duties of the doctor were to be found within and framed by the guidance itself, rather than the law:

> He would know that it was *his duty* to seek to persuade the girl to let him bring into consultation her parents (or one of them). If she refused, he (or a counsellor to whom the girl had gone) *must ask himself whether the case was one of those exceptional cases in which the guidance permitted a doctor to prescribe contraception* without the knowledge or consent of a parent *(provided always that in the exercise of his clinical judgement he thought this course to be in the true interests of his patient).* In my judgment the guidance clearly implies that in exceptional cases the parental right to make decisions as to the care of their children, which derives from their right of custody, can lawfully be overridden, and that *in such cases the doctor may without parental consultation or consent prescribe contraceptive treatment in the exercise of his clinical judgement.*[15]

His Lordship's conflation of the doctor's duty with the guidance, combined with the definition of the patient's best interests as a clinical judgement, suggest that Lord Scarman was preparing to hand responsibility for these matters to the medical profession and its ethics, and this he duly did. He noted that both 'exceptional cases' and 'clinical judgement' were not defined in the guidance, and that this left the 'two areas of the doctor's responsibility in some obscurity'.[16] Nevertheless, his Lordship did not see this as too problematic as long as the

---

[13] [1985] 3 All ER 402 at 417.
[14] [1985] 3 All ER 402 at 417.
[15] [1985] 3 All ER 402 at 417–18. Emphasis added.
[16] [1985] 3 All ER 402 at 418.

general message, that doctors would only be able to prescribe contraception to a girl under 16 without parental knowledge and consent in exceptional circumstances, was not obscured to the point of appearing to authorise the doctor to do so 'whenever he should think fit'.[17] As this condition was held by Lord Scarman to have been met in the guidance, the doctor could lawfully provide the advice and treatment to the minor. For reasons that were not explained, the decision as to when a situation constituted an 'exceptional case' thus also became a clinical judgement. The fact that the concept of clinical judgement was left undefined by the court was not seen as a problem – as the definition could be made by the medical practitioner herself. Indeed, 'there really can be no compulsion in law on a government to spell out to a doctor what is meant by "clinical judgement"'.[18]

Having decided that the guidance was lawful, Lord Scarman returned to the legal issues in the appeal, mostly involving the meaning of statutory provisions. Like Lord Fraser before him, he was reluctant to be seen to interfere with what he considered to be a clinical issue. Indeed, once the guidance was defined by Lord Scarman as medical in nature, his own role ended, to be usurped by the medical profession and, it must be presumed, its ethics. Given his judgment in *Sidaway* which, as I demonstrated in Chapter 4, was very sensitive to the ethical context and thus lessened the decision-making role of doctors, it is surprising that ethical principles did not play a greater part in Lord Scarman's judgment.

ii.   The Dissenters – Lords Brandon and Templeman

After Lord Bridge had delivered a short judgment that emphasised the public law aspects of the case and otherwise agreed with Lords Fraser and Scarman, it was the turn of the dissenting judges to provide their reasons. For Lord Brandon, the medicalisation of the majority was rejected in favour of legalisation of the issues. His Lordship identified the three 'activities relating to the sexual conduct of girls who are under the age of 16':[19] first, the provision of contraceptive advice to such minors by non-doctors (the example given was that of social workers); secondly, the physical examination of minors by medical practitioners with a view to the patient subsequently using a form of contraception; finally, the prescription of contraceptives by doctors, in particular the contraceptive pill. These issues raised two legal questions: whether the activities referred to could, in any circumstances, be engaged in and, if so, whether this could occur without the prior consent and knowledge of the minor's parents. According to his Lordship, the answers were a matter of public policy, and legal in nature. The medical profession would have to follow the legal provisions. After some consideration, he said that,

> the inescapable inference from the statutory provisions … to which I have referred is that Parliament has for the past century regarded, and still regards today, sexual

17   [1985] 3 All ER 402 at 418.
18   [1985] 3 All ER 402 at 418.
19   [1985] 3 All ER 402 at 428.

intercourse between a man and a girl under 16 as a serious criminal offence so far as the man who has such intercourse is concerned.[20]

In the light of this, encouraging, promoting or facilitating sexual intercourse by a minor under 16 must be contrary to public policy and the provision of contraceptive advice and treatment, 'necessarily involves promoting, encouraging or facilitating the having of sexual intercourse'.[21] He thus concluded that it would not be possible, under any circumstances, for any of the three activities to be sanctioned by law. Thus, Lord Brandon was dismissive of the medical profession and, by extension, its ethics. His sole concern was whether it was legally possible for *the minor* to engage in the activities he described. Only once he had determined that they could not did he then consider the position of those persons who may advise or treat her. Thus, his judgment may be considered to be the polar opposite of that of the majority, in the sense that he *de*medicalised the issues involved, and gave no decision-making authority to medical practitioners.

Despite arriving at, substantially, the same conclusion as Lord Brandon, Lord Templeman adopted a very different approach. For him, there was no question of ignoring the medical practitioner until the legal issues had been resolved. Rather, the medical practitioner was at the heart of the judgement. Indeed, in his first paragraph his Lordship identified that 'this appeal involves consideration of the independence of a teenager, the powers of a parent and *the duties of a doctor*'.[22] This conflation of the 'duties' of the doctor with the 'power' of the parents was repeated when, having held that minors under 16 could not consent to sexual intercourse, he stated that this would not 'prevent parents and doctors *from deciding*' that contraceptive facilities should be made available to her.[23] The main problem would arise when doctors and parents differed in opinion. Lord Templeman said that two definitions of the minor's best interests existed – the parents' claim to be able to decide what was best for their child, and the doctors' to decide what was best for their patients. He did not consider either claim to be any more influential than the other and said that, in the event of disagreement, the courts would be the ultimate arbiters regarding the legality of providing contraceptive advice and treatment. Furthermore, the judge would be entitled to modify the views of both parents and doctors in defining the minor's best interests.[24]

In emergency cases, however, when it was impractical or impossible to seek judicial or parental approval, the doctor would be able to act according to her own definition of the patient's interests; although she may have to justify her decision in court at a later time.[25] Just as the majority had done, he held that in

---

[20] [1985] 3 All ER 402 at 429. The statutes considered were the Criminal Law Amendment Act 1885 and the Sexual Offences Act 1956. The case was *R v Tyrrell* [1894] 1 QB 710.

[21] *Gillick v West Norfolk and Wisbech Area Health Authority* [1985] 3 All ER 402 at 429.

[22] [1985] 3 All ER 402 at 431. Emphasis added.

[23] [1985] 3 All ER 402 at 431. Emphasis added.

[24] [1985] 3 All ER 402 at 432.

[25] [1985] 3 All ER 402 at 432.

some instances it would be lawful for a doctor to carry out certain medical procedures with the consent of the minor and despite the objections of the parents. As an example, he stated that an intelligent 15-year-old could consent to the removal of tonsils or an appendectomy.[26] However no minor under 16 could possibly be mature enough to consent to sexual intercourse and contraception:

> ... any decision on the part of a girl to practise sex and contraception requires not only knowledge of the facts of life and the dangers of pregnancy and disease but also an understanding of the emotional and other consequences to her family, her male partner and to herself. I doubt whether a girl under the age of 16 is capable of a balanced judgement to embark on frequent, regular or casual sexual intercourse fortified by the illusion that medical science can protect her in mind and body.[27]

Like Lord Brandon, Lord Templeman demedicalised the issues in the case; however, he did so in a way that directly confronted the medical profession. He thus cast doubt on the notion that the decision could constitute a clinical judgement. Indeed, he even placed the word clinical in inverted commas in order to emphasise his point: 'a doctor, acting without the views of the parent, cannot form a "*clinical*" or any other reliable judgement that the best interests of the girl require the provision of contraceptive facilities'.[28]

Although his Lordship stated that in exceptional circumstances (such as the parents having abandoned or abused the minor) the doctor could provide advice and treatment without the knowledge and consent of the parents, the crux of the judgment prioritised the rights of parents over those of the doctor. This eventuality was seen by Lord Templeman as being extremely rare, and he was explicit in his desire to emphasise that this should not be considered to be a 'general discretion' provided to medical professionals.[29] Ultimately, parental rights could trump those of doctors, and the DHSS guidance was held by him to be inconsistent with the law as it did not respect this hierarchy. In this way, he reached the same conclusion as Lord Brandon, but for different reasons. What both judgments share, however, is an approach that demedicalised the issues involved.

C.   Medical Ethics

As might be expected, the divisions within the House of Lords regarding medical ethics and its role were the same as those with respect to the decision itself. Thus, in simple terms, the majority of their Lordships, having medicalised the issue before them, by definition had to have confidence in medical ethics as a regulatory force to police the discretion that they gave to the medical profession.

---

[26]   [1985] 3 All ER 402 at 432.
[27]   [1985] 3 All ER 402 at 432.
[28]   [1985] 3 All ER 402 at 432at 433. Emphasis added.
[29]   [1985] 3 All ER 402 at 434.

The minority, in contrast, did not engage with medical ethics – a course of action entirely consistent with their rejection of the decision as a clinical judgement and thus one to be made by doctors. For this reason, it is not surprising that Lords Fraser and Scarman had the most confidence in the medical profession to regulate the decisions made by medical practitioners. For Lord Fraser, indeed, the abrogation of responsibility for decisions to the medical profession was both explicit and absolute. His view was that not only was it appropriate to medicalise the issue, but also that the responsibility for regulating the decisions made rested with the medical profession:

> [My judgment] ought not to be regarded as a licence for doctors to disregard the wishes of parents on this matter whenever they find it convenient to do so. *Any doctor who behaves in such a way would, in my opinion, be failing to discharge his professional responsibilities, and I would expect him to be disciplined by his own professional body accordingly.*[30]

What is striking here is the way that Lord Fraser qualified his view that a doctor arbitrarily disregarding the views of parents would be in breach of her professional responsibilities. He said that this would be his *opinion* of such behaviour, but the ultimate arbiters would be the medical profession. Lord Scarman adopted a similar approach, equally confident in the power and efficiency of medical ethics to prevent abuses of the discretion he was granting to medical practitioners. Consequently, he felt able, like Lord Fraser, to abrogate responsibility to the medical profession at the expense of the law:

> It can be said by way of criticism of this view of the law that it will result in uncertainty and leave the law in the hands of the doctors ... I accept that great responsibilities will lie on the medical profession. It is, however, a learned and highly trained profession, *regulated by statute and governed by a strict ethical code which is vigorously enforced.* Abuse of the power to prescribe contraceptive treatment for girls under the age of 16 would render a doctor liable to severe professional penalty. *The truth may well be that the rights of parents and children in this sensitive area are better protected by the professional standards of the medical profession than by a priori legal lines of division between capacity and lack of capacity to consent.*[31]

Thus, Lord Scarman advocated a position that went further than Lord Fraser's when he stated that the 'professional standards of the medical profession' may be better placed than the law and, more perplexingly, parents to protect the rights of children. The minority judgments, meanwhile, virtually ignored medical ethics. Only Lord Templeman mentioned the word when he said that he accepted the warning from Lord Bridge 'against the involvement of the courts in areas of social and ethical controversy'.[32] This is not surprising, given that both Lord Brandon and Lord Templeman had rejected the medicalisation of decisions concerning

---

[30]   [1985] 3 All ER 402 at 413. Emphasis added.
[31]   [1985] 3 All ER 402 at 425. Emphasis added.
[32]   [1985] 3 All ER 402 at 436.

advice and treatment regarding providing contraceptives to minors. There are, however, differences in the approaches taken by their Lordships in doing this. For Lord Brandon, the public policy arguments were conducted within the shadow of the law and its principles, rather than medical ethics. On the other hand, Lord Templeman confronted the medical profession and specifically rejected its ability to make the relevant decisions. Indeed, his objection was that the doctor would not be the best placed person to form the judgements needed: 'a doctor, acting without the views of the parent, cannot form a "clinical" or any other reliable judgement that the best interests of the girl require the provision of contraceptive facilities'.[33] It would seem that the rejection of a role for medical ethics by the minority of the House went hand in hand with their refusal to medicalise the issues before them. Equally, the medicalisation undertaken by the majority made it inevitable that medical ethics was engaged with. Moreover, in order for the judgments to make sense, the judges had to have confidence that the medical profession could cope with the regulatory responsibility that it was given. Both Lord Fraser and Lord Scarman made it clear that they had this confidence in the profession and its ethics. In this respect, medical ethics was seen by them as a regulatory tool that might even replace the law. This approach can be identified more strongly in the following cases.

III.   *Re R* – Empowering Medical Ethics

A.   The Facts

R was a 15-year-old girl in local authority care. She had, throughout her life, suffered from periods of mental illness involving violent and suicidal behaviour. The episodes increased in severity with age, and she was detained under s 2 of the Mental Health Act 1983 in an adolescent psychiatric unit. It was proposed that R should take anti-psychotic drugs and, at first, the local authority consented to this. However, R's mental state fluctuated and during lucid intervals she indicated that she would refuse consent to such treatment. The complicating factor, however, was that when in a lucid state R demonstrated sufficient understanding of her illness and the treatment to be considered '*Gillick* competent', and thus have the power to consent to treatment on her own behalf. The local authority began wardship proceedings and applied for leave to allow the unit to administer the medication to R with or without her consent. The medical evidence indicated that unless R undertook the course of treatment she would return to her previous psychotic state. The two principal questions for the Court of Appeal were, first, whether the ability to consent gave rise to a corresponding right to refuse consent determinatively and, secondly, what rights the court had under its wardship

---

[33]   [1985] 3 All ER 402 at 433.

jurisdiction. The facts of *Re R* raise questions that involve the opposite side of the arguments considered in *Gillick*, in the sense that it was the ability to refuse rather than consent to treatment that was at issue. Thus, while further exploring the concept of autonomy, *Re R* does so in a different context.

B.   The Decision

The only judgment discussed here is that of Lord Donaldson, because it is generally considered to be the leading judgment in the case.[34] In terms of precedent, the Court of Appeal not only had *Gillick* to contend with, but also the judgment in *Re E*, which had considered and affirmed the decision in *Gillick* thus establishing a line of precedent.[35] Determined not to be bound by this, Lord Donaldson distinguished *Gillick* on the basis that it did not involve a ward of court,[36] and Mrs Gillick was 'not challenging the right of a wardship court to exercise its *parens patrie* jurisdiction'.[37] Thus, unencumbered by dicta from the House of Lords, he began his analysis with a now famous analogy: consent unlocks the door to treatment and, in the context of a minor, there are two keyholders, the parents, each holding a key that they can use jointly or separately:

> If the parents disagree, one consenting and the other refusing, the doctor will be presented with a professional and ethical, but not with a legal, problem because, if he has the consent of one authorised person, treatment will not without more constitute a trespass or a criminal assault.[38]

Thus, no one parent had a right of veto but neither, however, did the child, *Gillick* competent or not. None of those parties had a 'master key' that rendered their refusal determinative. Rather, as long as one party consented to the procedure, the door would be unlocked and the *doctor* allowed to make a judgement because the dilemma was medical and not legal in nature. Before this point, when the *legality* of the treatment was being ascertained, the doctor had no role to play. To decide this in any other way, he said, would be counter productive:

> If the position of the law is that upon the achievement of '*Gillick* competence' there is a transfer of the right of consent from the parents to the child and there can never be a concurrent right in both, doctors would be faced with an intolerable dilemma, particularly when the child was nearing the age of 16, if the parents consented but the child did not. On pain, if they got it wrong, of being sued for trespass to the person or possibly being charged with a criminal assault, they would have to determine as a

---

[34]   See, for example, JK Mason and GT Laurie, *Mason and McCall Smith's Law and Medical Ethics* (7th edn, Oxford, Oxford University Press, 2006) 369, and E Jackson, *Medical Law: Text, Cases and Materials* (Oxford, Oxford University Press, 2006) 239.

[35]   *Re E (A Minor)* [1991] 2 FLR 585.

[36]   *Re R (A Minor) (Wardship: Consent to Treatment)* [1991] 4 All ER 177 at 183.

[37]   [1991] 4 All ER 177 at 184.

[38]   [1991] 4 All ER 177 at 184.

matter of law in whom the right of consent resided at the particular time in relation to the particular treatment. I do not believe that that is the law.[39]

However, once the lawfulness of treatment had been ascertained the matter did not end, as the doctor still had to decide whether or not to treat the child. The decision would then become ethical so that a *Gillick* competent child's consent or refusal would not be determinative and, although a 'very important factor in the doctor's decision whether or not to treat, does not prevent the necessary consent being obtained from *another* competent source'[40] – in other words, another keyholder. If the child was a ward of court the situation would be different, as the courts were not limited by the scope of parental powers. Thus, the decision of a court taken on behalf of a child *would be* determinative, irrespective of whether the child was *Gillick* competent or not. In this situation, the doctor did not know best, but the court would:

> [T]he court should exercise its jurisdiction in the interests of the children 'reflecting and adopting the changing views, as the years go by, of reasonable men and women, the parents of children, on the proper treatment and methods of bringing up children'. This is very far from saying that the wardship jurisdiction is derived from, or in any way limited by, that of parents.[41]

Having established the power of the courts in cases of wardship to bindingly consent or refuse treatment on behalf of the minor, Lord Donaldson considered the parameters of when *Gillick* competence might be declared or rebutted. For him, the test did not rely on an approach that would give primacy to the maturity of the individual, and thus the ability to benefit from having an autonomous choice. Instead, a content/outcome approach was adopted, where competence was based on the choices made rather than the individual themselves. Thus:

> [W]hat is involved is not merely the ability to understand the nature of the proposed treatment – in this case compulsory medication – but a full understanding and appreciation of the consequences both of the treatment in terms of intended and possible side effects and, equally important, the anticipated importance of a failure to treat.[42]

There is a strong, if implicit, undercurrent in this that if the child were to refuse treatment believed to be in her best interests then that child *must* be doing so as a result of a lack of maturity.[43] Indeed, the underlying attitude is that it was best for minors to receive the treatment that doctors were offering, and the best way to ensure this was to medicalise the decision. Lord Donaldson thus held that R did not have sufficient understanding or maturity to consent to the treatment.

---

[39]   [1991] 4 All ER 177 at 185.
[40]   [1991] 4 All ER 177 at 186. Emphasis added.
[41]   [1991] 4 All ER 177 at 186.
[42]   [1991] 4 All ER 177 at 187.
[43]   See also, for example, C Bridge, 'Religious Beliefs and Teenage Refusal of Medical Treatment' (1999) 62 *MLR* 585, who argues that the minor's refusal represents a 'stance against authority' (p 590).

However the conclusions regarding the facts of the case are, in some respects, less important than the implications of the judgment. Lord Donaldson's limitation of the philosophy behind *Gillick*, that mature minors should be able to make their own healthcare decisions, to cover consent to treatment but not refusal of consent, made the right to autonomy of minors meaningless. What the judgment did do through its keyholder analogy, however, was empower doctors by maximising the opportunities that they had to obtain legally valid consent. Once this consent was obtained, the question of whether to treat on the basis of that consent fell to medical ethics rather than the law. Needless to say, the case was not popularly received.[44] Indeed, the judgment in *Re W* below, as we shall see, was something of a response to that criticism.

C. Medical Ethics

There is scant mention of medical ethics in his Lordship's judgment. Nevertheless, it is still possible to glean enough information from what the Master of the Rolls did say, particularly when it is combined with his views in *Re W*, to reach a conclusion concerning his views on medical ethics and its role. The irony that lies within Lord Donaldson's judgment is that he empowered medical ethics while, at other times, asserting the power of the court, through its wardship jurisdiction, to decide what was in the best interests of minors. Indeed, in several instances in both the present case and, as we shall see, in *Re W*, Lord Donaldson reserved his greatest concern for the medical practitioner. For example, as we have seen, he effectively rejected Lord Scarman's judgment in *Gillick*, not on the basis of the rights of the minor, or even the parents, but instead on the grounds that it may create difficulties for doctors. Thus it will be remembered that he noted that he was worried that doctors might find themselves in an 'intolerable dilemma', when minors near the age of 16 refused consent to treatment while the parents consented, '[o]n pain, if they got it wrong, of being sued for trespass to the person or possibly being charged with a criminal assault'.[45]

This concern to protect the medical profession appears more understandable when it becomes clear that Lord Donaldson was preparing the ground to medicalise decisions regarding the consent of minors. Indeed, the effect of the judgment was to give doctors the greatest possible chance of being able to provide treatment that, in their opinion, would be in the best interests of their patients. Not to protect them, having supported and encouraged their right to make such decisions, would be counter-productive. This would inevitably involve ethical decisions being made and, just as with the majority in *Gillick*, an

---

[44] Lord Donaldson was to cite some of it himself in his judgment in *Re W* and it includes: A Bainham 'The Judge and the Competent Minor' (1992) 108 *LQR* 194, 198; R Thornton 'Multiple Keyholders – Wardship and Consent to Medical Treatment' [1992] *CLJ* 34, 36; C Dyer, *Doctors, Patients and the Law* 60–61 (Ian Kennedy), 76 (Lawrence Gostin), 156–157 (Ian Dodds-Smith).

[45] *Re R (A Minor) (Wardship: Consent to Treatment)* [1991] 4 All ER 177 at 185.

unconditional confidence is apparently displayed by the judge towards medical ethics. That this is the case was made clear, in explicit terms, by the same judge only one year later in *Re W*.

IV.   *Re W* – Total Confidence in Medical Ethics

A.   The Facts

W was a 16-year-old girl with a tragic family history. Her father died when she was 5, and the aunt who was to care for her and her sister was unable to do so, as a result of which they were taken into local authority care. They were to be fostered by a family, but W was bullied by one of the foster family's existing children, and did not receive adequate protection from the parents. Three years later, W was suffering from depression and six months after this, W and her sister were moved to new foster parents. Less than two years later, however, her new foster mother developed breast cancer and her grandfather, to whom she was particularly attached, died.

Months later, W developed the symptoms of anorexia nervosa. The following year, when it became clear that her condition was not improving with outpatient treatment, she was admitted to a residential unit for treatment. Again, she was unfortunate, as the clinical psychologist she was working with left the area without being replaced for five months. The consultant treating her, who she had known for over three years, also suffered a heart attack and was not at work for some months. It is in the context of this catalogue of misfortune that W's condition worsened, and it was proposed that she be moved to a different unit that specialised in eating disorders. W made it clear that she would refuse to consent to this. Consequently, the local authority applied for leave to transfer her to the specialist unit irrespective of her lack of consent. The facts of the case therefore bring forth issues that are similar to those in *Re R*, in the sense that they involve the right of a minor to refuse treatment determinatively.

B.   The Decision

Despite all three judges in the case providing substantive comments, I do not propose to consider the judgments of Balcombe LJ or Nolan LJ. This is because they concentrated on a purely legal analysis of s 8 of the Family Law Reform Act 1969, the relevant statutory provision concerning the issue before them, and the inherent jurisdiction of the court. I will also only examine Lord Donaldson's judgment briefly, because much of it covers the same ground as the one that he delivered in *Re R*. Nevertheless, Lord Donaldson provided in this case some of the most revealing comments about how the judiciary view medical ethics, and for that reason it is included here.

Lord Donaldson began his judgment with the construction of s 8 of the 1969 Act and his decision in *Re R*. He noted that his view was not popularly received by academics,[46] or indeed the Department of Health, which in its 1991 Guidelines for Ethics Committees, published following *Re R*, stated that '[t]he giving of consent by a parent or guardian cannot override a refusal of consent by a child who is competent to make that decision'.[47] In the light of this, Lord Donaldson pledged to re-examine his interpretation of the law. After considering *Gillick*, he concluded that the central point in *W* could be distinguished from it because, just as in *R*, the House of Lords had not had to consider the inherent powers of the court. Thus he again declared himself unencumbered by precedent, and was free to consider the issues on their own merits.

Lord Donaldson began by exploring the purpose of consent to treatment. For his Lordship, there were two purposes to consent – one clinical and one legal. Clinically, consent was deemed important because the patient's co-operation would be 'a major factor in contributing to the treatment's success'.[48] Additionally, failure to obtain the patient's consent would 'make it much more difficult to administer the treatment,'[49] presumably in a physical sense. These justifications did not consider the patient at all; rather, consent was apparently required to make the job of the medical practitioner easier. This suspicion is strengthened by Lord Donaldson's opinion on the legal importance of consent. It was not because the patient was the ultimate arbiter of what happened to her body, nor that she was best placed to determine her own best interests. Instead, the legal purpose of consent was 'to provide those concerned in the treatment with a defence to a criminal charge of assault or battery or a civil claim for damages for trespass to the person'.[50] In other words, the purpose of the legal requirement was to protect *the doctor* from the law, rather than the patient from treatment she did not want. It is perhaps for this reason that Lord Donaldson amended his 'keyholder' analogy when outlining the effect of s 8 of the 1969 Act:

> I regret my use ... of the keyholder analogy because keys can lock as well as unlock. I now prefer the analogy of a legal 'flack jacket' which *protects the doctor from the litigious* whether he acquires it from his patient ... or from another person having parental responsibilities which include a right to consent to treatment of the minor.[51]

Again, his Lordship's first consideration thus appeared to be the protection of the *doctor* rather than the *patient*. This approach was also identifiable towards the end of his judgment when he noted that the wishes of a minor who was over 16 or *Gillick* competent would be 'of the greatest importance both legally and

---

[46]   *Re W (A Minor) (Medical Treatment: Court's Jurisdiction)* [1992] 4 All ER 627 at 632
[47]   [1992] 4 All ER 627.
[48]   [1992] 4 All ER 627 at 633.
[49]   [1992] 4 All ER 627 at 633.
[50]   [1992] 4 All ER 627 at 633.
[51]   [1992] 4 All ER 627 at 635. Emphasis added.

clinically'.[52] Both were important, however, to protect the doctor rather than the patient. Lord Donaldson's judgment is essentially a more explicit restatement of his decision in *Re R*. The starting point was a concern for the doctor, and in particular her ability to perform the procedures that she decided were in the best interests of the patient. She would thus have three chances to gain legally valid consent, as the competent child or either parent retained the ability to consent, and that consent was valid even if it constituted a minority of opinion amongst the three. Waiting in the wings was the judiciary, ready to consent on behalf of the child if all parties refused. The abrogation of responsibility to the medical profession was total, even retaining the right to give it the power to decide if nobody else did, but at least it was undertaken openly and consciously. This can be seen in his approach in the case to medical ethics.

C.   Medical Ethics

Lord Donaldson's views concerning the role of medical ethics in *Re W* are an explicit demonstration of his confidence in it as a regulatory tool. Moreover, they are, without any doubt, the strongest example of the way in which the courts felt able to abrogate responsibility to the medical profession as a result of this confidence. When framing his conclusion regarding s 8 of the Family Law Reform Act 1969, Lord Donaldson recognised that the issues before him were not only legal in nature, and therefore should not be considered only within that context. Thus '[m]edical ethics also enter into the question. The doctor has a professional duty to act in the best interests of his patient'.[53] What follows is perplexing, for Lord Donaldson continued by stating that what the law allowed would not actually happen in practice:

> It is inconceivable that ... [the doctor] should proceed in reliance solely upon the consent of an under-age patient, however '*Gillick* competent', in the absence of supporting parental consent and equally inconceivable that he should proceed in the absence of the patient's consent. In any event he will need to seek the opinions of other doctors and may be well advised to apply to the court for guidance.[54]

Why it was 'inconceivable' that the doctor should proceed in one of the scenarios mentioned, despite the fact that his judgment was in the process of concluding that it would be legal to do so, was not explained. Neither was the question of why the doctor should apply to the court for guidance when the legal answer was clear and the matter had been medicalised. This last point is made all the more pertinent, and ever less logical, when his Lordship continued by placing total faith in the ability of *medical ethics* to stop doctors acting in the manner that he describes:

---

[52]   [1992] 4 All ER 627 at 637.
[53]   [1992] 4 All ER 627 at 635.
[54]   [1992] 4 All ER 627 at 635.

Hair-raising possibilities were canvassed of abortions being carried out by doctors in reliance upon the consent of parents and despite the refusal of consent by 16- and 17-year-olds. Whilst this may be possible as a matter of law, *I do not see any likelihood taking account of medical ethics*, unless the abortion was truly in the best interests of the child. This is not to say that it could not happen.[55]

He provided an example of how the 'hair-raising possibility' could happen – the case of *Re D*.[56] This concerned an 11-year-old with Sotos syndrome and the question was whether to sterilise her. One doctor and D's parents thought it best that she be sterilised immediately, while other healthcare professionals strongly disagreed. The court had held that, as D may have become capable of consenting to marriage in future, it would not be in her best interests to perform the procedure. The court, furthermore, accepted that it would be preferable to abort any pregnancy until such time as she developed competence.

However, he proceeded to complicate matters by stating that in *Re D* 'medical ethics did not prove an obstacle, there being divided medical opinions'.[57] It is unclear what he meant by this. Perhaps Lord Donaldson meant that the fact that there were doctors who believed it to be ethical to perform an abortion on D meant that medical ethics would not be an obstacle to an abortion being performed on her. Otherwise, it is difficult to see what 'obstacle' medical ethics had the potential to be in that situation. As we shall see, he certainly did not mean ethical guidelines from the GMC or BMA. What Lord Donaldson did not do, though, is explain why the situation he described with the hypothetical 17-year-old and the abortion was different to that in *Re D*. Nor did he explain how medical ethics would *definitely* reach the conclusion that he thought it would. He did not cite guidelines, nor did he attempt to otherwise define what the medical ethics he referred to might be. He did not seem to appreciate or explore what this amorphous concept might be; rather, he seems to have *presumed* that medical ethics would do as he expected it to.

V.   *Axon – Gillick* Revisited

A.   The Facts

The facts of *Axon* are similar to those in *Gillick*, and the case thus provided an opportunity to reappraise the judgment of the House of Lords 20 years on, particularly in the light of the totally different approach subsequently taken by the Court of Appeal. Unfortunately, however, the court did not engage with this issue, perhaps because it is only a first instance decision. In July 2004 the

---

[55] [1992] 4 All ER 627 at 635. Emphasis added.
[56] *Re D (A Minor) (Wardship: Sterilisation)* [1976] Fam 185.
[57] *Re W (A Minor) (Medical Treatment: Court's Jurisdiction)* [1992] 4 All ER 627 at 636.

Department of Health published guidance on the provision of contraceptive advice and treatment for minors, including abortion services.[58] The disputed elements of the document can be divided into two categories. First, the statement in the guidance that the duty of confidentiality owed by doctors to patients under the age of 16 was, essentially, no different to that owed to adult patients:

> This is enshrined in professional codes. All services providing advice and treatment on contraception, sexual and reproductive health should produce an explicit confidentiality policy which reflects this guidance and makes clear that young people under 16 have the same right to confidentiality as adults.[59]

The guidance then went on to specify the doctor's duty with regard to the provision of contraception and sexual health services to minors. This constituted the second contentious issue:

> It is considered good practice for doctors and other health professionals to consider the following issues when providing advice or treatment to young people under 16 on contraception, sexual and reproductive health.
>
> If a request for contraception is made, doctors and other health professionals should establish rapport and give a young person support and time to make an informed choice by discussing:
>
> — The emotional and physical implications of sexual activity, including the risks of pregnancy and sexually transmitted infections.
> — Whether the relationship is mutually agreed and whether there may be coercion or abuse.
> — The benefits of informing their GP and the case for discussion with a parent or carer. Any refusal should be respected. In the case of abortion, where the young woman is competent to consent but cannot be persuaded to involve a parent, every effort should be made to help them find another adult to provide support, for example another family member or specialist youth worker.
> — Any additional counselling or support needs.
>
> Additionally, it is considered good practice for doctors and other health professionals to follow the criteria outlined by Lord Fraser in 1985, in the House of Lords' ruling in the case of Victoria Gillick v West Norfolk and Wisbech Health Authority and Department of Health and Social Security. These are commonly known as the Fraser Guidelines:
>
> — the young person understands the health professional's advice;
> — the health professional cannot persuade the young person to inform his or her parents or allow the doctor to inform the parents that he or she is seeking contraceptive advice;

---

[58] Department of Health, *Best Practice Guidance for Doctors and Other Health Professionals on the Provision of Advice and Treatment to Young People under Sixteen on Contraception, Sexual and Reproductive Health* (Department of Health, 2004): www.dh.gov.uk/assetRoot/04/08/69/14/04086914.pdf.

[59] *Best Practice Guidance for Doctors and Other Health Professionals* 2.

— the young person is very likely to begin or continue having intercourse with or without contraceptive treatment;

— unless he or she receives contraceptive advice or treatment, the young person's physical or mental health or both are likely to suffer;

— the young person's best interests require the health professional to give contraceptive advice, treatment or both without parental consent.[60]

The claimant, Ms Susan Axon, argued that the guidance was unlawful on five grounds, namely:

— it misrepresented the decision in *Gillick;*

— it gave the medical profession the power to decide what constituted a child's best interests,

— informing parents would become the exception rather than the rule;

— this would therefore exclude parents from decision-making regarding their children;

— and, finally, all of the above was a breach of Art 8(1) of the Human Rights Act 1998.

She sought the following declaration:

(1) doctors and other health professionals have a duty to consult the parents of a young person under 16 before providing advice and/or treatment in respect of contraception, sexually transmitted infections or abortions;

(2) parents have a right to be informed about the proposed provision of advice and/or treatment in respect of contraception, sexually transmitted infections or abortions.[61]

Ms Axon's argument was essentially the same as Mrs Gillick's – that parental rights should trump the doctors' power to decide what treatment to give to a minor. She therefore sought a demedicalisation of what she considered to be a non-medical issue The result of the case was to be the same, as Ms Axon was no more successful than Mrs Gillick had been.

B.   The Decision

Silber J. began with the House of Lords' decision in *Gillick.* He quoted Lord Fraser's guidelines regarding when doctors could provide contraceptive advice and treatment to minors without their parents' knowledge, and examined whether the rest of the majority in *Gillick* had agreed with them.[62] Just as in *Gillick,* the battle lines were drawn between the claimant's assertion that parental rights should supersede the powers of the doctor, and the Secretary of State for Health's argument that the opposite should be the case. Ms Axon was always

---

[60]   *Best Practice Guidance for Doctors and Other Health Professionals* 4.
[61]   *R (on the Application of Axon) v Secretary of State for Health* [2006] EWCA 37 at para 8.
[62]   [2006] EWCA 37 at paras 9–14.

fighting a losing battle, as even a cursory reading of *Gillick* should make it clear that the views of the majority countered Ms Axon's assertions in both content and spirit. Her only hope, then, was to argue that *Gillick* had been wrongly decided, which she did indirectly by arguing that it was 'misrepresented'.[63] The judge was unwilling to accept this argument.

Once Silber J had decided that Ms Axon's argument ran contrary to *Gillick*, and that it had not been misrepresented, then all other avenues were to fall away in swift succession. Indeed, all that was left was to argue that *Gillick* did not apply to abortions but only to contraceptive advice and treatment, and to attempt to invoke the Human Rights Act 1998. The former was forcefully rejected[64] and, with regard to the latter, it was held that there was 'nothing in the Strasbourg jurisprudence … [which suggests that] any parental right of control under Art 8 is wider than in domestic law'.[65] Thus, there was nothing in the guidance that could be said to interfere with the claimant's Art 8 rights. Silber J concluded by upholding Lord Fraser's guidelines in *Gillick* and declaring lawful the Department of Health guidelines that followed and supported the judgment. This was a predictable result. What the judge also did, however, was again prioritise the discretion of doctors over the rights of parents, just as the House of Lords had done in *Gillick*. Despite this it is noticeable that the concept of medical ethics played an insignificant part in the decision. Indeed, *Axon* did not trouble itself with the difference in philosophy between the courts in *Gillick* and then *Re R* and *Re W*. In a sense, though, this did not matter because, in each and every case considered in this chapter, the end result was the granting of discretion to doctors and their ethics. In this sense, at least, the case is consistent with all of those before it.

C.   Medical Ethics

As the above indicates, Silber J concentrated almost exclusively on the legal aspects of the case and there is little discussion or mention of medical ethics. Indeed, the word 'ethics' only appears three times in the judgment. The first time is in para 83 of 156, when Silber J noted that counsel for Ms Axon argued that abortion was different to contraceptive advice and treatment (and thus that *Gillick* should not apply), as 'a decision on whether to have an abortion raises potentially difficult non-medical issues such as moral, ethical, religious and cultural issues'. Silber J accepted that this was so, but found that Lord Fraser's guidelines in *Gillick* were nevertheless applicable to abortion as well as contraceptive issues. He further held that the minor should have the right to confidential treatment if she were found to be mature enough to make the decision herself

---

[63]   [2006] EWCA 37 at para 60.
[64]   [2006] EWCA 37 at paras 83–95.
[65]   [2006] EWCA 37 at para 132.

and have the ability to understand the issues concerned, and thus was *Gillick* competent. He continued, however, by noting that:

> This would constitute a high threshold and many young girls would be unable to satisfy the medical professional that they fully understood all the implications of the options open to them. These requirements would be underpinned by two matters of which the first is that the sanction for medical professionals was as explained by Lord Fraser that *a doctor who did not adhere to his guidelines could 'expect … to be disciplined by his own professional body'.*[66]

It was thus simply presumed that medical ethics would regulate such decisions, and do so effectively. The other two occasions arise in para 147 – very close to the end of the judgment. When giving reasons for his conclusion that the Department of Health guidelines were lawful, Silber J noted that in areas of social policy the 'Judiciary should show a substantial deference to the Executive'.[67] As authority for this, he cited with approval a quote from Lord Bridge in *Gillick*:

> In cases where any proposition of law implicit in a departmental advisory document is interwoven with questions of social and ethical controversy, the court should, in my opinion, exercise its jurisdiction with the utmost restraint, confine itself to deciding whether the proposition of law is erroneous and avoid either expressing *ex cathedra* opinions in areas of social and ethical controversy in which it has no claim to speak with authority or proffering answers to hypothetical questions of law which do not strictly arise for decision.[68]

Of course, when judges mention ethics, it is frequently unclear whether they are referring to medical ethics (in the sense of being the professional ethics of medical practitioners), or using the word as a synonym for morality. If it was the latter, then the courts are abrogating responsibility for a decision that has nothing to do with perceived medical expertise – as we are all equally able to judge morals. On the other hand, this may be one of those occasions in which the word refers to professional guidance. Indeed, given the fact that Silber J displayed enough confidence in medical ethics to trust it to make decisions, it cannot be discounted as a possibility. If that is the case, then the courts are still consciously abrogating responsibility for ethical matters to the medical profession. Such an approach would be consistent with that taken by the majority of the House of Lords in *Gillick*, and in *Re R* and *Re W*. Indeed, their Lordships' judgment in that case, including the parts referring to medical ethics shown above, was frequently cited as authority by Silber J for what he said. In such a scenario, then, medical ethics for Silber J is similarly a regulatory mechanism, with disciplinary powers, that the courts can entrust to police decisions of an ethical nature. It is unfortunate that the professional guidance does not justify this confidence.

---

[66] [2006] EWCA 37 at para 90. Emphasis added.
[67] [2006] EWCA 37 at para 147.
[68] *Ibid.*

VI.   Ethical Guidance

As might be expected, both the GMC and the BMA now have explicit guidance on the issue of consent with respect to minors, but that is a recent development. Traditionally, the GMC guidance has had little regard for the issue of the consent of minors. Indeed, the first mention of minors at all is to be found in the 1998 version of *Good Medical Practice*, well after *Re R* and *Re W*. In the section relating to consent, doctors were told that if a patient was under 16 and did not have the maturity to understand their condition and the treatment offered, then it would be appropriate to inform the person with parental responsibility of the prognosis.[69] No mention was made of the right of the minor to consent, although it is implicit in the guidance that if the minor was over 16 or did have the requisite maturity, she could make her own decisions without the need for parental involvement or knowledge. This advice was replicated in the 2001 version of the guidance, where it was starkly stated that '[i]n the case of children the situation should be explained honestly to those with parental responsibility and to the child, if the child has the maturity to understand the issues'.[70] The latest incarnation of *Good Medical Practice* emphasises that doctors must treat minors with respect, answer their questions and provide them with information that they can understand.[71] Readers are referred to the specific guidance on consent considered in detail in Chapter 4.[72]

The BMA guidance was similarly vague at first, with the 1980 *Handbook* simply telling doctors what was said in s 8 of the Family Law Reform Act 1969. However, it also contained a section considering a scenario where a girl under 16 requested an abortion. The doctor was advised that such a situation could not 'be resolved by any rigid code of practice', that attempts should be made to persuade the girl to tell her parents but that, if she refused, what the doctor should do 'will depend upon his judgment of what is in the best interests of the patient'.[73] As might be expected, by the publication of the 1988 guidance *Gillick* could not be ignored and the case was thus included. However, it was considered only in the context of whether contraceptive advice and treatment could be provided to a minor who was requesting it. Thus, the doctor was advised that she should attempt to convince the girl to inform her parents and, if she refused, to assess her maturity. If she were deemed by the doctor to be insufficiently mature, the doctor should refuse to offer the treatment. If she were found to be mature, the doctor should make a 'clinical decision' with regard to whether the treatment would be in the minor's best interests, and act accordingly.[74]

---

[69]   GMC, *Good Medical Practice* (GMC, 1998) para 12.
[70]   GMC, *Good Medical Practice* (GMC, 2001) para 22.
[71]   GMC, *Good Medical Practice* (GMC, 2006) paras 24–8.
[72]   GMC, *Seeking Patients' Consent: The Ethical Considerations* (GMC, 1998).
[73]   BMA, *The Handbook of Medical Ethics* (BMA, 1980) 28.
[74]   BMA, *The Philosophy and Practice of Medical Ethics* (BMA, 1988) 31.

By the time the 1993 guidance was published, *Re R* and *Re W* had already been decided. These decisions were noted, and said to mean that minors could consent, but not determinatively refuse consent, to treatment. However, the BMA did not view the cases as necessarily authorising ethical conduct. Thus, 'the tendency to regard mature young people as autonomous in their own right is a very welcome trend which should not be undermined'.[75] Indeed, readers were referred to an entire chapter concerning minors. In that chapter, doctors were told that it was a guiding principle that mature minors should be able to make their own treatment decisions.[76] After a discussion of *Gillick*, it was again emphasised that *Re R* and *Re W* had held that minors could not refuse consent to treatment. The BMA called this 'irreconcilable with the basic tenets of autonomy'.[77] It declared that 'doctors are unlikely to be happy' with Lord Donaldson's distinction between consent and refusal, and that competent minors should have the power to refuse treatment as well as consent to it.[78] However, the issue was somewhat left open as the guidance noted that doctors should explore 'all possibilities of a compromise solution' before seeking a court declaration authorising treatment.[79] The BMA's position in 1993 can therefore be seen to form something of a high water mark for ethical guidance in this area, despite the qualification at the end, in the sense that it again goes beyond the law in its protection of minors' autonomy. This was not to last.

It will be remembered that in *Re W* Lord Donaldson had sufficient confidence in medical ethics to state that although 17-year-olds could *legally* be forced to undergo treatment such as abortions that they did not want, *medical ethics* would prevent this from occurring:

> Hair-raising possibilities were canvassed of abortions being carried out by doctors in reliance upon the consent of parents and despite the refusal of consent by 16- and 17-year-olds. Whilst this may be possible as a matter of law, *I do not see any likelihood taking account of medical ethics*, unless the abortion was truly in the best interests of the child. This is not to say that it could not happen.[80]

However, as we have seen, neither the BMA nor the GMC guidance at the time contained anything that should have led his Lordship to have such confidence. The 1993 BMA guidance was written *after Re W*, and the situation is the same with the GMC, which did not publish its guidance on consent until 1998. Lord Donaldson cannot therefore be said to have had any justification for his confidence in medical ethics in his example. Unfortunately, since 1993 the ethics have developed in such a way as to undermine the autonomy of minors. Thus, if we

75 BMA, *Medical Ethics Today: Its Practice and Philosophy* (BMA, 1993) 14.
76 *Ibid* 70.
77 *Ibid* 80.
78 *Ibid* 85.
79 *Ibid*.
80 *Re W (A Minor) (Medical Treatment: Court's Jurisdiction)* [1992] 4 All ER 627 at 635. Emphasis added.

put Lord Donaldson's analogy to the test today, does it now do as he presumed that it would? As we have seen, *Good Medical Practice* does not refer to the question of whether the consent of the parents in such a situation would be ethically sufficient to allow the doctor to proceed. A doctor in a dilemma would therefore have to turn to the detailed document on consent in November 1998.[81] Paragraphs 23 and 24 consider the case of children, stating that:

> 23. You must assess a child's capacity to decide whether to consent to or refuse proposed investigation or treatment before you provide it. In general, a competent child will be able to understand the nature, purpose and possible consequences of the proposed investigation or treatment, as well as the consequences of non-treatment. Your assessment must take account of the relevant laws or legal precedents in this area. You should bear in mind that:
>
> — at age 16 a young person can be treated as an adult and can be presumed to have capacity to decide;
> — under age 16 children may have capacity to decide, depending on their ability to understand what is involved;
> — where a competent child refuses treatment, a person with parental responsibility or the court may authorise investigation or treatment which is in the child's best interests. The position is different in Scotland, where those with parental responsibility cannot authorise procedures a competent child has refused. Legal advice may be helpful on how to deal with such cases.
>
> 24. Where a child under 16 years old is not competent to give or withhold their informed consent, a person with parental responsibility may authorise investigations or treatments which are in the child's best interests. This person may also refuse any intervention, where they consider that refusal to be in the child's best interests, but you are not bound by such a refusal and may seek a ruling from the court. In an emergency where you consider that it is in the child's best interests to proceed, you may treat the child, provided it is limited to that treatment which is reasonably required in that emergency.[82]

This is both unhelpful and contradictory. Indeed, it suggests confusion on the part of the authors regarding whether to follow the philosophy espoused by *Gillick* or that of Lord Donaldson in *Re R* and *Re W*. On the one hand, the guidelines state that children under the age of 16 may have capacity to *decide*, depending on their ability to understand what is involved. The wording is very close to that in *Gillick*, and clearly suggests that the competent minor should have both the right to consent to *and* refuse medical treatment – indeed, the footnote at the end of the sentence refers to *Gillick* as authority for that point. Nevertheless, the very next bullet point undermines this interpretation when it notes that where a competent child refuses treatment, a person with parental responsibility or the court may authorise investigation or treatment that they feel is in the

---

[81]   GMC, *Seeking Patients' Consent: The Ethical Considerations* n 72.
[82]   *Ibid.*

child's best interests. This reflects Lord Donaldson's interpretation of the law in *Re R* and *Re W*. But which of these interpretations of the law must a doctor follow? The minor cannot both decide *and* have her decision subject to the acquiescence of her parents and/or the courts, for this would nullify any element of decision-making authority given to her in the first place. This would not grant the minor a right to make a decision; but merely offer the illusion of autonomy.

If the GMC guidance is inconsistent and confusing, then it is nothing if not an accurate reflection of the law and its interpretation of the autonomy of competent minors. Of course, as the guardians of formal medical ethics, it would be expected that the GMC's recommendations would at least be legally correct. However, in its desire to adhere to the law, the GMC has not helped the cause of medical practitioners seeking advice because advising doctors to adhere to inconsistent and contradictory law leads to inconsistent and contradictory medical ethics. As for the BMA, in 2000 it published a book solely concerned with the consent of minors to medical treatment.[83] The purpose of the book is to help medical practitioners with particular dilemmas, and it is structured in such a way as to make this possible:

> We envisage that readers may wish to dip into the book with a specific question in mind rather than read it in its entirety, [so] each chapter is designed to be free-standing and convey as complete a picture as possible.[84]

A quick look in the index finds that there is a section of the book that specifically considers abortion, and this might be the first place that a doctor would look in Lord Donaldson's scenario. Unfortunately, virtually the whole of the section presumes that the minor is seeking, rather than attempting to prevent, treatment. Only one sentence is therefore of use, stating that if the minor is deemed to lack capacity,

> a person with parental responsibility can *legally* consent to her undergoing the termination. In all cases, the patient's views must be heard and considered. If an incompetent minor refuses to permit parental involvement, expert legal advice should be sought. This should clarify whether the parents should be informed against her wishes.[85]

It is more than likely that the quote also presumes that the minor is attempting to consent to the termination, but cannot do so due to a lack of capacity. Nevertheless, it gives a sufficient amount of information to notify a reader of what the situation would be if the minor was attempting to refuse consent. Furthermore, it is interesting to note that, according to the BMA guidance, the test for whether the overriding of the minor's consent should occur is unequivocally legal rather than ethical in character. No attempt is made to engage the reader with any

---

[83] BMA, *Consent, Rights and Choices in Health Care for Children and Young People* (BMJ Books, 2000).
[84] *Consent, Rights and Choices in Health Care for Children and Young People* at (xxviii).
[85] *Ibid* at 172. Emphasis added, *Rights and Choices in Health Care for Children and Young People*.

notion that what is legal might not necessarily also be an ethical course of action. But what if a medical practitioner was not seeking legal advice, but rather the answer to an ethical question? Indeed, Lord Donaldson was clear that it would be medical ethics rather than the law that should protect the minor from the abortion. In this case, a doctor might head to the first chapter, which considers the ethical principles involved in the treatment of minors. The book notes that '[t]here is now consensus that from a young age children ought to be consulted and involved in health care choices'.[86] Nevertheless, such an approach 'does not necessarily mean they should be the sole decision makers or be able automatically to overrule the views of people caring for them'.[87]

Some pages later, the guidance states that a minor's 'informed and competent refusal of an elective or non-urgent treatment should *generally* be respected unless there are some exceptional arguments to the contrary, such as risk of damage in the long term or harm to other people'.[88] It argues that to override the refusal of a competent child would be against that child's best interests, but that this is not a universal principle. Indeed, yet again, the scale of the qualification renders the original principle almost meaningless:

> [T]he medical procedures that are least essential to … [the minor's] … wellbeing are generally the most amenable to informed refusal. *Where the law permits*, those [medical procedures] that are immediately life-prolonging or essential to maintain the young patient's health are least likely to be withheld simply on the basis of the child's refusal. In the latter case, questions arise about the child's *competence and moral authority* to make such a grave decision. Ultimately, the matter may need to be referred to the courts.[89]

An ethical dead end is therefore reached. It would seem from the guidance that a doctor's first thought, in Lord Donaldson's hypothetical scenario, should be to respect the valid refusal, but she should note that this is not a universal principle. The extent to which the refusal should be considered binding depends on the severity of the consequences for the minor, and the overriding of the refusal of consent may only occur 'where the law permits'. In other words, just as in the section on abortion, the exceptions to the ethical principle depend not on an ethical equation, but a legal one. Given this, it would then be necessary for a medical practitioner to turn to the chapter on the law to see whether she should overrule the refusal of consent of the minor.

As might be expected, the chapter concerning the law provides the reader with a précis of the relevant cases and statutes. Of course, due to the nature of the law in this area, the dilemma remains far from resolved. Nevertheless, there is also a section offering a commentary on the law, and it might be thought that it would

---

[86]   *Consent, Rights and Choices in Health Care for Children and Young People* 10.
[87]   *Ibid* at 10–11.
[88]   *Ibid* 18. Emphasis added.
[89]   *Ibid* 18–19. Emphasis added. The BMA guidance at this point appears not so much to strive to give autonomy to minors but, like the law, merely give the illusion that there is such autonomy.

be here that some sort of answer might be found. Unfortunately, this is not the case. The section begins by noting that the state of the law is not clear and that 'its apparent inconsistencies can be confusing'.[90] However, it does not then even attempt to form its own opinion on the matter. While recognising that to some commentators 'the power to refuse is the partner of the power to give consent, and it is logically inconsistent to credit competent children with only half of this pair';[91] the guidance also notes that '[s]ome distinction between consent and refusal is, however, defensible'.[92] Thus, 'other commentators have therefore commended the courts' position on refusal'.[93] Ultimately, the BMA guidance does not provide a resolution to the situation that Lord Donaldson described. The final paragraph states that:

> [t]he BMA's view is that there is a need for clarity about when it is acceptable to override a young person's wishes and when it is not. The legal issues could be clarified by the courts or statute ... Meanwhile, this book is the Association's attempt to provide as much guidance as it is presently possible to do.[94]

Nevertheless, the BMA guidance is at least consistent. At no stage does it tell doctors when they *should* override the refusal of consent of a minor. Rather, the reader is told when it is legally possible to do so, and then asked to make up her own mind. This approach was similarly adopted four years later in its update of *Medical Ethics Today*. In this guidance, the BMA asserts that minors have a somewhat equivocal right to autonomy:

> [W]hile recognising that autonomy has some limits ... we have strongly supported the view that judgements should be made by competent patients about their own situation. From an ethical viewpoint, therefore, a decision by a competent young person that is based on an appreciation of the facts demands respect. Both law and ethics stress that the views of children and young people must be heard. *In some cases, however, their views alone do not determine what eventually happens.*[95]

Later on, the same equivocation is repeated. After recognising that the right of minors to consent does not mean that there is a corresponding legal right to refuse treatment (justified by a box containing a précis of *Re W*), the guidance notes that '[d]octors are often unhappy' with this situation and that 'the BMA hopes that all possibilities of a compromise solution would be explored first'.[96] Moreover, it is 'difficult to envisage a situation in which it is ethically acceptable

---

[90]   *Ibid* 39.
[91]   *Ibid* 40.
[92]   *Ibid.*
[93]   *Ibid.*
[94]   *Ibid.*
[95]   BMA, *Medical Ethics Today: The BMA's Handbook of Ethics and Law* (BMA, 2004) 131. Emphasis added.
[96]   *Ibid* 141. Emphasis added.

to provide elective treatment when a competent, informed young person consistently refuses it'.[97] 'Difficult', of course, does not equate to impossible, and it thus cannot be said that the BMA position is that it is totally against proceeding against the patient's wishes. Indeed, the section states that doctors,

> must act within the law and balance the harm caused by violating a young person's choice against the harm caused by failing to treat. *In cases of doubt, legal advice should be sought.*[98]

It is thus possible to see that, in the specific situation considered by Lord Donaldson, the ethical guidance at the time of his decision in *Re W* did not do as he presumed that it would, and nor does it do so today. Rather, it presumes that *the law* is able and willing to regulate medical practitioners' behaviour and take responsibility for setting the boundaries around which the decision will be taken. This is the only possible reason that the ethical guidance is essentially a restatement of contradictory law. Unfortunately, as we have seen, in any cases the courts presume exactly the same thing of medical ethics. It is here that we may therefore identify a regulatory vacuum, where the law seeks to abrogate responsibility to medical ethics, and medical ethics seeks to abrogate responsibility back to the courts. This leaves the doctor free to do whatever her conscience dictates, as medical ethics and medical law cancel each other out. Moreover, the Bristol process can therefore be seen to have led to such a result.

VII.   Conclusion

The paradox identified in Chapter 4, where the more the ethical component was identified the less power was given to medical ethics, does not operate here. Rather, medical ethics is used by judges for their own ends, either to protect the autonomy of minors (as in *Gillick* and *Axon*), or to remove it (as per Lord Donaldson in *Re R* and *Re W*). They choose when to emphasise the ethical issues and when to ignore them. The only consistent element in the cases is that when medical ethics is used it invariably gives power and decision-making responsibility to medical professionals. In all the cases considered in this chapter, medical ethics was treated as a panacea which justified medicalisation and the consequent abrogation of responsibility to the medical profession. Even in *Re R* and *Re W* in the Court of Appeal, where Lord Donaldson sought to remove decision-making power from minors, he still gave ultimate control to medical professionals rather than to the minor's parents. In the light of this, it is instructive to see the faith shown in medical ethics by the judges in all of the cases. From the confidence expressed in *Gillick* and *Axon* that that the medical profession would discipline its own members for failing to heed guidelines to Lord Donaldson's insistence that

---

[97]   *Ibid.*
[98]   *Ibid.*

legal loopholes would not be exploited because medical ethics would prevent it, the role of ethics is idealised and presumed to be effective. This is the case in every judgment, whatever approach it actually takes to the question of the autonomy of minors.

Unfortunately, the contrast with the actual content of that guidance could not be starker. At the time of *Re W*, the ethical guidance did not do what Lord Donaldson presumed that it did, and that remains the situation today. Both the GMC and the BMA guidance seem to find difficulty in the lack of direction provided by the law, and their advice is therefore little more than a recommendation that legal advice is sought. This is particularly perplexing given the fact that both bodies demonstrated a willingness to go *beyond* the law in Chapter 4, and that the law leaves so much to the discretion of doctors. There is no good reason why they could not have done so here and, given the state of the law, it is arguable that they should have. Indeed, medical law thus abrogates decision-making responsibility to medical ethics, and medical ethics then seeks to give it back to the law. A regulatory vacuum ensues, in the sense that the two cancel each other out. What is left is the conscience of the individual practitioner. The confidence displayed in medical ethics in this area can therefore be seen to be very much misplaced, and the dangers inherent in fragmentation, as identified by the Bristol Inquiry Report, realised.

6

Sterilisation/Best Interests – Legislation Intervenes

I. Introduction

The previous two chapters have considered the issues of consent and patient autonomy. In English law, in order to be able to exercise autonomy it is first necessary to demonstrate that one is competent to do so. Of course, not everyone passes this test and for those who do not the question is then one of how they can receive the medical treatment that they need. The four cases in this chapter consider this question in relation to incompetent patients who, it was submitted to the courts, required sterilisations that they legally could not consent to.[1] The law is, prima facie, simple: the requirement of consent is waived if the patient is incompetent, and the doctor is entitled to act in the 'best interests' of that patient. This may be a narrow construct – if the patient is only temporarily incompetent, unconscious for example, her best interests are generally held to be to restore her to a position where she may make her own decision. For permanently incompetent patients, such as adults with learning disabilities, the definition of 'best interests' is more difficult to specify. Indeed, the notion of best interests is only simple on a superficial level, as the difficulty lies in creating an objective and fair definition that works well in all eventualities, or at least the majority of them.

The best interests test applies to all incompetent patients, and is also relevant to the end of life issues discussed in Chapter 7. In this chapter I focus on sterilisation because it was in these cases that best interests as a concept was created and modified, and the fact that there exists House of Lords dicta in the area. It therefore fits the criteria for inclusion outlined in Chapter 1. The facts of the cases all follow a similar path. In each example, a patient defined by the court as incompetent (though this is sometimes simply assumed by them) is seen to be at risk of beginning or continuing an existing sexual relationship. In all but one of the cases, there was a further risk of pregnancy – the exception being the one

---

[1] *Re B (A Minor)(Wardship: Sterilisation)* [1987] 2 All ER 206; *F v West Berkshire Health Authority* [1990] 2 AC 1; *Re A (Medical Treatment: Male Sterilisation)* [2000] 1 FLR 549; *Re SL (Adult Patient: Sterilisation)* [2000] 2 FCR 452.

reported case involving a man. In all of the cases considered here at least some of the medical practitioners involved supported the sterilisation, as did most of the parents. The courts were asked to provide declaratory judgments to the effect that it would be lawful to sterilise the patient. Needless to say, this involves an examination of how the courts have defined what a best interest is, and the implementation of that definition.

The ethical issues inherent in the decisions are clear. How do we treat the autonomy of a person who is unable to give consent? What is a 'best interest', and how do we ascertain what it is in a given situation? Is it to be limited to her best *medical* interests, or should other less tangible factors be considered? Is it justifiable to consider the foetus that may be created by any pregnancy, or even the sexual partner of the patient? As we shall see, the first instinct of the courts has been to medicalise the decision and, as the issues are ethical in nature, this meant once again abrogating responsibility not just to the medical profession, but also its ethics. In such a scenario, there is also the further question surrounding whether or not medical ethics is actually the correct forum for making these decisions. As the courts recognised in the 1970s, the right to reproduce is a fundamental human right, and there needs to be some justification for removing that right from a person.[2] While this was forgotten by the courts for a time afterwards, it does raise issues about whether the legislature should have been more proactive. In this respect, it is noticeable that the cases considered were decided in the midst of sporadic legislative activism in the area that led to the Mental Capacity Act 2005. This will also be considered here.

As the cases demonstrate, the courts have been inconsistent in their approach to medical ethics. Thus, in the beginning they chose to medicalise the issues and thus treat them as questions of technical medical practice. In later cases, however, there is something of a backlash against this view and the courts have begun to retake control of the decision. Indeed, it is noticeable that the paradox identified in Chapter 4, that the more the ethical dimension is recognised the less power is given to medical ethics, is operative again.

II.   *Re B* – Declining to Define Best Interests

A.   The Facts

B was a 17-year-old girl who had been diagnosed as having a learning disability at an early age and placed in local authority care at 4. She was prone to aggressive outbursts, and it was estimated that B's ability to understand speech equated to that of a 6-year-old. Her ability to express herself was equated by the court to that of a 2-year-old. The medical evidence suggested that B would never reach the

---

[2]   See Heilbron J in *Re D* [1976] 1 All ER 326.

stage where she might look after herself or return to her mother's care. It was suggested to the court that her mental capacity would never develop beyond a level that would equate with that of a 6-year-old. The council officers and B's mother were concerned that she had begun to show signs of sexual interest and awareness, and had made what were considered to be sexually provocative advances towards male members of staff. However, although she was capable of understanding the relationship between pregnancy and a baby, she was considered to be unaware of sexual intercourse and its causal link to pregnancy. Given the fact that she did not like small children, it was felt that a pregnancy would be disastrous for her. Moreover, the fact that her obesity and irregular periods would make it difficult to discover if B was pregnant before it was too late to abort added further complication.

It was contended that if she were sterilised, B would have much more freedom in the long term, as she would need less supervision if the risk of pregnancy was not so acute.[3] The local authority applied to the High Court to have B made a ward of court and, subsequently, for the court to authorise that a sterilisation operation be performed on her. This was supported by B's mother, but opposed in court by the Official Solicitor on behalf of B. The question for the court was whether B's welfare was best protected by authorising the sterilisation. At first instance, the application was granted. The Court of Appeal dismissed the Official Solicitor's appeal, and he then appealed to the House of Lords.

The judgments in the case are not the normal sort that one would expect to see from a House of Lords judgment. Indeed, four of the five judges in the case provided substantive judgments, yet they combine to take up just eight pages of the All England reports. In this sense, then, it might be expected that the judges would have seen the question that they had to answer in narrow terms, and that they would have ignored the wider issues inherent in the case. As we shall see, this is indeed the case, as the wider issues are identified but ignored. All were agreed that the sterilisation was in B's best interests, and dismissed the Official Solicitor's appeal. The case is notable for the fact that the House of Lords simply assumed that sterilisation would be in B's best interests, thus making for the complete medicalisation that was to occur two years later unsurprising.

B. The Decision

i. Lord Hailsham

In the first paragraph of his judgment, his Lordship stated that had it not been for the public interest in the case he would have been content to say that he agreed with every word of the judgments at first instance and in the Court of

---

[3] Given that B was deemed incapable of consenting to sexual intercourse, it is surprising that the courts did not recognise that this would constitute abuse. See S McLean, *Old Law, New Medicine: Medical Ethics and Human Rights* (London, Pandora, 1999) ch 5.

Appeal. This declaration made, he began his substantive judgment by defining what the case was about: 'the first and paramount consideration is the well-being, welfare or interests (each expression occasionally used, but each, for this purpose synonymous) of the ... ward'.[4] He continued by recognising and rejecting a wider context to the case, holding that,

> there is no issue of public policy other than the application of the above principle which can conceivably be taken into account, least of all ... any question of eugenics.[5]

Having limited the scope of his considerations, Lord Hailsham described B's mental state and the lack of alternative, less drastic options available to her (such as oral contraceptives), and analysed these in the narrow terms that he had constructed. He pointed out that B's mother, her social worker, a gynaecologist and a paediatrician (the latter three advising the local authority) all considered it to be in B's best interests that the procedure was performed. He noted with approval that sterilisation had been found by the lower courts to be the only 'viable' option, and that he did not see how the courts could 'sensibly' have reached any other decision 'applying as they did as their first and paramount consideration the correct criterion of the welfare of the ward'.[6] His preference for a narrow interpretation of the issues inherent in the case was highlighted in unequivocal fashion when he considered the argument put to him that the right to reproduce was a 'basic human right'.[7] He held that a Supreme Court of Canada case that had concluded that sterilisations should not be authorised for non-therapeutic purposes was 'in startling contradiction to the welfare principle'.[8] Moreover,

> [t]o talk of the 'basic right' to reproduce of an individual who is not capable of knowing the causal connection between intercourse and childbirth, the nature of pregnancy, what is involved in delivery, unable to form maternal instincts or to care for a child appears to me wholly to part company with reality.[9]

It would therefore appear that sterilisation was deemed to be in B's best interests without any objective criteria being used to reach this conclusion other than that others had defined them as such. Lord Hailsham would only give reasons to justify what was *not* in her interests – pregnancy and childbirth. Thus, he looked at the issue before him in the narrowest terms possible, and failed to justify his decision. The test to use in order to define the welfare of the ward, the court's 'paramount consideration', remained undefined. Nevertheless, on this basis, he issued the declaration sought that it would be in B's interests to be sterilised.

---

[4]   *Re B (A Minor)(Wardship: Sterilisation)* [1987] 2 All ER 206 at 212.
[5]   [1987] 2 All ER 206 at 212
[6]   [1987] 2 All ER 206 at 212
[7]   [1987] 2 All ER 206 at 213.
[8]   *Re Eve* (1986) 31 DLR (4th) 1, in *Re B (A Minor)(Wardship: Sterilisation)* [1987] 2 All ER 206 at 213.
[9]   [1987] 2 All ER 206 at 213.

ii. Lord Bridge

Lord Bridge's judgment was similar in both scope and tone. He began by recounting the parties who had given evidence in the case, stating that the facts emerged 'with the utmost clarity' from their contributions.[10] He emphasised that the Official Solicitor was right in appealing the first instance decision, and also in taking the case to the House of Lords, because of the public interest in the case and the judgment of the Supreme Court of Canada in *Re Eve*. The rest of his short judgment involved a very brief consideration of each, with the public interest questions comprising one paragraph.[11]

Like Lord Hailsham, Lord Bridge recognised the wider context of eugenics – or more correctly, he recognised that others saw the issue of eugenics in the case before him. Nevertheless, Lord Bridge was also dismissive of any notion that this point might need to be addressed, and it was batted away in unequivocal style, stating that eugenics had 'nothing whatsoever' to do with the present case.[12] He then turned to the judgment in *Re Eve*, providing a quote from that case in which La Forest J had held that non-therapeutic sterilisations could *not* be in the best interests of patients:

> The grave intrusion on a person's rights and the certain physical damage that ensues from non-therapeutic sterilization without consent, when compared to the highly questionable advantages that can result from it, have persuaded me that it can never safely be determined that such a procedure is for the benefit of that person. Accordingly, the procedure should never be authorised for non-therapeutic purposes under the parens patriae jurisdiction.[13]

Lord Bridge was unimpressed with this approach and called it a 'sweeping generalisation' that was 'entirely unhelpful', and that to state that a sterilisation would never be in the interests of the ward 'patently wrong'.[14] Moreover, to distinguish between therapeutic and non-therapeutic sterilisations would be counter productive as it would 'divert attention from the true issue, which is whether the operation is in the ward's best interest'.[15] His Lordship also rejected any notion that B had a human right to reproduce, holding that pregnancy would be an 'unmitigated disaster' for her, and that '[t]he only question is how she may best be protected' from it.[16]

The judgment was essentially built upon the presumption that it was not in B's best interests to become pregnant, and it followed from this that sterilisation was the only logical course of action. All else flowed from that foundation, and this is why Lord Bridge could not accept the decision in *Re Eve*. What Lord Bridge did

---

[10]   [1987] 2 All ER 206 at 213.
[11]   [1987] 2 All ER 206 at 213.
[12]   [1987] 2 All ER 206 at 213.
[13]   [1987] 2 All ER 206 at 214.
[14]   [1987] 2 All ER 206 at 214.
[15]   [1987] 2 All ER 206 at 214.
[16]   [1987] 2 All ER 206 at 214.

not do, again mirroring the approach of Lord Hailsham, was define *how* he reached his conclusion as to what B's best interests were. Rather, he stated that B's best interests were to undergo the procedure, and declined to provide any justification other than to argue that it was self-evident: 'I find it difficult to understand how anybody examining the facts humanely, compassionately and objectively could reach any other conclusion'.[17] The definition of best interests was thus again unexplored.

iii.   Lord Templeman

After Lord Brandon had concurred with the judgments of Lords Hailsham, Bridge and Oliver, Lord Templeman gave his reasons for also agreeing with the others. He was mostly concerned with the procedure for making such decisions, and emphasised that sterilisations of minors should only be carried out with a court's permission because it would prevent a doctor from being liable in 'criminal, civil or professional proceedings',[18] and the court, in the exercise of its wardship jurisdiction, was 'the only authority ... empowered to authorise such a drastic step'.[19] This was because all parties, including the ward, would be represented and, crucially, that all facts and factors could be disclosed and discussed:

> Expert evidence will be adduced setting out the reasons for the application, the history, conditions, circumstances and foreseeable future of the girl, the risks and consequences of pregnancy, the risks and consequences of sterilisation, the practicability of alternative precautions against pregnancy and any other relevant information.[20]

Ultimately, Lord Templeman held that 'a decision should only be made by a High Court judge',[21] because in the Family Division of the High Court judges are chosen for their 'experience, ability and compassion'.[22] Additionally, the range of issues involved meant that only such judges would be qualified to make decisions of this nature. On that basis, the courtroom was the most appropriate setting: '[n]o one has suggested a more satisfactory tribunal or a more satisfactory method of reaching a decision which vitally concerns an individual but also involves principles of law, ethics and medical practice'.[23] Lord Templeman's approach is thus different to that of those who preceded him. Indeed, his emphasis on the decision-making authority of the *judge*, and his view that the experts giving evidence were there for the benefit of the court, and not to

---

[17]   [1987] 2 All ER 206 at 214.
[18]   [1987] 2 All ER 206 at 214.
[19]   [1987] 2 All ER 206 at 214.
[20]   [1987] 2 All ER 206 at 214–5.
[21]   [1987] 2 All ER 206 at 215.
[22]   [1987] 2 All ER 206 at 215.
[23]   [1987] 2 All ER 206 at 215.

determine the outcome themselves, were approximately decade ahead of its time and certainly against the prevailing opinion of the moment.[24]

iv. Lord Oliver

The final judgment was delivered by Lord Oliver, and it is by far the longest. This is less to do with the amount of analysis offered and more reflective of the fact that he began it with a lengthy exposition of the facts of the case. Nevertheless, his judgment was the only one to show *how* he came to conclude that sterilisation would be in B's best interests, rather than simply assuming that it was. He said that it was important to emphasise the facts of the case because it was,

> essential to appreciate, in considering the welfare of this young woman which it is the duty of the court to protect, the degree of her vulnerability, the urgency of the need to take protective measures and the impossibility of her ever being able … to consent to any form of operative treatment.[25]

Thus he analysed the two different courses of action available to the court: sterilisation or the administration of a progestogen pill. He concluded that sterilisation was indeed in B's best interests not due to any particular advantage to that course of action, but because of the disadvantages of the only other viable option. Indeed, he identified reasons why the administration of the pill might be problematic, ranging from the length of time that the drug would have to be taken, the rest of B's fertile life, to the difficulty of administering it during B's violent moods. Consequently, he held that the judge at first instance was right to conclude that sterilisation was thus in B's best interests.

He ended his judgment, like the rest of their Lordships, by refusing to engage with the wider issues. Thus the human rights aspects were distinguished on the basis that B would never be capable of consenting to sexual intercourse. The distinction between therapeutic and non-therapeutic sterilisations made in *Re Eve* was also dismissed as irrelevant and unworkable. Lord Oliver concluded by adding his name to the list of judges who felt compelled to emphasise that the case was not 'about eugenics'.[26] While it is possible to disagree with his viewpoint, at least Lord Oliver spent time demonstrating how he came to decide that the sterilisation was in B's best interests. He was the only judge to do so.

C. Medical Ethics

The case is memorable not for its consideration of medical ethics and ethical issues, but for its lack of willingness to engage with them. The judges consciously

---

[24] Indeed, it is far closer to the view expressed in the final two cases in this chapter, *Re A (Medical Treatment: Male Sterilisation)* [2000] 1 FLR 549; *Re SL (Adult Patient: Sterilisation)* [2000] 2 FCR 452.
[25] *Re B (A Minor)(Wardship: Sterilisation)* [1987] 2 All ER 206 at 218.
[26] [1987] 2 All ER 206 at 219.

avoided discussing any wider context to B's situation, and thus the ethical components to the case. Indeed, there are only two points within the judgment at which it may be said that medical ethics was mentioned – in both cases it was Lord Templeman who made the comments. The first can be found at the beginning of his judgment, when he noted that a doctor performing a sterilisation on the basis of the consent of the parents of the patient 'might still be liable in criminal, civil *or professional* proceedings'.[27] The latter can only be a reference to the GMC, though it is unclear how Lord Templeman considered that this might be the case. Presumably he meant that, in the event of a successful criminal or civil prosecution the GMC would subsequently commence disciplinary proceedings. Indeed, it is interesting to note that in *Sidaway*, as demonstrated in Chapter 4, he was also the only judge in the House of Lords to make specific reference to medical ethics as a concept, rather than ethical principles, when he spoke of doctors being 'obedient to the high standards set by the medical profession.'[28] In this sense, then, it can be argued that he has a clear and considered view of what medical ethics is and how it operates, and a confidence in its role as a regulator of medical behaviour.

The second mention of ethics by Lord Templeman came near the end of his judgment, when he stated that the issues in the case encompass 'principles of law, ethics and medical practice'.[29] The quote is clear in the sense that it separates law from ethics and, perhaps more pertinently, ethics from medical practice. It can therefore be seen that for Lord Templeman at least medical ethics was not a matter of technical medical skill. Moreover, there is once again a precedent from his Lordship with respect to this position. When delivering his judgment in *Gillick*, as we saw in Chapter 5, his Lordship rejected the notion that the medical practitioner was best placed to make the decisions involved in that case – disagreeing with the notion that the issues were clinical in nature as propounded by the majority in that case.

The other judges in the case did not share Lord Templeman's appreciation of what medical ethics might be or do. Instead, it can be argued that they were conscious of and conscientious in their determination in failing to engage in the ethical elements of the case. The majority of the judges only mentioned the wider, ethical question of eugenics briefly before dismissing it. Furthermore, the refusal of the majority, Lord Oliver excepted, to explain *why* the sterilisation was found to be in B's best interests only adds to the suspicion that the answer to that particular question had simply been assumed before the case had been decided. Certainly, they tell us nothing about medical ethics other than that they chose to ignore them, although the implicit assumption that the sterilisation was in B's best interests makes the medicalisation in the next case more predictable.

---

27   [1987] 2 All ER 206 at 214. Emphasis added.
28   *Sidaway v Board of Governors of Bethlem Royal Hospital* [1985] 1 All ER 643 at 665.
29   *Re B (A Minor)(Wardship: Sterilisation)* [1987] 2 All ER 206 at 215.

III.   *F v West Berkshire* – Unabashed *Bolamisation*

A.   The Facts

Only two years after the House's decision in *Re B*, their Lordships had the opportunity to revisit many of the issues involved. The one significant difference was that, this time, the prospective patient was an adult. F was a 36-year-old woman who had been diagnosed with a serious learning disability since she was about 9 months old. From the age of 14, she had been a voluntary in-patient at a mental hospital. Lord Brandon stated that the medical evidence suggested that she had the verbal capacity of a 2-year-old child, and that her general mental capacity equated to that of a 4- or 5-year-old. Despite the court hearing that she had made significant progress while at the hospital, it was said there was no prospect of F's mental condition developing in any major way.

The reason for the application was that F had formed a relationship with another patient at the hospital – P. Lord Brandon noted that this relationship was 'of a sexual nature' and 'probably … [involved] sexual intercourse, or something close to it, about twice a month'.[30] He said that F did this voluntarily, and that she probably obtained some enjoyment from the liaisons, although he provided no proof of this.[31] However, F's fertility was that of a woman of her biological age and it was felt that, from a psychiatric point of view, it would be 'disastrous' for her to conceive a child as she could not understand the meaning of pregnancy or childbirth, let alone care for a child.[32] The two alternative contraceptive methods considered were each found to have major disadvantages. The contraceptive pill was discounted as an option as F could not be trusted to take it, and there were concerns about the effects on her health. The other option, an interuterine device, contained the risk of infection, and elicited concern that F would not be able to effectively communicate the symptoms of this to her carers in time for remedial action to occur.

Consequently, the judge at first instance had held that it would be in F's best interests for the sterilisation to take place, and this was unanimously upheld by the Court of Appeal. There were two issues that merited a further appeal to the House of Lords. The first, according to Lords Bridge and Brandon, was the question of whether the court should become involved in such a decision at all. Secondly, if the law did have a role to play, what principles should the court to decide whether such a procedure would be in F's best interests? Needless to say, this case contained many issues that overlap with those in *Re B*. Nevertheless, in *F* the question of *how* to reach a conclusion regarding what her best interests are is

---

[30]   *F v West Berkshire Health Authority* [1990] 2 AC 1 at 53
[31]   [1990] 2 AC 1.
[32]   [1990] 2 AC 1.

much more clearly defined. Four of the five judges in the case provided substantive judgments, of various lengths, although it is generally agreed that the leading judgments in the case were delivered by Lords Brandon and Goff. The judgment of Lord Jauncey is so short as to not merit consideration here, comprised as it is of only two short paragraphs. All were agreed that the sterilisation would be in F's best interests.

B.   The Decision

i.   Lord Bridge

The first judgment was that of Lord Bridge, and he announced that he had had the chance to read those of Lords Brandon and Goff, and concurred with their reasoning. He summarised the conclusions of the judges that he agreed with and said that the court did not have the jurisdiction to give or withhold consent on behalf of an incompetent adult patient in the same way that it would with a minor through the wardship jurisdiction.[33] The court did however have the power to make a declaration of lawfulness regarding the proposed procedure, on the basis that it was in the best interests of the patient. He also held that, while in strict legal terms the declaration was not necessary, in practice it should always be sought.[34] Finally, he specified the procedure to be used to obtain the declaration of lawfulness. The problem for the House of Lords was that, quite simply, there was no legal procedure for dealing with incapable adults. In this sense, there was nothing in the common law that provided doctors with a legal justification to treat. Lord Bridge referred to a 'paucity in clearly defined principles',[35] and noted that it was axiomatic that treatment necessary to preserve the life or health of an incapable adult could be lawfully given, but that a strict application of the common law principle of necessity would mean that many incapable patients 'may be deprived of treatment which it would be entirely beneficial for them to receive'.[36] His Lordship, in a way that his colleagues were to follow, thus set himself up to conjure some law from nothing. His main concern, quite openly stated, was to protect the medical professionals involved:

> It would be intolerable for members of the medical, nursing and other professions devoted to the sick that, in caring for those lacking the capacity to consent to treatment, they should be put in the dilemma that, if they administer the treatment which they believe to be in the patient's best interests ... they run the risk of being held guilty of trespass to the person, but, if they withhold that treatment, they may be in breach of a duty of care owed to the patient.[37]

---

[33] [1990] 2 AC 1 at 51.
[34] [1990] 2 AC 1 at 51.
[35] [1990] 2 AC 1 at 51.
[36] [1990] 2 AC 1 at 52.
[37] [1990] 2 AC 1 at 52.

The only way to resolve this conflict, he continued, was to ensure that the doctor was only required to conform to a single standard. Lord Bridge decided that the standard should be the professional one of due skill and care, and thus he held that the test for best interests should be the *Bolam* test – the sterilisation would therefore be in F's best interests if a 'reasonable body of medical opinion' declared that this was the case. Needless to say, this caused controversy, as academics criticised the judgment as medicalising a non-medical issue that doctors were not uniquely qualified to decide on, thus wrongly abrogating responsibility for the matter to the medical profession, particularly given the way that *Bolam* was interpreted at the time.[38] As the issue was ethical in nature, of course, that meant abrogating responsibility to medical ethics.

ii. Lord Brandon

Lord Brandon's judgment is generally considered to be one of the two leading judgments in the case, perhaps because it is among the two longest. Nevertheless, it is not particularly different from that of Lord Bridge in both tone and content. Indeed, Lord Brandon also divided his judgment into the elements that Lord Bridge had identified – the appropriateness of court involvement, the jurisdiction of the court if involvement were found to be appropriate, and the procedural issues that needed to be considered. Perhaps unsurprisingly, he decided the issues in substantially the same way as Lord Bridge. Lord Brandon thus began his analysis of the first question by stating that, as a general principle, when a patient lacked the capacity to make decisions, 'it is necessary that some other person or persons, with the appropriate qualifications, should take such decisions for them'.[39] Moreover, he noted that the principle of necessity would in some cases not just make it lawful for doctors to carry out such procedures, but actually furnish them with a common law *duty* to do so. This is because they will have assumed responsibility for the patient and thus created a legal duty of care to act in her best interests.[40] Therefore, the lawfulness of such treatment would not depend on any prior approval from a court, but instead on whether the treatment was considered to be in the best interests of the patient. In this way, Lord Brandon was able to conclude that the involvement of the courts would not be required as a matter of law. However, he emphasised several times that this did not mean that it would not be 'good practice' to obtain a declaration of lawfulness in situations such as that of F.[41] But this was not because he wished to maintain a level of judicial oversight with respect to that sort of decision; rather,

---

[38] See ch 1 of his book.
[39] *F v West Berkshire Health Authority* [1990] 2 AC 1 at 55.
[40] [1990] 2 AC 1 at 56.
[41] [1990] 2 AC 1 at 56.

it was emphatically and openly admitted by his Lordship, just as Lord Bridge had done, that the purpose was to 'protect the doctor or doctors ... from subsequent adverse criticisms or claims'.[42]

Lord Brandon continued by considering what jurisdiction the court had when considering applications for declaratory judgements. After examining the powers of the court, such as the nature of the *parens patrie* jurisdiction and its lack of applicability to adults such as F, Lord Brandon agreed with the Court of Appeal that the court did have the power to issue declaratory judgments. However, he disagreed with it on one vital point: they had held that the court had the power to approve or disapprove of procedures – issuing injunctions if necessary. Lord Brandon overruled this and stated that the court had no such jurisdiction, and could only issue declarations as to the lawfulness of the proposed procedure. Turning to the procedural issues, his Lordship considered the basis upon which treatment might be declared to be lawful by the court. He noted that the judge at first instance and the Court of Appeal had disagreed over what constituted the patient's best interests – the basis upon which procedures might be declared to be lawful. For Scott Baker J in the High Court, best interests were defined by the medical profession through *Bolam*. The Court of Appeal, however, found this to be 'insufficiently stringent' a test.[43] Lord Brandon, like Lord Bridge before him, agreed with the trial judge and held that:

> [i]f doctors were to be required ... to apply some test more stringent than the *Bolam* test, the result would be that some adults would ... be deprived of the benefit of medical treatment which adults competent to give consent would enjoy.[44]

As there was a responsible body of medical opinion that would sterilise F, he held that the procedure could be held to be in her best interests. Needless to say, the same criticisms that were made of Lord Bridge's judgment can also be made of Lord Brandon's. Indeed, the abrogation of responsibility to the medical profession of the issue is, if anything, more pronounced than it was by Lord Bridge. The combination of the overt protection of the doctors, the equally explicit medicalisation and the refusal to exercise oversight is what makes this case a prime example of a 'pro-doctor' judgment in a non-medical area. The rest of the judges took a similar approach.

iii.   Lord Griffiths

While Lord Griffiths eventually agreed with the judgment of Lord Brandon, he was clear and emphatic in his reluctance to do so. Indeed, he agreed with the previous judges in general terms with respect to the principle issues – that the court should be involved, and that treatment should be lawful if it were to be in the patient's best interests, as defined by the application of the *Bolam* test.

---

[42]   [1990] 2 AC 1 at 56.
[43]   [1990] 2 AC 1 at 67.
[44]   [1990] 2 AC 1 at 68.

However, he parted company with Lord Brandon with respect to whether court involvement was desirable or mandatory. Referring to Lord Brandon's view that it should only be 'good practice' to obtain a declaration of lawfulness before a sterilisation, Lord Griffiths felt compelled to voice his dissent:

> I cannot agree that it is satisfactory to leave this grave decision with all its social implications in the hands of those having the care of the patient with only the expectation that they will have the wisdom to obtain a declaration of lawfulness before the operation is performed. In my view the law ought to be that they must obtain the approval of the court before they sterilise.[45]

While he would therefore forbid the sterilisation of an incompetent adult without prior court authorisation, he accepted that the other judges deciding the case did not agree with him. In this way, he withdrew his interpretation of the law and accepted 'but as second best', the procedure put forward by Lord Brandon.[46] This judgment highlights the fact that the criticisms subsequently made of the decision were valid. Lord Griffiths was uncomfortable with granting all of the decision-making power to the medical profession. Indeed, his Lordship recognised the wider context that the others did not when he talked of the 'social implications'. Moreover, his quote emphasised the dangers of the medicalisation into which the rest of the House of Lords were headed. Consequently, it is perplexing that Lord Griffiths did not give a dissenting judgment instead of accepting the views of a majority with which he clearly did not agree. Perhaps he felt that he had made his point. His voice, however muted, was to be the sole voice of dissent.

iv. Lord Goff

The penultimate judgment, though the last substantive one, was delivered by Lord Goff. He began by agreeing with Lord Brandon that if there were to be a solution to F's situation then it must be found or, if it did not exist, created from within the common law. To this end, he adapted the concept of necessity to justify medical procedures without the consent of incapable adults. Like Lord Brandon, Lord Goff placed his faith in the 'good practice' of medical professionals criticised by Lord Griffiths. Thus, after stating that the lawfulness of the procedure would be tested with reference to the *Bolam* test, and therefore medicalising the issue, Lord Goff continued by making a distinction between what the law would require and what would happen in reality:

> No doubt, in practice, a decision may involve others besides the doctor. It must surely be good practice to consult relatives and others who are concerned with the care of the

---

45 [1990] 2 AC 1 at 70.
46 [1990] 2 AC 1 at 71.

patient … [W]here the decision involves more than a purely medical opinion, an inter-disciplinary team will in practice participate in the decision.[47]

He further held that, in practice, a declaratory judgement should be obtained by the medical professionals before any sterilisation such as that proposed for F would be carried out. Lord Goff also stressed that, in the absence of any *parens patrie* powers, the court simply had no jurisdiction to do anything but issue a declaration of lawfulness if one was sought. Nevertheless, it was here that contradictory signals began to emerge from the judgment. First, he held that such a declaration would constitute an 'independent, objective and authoritative view on the lawfulness of the procedure', and that this was the most appropriate way of protecting the interests of the patient, who would also be represented.[48] Yet, on the other hand, Lord Goff also remained keen to reassure medical practitioners that they had nothing to fear from the involvement of the court:

> I recognise that the requirement of a hearing before a court is regarded by some as capable of deterring certain medical practitioners from advocating the procedure of sterilisation but I trust and hope that it may come to be understood that court procedures of this kind, conducted sensitively and humanely by judges … are not to be feared by responsible practitioners.[49]

That said, he also emphasised the ultimate power of the court, rather than medical practitioners, to make decisions:

> In all proceedings where expert opinions are expressed, those opinions are listened to with great respect but, in the end, the validity of the opinion has to be weighed by the court … *For a court automatically to accept an expert opinion, simply because it is concurred in [sic] by another appropriate expert, would be a denial of the function of the court.*[50]

This is perplexing for two reasons. First, because it must be remembered that Lord Goff had earlier held that there was no legal requirement for doctors to first obtain court declarations, and that it was instead only desirable 'in practice', thus the power of the court to make decisions can only be defined as illusory. Second, his Lordship had held that whether the sterilisation was in the best interests of F would be decided with reference to the *Bolam* test, which in 1989 was interpreted precisely in the way that Lord Goff denied in the italicised part of the quote.[51] Indeed, he ended his consideration of the topic with another conciliatory gesture towards the medical profession when he assured it that when two doctors agree that a sterilisation is appropriate 'there is a high degree of likelihood that … [that

---

47   [1990] 2 AC 1 at 78.
48   [1990] 2 AC 1 at 79.
49   [1990] 2 AC 1 at 80.
50   [1990] 2 AC 1 at 80.
51   See generally M Brazier and J Miola, 'Bye-Bye *Bolam*: A Medical Litigation Revolution?' (2000) 8 *Medical Law Review* 85.

view] will be accepted'.[52] Given the express acceptance of *Bolam* by the House of Lords in the case, and the way in which it was interpreted at the time, it can only be concluded that Lord Goff's declarations of judicial oversight are somewhat empty, and that his approach was ultimately the same as that of his colleagues.

C. Medical Ethics

It is almost trite to compare the approach of the House of Lords in *F* to that of Lord Diplock in *Sidaway*. In both cases what was essentially an ethical issue was medicalised through an indiscriminate use of the *Bolam* test. Moreover, in both cases any suggestion that the issue before the court was not one of medical expertise was totally and deliberately rejected. Ultimately, both the House of Lords in *F* and Lord Diplock in *Sidaway* offered a full and unconditional abrogation of responsibility to the medical profession for non-technical, ethical issues. Another coincidence with *Sidaway* is that there was scant mention of the word ethics or its derivatives. In *F* there was only one, and it came as Lord Goff provided a quote from Lord Templeman in *Re B*. When considering the appropriateness of the court as a forum for making such decisions, Lord Templeman had stated that there was not 'a more satisfactory method of reaching a decision which vitally concerns the individual but also involves principles of law, ethics and medical practice'.[53] Again, the mention of the word was almost tangential to his main point, and there is certainly no impression given from that quote that ethics were being considered in a rigorous way. Indeed, as it is the only mention of the word in the entire judgment, it is more likely to be a throwaway comment than anything else. Nevertheless, there are other instances in the case where it can be seen that some of the House of Lords are aware of medical ethics as a concept. It could be argued, for example, that Lord Brandon's emphasis on 'good practice' demonstrates a confidence in the regulatory powers of medical ethics that is redolent of the approach taken by Lord Donaldson in *Re R* and *Re W* seen in Chapter 5. Indeed, there must have been something that allowed him to leave, like Lord Donaldson, a legal loophole safe in the knowledge that it would not be exploited. In *Re W*, Lord Donaldson had said that medical ethics would prevent minors having abortions forced upon them even if it were legal, while in *F* 'good practice' would ensure that doctors would seek the advice of the courts before proceeding even if it were not a legal requirement. Such an approach suggests that the judges had a vision of a medical profession bound by its own clear and rigorous standards of ethical conduct, backed by sanctions for non-compliance.

Further evidence for this comes from the judgment of Lord Goff. After stating that the origins of a common law power to act without a patient's consent can be found in the principle of necessity, his Lordship explained it in the following way:

---

[52] *F v West Berkshire Health Authority* [1990] 2 AC 1 at 80.
[53] [1990] 2 AC 1 at 80.

This can perhaps be seen most clearly in cases where there is no continuing relationship between doctor and patient. The 'doctor in the house' who volunteers to assist a lady in the audience who, overcome by the drama or the heat in the theatre, has fainted away is impelled to act by *no greater duty than that imposed by his own Hippocratic Oath.*[54]

It is thus clear that his Lordship, like Lord Brandon before him, saw the doctor as answering to more than one master – the law and his own profession and its ethical standards. Nevertheless, this does not appear to have overly concerned him, as he retained sufficient confidence in the power of the medical profession and its codes of conduct to openly allow it to regulate ethical as well as clinical decisions. Indeed, he said that his overall approach should apply 'as much in cases where the opinion involves a question of judgment as it does in ... a purely scientific matter'.[55] In this way, then, it can be seen that both ethical principles and medical ethics as a concept were identified by the judges. Having been identified, however, they were then deliberately and consciously medicalised. The fact that the decision was not one of technical scientific expertise was held to make no difference. Similarly, medical ethics was entrusted with a legal loophole in the same way as we saw in Chapter 5. The case of *F* is considered by some to epitomise *Bolam*isation and medicalisation. Its consideration of medical ethics does little to dispel that view. Indeed the concern to protect the doctors from litigation, rather than the rights of F, serve to emphasise this. It took a decade for that to change, but change it eventually did.

IV.   *Re A (Male Sterilisation)* – Reclaiming Control

A.   The Facts

A was a 28-year-old man with Down's syndrome. His intelligence impairment was found to be on the borderline between 'significant' and 'severe'.[56] The medical evidence stated that A did not have the mental ability to understand the link between sexual intercourse and pregnancy, and would never develop it. More-over, he did not have, and would never have, the capacity to understand the nature and purpose of a vasectomy, nor would he ever be capable of legally consenting to or refusing consent to such a procedure. Nevertheless, he had the sexual urges of any 28-year-old male. As the court noted,

[he] masturbates when he sees pictures of nude women. He has been involved in affectionate incidents with women of a sexual kind. He is fertile and might be physically capable of fathering a child.[57]

---

54   [1990] 2 AC 1 at 77–8. Emphasis added.
55   [1990] 2 AC 1 at 80.
56   *Re A (Medical Treatment: Male Sterilisation)* [2000] 1 FLR 549 at 550.
57   [2000] 1 FLR 549 at 550.

His mother had cared for him all of his life, with the exception of some short periods of respite care, and was 63 at the time of the hearing. The court noted that she had provided A with a high degree of supervision; however, her health was deteriorating and she needed operations on her back and hip.[58] A's mother recognised that she would not be able to provide such supervision for much longer and that A would have to go into local authority care. She was concerned that if A did not receive an adequate level of supervision while in local authority care, he might impregnate someone there; indeed, there had been instances in his day centre when A had acted inappropriately towards women and had had to be stopped from doing so. For this reason, and supported by a consultant psychiatrist, she applied to the High Court to have him sterilised despite the absence of consent on the part of A. This was because she disapproved of men walking away from their responsibilities, and would thus prefer to be sure that A could not impregnate anyone when he was in the care of the local authority. In the High Court Sumner J refused to issue the declaration. For a variety of reasons, far more comprehensively outlined than in either *Re B* or *F v West Berkshire*, he held that it was simply not in A's best interests to perform the vasectomy:

> I do not see that the advantages to A of a vasectomy are clear. It will not protect him from being exploited or from a risk of sexually transmitted diseases. It will not protect him from casual relationships which his mother would not like; it only prevents one possible but important result. It follows that because there are other risks involved in any sexual relationship that A may have with a young woman, the degree of vigilance and supervision is not likely significantly to decrease, whether he is or is not at home ... Thus I do not accept that the operation would add value to the quality of A's life to any significant extent ... Faced with the alternative of an invasive operation not without risk, I do not regard the risks that would otherwise face A as warranting such a course, nor the advantages to A as sufficiently positive. The operation is, in the words of Lord Goff of Chievely in *Re F*, not essential to A's future well-being.[59]

In part because it was the first time that the courts had been confronted with a male sterilisation, the Court of Appeal agreed to hear the appeal from A and his mother.

B.   The Decision

Just as the House of Lords decision in *F* can only be seen as a creature of its time, the same can be said of this case. Indeed, it was always going to be difficult for the old, descriptive interpretation of *Bolam*, and the subsequent medicalisation of sterilisation decisions, to survive the decision in *Bolitho* unscathed. In the case of *A* the Court of Appeal, led by Butler-Sloss P, signalled a significant change in direction. It was clear that the operation would be lawful if it was in A's best

---

[58]   [2000] 1 FLR 549 at 551.
[59]   [2000] 1 FLR 549 at 552–3.

interests, but the more difficult proposition was defining what those best interests actually were – particularly in the light of *Bolitho*, as noted above. Four grounds were put to the Court of Appeal, on behalf of A's mother, to demonstrate that the sterilisation should be seen as a form of contraception and thus in his best interests. They were similar to those often used in such cases: first, that A's mother was merely planning for his future; secondly, that sterilisation would give A the opportunity to enjoy deeper relationships, including in a sexual sense, and that he would enjoy this; thirdly, the option of a later application to revisit the situation if A were ever found to have formed a relationship was argued to be unrealistic; and, finally, that in the event that A should impregnate a woman, he would face disapproval from others and his freedom would be curtailed as a result.[60]

The Official Solicitor opposed the application and made several contrary submissions. These were, in some cases, different to the norm and particular to the case at the time. He began by stating that there was a presumption that non-therapeutic sterilisations should not be approved by the court, though this could be debunked by demonstrating that such a procedure would be in the best interests of the patient.[61] The next two points were more novel. First, he argued that the patient's best interests could not be determined by simple reference to the *Bolam* test, and that the two should therefore be seen as separate.[62] Secondly, the issues that were relevant to the proposed sterilisation of a female did not necessarily arise in the case of a man, since pregnancy would not be the result for A.[63] Consequently, to sterilise A might constitute a breach of his human rights. In this case, nothing was to be gained by sterilising A, and it could not, therefore, be said to be in his best interests to do so:

> A refusal [to grant the declaration sought] by the Court of Appeal would not adversely affect the care given by the mother to A nor would sterilisation displace the continuing necessary level of supervision imposed upon A ... The conclusion of the Official Solicitor was that the facts of the present appeal did not establish that the proposed operation was in the best interests of A, but that there might in future be a change of circumstances which might then establish a case for sterilisation.[64]

---

60   [2000] 1 FLR 549 at 553.
61   [2000] 1 FLR 549 at 553.
62   [2000] 1 FLR 549 at 553.
63   [2000] 1 FLR 549 at 553.
64   [2000] 1 FLR 549 at 553–4.

Thus A's case was different to that of F, in particular as there was significant doubt and disagreement concerning whether or not the sterilisation would actually be in his best interests. This point was explicitly recognised by Butler-Sloss P, who delivered the first judgment in *A*.

i. Butler-Sloss P

The President considered extracts from the House of Lords' judgment in *F*, and utilised the presumption that the sterilisation was in F's best interests as a justification for effectively distinguishing that case from that of A. In a foretaste of what was to come, she immediately questioned the notion that a patient's best interests equated to his best *medical* interests. She quoted herself in a previous case, not concerning sterilisation, stating that best interests were not limited to best medical interests, and then noted that 'best interests encompasses medical, emotional and all other welfare issues'.[65] Once this was established it was clear that the link between best interests and *Bolam* (and thus the medical profession and its ethics), so strong in *F*, would have to be reconsidered. Indeed, Butler-Sloss P wasted no time in moving on to that topic. She was typically clear and strident in her view that the two were separate entities, and that the courts would not therefore abrogate responsibility to the medical profession as the House of Lords had done in *F*:

> Doctors charged with the decisions about the future treatment of patients and whether such treatment would, in the cases of those lacking capacity to make their own decisions, be in their best interests, have to act at all times in accordance with a responsible and competent body of relevant professional opinion [in other words, conform to *Bolam*]. That is the professional standard set for those who make such decisions. The doctor, acting to that required standard, has, in my view, a second duty, that is to say, he must act in the best interests of a mentally incapacitated patient. *I do not consider that the two duties have been conflated into one requirement* ... In any event, in the case of an application for approval of a sterilisation operation, *it is the judge, not the doctor, who makes the decision that it is in the best interests of the patient that the operation be performed*.[66]

She concluded that it had to be proved to the court that the procedure would be in the best interests of the patient, and that this was particularly important since the situation involved a fundamental human right protected by law – the right to reproduce. She was also at pains to stress that, as a male, the considerations that were relevant to A were different to those in previous cases that concerned the sterilisation of women. Ultimately, she held that there would be no 'direct consequence' of sexual intercourse for A except the risk of contracting a sexually

---

[65] [2000] 1 FLR 549 at 555. The quote is from *Re MB (Medical Treatment)* [1997] 2 FLR 426 at 439.

[66] *Re A (Medical Treatment: Male Sterilisation)* [2000] 1 FLR 549 at 555. Emphasis added.

transmitted disease.[67] Moreover, the supervision that he currently received would continue whether he was sterilised or not, not least because the objects of his inappropriate attention would also require protection and sterilisation would not change that. For these policy reasons, Butler-Sloss P held that the procedure had not been shown to be in A's best interests and she dismissed the appeal on that basis.

ii.   Thorpe LJ

After Schiemann LJ had held, in two sentences, that he agreed with both of the other judges in the case, it was the turn of Thorpe LJ to deliver the final judgment in the case. It was much shorter than that of Butler-Sloss P, and he began by stating that he agreed with all that she had held. His judgment was thus necessarily similar in both tone and content to hers, as he too concentrated on piecing together what he termed the 'evidential jigsaw' from the experts that would lead him to a determination of what course of action could be said to be in A's best interests.[68] His conclusion was arrived at on substantially the same basis as that of the President, that sterilisation would not lead to any gain in freedom on the part of A and thus offered him no tangible advantages. The role of A's mother in this was key:

> A's mother effectively conceded that there would be no relaxation in the level of supervision were a vasectomy performed. As she explained that was a consequence of her basic distaste for sex outside marriage. As well as the control which she was able to exert within her own house she would not accept a placement at a home or day centre that adopted a permissive attitude to sexual intercourse between disabled people in their care.[69]

As this was the case, he held that the appellants had failed to prove that the procedure would be in A's best interests. He reached this conclusion by 'preferring' the evidence of one medical expert over the others.[70] This judgment is therefore the polar opposite of that of the House of Lords in *F v West Berkshire*. Indeed, the change in approach to the concept of best interests redefined it as a judicial, as opposed to medical, construct, albeit one that relied heavily on medical evidence in practice. Nevertheless, what is important from this case is the notion that a patient's best interests are much wider in scope than their best *medical* interests. This led inexorably towards an acknowledgment that the previous medicalisation of best interests was inappropriate, and the demedicalisation also served to lessen the role of medical ethics in the decision-making

---

[67]   [2000] 1 FLR 549 at 557.

[68]   [2000] 1 FLR 549 at 559. He continued by describing the cost-benefit 'checklist' that judges should compile in order to decide.

[69]   [2000] 1 FLR 549 at 559.

[70]   [2000] 1 FLR 549 at 560. He state that he was 'less impressed' with one expert, while finding the other's evidence "more realistic" (*Ibid*).

process. Nevertheless, despite relying heavily on medical evidence in an ethical issue, medical ethics was again conspicuous by its absence.

C. Medical Ethics

This case, like several others that have been considered thus far, presents a problem in writing about the treatment of medical ethics in the absence of any such consideration by the court. Indeed, the word 'ethics' and its variants do not appear at all in the entire transcript of the case. Nevertheless, there are some observations that can be made. The first concerns the desire of the court to reclaim the concept of best interests by emphasising the fact that it goes beyond the patient's best *medical* interests. Just as with the cases concerning risk disclosure in Chapter 4, the more that the patient's 'rights' are considered important, the less likely it is that the courts will abrogate responsibility to the medical profession and its ethics. This supports the argument that the case can only be seen as a creature of its time, as medical paternalism has become less and less acceptable – a point recognised by Lord Woolf.[71] In this case, it is the post-*Bolitho* reappraisal that is most evident in the effective reining in of *Bolam* and, by extension, medicalisation; however implicitly it is done.

The other interesting facet to the case is that the reassertion of control of the decision by the courts over the medical profession occurred *despite* almost all the evidence being from medical practitioners. Butler-Sloss P referred to evidence being heard from A's mother, two psychiatrists (one on each side), two urologists and A's carers at the day centre. The 'battle' between the experts, notably in the judgment of Thorpe LJ, was fought between the two psychiatrists. It might thus be expected that medical ethics would have been considered, since the two experts were considering an ethical rather than technical issue. Nevertheless, despite ethical issues being raised by them, such as the potential vulnerability of anyone that A might engage in intercourse with and the reasonableness of restricting A's freedom of movement, medical ethics as a concept was not considered at all. It can thus be seen that even when ethical issues are identified and discussed with medical professionals, just as with the later risk disclosure cases discussed in Chapter 4, medical ethics as a concept is, perhaps paradoxically, marginalised.

---

[71] Lord Woolf, 'Are the Courts Excessively Deferential to the Medical Profession?' (2001) 9 *Medical Law Review* 1.

V.   *Re SL (Adult Patient)(Sterilisation)* – Continuing the Approach

A.   The Facts

Only a few months after their decision in *Re A*, Butler-Sloss P and Thorpe LJ had the opportunity to expand upon their views regarding best interests in another sterilisation case to reach the Court of Appeal. S was a 28-year-old woman with a learning disability. Her mother sought a declaration from the court to the effect that it would be in S's best interests, and therefore lawful, to sterilise her. The reason for this was that her mother was finding caring for S more and more difficult as she got older, and saw it as inevitable that S would eventually move to sheltered accommodation. Furthermore, as S was an attractive woman, her mother feared that if she were to be removed from her careful supervision, S might form a bond with someone or be the victim of a sexual assault, and that either of these scenarios could lead to pregnancy. A medical concern, meanwhile, was that she suffered from heavy menstrual bleeding that she had difficulty in comprehending and which caused her some distress. S was represented by the Official Solicitor, who opposed the application.

At first instance, the judge identified two possible courses of action. The first was a laparoscopic subtotal hysterectomy and the second was the insertion of a Mirena coil, a much less invasive procedure. The medical evidence suggested that while it might be necessary to perform the hysterectomy, it was worth attempting the less invasive option to see if that worked before reverting to the more invasive procedure. Nevertheless, as demonstrated below, the trial judge found that to move directly to the hysterectomy would be *Bolam*-compatible, and held that both options would be lawful, thus granting the declaration sought by S's mother. The Official Solicitor took the case to the Court of Appeal. Two of the three judges delivered substantive judgments (Mance LJ agreeing with the others), and the first judgment was again provided by Butler-Sloss P.

B.   The Decision

After recounting the facts and identifying the grounds for appeal, the President continued by examining the evidence used by the judge at first instance to reach his conclusion. She noted that he had taken evidence from a variety of sources and that, with respect to the heavy menstrual bleeding, the conclusions could be divided into two groups – those of the medical experts and those of the non-medical witnesses. Essentially, all witnesses were agreed that it would be best for the menstruation to stop – although for differing reasons. The judge decided to concentrate on the medical evidence. One of the medical experts, Dr E (a consultant psychiatrist) was unhappy about the potential psychological effects of a hysterectomy.

The other medical experts, Dr K and Professor T, concluded that the Mirena coil, as the least invasive option, should be tried first. However, hysterectomy should not be discounted as an option, but should be used if the coil did not work. At first instance, Wall J had rejected the evidence of Dr E and approved that of Dr K. He had further held that while the fitting of the Mirena coil was the preferred option, he 'did not understand either Dr K or Professor T to say that to move immediately to surgery was outside the *Bolam* test'.[72] Wall J then emphasised that 'it is for the court to decide what is in the best interests of S'.[73] Furthermore, the medical evidence was merely advice for the court to consider and he thus declared both the fitting of the coil and the hysterectomy to be lawful as a first resort, even though the latter was not the first choice of any of the medical experts. Thus, the questions for Butler-Sloss P were, first, what constituted S's best interests (and whether the judge's conclusion was consistent with the evidence); and, secondly, how the *Bolam* test should be used in order to reach a decision.

With regard to the first ground of appeal, Butler-Sloss P approved of the philosophy behind the trial judge's decision, but not the decision itself. She agreed that any conception of the patient's best interests must encapsulate more than merely medical considerations, as they were 'wider in concept'.[74] She also strongly supported the trial judge's affirmation that it was for the courts rather than the medical profession to define best interests: '[i]t therefore falls to the judge to decide whether to accept or reject the expert medical opinion that an operation is, or is not, in the best interests of a patient'.[75] Even more interesting, however, was the nature of her recognition that what she and the trial judge were doing was curtailing medical dominance: '[i]t is relevant to remember that the focus of judicial decisions has been to rein in *excessive medical enthusiasm*'.[76] This was an explicit declaration of judicial reclamation of authority over the medical profession, and could not have been more strongly worded. In the light of this, it is surprising that she still found that the trial judge had been wrong to reject the medical evidence:

> Was there any countervailing evidence of equal weight upon which the judge could rely to offset the medical evidence? ... [T]he mother, has set out with care the evidence ... demonstrates the difficulties experienced by S and by those who care so well for her. But the understandable concerns of a caring mother and the problems of dealing with S during her menstrual periods do not, on the facts of this case, tilt the balance towards

[72] *Re SL (Adult Patient: Sterilisation)* [2000] 2 FCR 452 at 458.
[73] [2000] 2 FCR 452 at 458.
[74] [2000] 2 FCR 452 at 461.
[75] [2000] 2 FCR 452 at 461.
[76] [2000] 2 FCR 452 at 461. Emphasis added.

major irreversible surgery for therapeutic reasons when they are unsupported by any gynaecological, psychological or other medical evidence. The judge appears to have accepted the evidence of the family and friends on these issues in preference to the expert evidence to the contrary in circumstances in which the significance he attached to that family evidence was disproportionate.[77]

It may be argued that Butler-Sloss P was limiting the requirement of supporting medical evidence to *therapeutic* interventions. Nevertheless, it must be recognised that there is, prima facie, something of an incongruity in medical evidence being considered critical when the concept of best interests had been highlighted as being about much more than medical considerations. Her conclusion that the judge at first instance had insufficient grounds to reject the medical evidence can therefore be seen as a sign that while the courts have declared themselves the ultimate arbiters of best interests, medical professionals and their views on such ethical matters would not be marginalised by the change in judicial approach. This can be seen clearly with regard to her consideration of the second aspect of the appeal – the place of the *Bolam* test in deciding best interests. Butler-Sloss P. held that while *Bolam* (and thus the medical profession) were involved at the beginning of the decision-making process, it was for the court to further narrow down the options to arrive at the 'best interests' of the patient:

> I would suggest that the starting point of any medical decision would be the principles enunciated in the *Bolam* test and that a doctor ought not to make any decision about a patient that does not fall within the broad spectrum of the *Bolam* test. The duty to act in accordance with responsible and competent professional opinion may give the doctor more than one option since there may well be more than one acceptable medical opinion. When the doctor moves on to consider the best interests of the patient he/she has to choose the best option, often from a range of options. ... [T]he best interests test ought, logically, to give only one answer.[78]

Thus *Bolam*, through medical evidence, would narrow down the options available, as there would be a finite number of options that could conform to it. However, once the other, wider issues were added, the options would be further narrowed down to just one, and only then can it be said that the patient's best interests have been defined. Butler-Sloss P found that the trial judge had only applied the first of the two parts of the process, and had therefore misapplied the law. She therefore allowed the appeal. The judgment of Thorpe LJ concentrated on the technical legal aspects of the best interests test, and can be seen as complementary to that of the President, rather than a separate opinion. On that basis, it is unnecessary to discuss it here. Mance LJ simply declared that he agreed with the other two judgments.

---

[77] [2000] 2 FCR 452 at 461–2.
[78] [2000] 2 FCR 452 at 464.

C. Medical Ethics

Perhaps predictably, given the proximity in time and the fact that the same judges gave substantive opinions, the approach taken in this case is identical to that in *Re A*. Nevertheless, the word 'ethics' can at least be found in *Re SL* – not once but twice. The first time was when Butler-Sloss P was quoting Wall J, the judge at first instance, concerning the latter's view that best interests was a matter for the courts rather than the medical profession to establish. After emphasising that the medical evidence was merely advice for the court, she quoted Wall J as adding that '[p]lainly I could not declare lawful a course of action which ran counter to established medical ethics'.[79] It is not clear what Wall J meant by 'established medical ethics', nor did he state whether he had consulted any ethical guidance in reaching his decision. However, it may well be that what he meant was that the courts would not *force* medical practitioners to treat a patient in a way that, in their judgement, was not in that patient's best interests, only issue a declaration of lawfulness. Alternatively, he could have been saying that if there was no *Bolam* compliance then a course of action could not be lawful. Nevertheless, what it does demonstrate, at the very least, is a recognition on the part of Wall J that the issues in the case went beyond the technical medical. The other mention of the word was from Butler-Sloss P herself. Near the end of her judgment she held that 'best interests as applied by the court extends beyond the considerations set out in *Bolam*. The judicial decision will incorporate broader ethical, social, moral and welfare considerations'.[80] The list of broader considerations can include anything that the judge finds relevant, and there is perhaps a suspicion that the word 'ethical' as mentioned does not necessarily refer to medical ethics, but rather to morality.

However, in the first mention of 'medical ethics', by Wall J, it can be seen that the judge was clearly referring to a concept that is created by and for the medical profession. It is also clear that he was unwilling to force medical practitioners to act in a way that would be inconsistent with what they, as a profession, would consider to be these ethics. In this way, he remained deferential to what he saw as medical norms. That is not the case with Butler-Sloss P, and indeed her separation of the ethical aspect from the medical considerations decided by *Bolam* again demonstrates her view that doctors have no specific ethical expertise. Rather, the ethical considerations are a part of those to be decided by *the judge*, after the medical profession has given evidence. The case highlights the two views of medical ethics that come out of the judgment at first instance and then in the Court of Appeal. In the former, medical ethics was seen to be medical in nature, and this prevented too much judicial interference. In the Court of Appeal,

---

[79] [2000] 2 FCR 452 at 458.
[80] [2000] 2 FCR 452 at 464–5.

though, importance was placed on ethical *principles* rather than the *concept* of ethics, thus purporting to reclaim decision-making authority for the court.

VI. Law Reform

The period between the decision in *F* and *Re A* and beyond was marked by attempts at law reform. This began almost immediately after the decision in *F*, when the Law Commission was asked to examine the law in the area. It finally produced its report in 1995.[81] Entitled *Mental Incapacity*, it examined the 'ways in which decisions may lawfully be made on behalf of those who are unable to make decisions for themselves'.[82] Indeed, as the report explicitly stated, one of the reasons for the decision of by the Law Commission to investigate the issue was the view put to it that *F* had drawn attention to the issue but that the House of Lords 'could not provide a comprehensive solution'.[83]

The Law Commissioners did not approve of the judgment in that case, and they recognised that their approach would therefore 'involve a significant departure from the present state of the law'.[84] In particular, they were unequivocal in their condemnation of the use of the *Bolam* test as the sole method of ascertaining whether a particular treatment was in a patient's best interests. Noting that in *F* a doctor who acted in a *Bolam*-compliant way was both not negligent and deemed to be acting in the best interests of her patient, the report was scathing:

> The apparent conflation of the criterion for assessing complaints about professional negligence with the criterion for treating persons unable to consent has been the butt of vehement criticism. No medical professional or body responding to Consultation Paper No 129 argued in favour of retaining such a definition of 'best interests'. Many were extremely anxious to see some clear and principled guidance given as to what 'best interests' might involve. The British Medical Association, for its part, supported our provisional proposals for statutory guidance 'without reservation'.[85]

The Law Commission favoured an approach which they considered to be a compromise between the best interests test and the substituted judgment test exemplified by the approach of the Supreme Court of Canada in *Re Eve*. In that case, La Forest J had followed the US case of *Re Grady*, and held that, when deciding what course of action to pursue on behalf of an incapacitated adult, the court should,

> attempt to determine what decision the mental incompetent would make, if she was reviewing her situation as a competent person, but taking account of her mental

---

[81]   Law Commission, *Mental Incapacity* (Law Com 231, 1995).
[82]   *Ibid* para 1.1.
[83]   *Ibid* para 1.4.
[84]   *Ibid* para 3.26.
[85]   *Ibid* para 3.26.

incapacity as a factor in her decision. It allows the court to consider a number of factors bearing directly upon the condition of the mental incompetent.[86]

It also noted that no statute could offer an 'exhaustive account' of what would constitute a person's best interests in every situation.[87] To this end, the report recommended a checklist of four issues that 'regard should be had to' in determining a patient's best interests, and the influence of the substituted judgment test are plain to see:

(i) 'the ascertainable past and present wishes and feelings of the person concerned, and the factors that person would consider if able to do so';
(ii) 'the need to permit and encourage the person to participate, or to improve his or her ability to participate, as fully as possible in anything done for and any decision affecting him or her';
(iii) the views of other people who it is 'appropriate and practicable to consult about the person's wishes and feelings and what would be in his or her best interests';
(iv) whether an alternative course of action exists that would achieve the same ends 'in a manner less restrictive of the person's freedom of action'.[88]

The Law Commission report also mentioned sterilisation specifically and again parted company with the approach previously taken by the House of Lords. It will be remembered that, in the case of *Re B*, the House of Lords dismissed the distinction made in *Re Eve* between therapeutic and non-therapeutic sterilisations as unworkable and irrelevant. The Law Commission disagreed, recommending that any proposed sterilisation other than to 'treat a disease of the reproductive organs or relieve existing detrimental effects of menstruation' should first require court authorisation.[89]

Despite the report referring to them as a compromise between best interests and substituted judgment, its proposals reflect the approach of the latter far more than the former. In 1997, a consultation paper was issued by the Government, entitled *Who Decides?*[90] The results were collated and considered and, consequently, in 1999 a policy document was issued called *Making Decisions*.[91] This approved of the Law Commission's checklist of factors to determine best interests, but added two more. First, regard should be had to whether there 'is a reasonable expectation of the person recovering capacity ... in the foreseeable future'; and, second, the need 'to be satisfied that the wishes of the person without capacity were not the result of undue influence'.[92] Additionally, the

---

[86] *Re Eve* (1986) 31 DLR (4th) 1 at 27. *Re Grady* (1981) 426 A 2d 467.
[87] Law Commission, *Mental Incapacity* (Law Com 231, 1995) para 3.26.
[88] *Ibid* para 3.28.
[89] *Ibid* para 6.4.
[90] *Who Decides? Making Decisions on Behalf of Mentally Incapacitated Adults* (Cm 3803, 1997).
[91] *Making Decisions* (Cm 4465, 1999).
[92] *Ibid* para 1.12.

document argued that the list of factors should not be 'applied too rigidly' and thus 'exclude consideration of any relevant factor in a particular case'.[93] What can be seen from the general approach of the Law Commission, the consultation and the resulting policy document is, principally, a desire to involve incapacitated patients in their own care as much as possible. Further, however, the concept of best interests was reconfigured to be less a *medical* construct and more of an evaluation of what the patient would have wanted if she were competent.

While the later cases in this chapter were being decided, the process of law reform continued in a sporadic fashion, and in June 2003 a draft Mental Incapacity Bill was presented to Parliament.[94] It faced assessment by a Joint Scrutineering Committee of the House of Lords and House of Commons in the summer of 2003, which published a report in November of that year.[95] Chapter 7 of that report considered the concept of best interests. It noted that the submissions it received were broadly in favour of the four checklist items proposed by the Law Commission in 1995 and accepted following consultation. Indeed, the Joint Committee was in general agreement with the statute, only emphasising the fact that the checklist should not be seen as exhaustive.[96] It made small but insignificant recommendations regarding clarifications to the wording in certain areas, but none sought to change the substance or tone of the legislation.[97]

In February 2004, the Government issued a response to the report, with the concept of best interests again being seen as essentially uncontroversial: '[t]he Committee has pointed out that decision makers will need to be clear about what best interests requires of them. We recognise that this will be one area that the Codes of Practice will need to cover'.[98] In April 2005 the Bill received Royal Assent, and it came into force as the Mental Capacity Act 2005 in April 2007. Section 4 defines best interests and, as can be seen, the 'checklist' approach remains:

4 Best Interests

(1) In determining for the purposes of this Act what is in a person's best interests, the person making the determination must not make it merely on the basis of –

(a)   the person's age or appearance, or

---

[93]   *Ibid* para 1.12.
[94]   Draft Mental Incapacity Bill (Cm 5859–1).
[95]   *Report of the Joint Committee on the Draft Mental Incapacity Bill* (HL Paper 189–1, 2003).
[96]   *Report of the Joint Committee on the Draft Mental Incapacity Bill* at para 85.
[97]   See *Report of the Joint Committee on the Draft Mental Incapacity Bill* paras 86–96. The report rejects many of the recommendations for change that it highlights as having been suggested to it.
[98]   *The Government's Response to the Scrutiny Committee's Report on the Draft Mental Incapacity Bill*, at para 4. This can be found on the Department of Constitutional Affairs website at: www.dca.gov.uk/pubs/reports/mental-incapacity.htm.   A   detailed   response   is   available   at www.dca.gov.uk/pubs/reports/mental-incapacity.htm#part2 – see, in particular, the responses to recommendations 17–26.

(b)   a condition of his, or an aspect of his behaviour, which might lead others to make unjustified assumptions about what might be in his best interests.

(2) The person making the determination must consider all the relevant circumstances and, in particular, take the following steps.

(3) He must consider –

(a)   whether it is likely that the person will at some time have capacity in relation to the matter in question, and
(b)   if it appears likely that he will, when that is likely to be.

(4) He must, so far as reasonably practicable, permit and encourage the person to participate, or to improve his ability to participate, as fully as possible in any act done for him and any decision affecting him.

(5) Where the determination relates to life-sustaining treatment he must not, in considering whether the treatment is in the best interests of the person concerned, be motivated by a desire to bring about his death.

(6) He must consider, so far as is reasonably ascertainable –

(a)   the person's past and present wishes and feelings (and, in particular, any relevant written statement made by him when he had capacity),
(b)   the beliefs and values that would be likely to influence his decision if he had capacity, and
(c)   the other factors that he would be likely to consider if he were able to do so.

(7) He must take into account, if it is practicable and appropriate to consult them, the views of –

(a)   anyone named by the person as someone to be consulted on the matter in question or on matters of that kind,
(b)   anyone engaged in caring for the person or interested in his welfare,
(c)   any donee of a lasting power of attorney granted by the person, and
(d)   any deputy appointed for the person by the court,
as to what would be in the person's best interests and, in particular, as to the matters mentioned in subsection (6).

There is much for the decision-maker to ponder, but this may be seen as a disadvantage, because the Act only imposes a duty to take the criteria into account, and thus is more guidance than direction. Indeed, there is no duty to accept the information that has to be sought, and it is open to the decision-maker to disregard it completely if she so wished. Furthermore, contrary to what was proposed by the Law Commission and accepted afterwards following consultation, the influence of substituted judgment has been downplayed, and a return to objectivity sought. This is apparent in the explanatory notes, para 25 of which state that:

It is a key principle of the Bill that all steps and decisions taken for someone who lacks capacity must be taken in the person's best interests by applying an objective test. The best interests principle is an essential aspect of the Bill and builds on the common law while offering further guidance. Given the wide-range of acts, decisions and circumstances that the Bill will cover, best interests is not defined in the Bill. Rather *subsection (1)* makes clear that determining what is in an individual's best interests requires a consideration of all relevant (defined in subsection (11)) circumstances. The clause goes on to list particular steps that must be taken. Best interests is not a test of 'substituted judgement' (what the person would have wanted), but rather it requires a determination made by applying an objective test as to what would be in the person's best interests. All the relevant circumstances, including the factors mentioned in the clause must be considered, but none carries any more weight or priority than another. They must all be balanced in order to determine what would be in the best interests of the individual concerned. The factors in this clause do not provide a definition of best interests and are not exhaustive.

Thus the legislation provides mixed signals. On the one hand, it seeks to reject substituted judgment and return to an objective test. Yet, on the other hand, it emphasises that the checklist is not designed to be an exhaustive list of what may be considered. In this sense, it is hard to see how the concept of best interests can be described as objective at all, as the decision-maker can take any factors that she likes into account, and then accept or reject them according to her own conscience. Indeed, the equivocal language used in s 4 (such as 'regard will be had' and 'take into account') further allows the decision-maker leeway to impose her own will on the definition of the patient's best interests in a particular case.

Although the Act provides for others, such as those given power of attorney, to be given decision-making powers, in many cases it will still fall to doctors to make the decisions and thus determine the patient's best interests, as no such proxy will be designated. In such situations, it can be argued that the Act gives them power that is more reminiscent of *F* than it is of *Re A* and *Re SL*. It is thus imperative, given this flexibility, that medical ethics guidance should provide a solid base for decision-making. Unfortunately, this is not the case.

VII.   Ethical Guidance

The most notable aspect of the GMC's ethical guidance in this area lies is its absence. Indeed, the GMC does not provide specific guidance on sterilisations, and there is also little with respect to the best interests principle. All of the relevant guidance from the GMC can be found in the document concerning consent examined in Chapters 4 and 5.[99] There is no mention of incompetent patients in any of the editions of *Good Medical Practice* except for the latest version, where doctors are simply told that the further guidance on consent includes advice on consent regarding patients who are unable to give their own consent.[100] Written in 1998, *Seeking Patients' Consent* precedes the later cases of

---

[99]   GMC, *Consent: The Ethical Considerations* (GMC, 1998)
[100]   GMC, *Good Medical Practice* (GMC, 2006) para 36.

Re A and *Re SL*, as well as the results of the consultation that led to *Who Decides*, but it was written after the Law Commission report. Best interests are considered in para 25, and the GMC essentially follows the Law Commission's recommendations:

> In deciding what options may be reasonably considered as being in the best interests of a patient who lacks capacity to decide, you should take into account:
>
> — options for treatment or investigation which are clinically indicated;
> — any evidence of the patient's previously expressed preferences, including an advance statement;
> — your own and the health care team's knowledge of the patient's background, such as cultural, religious, or employment considerations;
> — views about the patient's preferences given by a third party who may have other knowledge of the patient, for example the patient's partner, family, carer, tutor-dative (Scotland), or a person with parental responsibility;
> — which option least restricts the patient's future choices, where more than one option (including non-treatment) seems reasonable in the patient's best interest.

The only mention of sterilisation comes in para 26, which suggests to doctors when they might wish to seek court approval before acting:

> Where a patient's capacity to consent is in doubt, *or where differences of opinion about his or her best interests cannot be resolved satisfactorily, you should consult more experienced colleagues and, where appropriate, seek legal advice on whether it is necessary to apply to the court for a ruling. You should seek the court's approval where a patient lacks capacity to consent to a medical intervention which is non-therapeutic or controversial, for example contraceptive sterilisation,* organ donation, withdrawal of life support from a patient in a persistent vegetative state. Where you decide to apply to a court you should, as soon as possible, inform the patient and his or her representative of your decision and of his or her right to be represented at the hearing.[101]

While the GMC's approach to best interests can be seen as proactive at the time, and it certainly preceded the courts' change of approach, it has not since been updated. Moreover, the italicised part of para 26 suggests that the definition of a patient's best interests is a medical decision to be made by doctors, which is less reflective of the tone of the Law Commission report. Overall, however, the concept of best interests is given little more than cursory consideration, and sterilisation itself is not considered at all.

The BMA was similarly reluctant to consider incompetent patients at first, with the 1980 *Handbook* stating that unless a guardian had been appointed, 'no individual or office holder has legal authority to consent to treatment' on behalf of a mentally incompetent adult.[102] No comment was passed on this state of affairs. In the 1988 guidance, this legal issue was also noted, and the BMA emphasised that the legal position led to 'enormous practical difficulties' and

---

[101]   Emphasis added.
[102]   BMA, *Handbook of Medical Ethics* (BMA, 1980) 13.

called for the law to be clarified.[103] However, it also noted that the decision in *Re B* had implied that while nobody could give valid consent on behalf of an adult, '[i]n these cases the courts may rule that the medical intervention will not act against the best interests of the individual'.[104] In terms of the definition of the patient's best interests, the book made it clear that this is for the 'doctor to decide'.[105] The 1993 book contained an entire section on the sterilisation of adults with learning disabilities, and this was divided into two sections, the first considering *Re B* and the right to reproduce, and the second *F v West Berkshire* and the best interests test. With respect to *Re B*, the BMA recognised that the decision had been criticised for its speed and because *B* was not sexually active at the time and thus sterilisation might have been premature.[106] However, it reserved its most stringent criticism for the very notion that contraception could be seen as part of the solution to the potential sexual abuse of incompetent adults, calling it 'perplexing' and referring to the issue as '[o]f continuing concern'.[107] With regard to best interests, the guidance emphasised that although only one judge had held that all sterilisations should receive prior court authorisation, such permission should be sought unless the procedure was performed on 'unambiguous therapeutic grounds'.[108] Moreover, it noted that there was a 'marked reluctance' among doctors to seek judicial authorisation, and that this had led to concern that sterilisations were being carried out unnecessarily.[109] Given the state of the law in 1993, it may be argued that judicial oversight would be more of a cosmetic exercise than anything else but, once again, the 1993 guidance can be seen to go beyond the law in terms of limiting medical practitioners' discretion.

The 2004 update of *Medical Ethics Today*, as might be expected given the size of the book, provides a more detailed examination of the issues, has a section on best interests, and another specifically on sterilisation. It also has the advantage of having been written after the later cases redefining the use of *Bolam* in deciding best interests and the Law Commission report. With regard to best interests, the book notes simply that 'many factors are important in deciding what may benefit … [patients] or be in their best interests'.[110] It continues by providing a list of factors to consider:

— the patient's own wishes and values (where these can be ascertained), including any advance statement
— clinical judgment about the effectiveness of the proposed treatment, particularly in relation to other options

103   BMA, *Philosophy and Practice of Medical Ethics* (BMA, 1988) 32.
104   *Ibid.*
105   *Ibid.*
106   BMA, *Medical Ethics Today: Its Practice and Philosophy* (BMA, 1993) 109.
107   *Ibid* 111.
108   *Ibid* 112.
109   *Ibid.*
110   BMA, *Medical Ethics Today* (BMA, 2004) 108.

— when there is more than one effective option, which option is least restrictive of [sic] the patient's future choices
— the likelihood and extent of any degree of improvement in the patient's condition if treatment is provided
— the views of people close to the patient, especially close relatives, partners, carers, or proxy decision makers about what the patient is likely to see as beneficial
— any knowledge of the patient's religious, cultural, and other non-medical views that may have an impact on the patient's wishes.[111]

What is striking here is the similarity between the BMA and the GMC's checklists, and that first proposed by the Law Commission that eventually became the Mental Capacity Act. Indeed, it would appear that the law and the medical ethics have converged, with the former following the lead of the latter on this point. Nevertheless, the same cannot be said for the BMA book's advice concerning sterilisation. In that section, there is a subsection that specifically considers the sterilisation of people with learning disabilities. It begins by noting that the 'rights of people with learning disabilities to enjoy sexual relationships in private has been an issue of historical debate, and sterilisation of those who lack capacity … has been controversial'.[112] It then states that there are several factors that warn against sterilisation, from the harm it seeks to prevent being insufficient justification, and the proposal being more for the benefit of carers to the risk that sterilisation could mask sexual abuse.[113] It is when the guidance turns to the law that the problems begin. It identifies the fact that Art 12 of the European Convention on Human Rights, incorporated into English Law by the Human Rights Act 1998, provides a right to reproduce, and highlights the fact that in 1976 the courts refused to sanction the sterilisation of a minor because of the 'frustration and resentment the patient would be likely to experience in later life, arising from her inability to have children'.[114] Then, however, it states that a 'similar point was made in the 1989 case of *Re F*,'[115] and that that case confirmed that incapable adults must be treated in their best interests. This was defined as:

— necessary to save life or prevent deterioration or ensure an improvement in the patient's physical or mental health and
— in accordance with a practice accepted at the time by a responsible body of medical opinion skilled in the particular form of treatment in question.[116]

Despite the next paragraph stating that non-therapeutic sterilisations should not be carried out without a court declaration, the above is still a poor representation of what the law on best interests is now, as it takes no account of the judgments in the later cases that sought to reclaim decision-making authority for the courts,

[111] *Ibid* 109.
[112] *Ibid* 235.
[113] *Ibid.*
[114] *Ibid* 236. The case being referred to is *Re D (a minor)* [1976] 1 All ER 326.
[115] *Ibid.*
[116] *Ibid.*

discussed earlier in this chapter. This is all the more perplexing because, on the very same page, a box is provided with a *précis* of the judgment in *Re A*. This concludes that the judgment 'made clear ... that the concept of best interests in such cases relates to the mentally incapacitated person, not to carers or other third parties'.[117] This definition of best interests is thus not only inconsistent with the modern law and the GMC guidance, but it is even inconsistent with what the book said in an earlier chapter! It is difficult to conceive of what a medical practitioner would make of this advice. The fact that the two considerations of best interests occur in different chapters means that some doctors might miss the version that *is* consistent with the law and the GMC. Moreover, best interests does not appear in the index (it is to be found instead as a subheading of 'incapacitated (incompetent) patients'), while 'sterilisation' does. In this regard, the BMA guidance can only be seen as problematic. With the exception of the BMA's inconsistent book, the guidance shown in this chapter tends to reflect the Law Commission's definition of best interests. However, while medical law in the form of the statute and medical ethics may look well integrated in this area of law, neither necessarily supports the more recent view of the courts that sterilisation decisions should contain less medical input. Indeed, this is the Trojan Horse contained in the statute and ethical guidance: that when doctors are asked to make decisions regarding best interests, they may well have more discretion than the later cases would grant them. The current guidance reinforces this approach, and the individual doctor's conscience becomes more, rather than less, important.

VIII. Conclusion

The paradox first identified in Chapter 4 is once again operative and there are similarities between the sets of cases in the two chapters. In both cases the courts began by *Bolam*ising the issue while marginalising the ethical content, and subsequently sought to regain control by recognising the ethical content while paradoxically lessening the role of medical ethics. Nevertheless, there are distinct differences in the two sets of cases, and they arise as a result of the content of the guidance. With risk disclosure, the guidance went beyond the law, and sought to give patients more autonomy than the law was, at first, prepared to grant. If anything, the law eventually caught up with the ethical guidance. With sterilisation, however, the law and the guidance essentially say the same thing, as law reform and ethical guidance seemed to develop in tandem. Indeed the approach taken by the Law Commission, and continued all the way up until the Mental Capacity Act, has been replicated by the ethical guidance from all bodies.

Thus the checklist of factors for determining best interests can be found in both the legal and ethical guidance. In neither case is it meant to be an exhaustive

---

[117]   *Ibid.*

list of factors, and the checklist in all cases has been left vague and open to interpretation. This is, ostensibly, so that all relevant factors can be taken into account in individual cases. The language used bears this out. The wording used in the Mental Capacity Act is even more equivocal. Thus in s 4, for example, it is permissive rather than directive. Subsection (2) provides that the decision-maker must '*consider* all the relevant circumstances'. Subsection (3) provides factors that a doctor 'must *consider*'. In sub-s (4) the decision-maker must 'so far as is reasonably practicable' encourage the patient to participate in decisions. In sub-s (6), she must '*consider*, so far as is reasonably practicable' the patient's past and present wishes. Finally, in sub-s (7), she must '*take into account*, if it is practicable to consult them' the views of carers, relatives, court-appointed deputies and others with decision-making powers.

When the doctor is the decision-maker (although, as previously mentioned, the Act does at least provide for others to fill that role, such as a person granted power of attorney by the patient), then the specific legal requirement is *to think about* the information. She is still left with discretion with respect to whether to comply with it. This may be seen as an even less exacting standard than that used by the courts, in the sense that if the doctor is making the decision she does so effectively unfettered by the information provided about what the patient would have wanted. The element of control sought by the courts in the more recent cases may even be undermined.

This is replicated in the ethical guidance. Paragraph 25 of the GMC document advises doctors of a list of factors that they should 'take into account', and the BMA guidance provides doctors with 'a list of factors to consider'. Once again, the wording is equivocal and permissive. The danger with the language used in the statute and the ethical guidance is that, on the occasions that such decisions need to be made, the decision-makers will feel emboldened to make the choices that their consciences tell them to. As mentioned above, their only duty is to consider rather than to accept and act on information from others, and the ethical guidance has always said that decisions regarding patients' best interests are for *doctors* to make. In turn, the courts might feel bound by the wording of the Act. This would effectively undo what the courts have achieved over the past few years in reclaiming decision-making authority in this area from medical professionals.

Essentially, the sterilisation cases and the law reform in the area tell a story that is far from complete. Just as with risk disclosure, the original *Bolam*ite philosophy of the courts has been replaced by a more patient friendly approach. However, the Mental Capacity Act calls into question whether that new approach will remain. It will be impossible to tell until the Act is tested in court. The medical ethics, again reflecting the situation with risk disclosure, were ahead of the law to begin with when championing the Law Commission's checklist over *Bolam*, and the law has had to catch up. In Chapter 5, we saw medical law and medical ethics cancel each other out. Here, the wording of the ethical guidance and the Mental Capacity Acts cancels itself out. It is just as amorphous as the law and the wording in both the GMC and BMA documents does nothing to stop medical professionals acting on the basis of their own consciences, as all of the fragments of discourse leave the ultimate decision to the discretion of the decision-maker. As Chapter 3 has argued, since Nuremburg this has ceased to be acceptable.

7

The End of Life – Total Abrogation

I. Introduction

If ever there was a topic that self-evidently contained a clear and intrinsic ethical content it is that of issues at the end of life. The cases examined here are examples of instances where the courts have had to adjudicate on questions concerning the withdrawal of life sustaining medical treatment.[1] In this situation, the ethical principle of the sanctity of life may conflict with such a withdrawal and some medical practitioners consider such activities to go against their conception of what it means to be a doctor. That is not to say, however, that in all of the cases the doctors are against the withdrawal. Rather, the cases constitute an eclectic mix, ranging from situations where the patient is incompetent (*Bland*) to those when she is competent at the time of the decision but will become incompetent (*Burke*); and from scenarios where the patient wishes treatment to be discontinued against the advice of medical practitioners (*Ms B*) to ones where they wish to continue treatment but the doctors believe it would be fruitless (*Burke*). Then, the ethical principle of autonomy considered in Chapters 4 and 5 also becomes engaged. A complicating factor in one of the cases is the fluctuating capacity of the patient, in the sense that even if he is competent at the time of the court hearing, he may be incompetent before he dies. Thus, the weight to give the advance wishes of the patient and the opinions of relatives also becomes important.

This chapter therefore contains, in ethical terms, a mixture of old and new. Issues surrounding consent and best interests will again become operative and relevant, while the concept of the sanctity of life will be introduced. It is axiomatic that they will, at times, conflict with each other. Equally predictable is the fact that in this area there is no shortage of ethical guidance and in one of the

---

[1] *Airedale NHS Trust v Bland* [1993] 1 All ER 821; *Re G (Persistent Vegetative State)* [1995] 2 FCR 46; *Ms B v An NHS Hospital Trust* [2002] EWCH 429; *R (on the application of Burke) v General Medical Council* [2004] EWCH 1879; *R (Burke) v General Medical Council* [2005] EWCA Civ 1003.

cases (*Burke*) the GMC's guidance is specifically challenged. When this is combined with the admission by the House of Lords in *Bland* that they had a 'clean slate' on which to create law, it is clear that there is much for this chapter to consider.

II.   *Airedale NHS Trust v Bland* – An Eclectic Mix

A.   The Facts

Anthony Bland was injured in the Hillsborough disaster of 1989. Due to being crushed, his brain was starved of oxygen and he suffered hypoxic brain damage. He was diagnosed as being in a persistent vegetative state (PVS) and had to be fed by naso-gastric tube. He could not see, hear or feel anything, and there was no prospect of recovery. The court was asked to issue a declaration as to the lawfulness of discontinuing the medical care received by Anthony, which would effectively cause his death. The problem was that, as Lord Browne-Wilkinson recognised at the beginning of his judgment, the *Bland* case fell beyond a mere question of legal reasoning due to the fact that medical technology seemed to progress at a faster rate than the common law:

> … behind the questions of law lie moral, ethical, medical and practical issues of fundamental importance to society. As Hoffman LJ in the Court of Appeal emphasised, the law regulating the termination of artificial life support being given to patients must, to be acceptable, reflect a moral attitude which society accepts. This has led judges into the consideration of the ethical and other non-legal problems raised by the ability to sustain life artificially which new medical technology has recently made possible. But in my judgement in giving the legal answer to these questions judges are faced with a dilemma. The ability to sustain life artificially is of relatively recent origin. *Existing law may not provide an acceptable answer to the new legal questions which it raises.*[2]

Thus, the problems confronting the House of Lords were those of a blank canvass and recognition that the questions put to them were intrinsically moral and ethical. There were also legal difficulties to navigate, chief among them the law relating to murder, the 'existing law' referred to above. Indeed, in order for the removal of life-sustaining treatment to be lawful, their Lordships had to make several leaps of logic that were not always strictly credible. First, life-sustaining measures including artificial nutrition and hydration had to be defined as medical treatment rather than care. In this way, once it was determined that continuation of this treatment was not in the patient's best interests, there was no duty to continue to provide it. Such a medicalisation of basic humanitarian care would lead to the *Bolam*isation of the issue. Secondly, a leap had to be made as a direct consequence of this interpretation. Once it was determined that the

---

[2]   *Airedale NHS Trust v Bland* [1993] 1 All ER 821 at 877–8. Emphasis added.

treatment was not in the patient's interests, it still had to be discontinued. The removal of naso-gastric tubes or the switching off of artificial ventilation, for example, would involve acts that intentionally caused death, and thus would constitute murder. The leap undertaken by House of Lords was that they reclassified the removal of such treatment as an omission to treat rather than an act that caused death. This highly controversial definition perhaps defies logic, but was necessary in order to legally justify what the courts were doing. The fact that the decisions involved were ethical rather than clinical is self evident, but for the court to reach its desired conclusion it had to medicalise the issues, and thus abrogate responsibility to medical ethics. All of the judges held that it would be lawful to remove the treatment being given to Anthony Bland.

B. The Decision

i. Lord Keith of Kinkel

The starting point for Lord Keith was what he considered to be the complicating factor in the case, namely that 'it very commonly occurs that a person, due to accident or some other cause, becomes unconscious and is thus not able to give or withhold consent to medical treatment'.[3] His Lordship stated that in this situation under the principle of necessity medical practitioners could apply treatment that was in the best interests of the patient. Here then, according to Lord Keith, was the crux of the issue: in a situation such as that in which Anthony Bland found himself, how could his best interests be calculated?

His Lordship was careful to ensure that his judgment could not be interpreted as advocating euthanasia. Thus, he rejected the arguments by both parties that Anthony Bland's best interests 'favour[ed] discontinuance'.[4] He did not profess to disagree with the statement in itself; rather, he felt doubt about 'this way of putting the matter'.[5] Thus Lord Keith found himself in a quandary. While sympathising with the argument that the best interests of the patient were that he should be allowed to die, he also appeared to feel unable to say so explicitly, and thus his Lordship could not advocate a right to die on the part of Anthony Bland, as it could open the door to euthanasia. Yet he wanted to allow the treatment to be discontinued, and to this end held that it was impossible to 'make any relevant comparison between continued existence and the absence of it' in this case.[6] Indeed,

---

[3]   [1993] 1 All ER 821 at 860.
[4]   [1993] 1 All ER 821 at 860.
[5]   [1993] 1 All ER 821 at 860.
[6]   [1993] 1 All ER 821 at 861.

to an individual with no cognitive capacity whatever, and no prospect of recovering any such capacity in this world, it must be a matter of complete indifference whether he lives or dies.[7]

Lord Keith therefore needed an opening through which he could arrive at his desired conclusion without endorsing euthanasia. The opening he found was the *Bolam* test. Lord Keith defined medical treatment as widely as possible, encompassing the feeding of Anthony Bland. If it was a form of medical treatment, then the *Bolam* test applied, so 'a medical practitioner is under no duty to continue to treat such a patient where a large body of informed and responsible medical opinion is to the effect that no benefit at all would be conferred by continuance'.[8] The issue could thus be resolved to his satisfaction through medicalisation.

However, one final obstacle remained: that of the principle of the sanctity of life. As his Lordship recognised, it was a concern of the state and thus the judiciary, but this was not a problem, because the principle was not absolute:

> It does not compel a medical practitioner on pain of criminal sanctions to treat a patient, who will die if he does not, contrary to the express wishes of the patient. It does not authorise forcible feeding of prisoners on hunger strike. It does not compel the temporary keeping alive of patients who are terminally ill where to do so would merely prolong their suffering … it does no violence to the principle to hold that it is lawful to cease to give medical treatment and care to a PVS patient who has been in that state for over three years, considering that to do so involves invasive manipulation of the patient's body *to which he has not consented* and which confers no benefit upon him.[9]

This was an odd way to frame his conclusion. As he had stated earlier in his judgment, the principle of necessity allowed medical practitioners to give treatment in the best interests of the patient if she was unable to consent. While it was true that, using the *Bolam* test, continued treatment was not in Anthony Bland's best interests, to argue that treatment should be discontinued because he had not consented to it was illogical as there is no way that Anthony could indicate his consent or refusal with regards to anything. Indeed, as mentioned above, his Lordship had argued that, for Anthony Bland, continued existence would be a matter of 'complete indifference' to him. Legal and ethical principles were therefore a means to an end for Lord Keith, allowing him to justify his decision without coming too close to advocating euthanasia. Thus, in order to reach his desired conclusion, he had to *Bolam*ise the issue, and thus abrogate decision-making authority to the medical profession and its ethics.

ii.   Lord Goff

Lord Goff's judgment lacked nothing in comprehensiveness. In considering the legal and ethical aspects of the case, he explored the law and medical ethics

---

7   [1993] 1 All ER 821 at 861.
8   [1993] 1 All ER 821 at 861.
9   [1993] 1 All ER 821 at 861. Emphasis added.

discourse published by the BMA (in the form of a discussion paper that he held constituted the prevalent ethical view[10]) and the views of academics. He thus examined both unofficial and semi-formal medical ethics. The GMC's absence can be explained by the fact that it had published no advice on the issue. Perhaps more than Lord Keith, Lord Goff recognised the practical ramifications that an unclear or ill-considered judgment would have on the medical profession:

> It would, in my opinion, be a deplorable state of affairs if no authoritative guidance could be given to the medical profession in a cases such as the present, so that a doctor would be compelled either to act contrary to the principles of medical ethics established by his professional body or to risk a prosecution for murder. As Compton J said in *Barber* v *Superior Court of Los Angeles County* (1983) 147 Cal App 3d 1006 at 1011: 'a murder prosecution is a poor way to design an ethical or moral code for doctors who are faced with decisions concerning the use of costly and extraordinary "life support" equipment'.[11]

Thus, his presumption was that to continue to treat Anthony was unethical, and that the law should therefore allow the ethical course of action to be taken. In order to achieve this, the first issue that he examined was that of the sanctity of life, which he defined as a non-medical issue.[12] He referred instead to the protection given to the principle in Art 2 of the European Convention on Human Rights,[13] and Art 6 of the International Covenant on Civil and Political Rights.[14] He continued by stating that: 'the principle of the sanctity of life must yield to the principle of self-determination ... and, for present purposes perhaps more important, the doctor's duty to act in the best interests of his patient must likewise be qualified'.[15] This led Lord Goff, to conclude that,

> there is no question of the patient having committed suicide, nor therefore of the doctor having aided or abetted him in doing so. It is simply that the patient has, as he is entitled to do, declined to consent to treatment which might or would have the effect of prolonging his life and the doctor has, in accordance with his duty, complied with his patient's wishes.[16]

Lord Goff distinguished this from euthanasia by arguing that the latter occurred when the doctor *actively* ended the life of the patient, such as with a lethal injection. However, he recognised the theoretical flaw in what the House of Lords was doing in trying to distinguish the decision in *Bland* from euthanasia:

> It is true that the drawing of this distinction may lead to a charge of hypocrisy, because it can be asked why, if the doctor, by discontinuing treatment, is entitled in consequence

---

[10]   BMA, *Treatment of Patients in Persistent Vegetative State* (BMA, 1992).
[11]   *Airedale NHS Trust v Bland* [1993] 1 All ER 821 at 865.
[12]   *Ibid.*
[13]   Convention for the Protection of Human Rights and Fundamental Freedoms (Rome, 4 November 1950; TS 71 (1953); Cmnd 8969), now the Human Rights Act 1998.
[14]   New York, 19 December 1966; TS 6 (1977) Cmnd 6702.
[15]   *Airedale NHS Trust v Bland* [1993] 1 All ER 821 at 866.
[16]   [1993] 1 All ER 821 at 866.

to let his patient die, it should not be lawful to put him out of his misery straight away, in a more humane manner, by a lethal injection, rather than let him linger on in pain until he dies. But the law does not feel able to authorise euthanasia, even in circumstances such as these, for, once euthanasia is recognised as lawful in these circumstances, it is difficult to see any logical basis for excluding it in others.[17]

In setting out the parameters of how far the law was willing to extend itself in these circumstances, Lord Goff was implicitly referring to the doctrine of double effect, a central point of debate for moral philosophers and applied ethicists.[18] The fact that Lord Goff had given consideration to academic material was demonstrated in the following paragraph when, in answering the theoretical question posed by the distinction he had made, he relied on the work of Professor Glanville Williams to explain that when the doctor switched off a life-support machine, it was 'in substance not an act but an omission to struggle' and that 'the omission is not a breach of duty by the doctor, because he is not obliged to continue in a hopeless case'.[19] In utilising an academic text in this way, and indicating that he has read others, Lord Goff showed a great willingness to deliver the comprehensive judgment that he felt was needed in this case by building his judgment from founding principles rather than trying to fit it into existing law. Furthermore, he was comfortable not only with purely legal discussions, but also with more philosophical ones. Indeed, he continued by further exploring the philosophical distinction between euthanasia and discontinuing treatment, and how in some cases the hastening of death under the doctrine of double effect may in fact be in the patient's best interests.[20]

Only when these philosophical and theoretical issues had been considered did his Lordship turn to the question before him, but he was anxious that the question should be correctly framed:

> The question is sometimes put in striking or emotional term, which can be misleading. For example, in the case of a life support system, it is sometimes asked: should a doctor be entitled to switch it off, or to pull the plug? And then it is asked: is it in the best interests of the patient that a doctor should be able to switch the life support system off, when it will inevitably result in the patient's death? Such an approach has rightly been criticised as misleading, for example by Professor Ian Kennedy (in his paper in *Treat Me Right, Essays in Medical Law and Ethics* (1988)), and by Thomas J in *Auckland Area Health Board v A-G* [1993] 1 NZLR 235 at 247. This is because the question is not

---

[17]   [1993] 1 All ER 821 at 867.

[18]   For a fuller, yet refreshingly simple, explanation of double effect see Glover J, *Causing Death and Saving Lives* (Penguin, 1990) 86–91.

[19]   *Airedale NHS Trust v Bland* [1993] 1 All ER 821 n 1 at 867. Lord Goff quoted from p 282 of Glanville Williams, *Textbook of Criminal Law* (2nd edn, London, Stevens, 1983). Although this is essentially a legal text, the discussion examined by his Lordship is one that can be considered philosophical in nature. Indeed, much of medical law (and thus the lawyers' contribution to unofficial medical ethics) is a criminal law/law of torts hybrid. As a result, this section classifies such comments as unofficial medical ethics.

[20]   *Airedale NHS Trust v Bland* [1993] 1 All ER 821 at 868–9.

whether it is in the best interests of the patient that his life should be prolonged by the continuance of this form of medical treatment or care.[21]

Thus, Lord Goff provided further evidence of his reading and his comfort in discussing the subject was similarly evident. The judgments of Lords Goff and Keith can therefore be seen as markedly different. Lord Goff was more honest about what he was saying, and this can perhaps be attributed to his greater use of ethical principles. Indeed, his building of his judgment from the bottom up, in the sense of looking at the principles then framing the law around it, meant that it would be impossible to do otherwise. However, he also concluded by deferring the decision to *Bolam*.[22] Indeed, his starting point had been that it was unethical to continue to treat Anthony, and his use of unofficial and semi-formal medical ethics was designed to ensure that the law agreed. In this sense, he not only abrogated responsibility to the medical profession and its ethics, but actually changed the law to fit in with what he perceived as the medical ethics. In his ultimate deference to the medical profession, however, he was not alone.

iii.   Lord Browne-Wilkinson

Lord Browne-Wilkinson also recognised the ethical dimension to the case and confronted it directly. Indeed, he appeared comfortable referring to philosophical questions that would have taxed many a professional philosopher. For example, one of the ethical problems he referred to was '[w]hat is meant now by "life" in the moral precept which requires respect for the sanctity of human life?'[23] Furthermore, he also recognised that the answers to the ethical and moral questions posed by the case were entirely subjective, and differences of opinion existed not only in society, but also within the medical profession itself.

   Difficulties arose, however, as he sought to answer the questions that he had identified as being important to the case. Thus, after stating that differences of opinion on these matters were bound to occur, his Lordship recognised that if judges were to develop new law to regulate these circumstances, then the new law would necessarily reflect those individual judges' personal morality and ethical codes. However, in his view this would be an undesirable prospect:

> Where a case raises wholly new moral and social issues, in my judgement it is not for the judges to seek to develop new, all-embracing, principles of law in a way which reflects the individual judges' moral stance when society as a whole is substantially divided on the relevant moral issues. Moreover, it is not legitimate for a judge in reaching a view as to what is for the benefit of the one individual whose life is in issue to take into account the wider practical issues as to allocation of limited financial resources or the impact on third parties of altering the time at which death occurs.[24]

---

[21]   [1993] 1 All ER 821 at 869.
[22]   [1993] 1 All ER 821 at 871.
[23]   [1993] 1 All ER 821 at 878.
[24]   [1993] 1 All ER 821 at 878.

This led Lord Browne-Wilkinson to conclude that until Parliament could intervene the courts had to make use of the existing law. However, an issue that his Lordship could not avoid was that *someone* had to make such decisions until Parliament intervened, and it was at this stage that he considered the medical profession and its ethics. He started his analysis by declaring his lament that the medical profession could not make these decisions unhindered any more:

> In the past, doctors exercised their own discretion, in accordance with medical ethics, in cases such as these. To the great advantage of society, they took the responsibility of deciding whether the perpetuation of life was pointless. But there are now present amongst the medical and nursing staff of hospitals those who genuinely believe in the sanctity of human life, no matter what the quality of that life, and report doctors who take such decisions to the authorities with a view to prosecution for a criminal offence. I am not criticising such people: they are acting in accordance with their own moral standards But their actions have made it extremely risky for a doctor to take a decision of this kind when his action may lie on the borderline of legality.[25]

What is notable here is the automatic and instinctive confidence in medical professionals, and lack of trust in the judiciary, to make such decisions. Indeed, why was it not the place of judges to create new law on this area because it may reflect their personal morality, yet doctors could make them at will without the same danger? If the actions of doctors were on the 'borderline of legality', then surely it was imperative that the judiciary settled the legal position, even if it meant creating new law. Furthermore, the lack of clarity in the law also made it *even more* desirable that these cases were reported. If doctors were breaking the law, it must be in the best interests of society that they are brought to justice. It would seem from this Hippocratic confidence in the individual morality of doctors that his Lordship was preparing to abrogate responsibility to the medical profession and its ethics. He duly did so by agreeing that the test in this case should be that of the best interests of the patient, to be decided by the medical profession subject to the *Bolam* test.[26] Such a simplistic approach, designed to take responsibility away from the courts and give it instead to the medical profession, was explicitly stated with reference to the BMA discussion paper and his Lordship held that compliance with this, in itself, would satisfy the *Bolam* requirement.[27] Thus his Lordship considered the ethics of the medical profession as quasi-legal in status, even if it did not come from the GMC. Nevertheless, it is the reasons for this that are interesting. By lamenting that, on a legal issue, those unhappy with the actions of doctors were complaining about them, his Lordship effectively stated that the issue was one for medical ethics rather than law. For Lord Browne-Wilkinson, judicial oversight was not a priority, and indeed was to be discouraged.

[25]   [1993] 1 All ER 821 at 880.
[26]   [1993] 1 All ER 821 at 882.
[27]   [1993] 1 All ER 821 at 883.

iv.   Lord Mustill

Lord Mustill's judgment is something of a paradox. Although stating that the ethical arguments had been well covered by his colleagues and that he would not consider them himself he did do so, and his Lordship's comfort with them was clear. Indeed, his was the most sensitive judgment in the case, and while it addressed many of the same issues as Lord Browne-Wilkinson, it arrived at its conclusion by a completely different route. Lord Mustill began by identifying two questions which his judgment would consider:

> First, the role of the court, that the nature and function which the court is being called upon to perform, and the suitability of the court to perform it. Second, the consistency of the steps authorised by the two declarations now under appeal ... with the existing criminal law.[28]

It is the first of these questions that is of interest to this chapter, as his Lordship considered, under this heading, the place of the medical profession and its ethics with regards to the courts. Before turning to the issues surrounding the medical profession, however, his Lordship first thought it necessary to inject some much-needed honesty into his analysis of events. Anxious to clarify exactly what was proposed in the decision the court had to make, he argued that the distinction between letting someone die and euthanasia amounted to little more than a semantic one, and that 'however much the terminologies may differ the ethical status of the two courses of action is for all relevant purposes indistinguishable'.[29] Lord Mustill, with that argument, succeeded in bringing into perspective exactly what it was that the court was considering. It is perhaps therefore unsurprising that, given the importance of the matter, his Lordship was unwilling to abrogate responsibility to the medical profession in the way that Lord Browne-Wilkinson and the others had done. Indeed, he considered that despite the ethical nature of the case, the issues pertained to general ethics rather than medical ones. This led him to a different conclusion than his colleagues, in that in Lord Mustill's view the court should maintain a modicum of control over such decisions:

> If the criteria for the legitimacy of the proposed conduct are essentially factual, a decision upon them is one which the courts are well accustomed to perform, and may properly be obtained through the medium of an application for declaratory relief. If however they contain an element of ethical judgement, for example if the law requires the decision-maker to consider whether a certain course of action is 'in the best interests' of the patient, the skill and experience of the judge will carry him only so far. They will help him to clear the ground by marshalling the considerations which are said to be relevant, eliminating errors of logic, and so on. But when the intellectual part of the task is complete and the decision-maker has to choose the factors which he will take into account, attach relevant weights to them and then strike a balance *the judge is no*

---

[28]   [1993] 1 All ER 821 at 885.
[29]   [1993] 1 All ER 821 at 885.

better equipped, though no worse, than anyone else. In the end, it is a matter of personal choice, dictated by his or her background, upbringing, education, convictions and temperament. Legal expertise gives no special advantage here.[30]

The difference between that statement and the approach of, for example, Lord Browne-Wilkinson is striking. Lord Mustill did not agree that the medical profession was the best arbiter of these issues, and that the courts should grant responsibility for them to the doctors. Judges, according to Lord Mustill, had no advantage but also no disadvantage over anyone. This also highlights the contrast in what their Lordships considered to be the reason for the medical profession to go to court to obtain declarations. While Lord Browne-Wilkinson saw the courts as effectively a rubber stamp, Lord Mustill viewed this as the courts being anxious to 'ensure that the doctors act, as they themselves wish to act, only in accordance with the law'.[31] The implication was that ethics should thus follow the law, rather than the reverse. In other words, the level of oversight envisioned was much greater. This argument shifted the balance from 'doctor knows best' to a recognition that doctors were not better qualified than others to make non-medical judgements. This was further highlighted when Lord Mustill objected to the *Bolam* test on the grounds that 'the decision is ethical, not medical, and ... there is no reason why on such a decision the opinions of doctors should be decisive'.[32] He declined, however, to expand on what he would have done himself, stating that to do so would make 'no difference to the outcome of the appeal'.[33]

Thus the ethics of which Lord Mustill spoke were not those of the medical profession; indeed, he did not mention or consider the BMA guidelines given such weight by his colleagues in the case. In part, this may be because he was uncomfortable with a simple application of the *Bolam* test in order to decide such issues. This, in turn, was because his Lordship did not consider the matter to be medical in nature. In essence, Lord Mustill was the only judge who gave primacy to the law, and this is drawn directly from his recognition that the decision to be made was not a technical medical one. Equally, he was unique in setting out openly and sensitively exactly what the case involved. Unfortunately, in the context of the other judgements, his 'maverick' view that the issues were not medical in nature is outnumbered; yet he deserves credit for recognising that in matters pertaining to medical treatment the word 'ethical' does not always have to have the prefix 'medical' attached to it.

[30]   [1993] 1 All ER 821 at 886. Emphasis added.
[31]   [1993] 1 All ER 821 at 886.
[32]   [1993] 1 All ER 821 at 895.
[33]   [1993] 1 All ER 821 at 895.

C. Medical Ethics

Two aspects stand out with respect to the House of Lords' views on medical ethics in this case. The first is that there is a wide range of approaches regarding the amount of ethical guidance that the judges cited. Lords Keith and Mustill, for example, did not refer to the BMA document. This is in marked contrast to Lords Browne-Wilkinson and Goff, who variously took the BMA discussion paper to be quasi-legal, or considered it to be the philosophical underpinnings of what they were considering. The second aspect is a consequence of the first: there is a variety in how much law *creation* the judges were engaged in, and how they reached their conclusions. Nevertheless, all of the judges except Lord Mustill agreed that *Bolam* should apply to the determination of whether the continuation of treatment would be in Anthony Bland's best interests. In this way, they effectively abrogated responsibility for the matter to medical ethics. The judgment of Lord Browne-Wilkinson most explicitly reflected this, in the sense that, despite recognising the ethical issues, he not only disqualified himself from decision-making, but gave total control to the medical profession and its ethics. For Lord Keith, the ethics were basically ignored. Medicalisation was a means to an end. Lord Goff took a far more expansive approach, but was ultimately no less deferential to the medical profession. He argued that in such an important issue advice for the profession (albeit from the semi-formal sector) was to be desired and expected, and the medical profession had it in the BMA's discussion paper. Issued in 1992 by the BMA's medical ethics committee, his Lordship summarised the four safeguards which it says should be observed before discontinuing life support:

> (1) every effort should be made at rehabilitation for at least six months after the injury; (2) the diagnosis of irreversible PVS should not be considered confirmed until at least 12 months after the injury, with the effect that any decision to withhold life-prolonging treatment will be delayed for that period; (3) the diagnosis should be agreed by two other independent doctors; and (4) generally, the wishes of the patient's immediate family will be given great weight.[34]

Lord Goff attached great weight to the advice and appeared unconcerned by the lack of guidance from the GMC. He appeared content to rely on this semi-formal document in the absence of any from the formal sector of discourse. The danger for the courts lay in giving undue importance to documents advising medical professionals on the basis that they constituted satisfaction of the *Bolam* test. This is particularly true if the guidance does not emanate from the GMC, as the law then exacerbates fragmentation and surrenders oversight. Indeed, the BMA document was not even guidance but a discussion paper. But Lord Goff did not recognise this, and this is precisely what he did:

---

[34] [1993] 1 All ER 821 at 871.

Study of this document has left me in no doubt that if a doctor treating a PVS patient acts in accordance with the medical practice now being evolved by the medical ethics committee of the British Medical Association he will be acting with the benefit of guidance from a responsible and competent body of relevant professional opinion, as required by the *Bolam* test.[35]

However, the *Bolam* test has not always encouraged good practice over common practice, and certainly did not do so when *Bland* was being heard. Indeed, it is a recipe for paternalism, something that did not appear to perturb his Lordship. Thus Lord Goff accepted the committee's view that the relatives of the patient should have no determinative say over the final decision regarding the withdrawal of treatment: 'if that were not so, the relatives would be able to dictate to the doctors what is in the best interests of the patient, which cannot be right'.[36] The issue was thus medicalised, and the focus of his Lordship's judgment turned to the medical profession and how it could interact with the law:

In these circumstances, what is required is an understanding by both the judges and the doctors of each other's respective functions, and *in particular a determination by the judges not merely to understand the problems facing the medical profession in cases of this kind, but also to regard their professional standards with respect*. Mutual understanding between doctors and the judges is the best way to ensure the evolution of a sensitive and sensible legal framework for the treatment and care of patients, with a sound ethical base, in the interests of the patients themselves.[37]

The sound ethical base being referred to here was that of the medical profession. The subtext of the quote is that the medical profession, if it had an ethical position on a certain situation, could now expect that the courts would do all they could to accommodate it within the law. In the final analysis, medical ethics had the determinative say for Lord Goff. Nevertheless, at least he recognised the importance of examining them, thus maintaining some pretence at oversight. In this kind of case, the first in the United Kingdom to deal with this issue, the views of the medical profession were naturally of great importance, as principles were being developed rather than applied. Perhaps due to this, Lord Goff went to some lengths to study the legal and philosophical background to the issues in this case, and indeed some categorisation of discourse is evident. While aware of unofficial medical ethics, his Lordship prioritised the semi-formal document emanating from the BMA. The unofficial ethics he considered was there to give his reasoning background, but he still appeared to view medical ethics as something for the medical profession.

Lord Mustill was less deferential to medical ethics because he refused to abrogate decision-making responsibility to the medical profession. Thus, he did not support the use of *Bolam*, and he saw the case as a matter for the criminal

---

[35] [1993] 1 All ER 821 at 872.
[36] [1993] 1 All ER 821 at 872.
[37] [1993] 1 All ER 821 at 872. Emphasis added.

law. It is therefore of no surprise that he too did not mention the BMA guidelines, as they were irrelevant to his legalistic approach. That is not to say, however, that he did not recognise the ethical parameters to the case. On the contrary, it is precisely this recognition that led him to conclude that the case was for the courts rather than doctors to judge.

Lord Mustill apart, despite still not seeing their way clear to question the authority of the medical profession in matters pertaining to medical treatment, at least the judges were widening the spectrum of what they would consider, in contrast to other cases at around the same time such as *F v West Berkshire*. This may have been because they could not avoid doing so in *Bland*. Yet, while the judges showed an increased willingness to discuss the ethical issues underlining cases, they retained a propensity to capitulate to the medical profession. As the next case demonstrates, this capitulation was not an isolated event.

III.   *Re G –* More Unabashed Abrogation

A.   The Facts

The High Court reconsidered the problem of patients in PVS three years after *Bland*, albeit with a slightly different question to examine. In *Re G*, the issue was the weight, if any, to be given to the views of the patient's relatives.[38] G was injured in a motorcycle accident and diagnosed as being in PVS by five separate consultant neurologists. The accepted medical view was that G was in an even deeper state of PVS than Anthony Bland; however, G's family did not agree. Some, in particular his mother, felt that, having seen media reports, G's case was not hopeless, and thus resisted efforts made by the treatment team to withdraw his artificial nutrition. G's wife, on the other hand, had accepted that the feeding might be withdrawn. The hospital, believing continued treatment not to be in his best interests, sought a declaration concerning the lawfulness of withdrawing the feeding regime despite the disagreement of G's mother. The case is chosen because it demonstrates just how far *Bolam*isation was allowed to go, and how deferential the courts were to any ethical guidance that they identified.

B.   The Decision

As in *Bland*, BMA guidelines were considered, and Sir Stephen Brown P began his judgment by considering the guidelines that were issued after the House of Lords decision in *Bland*. In particular, the President drew attention to para 5, which considered the 'views of people close to the patient':

---

[38]   *Re G (Persistent Vegetative State)* [1995] 2 FCR 46.

> It is *good practice* for the doctors to consult the wishes of people close to the patient but their views alone cannot determine the treatment of the PVS patient. People close to the patient may be able to throw light on the wishes of the PVS patient regarding the prolongation of treatment and this is likely to be helpful in decision making. *Treatment decisions however must be based upon the doctors' assessment of the patient's best interests.*[39]

Two points are apparent: first, the final decision as to the patient's best interests was deemed a medical rather than social construct; secondly, it was determined to be 'good practice' to consult the views of relatives. This was not therefore an unequivocal requirement, but merely an indication of what the doctor should do. The aim of the consultation was to ascertain the wishes of the patient, which may be 'helpful' in the decision-making process. In this sense, it is a reflection of the 'checklist of factors' approach that has found favour with respect to determining a patient's best interests in Chapter 6. Nevertheless, the final sentence appears to suggest that even if the views of relatives were sought, and the wishes of the patient ascertained, the decision remained medical in nature. Sir Stephen Brown accepted both of these points without analysis or criticism, and made them the legal basis of his judgment. Thus, after demonstrating that the treatment team had consulted G's relatives, the President noted that 'the difficulty [in the case] is made plain when one has to consider where the responsibility lies for the treatment of Mr G'.[40] Further, 'I have no doubt that the law requires, as the BMA guidelines indicate, that treatment decisions must be based on the doctor's assessment of the patient's best interests'.[41] Therefore, having accepted that the decision was for the medical practitioners and their ethics, all that was left for Sir Stephen Brown was to verify that consultation had taken place:

> I have had to consider very carefully how the mother's opposition should be treated for, as the BMA guidelines make clear, it is very important that all those who have to consider the future treatment of a PVS patient should take into account the views of close relatives.[42]

For the judge, then, once the BMA guidance was complied with, the law would merely be a rubber stamp. In this way, it can be seen that the legal standard was totally subsumed by the ethical. Indeed, this was to become the basis of the decision to grant the declaration. Sir Stephen Brown held that the treatment team had sought the opinion of the relatives, and reiterated that the final decision was medical. As he noted, the hospital's 'application is well-founded in seeking to give effect to the patient's best interests'.[43]

---

[39]   [1995] 2 FCR 46 at 49. The BMA document quoted is BMA, *Guidelines for the Treatment of Patients in a Persistent Vegetative State* (BMA, 1993). Emphasis added.

[40]   *Re G (Persistent Vegetative State)* [1995] 2 FCR 46 at 50.

[41]   [1995] 2 FCR 46 at 50.

[42]   [1995] 2 FCR 46 at 50.

[43]   [1995] 2 FCR 46 at 51.

C.   Medical Ethics

The noticeable factor in the court's treatment of medical ethics is the confidence displayed in it to regulate the behaviour of the treatment team. It made no difference that it came once again from the semi-formal sector. There was, moreover, a Hippocratic confidence displayed in the individual morality of doctors. For example the head of the treatment team, a consultant referred to as Mr J, had said in evidence that he would not withdraw the feeding regime if G's wife changed her mind and refused consent to that course of action. Sir Stephen Brown nevertheless held that a declaration by the court that it would be lawful to withdraw artificial nutrition could still be appropriate as he had 'no doubt that all these matters will be carefully taken into account and that the wishes of the patient's wife in that regard will be fully respected and implemented'.[44] Like Lord Donaldson in *Re W*, as we saw in Chapter 5, the confidence in medical ethics extended to presuming that the doctor's ethics or morality would prevent her from behaving in a way that *the law* would allow.

Thus, the only way that the respect for G's wife's wishes could be ensured was if *medical ethics* was to prevent Mr J and his team from disregarding them. Indeed, the President was granting a declaration allowing the team to stop feeding G. The basis of that decision was the fact that the ultimate arbiters of the patient's best interests were the treatment team. If Mr J and G's wife were subsequently to disagree with respect to further treatment, there would be no legal bar to Mr J proceeding with any treatment option that he considered to be in G's best interests – notwithstanding any disagreement on the part of G's wife. Rather, just as in *Re W*, the onus would fall on medical ethics to prevent a development that was legally possible from occurring, even though the medical ethics that he himself cited did not do this. After the sensitivity to principle demonstrated by some of the House of Lords in *Bland*, it was unfortunate to see that approach ignored so soon afterwards. Nevertheless, it is clear in this case that Sir Stephen Brown demonstrated an uncritical confidence in medical ethics akin to that of Sir John Donaldson MR in *Re W*. In *Re G* the court had a clean slate similar to that in *Bland*, and chose to follow the ethical advice rather than seek to formulate comprehensive legal principle. The danger inherent in the decision in *Bland*, that the law's high regard for medical ethics might allow ethics to subsume law and thus eradicate judicial oversight, can therefore be seen to have materialised in *Re G*. Medical ethics was given a level of trust by the judge that we have not seen made so explicit since Chapter 5. In this most sensitive of issues, such an approach can only be seen as perplexing. Furthermore, as the next case demonstrates, not all doctors can be trusted to follow ethical guidance.

---

[44]   [1995] 2 FCR 46 at 50.

IV.   *Ms B* – When Ethics are not 'Ethics'

A.   The Facts

If any case in this area can correctly be termed a 'right to die' case, then it is this one.[45] Ms B suffered a cavernoma in 1999 due to a malformation of blood vessels in her spinal column. After being informed by her doctors of the possibility of a further bleed, and the need for further surgery which might result in severe disability, she composed and executed a living will. This stipulated that, in the event that she was to suffer from a 'life threatening condition, permanent mental impairment or permanent unconsciousness' treatment should be withdrawn.[46] Her condition improved and she left the hospital and returned to work. However, in 2001 the left side of her body weakened and she was readmitted to hospital. She had suffered an intramedullary spine cavernoma, which left her tetraplegic. A few days later, she was transferred to the intensive care unit of the hospital where she began to experience respiratory problems. She was treated with a ventilator, which she became reliant upon until the hearing in 2002.

Less than ten days after being transferred to the intensive care unit (ICU), Ms B informed her doctors about the existence of the living will and that she did not wish to be ventilated. She was told that the living will was not specific enough to cover the situation that she was in and a month later she underwent an operation to remove the cavernoma. This was a partial success. Ms B regained the ability to move her head and to articulate words. Nevertheless, she was disappointed in the results and for the first time specifically asked for the ventilator to be switched off. Three days later, having been assessed by a consultant psychiatrist, she was returned to the ICU, where she remained until the case was heard. She again requested that the ventilator be switched off and a week later asked her solicitors to formally request this again. Following psychiatric assessments, it became apparent that there were fluctuating opinions concerning her competence to make her own decisions.

Consultant psychiatrists Dr L and Dr E examined her separately on 10 and 11 April 2001 and both found that she had capacity. However, on 12 April Dr E amended her report to conclude that Ms B did not in fact have capacity and Dr L then did the same. Preparations that had been agreed with Ms B, such as arranging for her to say goodbye to her family, to prepare her for the withdrawal of the ventilator, were cancelled at this point. More disagreements followed about her care and the hospital's assessment of her mental capacity was reconsidered. By August 2001 the hospital felt that Ms B had regained the mental capacity to make her own decisions, but was unwilling to switch off the ventilator. As a compromise, she was offered referral to a weaning centre to pursue a programme

---

[45]   *Ms B v An NHS Hospital Trust* [2002] EWCH 429.
[46]   [2002] EWCH 429 at para 4.

of one-way weaning. This would have reduced the breaths given by the ventilator over a period of time in an attempt to urge her body to breath on its own. However, in contrast to two-way programmes, if her body did not respond the frequency of breaths from the ventilator would not be increased, with the effect that Ms B would die. She rejected this for two reasons; first, the length of time which this would take, approximately three weeks, and, secondly, the fact that no pain killers would be provided within this treatment.

B. The Decision

The case was finally heard in March 2002. As Butler-Sloss P noted, the crucial issue was whether Ms B had the mental capacity to make her own decisions. The President began her analysis with the principle of autonomy and she highlighted the fact that it was well established in English law.[47] She noted that '[t]his approach is identical with the jurisprudence in other parts of the world'[48] and, in support of this, cited the case of *Cruzan v Missouri Department of Health*.[49] She quoted the US Supreme Court as holding that:

[n]o right is held more sacred, or is more carefully guarded ... than the right of every individual to the possession and control of his own person, free from all restraint or interference of others, unless by clear and unquestionable authority of law.[50]

Butler-Sloss P thus appeared to define the concept of autonomy as legal in nature, and certainly it was emphatically one that has traditionally been protected by law.[51] This became important when the President considered her next, competing principle: the sanctity of life. She not only recognised that the two principles were in conflict with each other in the case before her, but she also categorised the latter as separate in nature to the former:

Society and the medical profession in particular are concerned with the equally fundamental principle of the sanctity of life. The interface between the two principles of autonomy and sanctity of life is of great concern to the treating clinicians in the present case.[52]

Thus, the principle of the sanctity of life, rather than being of concern to the law in the way that autonomy was deemed to be, was instead of concern to 'society and the medical profession'. The President did not elaborate on what this might mean, but it is at least arguable that the reference to the medical profession was

---

[47]   She gave quotes from *S v McC: W v W* [1972] AC 25; *Re F (Mental Patient: Sterilisation)* [1990] 2 AC 1; *Re T (Adult: Refusal of Treatment)* [1993] Fam 95 and *Re MB (Medical Treatment)* [1997] 2 FLR 426 (see *Ms B v An NHS Hospital Trust* [2002] EWCH 429 at paras 17–20).

[48]   *Ms B v An NHS Hospital Trust* [2002] EWCH 429 at para 21.

[49]   *Cruzan v Missouri Department of Health* (1990) 110 S Ct 2841.

[50]   In *Ms B v An NHS Hospital Trust* [2002] EWCH 429 at para 21.

[51]   *Ms B v An NHS Hospital Trust* [2002] EWCH 429 at para 21.

[52]   [2002] EWCH 429 at para 22. Emphasis added.

meant to refer to medical ethics. This is supported by the fact that, as discussed below, she later mentioned more than once that the doctors treating Ms B considered the removal of ventilation to be 'unethical'.

Butler-Sloss P was thus presented with something of a dilemma. On the one hand, the law subscribed to the primacy of autonomy, yet on the other 'society and the medical profession' were concerned with the sanctity of life. In the case before her, the two principles could only be seen as mutually exclusive and she would have to choose between them. Thus, if the reference to the 'medical profession' referred to medical ethics, the President had to choose between the law and those ethics. To justify her preference for the former, she provided several quotes from cases including one from Lord Goff in Bland:

> [I]t is established that the principle of self-determination requires that respect must be given to the wishes of the patient ... To this extent, the principle of the sanctity of human life must yield to the principle of self-determination ... and for present purposes perhaps most important, the doctor's duty to act in the best interests of his patient must likewise be qualified. On this basis, it has been held that a patient of sound mind may, if properly informed, require that life support should be discontinued ... It is simply that the patient has, as he is entitled to do, declined to consent to treatment ... and the doctor has, in accordance with his duty, complied with his patient's wishes.[53]

So the legal principle of autonomy clearly trumped the ethical one of the sanctity of life. Thus, the potential conflict was immediately and easily resolved. Indeed, the ethical aspects to the decision were never actually examined in detail in the judgment. Certainly, there was no examination of ethical principle and discourse in the way that there was in *Bland*. The closest that the court came was to examine an article considering the concept of autonomy.[54] Yet, of course, the principle of autonomy had already been defined as legal rather than ethical in nature, and there was also no discussion of the principle of the sanctity of life, other than its categorisation as less important than autonomy. However, that is not to say that medical ethics was absent from the judgment.

C. Medical Ethics

On more than one occasion in the judgment, as we shall see, it was stated that some of the doctors had 'ethical' objections to acceding to Ms B's wishes. Nevertheless, in 1999 the BMA had issued guidelines that considered the issue before the President.[55] Part two of that document considered a contemporaneous refusal of treatment by a competent patient:

---

[53]　[2002] EWCH 429 at para 23. Emphasis added.

[54]　[2002] EWCH 429 at paras 81–83, including quotes from K Atkins, 'Autonomy and the Subjective Character of Experience' (2000) 17 *Journal of Applied Philosophy* 71.

[55]　BMA, *Withholding and Withdrawing Life-Prolonging Medical Treatment: Guidance for Decision Making* (BMA, 1999).

It is well established in law *and ethics* that competent adults have the right to refuse any medical treatment, even if that refusal results in their death ... Procedures such as artificial nutrition and hydration and sedation may be refused by a patient who is competent to make that decision but they should continue to be available if the patient changes his or her mind.[56]

Thus, for the BMA at least, the ethical component of the situation was as settled as the law. In the light of this, what, then, was the basis for the 'ethical' objections of the doctors involved in the case? For Dr R, Ms B's request was simply inimical to her own view of what medical practice should achieve. As Butler-Sloss P noted, she 'had studied and spent her professional life trying to do her best to improve and preserve life. She did not feel able to agree with simply switching off Ms B's ventilation'.[57] She had only agreed to the one-way weaning process with the greatest reluctance. Mr G, a consultant, did not doubt Ms B's competence but felt that her refusal to even consider rehabilitative treatment at a specialist spinal cord centre meant that she did not have the 'experience of those aspects in order to know what life would be like'.[58] The President stated that, in this regard, she had 'the gravest doubts as to ... [its] legal validity', and thus rejected that view.[59] For Dr I, a consultant psychiatrist, the fact that Ms B was in the ICU rather than a rehabilitation unit may have influenced her psychological state. On this basis, he had reservations about her capacity due to her specific, temporal psychological state, though he had no doubts about her general capacity to make her own decisions. After conferring with the psychiatrist instructed by the Official Solicitor, however, he withdrew his concerns, and declared that he felt her to be competent without reservations.[60]

These, then, were the stated objections of Ms B's treatment team – two felt that she lacked capacity, and one that she was unwilling to accede to the patient's wishes because it was the opposite of the reason for which she became a medical practitioner. Dr Sensky, the psychiatrist instructed by the Official Solicitor, considered the views of the treatment team, and the President noted how this illustrated the 'conundrum and how difficult it is ethically and personally' for the treatment team to accept Ms B's wishes.[61]

This takes us to the root of the problem because, according to the BMA, there *was* no ethical conundrum. The court decided that there was no reason to doubt Ms B's competence; and yet Butler-Sloss P not only ignored the ethics to which she had just referred, but she again repeated the view of the medical practitioners that they found the removal of ventilation 'unethical'. Noting that doctors are 'trained to save life', she added that removal of ventilation was considered by

---

56   *Ibid* at para 9.1. Emphasis added.
57   *Ms B v An NHS Hospital Trust* [2002] EWCH 429 at para 57.
58   [2002] EWCH 429 at para 62.
59   [2002] EWCH 429 at para 63.
60   [2002] EWCH 429 at paras 64–71.
61   [2002] EWCH 429 at para 80.

some members of the treatment team to be 'killing the patient or assisting the patient to die and ethically unacceptable'.[62] But what kind of ethics were these? The semi-formal sector of ethical discourse was on the side of Ms B. The President can only have been referring to some unofficial sector sources read by the doctors treating Ms B or, as is most likely in the case of Dr R, the personal morality of the individual physicians.

While it is therefore undeniable that the law did not avoid its responsibility to formulate legal principle, as the judge prioritised it over the ethical principles and the 'ethical' objections of the doctors, it is interesting in the case that the process of ethical decision-making by Ms B's treatment team was not scrutinised. In finding for Ms B, the court sent out a clear signal that the law did take priority over the ethics. However, such an interpretation does not take into account the lack of critical analysis of the medical ethics espoused by the medical practitioners. Indeed, the President was keen to emphasise her praise for doctors:

> [A]ll those looking after Ms B have cared for her to the highest standards and with devotion. They deserve the highest praise. Ironically this excellent care has contributed to the difficulties for the Hospital. Ms B has been treated throughout in the ICU in which the medical and nursing team are dedicated to saving and preserving life ... The request from Ms B, which would have been understood in a palliative care situation, appears to have been outside the experience of the ICU in relation to a mentally competent patient.[63]

Such an argument allows the Trust a benefit of the doubt that it perhaps does not deserve. Indeed, as Butler-Sloss P noted in the same paragraph, the Trust had sought legal advice in April and thus were aware of the legal position. Those of a cynical disposition may wonder whether there was a connection between this legal advice and Drs L and E changing their reports concerning Ms B's competence only a day after finding, separately, that she had capacity. If this legal advice was on file then it should have been followed when Ms B was found to be competent. The finding by the President that the letter was simply 'not reread' in August, when she was found to be competent again, may not convince some.[64]

Furthermore, it is hard to believe that if Ms B's request was 'outside the experience' of the ICU team they never sought to examine their duties with respect to it. The fact that legal advice was commissioned suggests that some effort was made to engage with the wishes of Ms B; indeed, there is reference made in the judgment to the views of 'outside sources' being sought. The nature of these sources is not explained, but it would seem probable that some ethical sources were examined for a decision to be reached that to withdraw ventilation would be 'unethical'.[65] Despite this, as we have seen, the BMA at least was

---

[62]   [2002] EWCH 429 at para 97.

[63]   [2002] EWCH 429 at para 97.

[64]   [2002] EWCH 429 at para 97.

[65]   In para 10, it is noted that the Medical Director thought that the advice of an ethics committee should be sought, but that this was not possible as the hospital did not have one.

emphatic in its view that there was no ethical controversy, and that Ms B's wishes should have been adhered to once she was considered competent.

I would argue that the true situation was that the treatment team did not want to adhere to Ms B's request, and that this was for *moral* rather than *ethical* reasons. Indeed there is little reference in the judgment to ethical principles, and the only time that it was mentioned by a member of the treatment team, indirectly, was when Butler-Sloss P noted that the issues of concern to Dr R were the 'legal and ethical' ones regarding the removal of ventilation.[66] Thus the clinicians' reluctance to withdraw the ventilation was simply *presumed* to be ethical rather than moral in nature, when it was no such thing. Even a cursory glance at the ethics would have led them to question their position.[67] Once again, then, the court's view of medical ethics is difficult to determine. While the court engaged with ethics on a superficial level, the analysis was based on the law and the 'ethical' stance taken by the treatment team was imputed by the President and not critically evaluated. Indeed, it is perplexing that the doctors' 'ethical' objections were not subjected to scrutiny, as there was nothing in the ethical guidance that would suggest that they should have done anything other than accede to Ms B's wishes. This would suggest that the courts consider that more than one ethical position can be acceptable. If this is the case, then fragmentation can be seen to have taken a hold, and 'ethics', as defined by the court in *B*, is no more than a synonym for morality. Once again, the GMC was notable by its absence. In the final case in this chapter, however, that was not so.

V. *Burke* – Two Contrasting Judgments

A. The Facts

Six months after Ms B's case, the GMC published its first specific advice on the issue of withholding life-prolonging treatments,[68] and this was challenged in *Burke*.[69] The decisions at first instance and in the Court of Appeal are explored here, as the approaches taken to both law and ethics are radically different. Since 1982 Leslie Burke has suffered, and continues to suffer at the time of writing, from a spino-cerebellar ataxia with peripheral neuropathy. This is a progressive degenerative disorder and by 2004 Mr Burke was confined to a wheelchair, and would later become totally dependent on others for his care. His condition will

---

[66]   *Ibid* at para 56.

[67]   The BMA guidance notes that, if a doctor conscientiously objects to such a course of action, they should withdraw and allow the patient to be treated by a colleague who does not: *Withholding and Withdrawing Life-Prolonging Medical Treatment, op cit* n55, at para 24.1.

[68]   GMC, *Withholding and Withdrawing Life-prolonging Treatments: Good Practice in Decision-Making* (GMC, 2002).

[69]   *R (on the application of Burke) v General Medical Council* [2004] EWCH 1879.

degenerate to the point where, due to an inability to swallow, artificial nutrition and hydration will be required. However, he will retain full cognitive faculties, including the ability to feel pain, until almost the very end, at which point he will enter a semi-comatose state from which he will not recover. Essentially, there are three phases to the illness. During the first, he will have his cognitive function and an ability to communicate his wishes. In the second, although retaining cognitive faculties, he will be unable to communicate his wishes. Finally, in a semi-comatose state, he may lose his cognitive capabilities.[70] Mr Burke does not want his artificial nutrition and hydration to be withdrawn, in particular while he maintains cognitive faculties. As Munby J. noted at first instance, he 'does not want a decision to be taken by doctors that his life is no longer worth living'.[71] Mr Burke's complaint focused on the GMC advice which he believed did not allow him to make his own decisions and was not compatible with the law. In particular, attention was drawn to paras 32, 38, 81 and 82 of the document.[72] Under these paragraphs, the ultimate responsibility for decisions was given to the treatment team rather than the patient.

Paragraph 32 informs consultants that 'it is your responsibility to make the decision about whether to withhold or withdraw a life-prolonging treatment'. Paragraph 38 states that where the doctor was unsure about how to proceed, she should consult 'another clinician', but that ultimately the decision regarding the withdrawal of artificial nutrition and hydration (ANH) remained one to be taken by the treatment team. Paragraph 81 tells doctors that, even when the patient's death is not imminent, the withdrawal of ANH might be felt to be appropriate. In such 'sensitive' cases the doctor is advised to 'consult' the treatment team, those close to the patient, and a 'second or expert opinion from a senior clinician'. Finally, para 82 advises that in the event of irreconcilable differences of opinion, either with the patient's family or indeed within the treatment team, it may be necessary to obtain legal advice with a view to seeking a court ruling.

Paragraph 16 was also relevant:

> Applying these principles may result in different decisions in each case, since patients' assessments of the likely benefits and burdens or risks, and what weight or priority to give to these, will differ according to patients' different values, beliefs and priorities. Doctors must take account of patients' preferences when providing treatment. However, where a patient wishes to have a treatment that – in the doctor's considered view – is not clinically indicated, there is no ethical or legal obligation on the doctor to provide it. Where requested, patients' right to a second opinion should be respected.[73]

The paragraph is clear that, whatever the wishes of the patient, the final decision regarding medical treatment is one for the clinical team – the patient may not therefore demand treatment. Secondly, it asserts that neither the law nor medical

---

[70] [2004] EWCH 1879 at para 5.
[71] [2004] EWCH 1879 at para 6.
[72] These are quoted in *Burke* at [2004] EWCH 1879 at paras 10–13.
[73] [2004] EWCH 1879 at para 15. Emphasis added.

ethics is a bar to this. This view is mirrored in para 42 of the advice, which notes that if 'a specific treatment is requested which, in your considered view is clinically inappropriate, you are not legally or ethically bound to provide it'. If Mr Burke were to be successful, he would have to challenge not just medical ethics, but the formal sector of ethical discourse. Ironically, this was to be to his advantage at first instance. In the Court of Appeal, however, things would be different.

B.   The Decision at First Instance

The first issue for Munby J was whether there was a clinical justification for removing ANH. After examining the medical evidence, he decided that there could be in certain situations,[74] and it fell on the court to consider the precise nature of Mr Burke's claim. A primary issue for the court was whether it was within its jurisdiction to challenge GMC guidelines: was it within the ambit of the law to interfere with formal medical ethics? The court confronted medical ethics head on and Munby J not only considered the status of the advice from the GMC, but also the status of the organisation itself. He noted that the GMC was governed by the Medical Act 1983, s 35 of which, as we have seen, provides the GMC with the power to give ethical advice to the medical profession.[75]

The GMC was thus a public authority and therefore amenable to judicial review. Additionally, any advice that the GMC provided had to be consistent with the provisions of the Human Rights Act 1998. Munby J defined the conceptual nature of any such 'advice' and drew this from the case of *R v Secretary of State for the Environment ex parte Lancashire County Council*.[76] In that case, Jowitt J formulated a distinction between 'advice' and 'guidance':

> [Advice will] suggest how different factors might be weighted in relation to one another … [even if this] may have the effect of steering a conclusion in one direction rather than another. The concept of guidance goes beyond simply providing a checklist of factors which the commission should take into account. To guide someone is to lead, steer or point someone in a particular direction.[77]

In adopting this distinction, Munby J accepted that 'advice', which was less directive than 'guidance', remained challengeable if it was inconsistent with the law. As it was challengeable, ethical advice could properly be examined for consistency with the law. It is only at this point that ethics were introduced to the judgment. However, perhaps surprisingly, these were not medical ethics but,

---

[74]   [2004] EWCH 1879 at paras 18–20. Further, Munby J later noted that the provision (and, by implication, removal) of artificial nutrition and hydration was compatible with the *Bolam* test (see para 29).

[75]   *Ibid* at para 31.

[76]   *R v Secretary of State for the Environment ex parte Lancashire County Council* (1994) 93 LGR 29.

[77]   *R (Burke) v General Medical Council* [2005] EWCA Civ 1003 at para 32.

rather, the 'ethical basis of the law', to which an entire section was devoted.[78] Three key principles were identified and discussed: the sanctity of life, autonomy, and dignity; and Munby J was unequivocal in his view that, despite not being legal in nature, they informed the law:

> These may at root be ethical rather than merely legal principles but each is, of course, recognised by our law – both by our common law and by our human rights law derived by the Human Rights Act 1998 from the Convention.[79]

The judge then considered, at length, how these principles operated in domestic law and within the confines of the Human Rights Act 1998. He concluded that the GMC guidelines were not consistent with the law as it stood, as they gave insufficient weight to the patient's autonomy. What appeared, then, was a clash between medical law and formal medical ethics, and the judge decided that priority must be given to the former. This was not a decision that was arrived at lightly:

> The Guidance is not a legal textbook or statement of legal principles. It consists primarily of professional and ethical guidance for doctors provided for them by the professional body which is responsible for such matters. It is not my task to go on to advise the GMC how it should go about amending or revising the Guidance, save to direct the GMC's attention to the [relevant legal] principles ... Parliament has conferred on the GMC the statutory function of providing advice for members of the medical profession 'in such manner as the Council think fit' and I must be careful not to trespass upon that function. Equally I must be careful not to stray beyond the proper bounds of my task.[80]

Yet, despite the stated reluctance to infringe upon the role of the GMC, this is precisely what Munby J did. In finding that sections of the advice were inconsistent with the law, the primacy of medical law over medical ethics was not just stated as a hypothesis, but turned into a reality, something that we have not seen too often in this chapter so far.

C. Medical Ethics

In *Burke* at first instance there was a complete *volte face* from the position adopted in *Re G*. In the latter, medical ethics in the form of BMA guidance were considered without critique. In the former, however, the GMC guidance was not only tested for compatibility with the law, but found wanting in this regard. The view, expressed in *Bland* by Hoffman LJ in the Court of Appeal, that the law should instruct medical ethics, rather than the reverse, finally found favour with judges.

---

[78]   [2005] EWCA Civ 1003 at paras 51–80.
[79]   [2005] EWCA Civ 1003 at para 52.
[80]   [2005] EWCA Civ 1003 at para 215.

Nevertheless, it is interesting that, once again, there was written evidence taken from the BMA – despite the guidance in question being that of the GMC.[81] The BMA clearly commands the judiciary's respect in this area, and this is an indication that they might even be seen as more influential than the GMC. Again, this encourages fragmentation. Furthermore, in contrast with the GMC guidance, a section of the BMA version is cited with approval in the judgment![82] Nowhere, however, is it noted that the difference in approach between the two bodies may be problematic even though it cannot be appropriate that the two most important medical organisations in the country provide guidance that cannot be reconciled with that of the other. Again, the danger of fragmentation is heightened. However, it would not be accurate to say that ethical principles were ignored. On the contrary, they were considered in detail. But the ethical examination was undertaken in the context of the law, rather than medical ethics. The medical ethics model was then scrutinised to ensure that it was consistent with the conclusions surrounding the legal ethics. While this may appear to be an obvious way of proceeding, we have seen in previous sections in this chapter, and earlier chapters of this book, that such an approach cannot be taken for granted, and indeed has not occurred in the majority of cases considered.

What is disappointing in the case is that fragmentation and its dangers were not identified by Munby J. No attempt was made to engage with the question of whether, on a general level, this issue should be addressed. Munby J did not comment on the fact that he had found formal guidance to be inconsistent with the law, but not the semi-formal guidance that he praised. Nevertheless, this places medical professionals in a difficult situation – do they follow the GMC or BMA approach? This question goes to the heart of the issue in this book, and is an example of the lack of coherence in medical ethics, and the problems that fragmentation can cause.

D.   The Decision of the Court of Appeal[83]

The GMC appealed, and the Court of Appeal heard the case a year later. Unfortunately, the lack of coherence in medical ethics was not addressed. Rather, the judgement at first instance was, in effect, summarily dismissed and the GMC handed a resounding victory. David Gurnham, for example, has argued that:

> Munby J sought to invoke law, and especially Convention rights, to lay out the enforceability of patient wishes and medical duties, [but] the Court of Appeal's approach is to rely on the good faith and self-regulation of the medical profession.[84]

[81]   [2005] EWCA Civ 1003 at para 22.
[82]   [2005] EWCA Civ 1003 at para 112.
[83]   [2005] EWCA Civ 1003.
[84]   D Gurnham, 'Losing the Wood For the Trees: *Burke* and the Court of Appeal' (2006) 14(2) *Medical Law Review* 253 at 263.

Thus, the judgment of the Court of Appeal is notable for its absolute refusal to consider any wider implications, and also striking is the extent to which medical ethics was explicitly defined as belonging to the medical profession, and that decision-making responsibility was then fully abrogated to it.

The judgment of the Court of Appeal is a total departure from what Munby J had decided at first instance, so much so that Lord Phillips stated that the view of the Court was to 'counsel strongly against selective use of Munby J's judgment in future cases'.[85] Indeed, at every step the Court of Appeal disagreed with the judgment at first instance, and did so in a manner that gave discretion back to the medical profession. In part, the source of the disagreement was the insistence of the court that any questions surrounding the care that Mr Burke might receive when incompetent were premature and thus irrelevant to the present considerations.

The first issue considered by the Court of Appeal was that of best interests. Lord Phillips began by noting that Munby J had held that *Bolam* and best interests were distinct, as the former considered only clinical perspectives and did not involve 'a welfare appraisal in the widest sense, taking into account … a wide range of ethical, social, moral emotional and welfare considerations'.[86] Such a notion was immediately rejected by Lord Phillips who held that what he called a 'lengthy passage of intense jurisprudential analysis' by Munby J, derived from sterilisation cases, was quite simply not 'helpful' with regard to patients requiring ANH.[87] This was because the concept of best interests 'depends very much in the context in which it is used', and thus dicta from sterilisation cases was unlikely to be of use.[88]

This led to Lord Phillips medicalising and effectively re-*Bolam*ising the concept of best interests for Mr Burke. He stated that, in *Bland*, it had been held by Lord Goff that a patient's wishes may conflict with her best interests. Thus, 'it is best to confine the use of the phrase "best interests" to an objective test, which is … easiest to apply when confined to a situation where the relevant interests are medical'.[89] In terms of withdrawing ANH, the Court of Appeal recognised that the most problematic area for the law was when there was an incompetent patient and it had ceased to be in her best interests to continue that treatment. In the specific case of Mr Burke, Lord Phillips was able to avoid consideration of this point by noting that no such problem arose for Mr Burke as he was a competent patient wishing to be kept alive.

After considering whether the provisions of the Human Rights Act 1998 might be violated by the removal of ANH when he was incompetent, and concluding that they would not, Lord Phillips turned to the question of the lawfulness of the

[85]   *R (Burke) v General Medical Council* [2005] EWCA Civ 1003 at para 24.
[86]   [2005] EWCA Civ 1003 at para 28.
[87]   [2005] EWCA Civ 1003 at para 29.
[88]   [2005] EWCA Civ 1003 at para 29.
[89]   [2005] EWCA Civ 1003 at para 29.

GMC guidelines. This was given short shrift, again due to the fact that he limited his examination to 'the only relevant question in the guidance', which was whether it was 'compatible with the duty of a doctor to administer ANH to a *competent* patient' who wishes to be kept alive.[90] Thus, in all but two of the paragraphs of the guidance at issue, Lord Phillips simply declared that they were not relevant to Mr Burke's predicament as they either did not refer to ANH or did refer to incompetent patients. In the other two paragraphs, his Lordship simply put his faith in the medical profession and its ethics. In considering para 32 of the GMC guidance, for example, Lord Phillips accepted that the wording might imply that doctors could withdraw ANH despite the expressed wish of a competent patient not to do so. He held, however, that 'in the context of the guidance as a whole … we do not consider that any reasonable doctor would conclude' that this should be acceptable.[91] Similarly, when referring to para 42 of the document, Lord Phillips referred to the very notion of a doctor considering it inappropriate to continue giving ANH despite the wishes of the patient as 'totally unrealistic', while declaring it legal to do so, and despite the ethics saying the same![92]

Lord Phillips also explored what he termed the wider implications of the first instance judgment.[93] The first was the question of whether patients had a right to select the treatment that they would receive. As his Lordship noted, the GMC were concerned that Munby J had suggested that doctors might be obliged to provide treatment to a patient even though that treatment might, in the doctor's clinical judgment, not be in that patient's best interests. His Lordship said that Munby J's judgment should not be read in such a way as his Lordship was concerned specifically with life-prolonging treatment. In general, according to Lord Phillips, the doctor would offer treatment options to the patient, who would then either consent to one of them or refuse them. The doctor's duty was to offer options which were in the patient's interests. Thus,

> the right to choose is no more than a reflection of the fact that it is the doctor's duty to provide a treatment that he considers to be in the interests of the patient and that the patient is prepared to accept.[94]

In terms of ANH, Lord Phillips could conceive of only one scenario where ANH might lawfully be withdrawn despite the contrary wishes of a competent patient, and that was at the very last stages of life where the provision of ANH might actually hasten death.[95] For Munby J, as we saw, in such a scenario the patient's wish should be determinative. Lord Phillips disagreed, as 'a patient cannot demand that a doctor administer a treatment which the doctor considers is

---

[90] [2005] EWCA Civ 1003 at para 41. Emphasis added.
[91] [2005] EWCA Civ 1003 at para 44.
[92] [2005] EWCA Civ 1003 at para 46.
[93] [2005] EWCA Civ 1003 at paras 47–8.
[94] [2005] EWCA Civ 1003 at para 51.
[95] [2005] EWCA Civ 1003 at para 54.

adverse to the patient's clinical needs'.[96] He found such a scenario, however, to be 'extremely unlikely to arise in practice'.[97] Thus, the doctor's discretion would be maintained, at the expense of the competent patient's wishes. He continued by considering the position of the incompetent patient and how to determine best interests at the end of life. Essentially, Lord Phillips held that the lives of such patients were as valuable as any other, but rejected any attempt to define best interests in general because each case must be examined in its own context, taking account of all the relevant circumstances that made it unique. He held that the GMC guidance supported this view,[98] and stated that Munby J's declaration that parts of the GMC guidance were unlawful was erroneous.[99]

Finally, Lord Phillips examined whether there was a legal duty to obtain court authorisation before withdrawing ANH. Yet again he deferred to the medical profession, stating that while it should be good practice to seek court approval it was not a legal requirement. The reasons were twofold, one technical and one more practical. The technical reason was that a declaration of lawfulness did not constitute a granting of permission or authorisation; rather, it simply declared whether the proposed act would be lawful. The court, he said, 'does not 'authorise' treatment that would otherwise be unlawful'.[100] Indeed, the withdrawal of ANH in a given circumstance would have the same legal status whether a declaration was issued or not. The second reason was more controversial. Lord Phillips cited evidence provided by the Intensive Care Society that approximately 15,000 people die in intensive care units or on wards before discharge every year. 'Most', he added, 'die because treatment is withdrawn or limited'.[101] He admitted that there 'is not always agreement', but nevertheless noted that the courts would be unable to cope with the volume of referrals if there were a legal duty to consult them first.[102] Thus Lord Phillips overturned the decision of Munby J. There was little of the first instance decision that can be said to have remained unchallenged by the Court of Appeal. The tone of the judgments is also totally different. Where Munby J had recognised the ethical component to the case, Lord Phillips had denied it and left the issue in the hands of the doctors. Moreover, this was clearly a conscious decision.

E.   Medical Ethics in the Court of Appeal

Given that Lord Phillips was content with the GMC guidelines that would appear to allow medical practitioners to decide when to remove ANH from Mr Burke, it

---

96   [2005] EWCA Civ 1003 at para 55.
97   [2005] EWCA Civ 1003 at para 55.
98   [2005] EWCA Civ 1003 at paras 56–63.
99   [2005] EWCA Civ 1003 at paras 64–6.
100   [2005] EWCA Civ 1003 at para 80.
101   [2005] EWCA Civ 1003 at para 69.
102   *Ibid.* He stated that there might be ten per day.

is no surprise that his confidence in medical ethics appeared to be akin to that of Lord Donaldson in *Re R* and *Re W*. Thus, for example, there was a reluctance to engage with the issues at all, with his Lordship warning of the 'danger ... that the court will enunciate propositions of principle without full appreciation of the implications that these will have in practice, throwing into confusion' those doctors who would have to apply them.[103] Indeed, it might even be argued that Lord Phillips moved beyond the position of Lord Donaldson, in that he trusted the conscience of individual medical practitioners enough to leave loopholes in *both* the law and ethics. This was the case with para 42 of the GMC guidance, for example. The key part of that paragraph states that if 'a specific treatment is requested which, in your considered view is clinically inappropriate, you are not legally or ethically bound to provide it'. As previously mentioned, Lord Phillips rejected Mr Burke's challenge to that statement by stating that it would only be relevant 'if one postulates that a doctor might consider it "clinically inappropriate" to keep him alive by administering ANH despite his wishes and that this should be done. *We consider such a scenario to be totally unrealistic*'.[104]

Indeed, this incredulity that what Mr Burke was afraid of might occur, even as he declared that it would be legal if it were to, is astounding. His Lordship was not just content to leave a legal lacuna like Lord Donaldson in Chapter 5, and *Re G* in this one. Rather, he also left an *ethical* one, trusting in the conscience of individual medical practitioners to prevent them withdrawing treatment. In the wake of Harold Shipman and other medical scandals, not to mention Plato and Nuremburg as discussed in this book, such naiveté is scarcely credible.

VI. Ethical Guidance

The ethical guidance in this area is predictably voluminous. Surprisingly, however, it took time for the medical profession to identify the issue as meriting consideration, and thus its existence is a relatively recent occurrence. In this regard, the BMA was the only body to have published anything at the time of the House of Lords' judgment in *Bland*, and that was only a discussion paper. The GMC finally provided its own guidance in 2002. That document, as we have seen, was challenged by Leslie Burke. With even a cursory glance at the GMC's book it is easy to understand Mr Burke's preoccupation with the way that it is phrased. Indeed, it undeniably places much of its emphasis on the responsibility of the clinicians to make the decisions. References to this punctuate the document. Thus, even as it sets out its guiding principles, there is an implicit presumption that the decisions concerning withholding treatment are for doctors to make, even though they are not medical in nature. Paragraph 10, for example, states that,

---

[103] [2005] EWCA Civ 1003 at para 21.
[104] [2005] EWCA Civ 1003 at para 45. Emphasis added.

[b]enefits and burdens for the patient are not always limited to purely medical considerations, and *doctors should be careful,* particularly when dealing with patients who cannot make decisions for themselves, *to take account of all the other factors relevant to the circumstances of the particular patient.*[105]

The language is reminiscent of the Mental Capacity Act 2005, as we saw in Chapter 6, in its limitation of the doctor's duty to merely 'take into account' certain factors, and clearly envisions the final decision as belonging to the medical practitioner. This is made explicit a few paragraphs later, when considering decisions regarding incompetent patients, where there must be:

> an assessment of the benefits, burdens and risks, and the acceptability of proposed treatment must be *made on their behalf by the doctor, taking account of their wishes, where they are known.* Where a patient's wishes are not known *it is the doctor's responsibility to decide what is in the patient's best interests.* However, this cannot be done effectively without information about the patient which those close to the patient will be best placed to know.[106]

Again, the doctor need only 'take account' of the wishes of the patient, and there is no specific requirement to follow them. Where the patient's wishes are not known, responsibility is explicitly given to the doctor. Moreover, the doctor is only under a duty to respect refusals of treatment. With regard to patients expressing a desire, like Mr Burke, to continue to receive treatment, the position is clear: 'where a patient wishes to have a treatment that – in the doctor's considered view – is not clinically indicated, there is no ethical or legal obligation on the doctor to provide it'.[107] Where there is disagreement about the patient's best interests with other medical professionals, the patient or her relatives, the guidance suggests that the doctor should first try to reach agreement. This might even take the form of 'clinical or ethical review' from outside the healthcare team.[108] If no agreement is reached at this point, the guidance suggests that the doctor take legal advice regarding the necessity of seeking a court ruling which, as shown in *Burke,* would support the guidelines in the view that the decision rests with the doctor.[109]

The approach of the guidance is similar with respect to ANH. Removal of this can be upsetting for relatives of the patients, according to the guidance, because they may not understand the 'benefits and burdens' of ANH, and that it might be a part of the 'natural dying process'.[110] The decision is again left to the doctor, although the guidance at least recommends that she explain why ANH is being

---

[105]   GMC, *Withholding and Withdrawing Life-Prolonging Treatments: Good Practice in Decision-Making, op cit,* at para 10. Emphasis added.
[106]   *Ibid* at para 15. Emphasis added.
[107]   *Ibid* at para 16. See also para 42.
[108]   *Ibid* at para 58.
[109]   *Ibid* at paras 17–18.
[110]   *Ibid* at para 22.

removed to the patient's relatives.[111] Indeed, the balance of power envisioned by the guidance is made clear a little later, when 'clinical responsibility for decisions' is considered:

> If you are the consultant or general practitioner in charge of a patient's care, it is your responsibility to make the decision about whether to withhold or withdraw a life-prolonging treatment, taking account of the views of the patient or those close to the patient as set out in paras 41–48 and 53–57. Exceptionally, in an emergency where the senior clinician cannot be contacted in time, if you are an appropriately experienced junior hospital doctor or deputising general practitioner you may take responsibility for making the decision, but it must be discussed with the senior clinician as soon as possible.[112]

It thus appears that Mr Burke feared, and continues to have reason to be fearful of, the guidance. Indeed, it is a document that presumes from beginning to end that the doctor is the ultimate arbiter of the patient's best interests and when and how she will die. The views of others are there to be 'taken into account' but, like the wording of the Mental Capacity Act's definition of best interests, for information rather than direction. There is thus absolutely nothing to suggest that Lord Phillips was correct to state that Mr Burke's fears were 'totally unrealistic'. The BMA, although quicker to identify and respond to the issues,[113] has traditionally held a similar view. Thus, the discussion paper referred to with approval in *Bland* stressed that although the views of relatives should be considered, the determination of the patient's best interests was still to be considered a clinical judgement.[114] Neither the 1980 or 1988 guidance examined issues at the end of life, other than to briefly consider euthanasia.[115] The 1993 book, however, contained a chapter examining such issues, which argued that although there was sometimes a disconnection between legal and ethical imperatives, there was a 'commonality between law and ethics' in this area.[116] Indeed, the judgment in *Bland* was approved of, as was a GMC press release in 1992 that stated that treatment whose only purpose was to shorten a patient's life would fall short of a doctor's duty to her patient.[117] Furthermore, it was explicitly stated that the refusal of consent of a competent patient should be respected, and so should clear advance directives, despite voicing its opposition to the latter.[118] In terms of who should make the decision to withdraw treatment the guidance was more circumspect. Although

---

[111]   *Ibid* at paras 23–4.

[112]   *Ibid* at para 32.

[113]   They issued reports into euthanasia in 1971 and then again in 1988 (see BMA, *Euthanasia* (BMA, 1988)). See generally, BMA, *Handbook of Medical Ethics* (BMA, 1980) 90.

[114]   See BMA, *Discussion Paper on Treatment of Patients in Persistent Vegetative State* (BMA, 1992), and Lord Goff in *Airedale NHS Trust v Bland* [1993] 1 All ER 821 at 872.

[115]   See the 1980 *Handbook* (*op cit* n114) 30–1; and BMA, *Philosophy and Practice of Medical Ethics* (BMA, 1988) 90–2.

[116]   BMA, *Medical Ethics Today: Its Practice and Philosophy* (BMA, 1993) 156.

[117]   *Ibid.*

[118]   *Ibid* 162–3.

the past views of the patient and the views of relatives were said to be of value, the book reflects the law in its definition of best interests as a clinical decision to be taken by the treatment team.[119]

In 1999 the BMA issued a separate document considering issues at the end of life.[120] Standing at over 80 pages in length, this comprehensive booklet considered all aspects of the removal of treatment to dying patients, providing guidance on 'the type of factors that should be taken into account, the process which should be followed and the safeguards that should be in place' to ensure that decisions to withhold treatment were made 'appropriately'.[121] The booklet was written in response to what the BMA perceived as confusion following legal decisions that specifically referred only to cases of PVS, and the BMA had decided to provide the guidance as it did 'not believe that ... [non-PVS] cases should routinely be subject to Court review', but considered that guidelines should be published instead.[122] As the GMC had not yet provided theirs at that time, this was the BMA's attempt to fill the vacuum. The booklet essentially provides the same guidance that the GMC was to provide. The best interests of the patient were to be defined by the treatment team, and the legal rules should be followed. Indeed, an identical approach was adopted by the 2004 version of *Medical Ethics Today*.[123] In this regard, the BMA guidance up to then was just as paternalistic as that of the GMC, and Mr Burke would find as little solace in the approach of the BMA. However, the BMA was to change its mind, and it altered its policy to one that Mr Burke would presumably approve of:

> At the British Medical Association's Annual Representative Meeting in July 2004 the following policy statement was approved: 'That *this Meeting believes that patients who lose their capacity but who have indicated in advance that they wish to receive artificial hydration and nutrition should have their wishes respected*'. This expands on the more general statement on page 353 of Medical Ethics Today that: 'If the patient is known to have held the view that there is intrinsic value in being alive, then life-prolonging treatment would, in virtually all cases, provide a net benefit for that particular individual'.[124]

The current BMA policy therefore once again goes beyond the law in its protection of patient autonomy, as the Court of Appeal in *Burke* was to determine that there was no need to respect such advance indications. However, what is significant here is not just that it also goes beyond the guidance issued by the GMC, but also that the GMC went to court to guard against exactly what the

---

[119]   *Ibid* 166–7.
[120]   BMA, *Withholding and Withdrawing Life-Prolonging Medical Treatment: Guidance for Decision Making* (BMA, 1999). A second edition was published in 2001.
[121]   *Ibid* (x).
[122]   *Ibid* (ix).
[123]   BMA, *Medical Ethics Today* (BMA, 2004). See generally pp 351–388, and in particular pp 356–7.
[124]   www.bma.org.uk/ap.nsf/Content/WW2update05. Emphasis added.

BMA addendum tells doctors to do. On this specific issue, the GMC and BMA guidance can only be said to be at odds with each other.

VII. Conclusion

Once again, the pattern in the cases considered in previous chapters can be seen. First, the House of Lords case both identifies and engages with ethical principles, if not always with medical ethics. Then, there is a regression to 'doctor knows best', and a purely legal consideration of the issues – almost a denial of the ethical component. This occurred in *Bland* and, subsequently, *Re G*. Yet the trend is also for the ethical dimension to be rediscovered, and it was in both *Ms B* and *Burke* at first instance. Nevertheless, the ethical dimension in *Burke* was entirely considered within a legal rather than ethical framework, while in *Ms B* this was partially the case. Additionally, in *Ms B*, the principle of the sanctity of life was considered medical and autonomy legal, while in *Burke* at first instance both were categorised as the latter. This highlights that, as we have seen with the other issues considered in previous chapters, there is no common link between the judges' conceptualisations of medical ethics from one case to the next. Indeed, I would suggest that words such as 'medical ethics' and 'ethics' are used interchangeably without much thought being given to their meaning. Such an analysis is strengthened by the judgment in *Ms B*, where it is difficult to escape the conclusion that 'ethics' was used as a synonym for morality.

Moreover, it cannot even be argued that there is consistency between the cases regarding the authority of medical ethics. In *Re G*, and to an extent in *Bland*, medical ethics somewhat subsumed medical law. Despite the protestations of Lord Hoffman in the Court of Appeal in *Bland* that he would,

> expect medical ethics to be informed by the law rather than the reverse ... [t]his is a purely legal (or moral) decision which does not require any medical expertise and is therefore appropriately made by the court

in neither case can this be said to ring true.[125] Indeed, Munby J in *Burke* felt compelled to note that, given this statement, it 'makes all the more surprising the House of Lords' enthusiastic references ... to the "Bolam" test [in *Bland*].'[126]

Yet herein lies the crucial aspect of the consideration of medical ethics in these cases: there is inconsistency in how medical ethics is viewed and treated, both in terms of its definition and purpose. Once again we may divide the cases into those which support medical dominance (Lord Mustill's judgment in *Bland* excepted), and the one, *Burke* at first instance, that does not. What is perplexing is the return to instinctive abrogation of responsibility, in such a sensitive issue, that we saw in the Court of Appeal in *Burke*. This is different to the pattern in the

---

[125] *Airedale NHS Trust v Bland* [1993] 1 All ER 821 at 834.
[126] [1993] 1 All ER 821 at para 96.

previous chapters of this book, where once a more patient-centred judgment occurred, the rest followed that path. Just as baffling, in the context of such an important issue as the end of life, is the seeming primacy of the BMA over the GMC in some of the cases. In *Bland, Ms B* and *Burke* at first instance, evidence was provided to the court or guidelines considered from the BMA. As the court recognised in *Burke*, the GMC is the only body with statutory authority to provide ethical advice to medical professionals, yet the only role that the GMC had in that case was to have its guidance tested for compatibility with the law and found wanting at first instance! Yet the BMA provided written evidence to the court. The decision of the Court of Appeal to reverse the decision in *Burke* returned the law to its policy of displaying total confidence in medical ethics, yet the BMA's addendum contradicts both the law and the GMC. Although it might be argued that the disagreement comprises a specific situation, the difference in the guidance would hold significance for Mr Burke. Indeed, he would certainly wish for the BMA's primacy over the GMC to continue. Nevertheless, fragmentation can be seen to have taken hold in this area, and the courts' reversion to abrogating responsibility to medical ethics is all the more regrettable. Moreover, that fragmentation can also be seen to be creating a problem, in that the more influential sectors of discourse now offer conflicting advice. The law's confidence in medical ethics in this matter, then, can be seen to be even more misplaced.

8

Medical Ethics in Government-Commissioned Reports

I. Introduction

As the last chapters have demonstrated, the courts have not yet established a consistent conception of medical ethics and how it might work in conjunction with the law. Rather, the approach has been to either abrogate responsibility to medical ethics (sometimes without verifying that some exist), or to identify the ethical component to a case but then claim it as a legal issue and thus marginalise medical ethics. This chapter considers the reports of three committees asked to examine specific areas containing a significant ethical content. One is chosen from the 1980s, one from the 1990s and one from the 2000s, and each can be said to be the defining report of its decade. The Warnock Committee report, published in 1984, looked at issues relating to human fertilisation and embryology, and was eventually to form the basis of the Human Fertilisation and Embryology Act 1990.[1] The report of the House of Lords Select Committee on Medical Ethics was convened to consider whether euthanasia should be legalised, and published its report in 1994.[2] Finally, in 2005 a new House of Lords Select Committee examined Lord Joffe's Assisted Dying for the Terminally Ill Bill.[3] The inherent ethical component to each issue is obvious, and I will examine whether these committees have been any more consistent in their conceptualisations of what medical ethics might be and how it might fit in with the law.

The appreciation of medical ethics displayed by these committees might be expected to be more sophisticated than those of the judges in the cases, because they held several advantages over them. Chief among these was the fact that the committees were not constrained by the law. Whereas the judges were, by and large, forced to consider the ethics in light of existing legal rules, in the reports there was no such requirement; rather, the committees were charged with

---

[1] *Report of the Committee of Inquiry into Human Fertilisation and Embryology* (*Ibid*) (Cmnd 9314, 1984).
[2] *Report of the Select Committee on Medical Ethics* (HL Paper 21-I, 1994).
[3] *Report of the Select Committee on the Assisted Dying for the Terminally Ill Bill* (HL Paper 86-I, 2005).

suggesting what *future* law might contain. In this sense, they could give medical ethics as much or as little of a role as they saw fit. Indeed, without such legal encumbrances it was open to the committees, if they so chose, to prioritise the ethics and thus fit the law around them, or *vice versa*. The committees could essentially do whatever they liked with medical ethics, however they defined them and their purpose. Another advantage that they had was that they were not limited by the facts of cases. In Chapters 4–7, the judges had to answer specific questions regarding facts and circumstances. With the reports, on the other hand, the committees had the luxury of examining their subjects in the widest sense, allowing them to create founding principles and build upon them. Indeed, it might also be expected that the medical profession and its ethics would be seen as influential in setting the parameters of the law and how far medical ethics would have a role to play in decision-making. If anything, these committees had the opportunity to define and develop their own relationship between medical law and ethics, allowing them to design a legal framework in which they could work in tandem.

The committees also had the further benefit of time. In the courts there was pressure to decide cases within as short a timeframe as possible, and the judges were limited to hearing the evidence brought before them by the barristers. In the committees, however, there was less time pressure, and the members could call on whoever they liked to give evidence. As nothing was already decided, they could also hear from all sectors of ethical discourse and make their own decisions based not on who they were but on whether they liked what they heard from them. Finally, it might be expected that medical ethics would play a more prominent role in the committees simply because, just as with the evidence, the members were not all lawyers. Indeed, the Warnock Committee which, as we shall see, delivered the report that was most sensitive to the problems identified by this book, was chaired by a philosopher, Dame Mary Warnock, who had published in the field of medical ethics. This is perhaps no coincidence.

All of these factors suggest that the views of the committees regarding medical ethics should have been more sophisticated than those of the courts, with a greater appreciation and consideration of the nature and role of different ethical discourses. Furthermore, the position of medical ethics with regard to the law should have been expected to have been considered by the committees, and the blank canvass presented to them should have encouraged them to have been proactive rather than worried about upsetting any status quo. In this regard, the committees cannot be said to have been totally successful.

II. The Warnock Committee Report – Merging the Fragments

A. Introduction

The Warnock Committee faced an unenviable task. Established in 1982, its terms of reference were wide ranging. The committee was charged with considering:

> recent and potential developments in medicine and science related to human fertilisation and embryology; to consider what policies and safeguards should be applied, including consideration of the social, ethical and legal implications of these developments; and to make recommendations.[4]

It was thus asked not just to look at current developments in human fertilisation and embryology, but also to *potential* ones. The report stated that progress in this area was swift and unpredictable, and said that it would interpret potentiality as 'what we could realistically foresee' could be developed in the near future.[5] The scope of the report thus covered artificial insemination, surrogacy, and new processes of artificial reproduction. Abortion and contraception were, however, outside the ambit of the brief.[6] The ethical aspect to the committee's terms of reference is obvious and intrinsic to it. Indeed, there are few ethical issues that are more controversial than questions arising from the beginning of life and, in particular, when life begins and what it means to be human. The committee recognised this when it emphasised that the 'common factor linking all the developments, recent or potential, medical or scientific, was the anxiety that they generated in the public mind'.[7] Consequently, the committee decided to take a generalist view, providing general principles rather than specific rules, and leaving it to the Government to fill in the details. In this respect, the report thus sought to provide a skeleton that the future legislation could flesh out.

This was all the more critical since some of the procedures covered, such as artificial insemination, were already practiced in the UK despite not being 'universally accepted ethically, nor indeed regulated by law'.[8] It fell to the committee to make order out of the chaos, and even the generalist approach it adopted required it to construct a coherent ethical and legal base that would achieve as close to consensus as was possible. Thus, 'people generally want *some principles or other* to govern the development and use of the new techniques. The must be *some* barriers ... *some* limits fixed, beyond which people must not be allowed to go'.[9] Moreover, not to set such limits would be the sign of 'a society

---

[4] *Ibid* at para 1.1.
[5] *Ibid* at para 1.5.
[6] *Ibid* at para 1.3.
[7] *Ibid* at para 1.3.
[8] *Ibid* at para 1.3.
[9] *Ibid* at p 2. Emphasis added.

without moral scruples'.[10] However, such consensus would never realistically be achieved and 'in our pluralistic society it is not to be expected that any one set of principles can be enunciated to be completely accepted by everyone'.[11] For this reason, perhaps, it was decided that the agent responsible for guarding the moral scruples would be the law, as '[t]he law itself, binding on everyone in society, whatever their beliefs, is the embodiment of a common moral position. It sets out a broad framework for what is morally acceptable within society'.[12] With the ethical and legal positions yet to be ascertained, the generalist approach taken and the inevitability of a lack of consensus, the committee was being asked to build a moral and legal framework under which doctors and scientists would operate. This would involve outlining the position and role of medical ethics also.

B.   The Report

After an introductory chapter, the report examined the scope and organisation of existing services (Chapter 2), and the various techniques for the alleviation of infertility (Chapters 3–8). With each technique, arguments for and against the continued provision of such services were considered, and the inquiry's view was then disclosed and recommendations made. Roles for the technologies other than for the alleviation of infertility such as the prevention of the transmission of hereditary diseases and sex selection were also examined (Chapter 9), as were issues surrounding the freezing and storage of human gametes and embryos (Chapter 10). Chapter 11 was concerned with research on embryos and Chapter 12 looked at possible future developments. The most relevant section of the report for the purposes of this book is Chapter 13, which concerned the regulation of infertility services and research.

Chapter 2 contained the first indication that the committee viewed the role of consultants, and their consciences, to be of critical importance to their framework. In considering the question of eligibility for treatment, for example, the report divided the role of consultants into two: one clinical and one non-clinical. The clinical judgement would involve 'such considerations as the patient's age, the duration of infertility and the likelihood that the treatment will be successful'.[13] However, there were also other judgements to be made regarding, for example, the availability of treatment for single women, gay men and women,

---

[10]   *Ibid* at p 2.
[11]   *Ibid* at p 2.
[12]   *Ibid* at pp 2–3.
[13]   *Ibid* at para 2.12.

and women who had already had children.[14] In such cases, although the committee's own preference was for children to belong to a 'two-parent family, with both father and mother', it still recommended that 'everyone should be entitled to *seek expert advice*'.[15]

Thus the gatekeepers of entitlement would be the consultants, who would ultimately decide who to provide treatment to, and the committee recognised that it was asking them to make non-technical decisions, noting 'that this will place a heavy burden of responsibility on the individual consultant who must make social judgments that go beyond the purely medical'.[16] Furthermore, the committee asked itself whether it was possible to set out 'wider social criteria' for use by consultants in deciding whether to provide treatment, and decided that it was not because they could not be 'sensitive to the circumstances in every case'.[17] There was no mention of the medical profession and its ethics, though there was a presumption that, in making decisions regarding eligibility, consultants might speak to their 'professional colleagues'.[18] The inquiry thus envisioned discretion in such a fundamental area to be exercised not by the medical *profession*, but by the consciences of *individual practitioners*.

In the chapters describing the individual techniques and making recommendations (Chapters 3–8) there was little consideration of medical ethics as a concept or how regulation should occur. Nevertheless, the snippets that are there support the attitude displayed in Chapter 2. In Chapter 5, for example, when discussing the provision of *in vitro* fertilisation (IVF), consultants were again asked to make decisions beyond purely medical issues. Thus, the number of embryos to be transferred on each occasion was rightly described as being 'a matter of clinical judgment'.[19] However, and more controversially, medical practitioners were again charged with making non-technical decisions:

> In addition to the technical arguments we have outlined, a practitioner must also give very serious consideration to the social problems for the family that may follow the birth of more than twins, problems that may affect the continuing health and wellbeing of the mother in looking after the children and may adversely affect the children themselves.[20]

The committee thus envisioned medical practitioners assessing the social implications of treatment not just on the patient but also on any resulting child or children. Interestingly, there was no indication that the inquiry would expect the medical profession to publish ethical guidance to aid individuals having to make such decisions. Indeed in Chapter 10, which concerned the freezing and storage

---

[14] *Ibid* at paras 2.8 to 2.11.
[15] *Ibid* at para 2.11. Emphasis added.
[16] *Ibid* at para 2.13.
[17] *Ibid* at para 2.13.
[18] *Ibid* at para 2.13.
[19] *Ibid* at para 5.4.
[20] *Ibid* at para 5.4.

of gametes and embryos, directive regulation is again noticeable by its absence. Thus, the report stated that donors should have 'no rights or obligations with regard to their donations', and that the question of disposing of such material would be the responsibility of those who were storing it.[21] However, it then suggested that as 'a matter of good practice' the donors should be consulted to 'ascertain their wishes well in advance of the expiry' of the time limit for donations.[22] The committee recommended that this should be every five years. If at this point the donors could not be found, it would be 'good practice' to 'bear in mind' any previously expressed wishes relating to disposal.[23] As argued in Chapter 6 of this book with regard to the concept of best interests, 'good practice' is an ambivalent term that *suggests* what the medical practitioner should do without actually *requiring* that it should be done. It states a preference rather than being directive, and there is no indication that the inquiry expected the medical profession to produce its own guidelines. Thus, it can be seen that there was a familiar, Hippocratic confidence displayed in the ability of individuals to regulate their own behaviour.

However, the tone changed markedly when the report moved on to consider the use of embryos in research. In Chapter 11, then, the recommendation was that research on embryos should only be permitted under licence because such controls were 'essential to safeguard the *public interest* and to allay widespread anxiety'.[24] Equally, in the following chapter, which looked at possible developments in research such as nucleus replacement, the inquiry went further and recommended that the licensing body should 'promulgate guidance on what types of research, apart from those precluded by law, would be considered ethically acceptable in any circumstances'.[25] The guidance should be reviewed 'from time to time to take account of both changes in scientific knowledge and changes in public attitudes'.[26] The decision-making power with respect to research would rest with the licensing body rather than the researchers. As can be seen, the confidence in the conscience of individual medical professionals would not seem to extend to the research scientists, perhaps as a consequence of Nuremburg.

Chapter 13 contained the recommendations regarding the regulation of infertility services and research. This was where the dichotomy between the confidence displayed in individual medical practitioners and the suspicion of the motives of researchers was resolved. The committee essentially prioritised the need to reassure the public over the freedom of doctors and researchers. It recognised that the public concern they identified had to be 'reflected in public

---

[21]   *Ibid* at para 10.5.
[22]   *Ibid* at para 10.8.
[23]   *Ibid* at para 10.8.
[24]   *Ibid* at para 11.18. Emphasis added.
[25]   *Ibid* at para 12.16.
[26]   *Ibid* at para 12.16.

policy ... such restrictions may be regarded as infringing clinical or academic freedom'.[27] Moreover, 'doctors and scientists work within the moral and legal framework determined by society'.[28] In this sense, then, the committee can be seen to have lacked confidence in the medical profession and its ethics to decide what researchers could do, preferring to allow society to determine the limits. Nevertheless, it was also keen to stress that it did not seek to deprive the medical profession of decision-making authority any more than it had to:

> [I]t is not our intention to interfere with the duty of the doctor to exercise clinical judgement in treating patients. Indeed *we accept and expect the doctor to be the person who makes the final decision* about whether a treatment is likely to succeed and *whether it should be used.* Similarly, we accept that scientists must not be unduly restricted in pursuing their research interests.[29]

The inquiry's recommended framework thus stated that the 'interests of those directly concerned, as well as those of society in general, demand that certain legal and ethical safeguards should be applied'.[30] What it envisioned was a body designed to protect the public, which they defined as the 'primary objective of regulation'.[31] This body (which was to become the Human Fertilisation and Embryology Authority) would not be 'exclusively, or even primarily, a medical or scientific body'.[32] It would be a public body charged with protecting the public. Moreover, it would essentially conflate the legal and ethical requirements because it would not give a licence to unethical treatment or research, which, in turn, would be illegal without one. Thus, the committee saw the new body as having two functions, one advisory and one executive. The advisory function would essentially be ethical, issuing 'general guidance ... on good practice in infertility service provision ... it finds broadly ethically acceptable'.[33] The executive function would be more legal in nature, covering the granting of licences and ensuring that licence holders kept to the terms of those licences. In this way, then, the ethico-legal dichotomy could be reconciled. It would have a *legal* function in defining certain conduct as unacceptable and thus refuse to issue licences. It would also ensure that the licence holders did not deviate from its terms. However, beyond that minimum standard of acceptability, the body's role would then move onto a more advisory capacity, advising and guiding doctors and scientists. In this *ethical* function, doctors would be given as much discretion as possible, but only within the boundaries already set by the legal function.

Ultimately, the Warnock Committee saw medical ethics as something that would only become relevant when the question of legality had been settled. The

---

27   *Ibid* at para 12.16para 31.1.
28   *Ibid* at para 12.16para 13.2.
29   *Ibid* at para 13.1. Emphasis added.
30   *Ibid* at para 13.2.
31   *Ibid* at para 13.3.
32   *Ibid* at para 13.4.
33   *Ibid* at para 13.5.

first paragraph of the foreword to the report identified that the definition of the word 'ethical' 'is not absolutely unambiguous', and that it would be used in a wide sense to effectively denote morality.[34] It distinguished this from legal and medical ethics, which referred to 'professionally acceptable practice'.[35] Yet it did not specify that such practice had to be defined by the professions themselves, and the framework they recommend is an indication of that. The committee's vision of regulation involved the non-medical body rather than the medical profession overseeing both legality *and* good practice. This is markedly different from what was seen in the courts in Chapters 4–7 of this book, where decisions were often delegated to medical ethics without oversight. The Warnock Committee's approach can therefore be seen as sensitive to the different purposes of the law and ethics. The law would tell the medical profession what was acceptable, and medical ethics could then work within that framework. In this way, the different functions of medical law and medical ethics could be respected, without the abrogation of responsibility seen in the courts. Furthermore, the clearly-defined differentiation between the roles would aid in the defragmentation of responsibility and discourse. This approach was not to be replicated a decade later.

III.   The House of Lords Select Committee on Medical Ethics – Total, Hippocratic Confidence

A.   Introduction

The House of Lords Select Committee was established to consider:

> the ethical, legal, and clinical implications of a person's right to withhold consent to life-prolonging treatment, and the position of persons who are no longer able to give consent;

> And to consider whether and in what circumstances actions that have as their intention or a likely consequence the shortening of another person's life may be justified on the grounds that they accord with that person's wishes or with that person's best interests.[36]

Like the Warnock Committee, it was presented with a clean slate in that the committee was allowed to suggest either the maintenance of the status quo or changes in the law. It was thus not constricted by any existing legal rules. Additionally, it was asked to deliberate on an inherently ethical subject, as noted in Chapter 7 of this book. Indeed, the decision of the House of Lords in *Bland*, two years before the publication of the report, was cited in the introduction by the committee as one of the catalysts for it having been commissioned in the first

---

[34]   *Ibid* at p 1.
[35]   *Ibid* at p 1.
[36]   *Report of the Select Committee on Medical Ethics* (HL Paper 21-I, 1994) at 7.

place.[37] Others included the trial of Dr Cox for administering a lethal dose of drugs to a suffering patient, advances in medical technology, demographic changes and a change in the nature of the doctor–patient relationship.[38] The remit of the committee was wide. In ethical terms, the rights of both competent and incompetent patients were to be considered. Issues surrounding consent, autonomy and best interests, already considered in Chapters 4–7, again came to the fore. Yet the committee also had to examine issues such as what it meant to be alive, personhood, the value of life and the potential acceptability of proxy decision-making. For the purposes of this book, however, it is how the committee defined medical ethics, and saw its role in relation to the function of the law and practice in the area, that is of interest.

B.   The Report

The report was structured so that, after an introductory section (labelled 'Part 1'), it presented representative examples of the evidence given to it with respect to each issue (Part 2), which formed the bulk of the document. The committee's opinions and recommendations were then set out in the final section (Part 3). The definition and role of medical ethics was not the focus of the Select Committee's inquiry but from the evidence given it is possible to provide a snapshot of what some of the witnesses, and indeed the committee itself, were thinking.

As might be expected, the evidence presented in Part 2 of the report provided an eclectic mixture of opinions, agendas and viewpoints. Also, predictably, the word 'ethics' or its derivatives was used in several instances when, in reality, the witness was referring to a moral judgment. For example, the Society for the Protection of the Unborn Child (SPUC) managed to misuse the word twice in two sentences quoted by the committee with regard to refusing life-saving treatment:

> Even if there is an absolute legal right to refuse all medical treatments, there is no such absolute moral *or ethical* right … Where consent is refused simply in order to hasten death, it amounts to suicide and is *unethical.*[39]

Despite SPUC's seeming distinction between morals and ethics, the ethics to which they referred were certainly not *medical* ethics. Despite being the most persistent party in misusing the word ethics, they were not alone in doing so.[40] Nevertheless, they help to emphasise the point that the notion of the definition of ethics remained as amorphous as ever in 1994.

---

[37]   *Ibid* at para 7.
[38]   *Ibid* at paras 1–10.
[39]   *Ibid* at para 43. Emphasis added.
[40]   See also, for example, paras 167 and 200.

In terms of the medical ethics itself and its role, once again opinions diverged. On the one hand, there was strong representation by some witnesses who believed that decisions at the end of life should not be left to the medical profession and its ethics. Senior members of the legal profession, for example, were quoted as seeking a role that would oversee doctors. Thus Sir Stephen Brown, President of the Family Division of the High Court, stated that it would be appropriate for the courts to examine cases at the end of life, and the Official Solicitor expressed the view that he would be 'prepared to shoulder the burden' of representing incompetent patients.[41] Some welcomed the legal profession's view, arguing that many of these decisions in the courts were not medical at all, and thus should be left to the judiciary rather than the medical profession. Thus the Guild of Catholic Doctors, for example, was of the opinion that doctors should be required to 'submit their views for legal interpretation'.[42] Similarly, Professor Sheila McLean, an academic medical lawyer, stated that it was for 'the law and not the clinician' to make such decisions. Most pertinently, the committee cited ENABLE (a charity concerned with the welfare of people with learning disabilities) as recognising that 'there should be a distinction between the medical prognosis and the ethical decision on treatment'.[43] Medical ethics was not trusted, then, and the unique competence of doctors to decide such issues denied. In this way, it can be seen that there was no abrogation of responsibility to medical ethics as happened so often in the courts.

Many of those same witnesses, though, also expressed a lack of confidence in the law as it stood at the time to regulate medical practitioners' behaviour. ENABLE criticised as 'misconceived' the 'unique status given to the views of medical professionals', and argued that the courts were not a 'genuinely independent safeguard. Almost invariably they have either explicitly followed medical opinions or simply referred decisions back to doctors'.[44] McLean argued that such issues 'are not ultimately referable to current, reasonable or even responsible medical practice'.[45] The committee recognised that many witnesses saw the courts' 'reliance on medical opinion' as a reason for disenchantment with judicial involvement, citing *Bolam* as a 'notable' example.[46] Others, however, were more equivocal and saw a role for medical ethics. The BMA, for example, stated that decisions regarding withdrawal of life-sustaining treatment should be subject to '*various* forms of review'.[47] The Department of Health, meanwhile, said that the courts should become involved only when 'existing legal principles *or professional*

---

[41]   *Ibid* at para 83.
[42]   *Ibid* at para 84.
[43]   *Ibid* at para 86.
[44]   *Ibid* at para 86.
[45]   *Ibid* at para 86.
[46]   *Ibid* at para 85.
[47]   *Ibid* at para 82. Emphasis added.

protocols were insufficient to guide a doctor's decision'.[48] With respect to living wills, Scottish Action on Dementia argued that,

> there would not be the current interest in and demand ... in the United Kingdom if *current codes of professional ethics* were meeting patients' needs ... [although it is] still the case that many United Kingdom doctors do not respect patient autonomy,[49]

suggesting that the answers lay in the codes themselves.

The wide range of opinion on offer was completed by a group of witnesses who appeared to see the issues before them as most appropriately controlled by the medical profession and, by extension, its ethics. This was most evident in the discussions surrounding advance directives. Christian Action Research and Education (CARE), for example, objected to living wills on the grounds that 'it would be bizarre in the extreme to require a skilled, professional doctor to adhere to the stipulations of a living will which did not accord with his/her expert opinion of what would be in the best interests of the patient's health'.[50] Dr David Cook, a Fellow and Chaplain of Green College and Director of the Whitefield Institute, Oxford went even further, stating that to allow advance directives binding status would 'gravely undermine the professional expertise and judgement of doctors. *It would make doctors nothing more than slaves of society*'.[51] Even the BMA was of a similar opinion. In arguing that legislation was unnecessary, it is quoted by the committee as stating that this was because where the advance directive was sufficiently clear doctors should 'regard the patient's wish as determinative'.[52] However, it then continued by arguing that 'it should be possible for a directive to be overridden by clinical judgement', which undermined its previous position.[53] Needless to say, such views are reminiscent of the warnings of Thomas Szasz and Ian Kennedy that we saw in Chapters 2 and 3 that the medical profession was always willing to assume responsibility for non-technical issues, and would then be reluctant to relinquish it.

Part 3 of the report, which contained the committee's recommendations, featured what was essentially a victory for this last group's opinions, as the medical profession was entrusted with significant decision-making power. Indeed, in almost all cases it was entrusted with discretion. Thus, for example, when referring to voluntary euthanasia, the committee stated that it did not support a change in the law in order to allow the practice. This was, in part, because it envisaged that medical ethics could adequately regulate behaviour. It welcomed 'moves by the medical professional bodies to ensure more senior oversight of practice in casualty departments, as a step towards discouraging

---

[48] *Ibid* at para 82.
[49] *Ibid*, at paras 185–6. Emphasis added.
[50] *Ibid* at para 196.
[51] *Ibid* at para 196. Emphasis added.
[52] *Ibid* at para 212.
[53] *Ibid* at para 212.

inappropriately aggressive treatment by less experienced practitioners'.[54] This effectively allowed the medical profession and its ethics unfettered discretion in deciding who to strive to keep alive and who to allow to die. This discretion was even extended when the committee found that there was no 'significant ethical difference' between decisions to discontinue treatment that had already begun and those involving neglecting to begin treatment at all.[55]

The same occurred with respect to the principle of double effect, which allows a doctor to administer drugs with the intention of pain relief even if it shortens the life of the patient. The report labelled this a clinical judgement and stated, in language indicative of *Bolam*, that the doctor must act 'in accordance with responsible medical practice'.[56] In response to the notion that this would amount to 'widespread euthanasia' by the back door, the same attitude towards the medical profession and its ethics was again displayed, with the committee emphasising its 'confidence in the medical profession to discern when the administration of drugs has been inappropriate or excessive'.[57] Indeed, confidence in the medical profession was so high that the committee even rejected calls for the law to provide 'clearer general guidance' as to when discontinuation of treatment might be appropriate.[58] Rather, the committee was happy to note that 'doctors who act responsibly ... have adequate protection under existing law', giving further weight to the suspicion that the committee's first aim was to *protect* medical discretion.[59] This suspicion becomes even stronger upon reading the committee's views on advance directives. Once again, legal regulation was rejected in favour of medical discretion. Thus,

> [i]nstead of legislation ... we recommend that the colleges and faculties of all the health-care professions should jointly develop a code of practice to guide their members. The BMA's Statement on Advance Directives has much to recommend it as a basis for such a code.[60]

Ultimately, then, the abrogation of responsibility was virtually complete. While the committee supported the creation of a judicial forum with the power to choose between alternatives,[61] the amount of discretion given to medical practitioners and their ethics was still significant. Indeed, this was a point that was recognised by the committee itself, who noted that some 'may consider that our conclusions ... give too much weight to the role of accepted medical practice, and that we advocate leaving too much responsibility in the hands of doctors'.[62] Furthermore, they 'may argue that doctors ... are no better qualified than any

---

[54] *Ibid* at para 239.
[55] *Ibid* at para 251.
[56] *Ibid* at para 242.
[57] *Ibid* at para 243.
[58] *Ibid* at para 256.
[59] *Ibid* at para 256.
[60] *Ibid* at para 265.
[61] *Ibid* at paras 245–6.
[62] *Ibid* at para 272.

other group of people to take ethical decisions about life and death'.[63] However, the committee held a Hippocratic view of the morality of individual doctors, and this allowed them to dismiss such fears: '[b]y virtue of their vocation, training and professional integrity ... [doctors] may be expected to act with rectitude and compassion'.[64] What is most perplexing is that, in the very next paragraph, the committee recognised that 'doctors are not a homogenous group' but have 'a variety of philosophical views'.[65] Rather than call into question whether doctors could all be trusted as individuals, the committee saw this as a positive as no single view could 'dominate accepted practice in a way that might prejudice the interests of an individual patient'.[66] There was thus, on the part of the committee, confidence in *both* the conscience of individual medical practitioners *and* medical ethics to regulate them, despite recognising the fact that there was no homogencity within the medical profession.

This somewhat confused vision of how ethical dilemmas might be resolved is a metaphor for the general approach taken by the committee. Medical ethics were for the medical profession to regulate, and the law should remove itself and let doctors evaluate their own behaviour. This makes even less sense when one considers the lack of involvement from the only medical body with statutory authority to regulate doctors – the GMC. Thus, not only did the report suggest that BMA guidance form the basis of the code of practice on advance directives, but the GMC did not even appear in the list of those who provided written evidence. The GMC's president at the time, Sir Robert Kirkpatrick, did provide evidence, but in a personal capacity.[67] The overall picture with regard to medical ethics is thus one of ambivalence borne of a fear of being seen to interfere. Once the committee had identified the issues as pertaining to medical ethics, it immediately deferred decision-making authority to the medical profession. Far from being the 'slaves of society', the Select Committee Report saw them as the kings of the castle.

IV. The Joffe Bill Select Committee Report – Avoiding the Question

A. Introduction

Although it engaged with many of the same issues as the House of Lords Select Committee on Medical Ethics, this Select Committee was formed to consider a specific piece of potential legislation: the Assisted Dying for the Terminally Ill Bill

---

[63] *Ibid* at para 272.
[64] *Ibid* at para 272.
[65] *Ibid* at para 273.
[66] *Ibid* at para 273.
[67] *Ibid* at para 273. See fn 2 on p 19.

proposed by Lord Joffe. Its remit was far ranging, allowing it not only to make amendments to the Bill itself but to also decide whether or not it should proceed at all. The Bill:

> seeks to legalise, for people who are terminally ill, who are mentally competent and who are suffering unbearably, medical assistance with suicide or, in cases where the person concerned would be physically incapable of taking the final action to end his or her life, voluntary euthanasia.[68]

Within such a framework, then, ethical issues arose in abundance. In order to fulfil its role, the report had to look not just at the Bill itself, but also examine the philosophy behind it in order to arrive at a judgement with respect to its adequacy. This is precisely what it did. It began by considering what it termed the 'Underlying Ethical Principles' (autonomy and the sanctity of life), then went on to look at 'Practical Issues' (such as covert euthanasia and the slippery slope argument), before examining both the 'Overseas Experience' and 'Public Opinion'. As can be seen from this structure, then, the Select Committee decided to look at philosophical and practical issues separately. Indeed, the chapter of the report concerning the ethical principles contained a sizeable amount of evidence from academic philosophers, while the chapter on the practical issues was, in general (though not exclusively), the preserve of medical witnesses. While this might be expected, it is somewhat reminiscent of the view of medical ethics as a pedantic irrelevance that we saw in Chapter 3 that typifies contemporary relations between doctors and ethicists. The committee's report contained elements that have been discussed in Chapters 2 and 3 of this book. In particular, themes such as the definitional problem inherent in medical ethics, and the influence of the various sectors of discourse, appeared again.

The key issues for the purposes of this section, however, and what is therefore unique in this report, are those of responsibility and the permanence of ethical principles. With respect to the former, my discussion of Plato in Chapter 2 highlighted Thomas Szasz's view that the medical profession is a willing recipient of responsibility for non-medical issues. Further, as I argued in Chapter 3, once it obtains such responsibility, it is utterly resistant to any attempt to remove it. The decision of the GMC to defend its guidelines in the *Burke* case is evidence of this, as it sought to defend the discretion its guidance gave to doctors to determine when a patient's life ceased to be worth living, and the theme is repeated in this report. Here the issue was that for some witnesses from the medical profession, there was a preference for an unregulated system of covert euthanasia (thus empowering the doctor and her discretion) rather than a system that would be based on legislation and containing substantial judicial oversight. The permanence of ethics concerned the way in which some witnesses to the committee appeared to think that ethical principles, once developed, somehow became

---

[68]   *Report of the Select Committee on the Assisted Dying for the Terminally Ill Bill* (HL Paper 86-I, 2005).

permanent and could not be changed. In such a scenario an inevitable tension would be created if the law was changed and medical ethics did not evolve with it.

B.   The Report

The Bill itself may be seen as a mechanism for society to regain control of end of life issues from the medical profession. Tensions arose precisely with regard to Kennedy and Szasz's argument, in the sense that the medical profession was unwilling to cede control of what are essentially non-medical issues. The starting point for an explanation of this must lie in the practical, rather than ethical, issues identified by the Select Committee. This is because, as the report noted, assisted suicide already occurred in this country, despite its illegality. Indeed, the figures cited in the report suggested that over 10 per cent of medical practitioners had either assisted a patient to die, or personally knew of one who had. A survey conducted by the *Sunday Times* newspaper in 1998 found that one in seven general practitioners had helped a patient to end their life. Similarly, a larger study by McLean in 1996 (with 1,000 respondents rather than 300 for the *Sunday Times*) found that 12 per cent of respondents personally knew a doctor who had helped a patient to kill themselves. The same number was found by Ward and Tate in the *British Medical Journal* in 1994 to have complied with a patient's request to hasten death.[69] What the figures demonstrate is that assisted dying *was already happening*, despite what the law and medical ethics might have said. Thus, Lord Joffe's Bill could be seen as an attempt to regain control over medical behaviour that was illegal, unethical (according to GMC and BMA guidelines), but nevertheless occurring.

Perhaps inevitably there was some attempt on the part of the medical establishment (specifically, the formal and semi-formal sectors of ethical discourse) to deny that this was the case. Dr Michael Wilks of the BMA, for example, argued that there was 'no evidence' of covert euthanasia,[70] and Professor Sir Graeme Catto of the GMC was also dismissive of the claims, albeit in a more qualified manner:

> [W]e have no evidence that this is the case, and we have had a discussion ... about the anecdotal nature of some of these reports. No doubt there is some truth behind them, but we have no objective evidence of which I am aware that this exists.[71]

The conclusion arrived at by the Committee was similar to the evidence provided by Professor Catto. It found that while the surveys may have exaggerated the extent of covert euthanasia, and 'would be surprised if ... [it] were being

---

[69]   *Ibid* at p 31.
[70]   *Ibid* at p 32.
[71]   *Ibid* at p 32.

practiced on anything like the scale of some of these surveys suggest',[72] neverthe-less 'all laws are flouted to a greater or lesser extent, and we would be surprised if … this … were an exception'.[73] The Select Committee appeared to be uncon-cerned both that this practice existed, and that neither the law nor medical ethics had prevented its occurrence. Indeed, it felt that much of what might be termed covert euthanasia was actually doctors using the principle of double effect.[74] The lack of concern on the part of the BMA and GMC was less surprising, however, as it is consistent with Szasz's arguments, and those of both Ian Kennedy's academic writing and the Bristol Inquiry Report, that the medical profession might prefer an informal, secretive system where they retained control in their autonomous, unregulated silos, rather than an objective standard imposed from outside its 'boundaries'. Moreover, it is also consistent with the attitude of some of the medical witnesses 10 years earlier in the House of Lords Select Committee on Medical Ethics in 1994.

The position of the main medical organisations is best summed up with reference to the 'policeman's dilemma' introduced in evidence to the Select Committee. Professor John Harris, a bioethicist, provided a hypothetical, analo-gous situation to the one envisioned in the Bill. This envisioned an accident in the United States in which a motorist was trapped in his burning vehicle, and where it was clear that he would burn to death before he could be freed. The dilemma revolved around whether a policeman on the scene should comply with a request from the motorist to shoot him before he burned to death.[75] Harris was using this to demonstrate a philosophical point, which was that it may sometimes be morally justifiable to kill somebody in order to prevent their further suffering. It also highlighted the favoured position of the medical organisations, which would prefer a model where assisted suicide was officially illegal, but would unofficially continue to occur in rare circumstances without sanction. Needless to say, if rules were not objectively laid down ultimate control would rest instead with individual medical professionals, as there would be no system to regulate them.

Indeed, in the policeman's dilemma, it was the policeman who judged whether the remaining life of the driver was sufficiently intolerable that it would be permissible to end it. It would also be the conscience (or ethics) of the policeman that dictated whether she was willing to comply with the wishes of the suffering driver. In rejecting a change in the law, the medical bodies were essentially seeking to keep control of those two key decisions made by the policeman, thus providing a central role for the medical profession and its ethics. Furthermore, the logic expressed by the GMC in disapproving of the Bill as a whole cannot be

---

[72]   *Ibid* at p 82.
[73]   *Ibid* at p 82.
[74]   *Ibid* at p 81.
[75]   *Ibid* at pp 21–2.

reconciled with its position in the *Burke* case discussed in Chapter 7. Thus, Professor Catto expressed the following view on behalf of the GMC:

> We understand the view that there is no moral difference between withholding life-prolonging treatment and taking active steps to end a patient's life or that there is a continuum which spans both withholding treatment or providing drugs which may have a double effect and taking active steps to end a patient's life. We understand that view but we do not share it. We believe that active steps to end a life raise questions for society on the value it attaches to human life and the role and responsibilities of those curing or restoring health; indeed, those who are responsible for caring for individuals who are nearing death bear special responsibilities.[76]

Yet, as argued with respect to *Burke*, the medical profession appears to wish to maintain control both within the context of providing treatment *and* regarding its withdrawal. As Harris demonstrated with his policeman's dilemma, if society accepts the case of the trapped driver, then 'we concede the principle of assisting death in extreme distress'.[77] Yet the GMC did not seem to see that once it argued for the removal of artificial nutrition and hydration from Mr Burke, it could not then object to the proposed Bill on the grounds that it disapproved of taking active steps to end life.

Thus the preferred model of the medical profession, in particular the GMC, would place almost all of the decision-making burden onto medical ethics at first instance. The policeman's dilemma validates an unofficial and non-objective method of identifying the exceptional situations in which the law may be disregarded. The question of whether the situation was indeed exceptional would thus fall to the medical profession (in the case of assisted suicide) and therefore its ethics. The view of the committee was that once 'anyone takes upon him or herself the responsibility for ending someone's life in order to prevent suffering, he or she must let the courts examine all the facts of the case and reach a judgement on guilt or innocence'.[78] In this way, it can be seen that the committee therefore identified a two-tiered approach to making decisions in such a scenario. First, medical ethics would allow the medical practitioner to make a decision regarding exceptionality. Although that decision might then be examined retrospectively by the courts (the second tier), it remained, essentially, one for the individual doctor to make. Only within such a model could the position of the GMC be justified, in that it retained the definition of the decision as, primarily, medical. Moreover, it allowed it to oppose the concept of assisted suicide, while not only conceding that it might go on but also, perhaps, condoning it at times (indeed, in *Burke* it might even be said by some to have gone even further and dangerously close to involuntary euthanasia).

---

[76]   *Ibid* at p 23.
[77]   *Ibid* at p 22.
[78]   *Ibid* at p 28.

If any control at all is to be exerted on individual practitioners, it must come through a fear of the courts, and/or a fear of the medical profession's disciplinary procedures. In this regard, the law and medical ethics must work in conjunction with each other to prevent decisions being based on a doctor's individual morality. Ultimately, as we have seen, it was almost identical to the attitude of some seen a decade earlier in the Report of the House of Lords Select Committee on Medical Ethics. Another issue specific to this report is that of the perceived impact on medical ethics of a fundamental change in the law. Indeed, it has long been a staple of ethical guidance that assisted suicide is unethical. If the law were to be changed to allow it, though, might this also signify that it might be ethical to comply with a patient's request to aid her suicide? Contradictory approaches to answering this question were suggested to the committee. The first of these was to identify principles through which the provisions of the Bill may be either supported or disapproved of, then frame the response accordingly. This would dislocate ethical principles from their sources and purpose. For example, the report began by considering the principles of autonomy and the sanctity of life.[79] The variety of sources used was wide, including philosophers, lawyers, religious groups (both Christian and Jewish), pressure groups alongside doctors speaking in a personal capacity, the GMC and BMA.

However, the ethical principles were discussed in a way that suggested that they existed on their own, rather than in conjunction with the law and thus the society around it, and were therefore unchanging absolutes. Thus, for example, the GMC opined that the Bill, if enacted, would be 'difficult to reconcile with the medical ethical principles of beneficence and non-maleficence'.[80] Similarly, Professor Leigh of the Association of British Neurologists was quoted as saying that hastening the death of a patient 'is traditionally – and probably always will be – against the medical ethic'.[81] These statements suggest that the ethical principles they referred to existed independently of any change in the law or, indeed, professional guidance. There was no indication or recognition that the 'medical ethic' may have to change if the Bill were to be enacted. Therefore, for some medical practitioners at least, medical ethics was a concept that was not just internal to the medical profession, but also one that could not be divorced from the self-image that doctors had with regard to their profession, and a change in the law would therefore have no effect on it. In this way, then, Professor Maughan, an oncologist at the University of Cardiff, began his evidence with the words '[t]o me as a doctor'.[82] The implication from these examples is that the Bill was not just contrary to their vision of their profession and its ethics, but also that the ethics were not negotiable or liable to change. In this approach, then, medical ethics becomes detached from everything outside the profession. It

---

[79]   *Ibid* at Chapter 3.
[80]   *Ibid* at p 42.
[81]   *Ibid* at p 22.
[82]   *Ibid* at p 22.

belongs to, and becomes crucial to, the professional self-image of the individual doctor. The ethics thus preceded the Bill and would continue to exist irrespective of whether it became law. The law would therefore have to conform to medical ethics to be acceptable, rather than the reverse.

Another approach, however, suggested that medical ethics be seen as a more flexible concept. It differed from the first in the sense that it envisaged medical ethics not as an absolute or immovable concept, but as one that was sensitive to outside influences such as the law. Rather than medical ethics imposing principles on others, this view saw medical ethics as being receptive to changes in the society around it. This may be summed up by the view of the committee, early on in its report, that the 'perceived problem ... is more about the *impact of the law* along the lines of the Bill *on medical ethics* as a whole'.[83] The report referred to this as a paradigm shift, with respect to the notion that the Bill would introduce death as a further treatment option, and the presumption was that medical ethics would also therefore change.

Indeed, the committee strengthened the credentials of this approach by concluding that 'the acceptability or otherwise of a change in the law is a matter for society as a whole to decide through its legislators in Parliament'.[84] The medical profession, while influential, would not have a determinative say in the potential change in the law. Given this, it is not surprising that some professional bodies had a 'neutral stance' on the 'underlying principles' of the Bill.[85] But this view was not universal. The report highlighted the fact that the BMA and the Royal College of Nursing both voiced opposition to the change in the law, as did some individual doctors. Of course, individual doctors and professional groups were entitled to voice their opinions. That, after all, is what is what the Select Committee would wish them to do. Nevertheless, the second approach left open the question of whether medical ethics might be forced to change with the law. Under the first approach, the ethical standard was an inflexible absolute. However, since medical ethics should be consistent with the law, it could not be inflexible. This was something that was recognised by the GMC, who noted that their guidance 'will always be consistent with the law'.[86]

Perplexingly, having identified the two approaches, the committee declined to choose between them, and thus there was no resolution to what is a fundamental difference in opinion regarding the definition and role of medical ethics. Indeed, all that can be done here is to recognise that such a dispute existed. The committee concluded that the Bill should be returned to Parliament to be reconsidered, but with some provisos. They included, for example, that a clear distinction be made between assisted suicide and voluntary euthanasia and that

---

[83]   *Ibid* at p 40. Emphasis added.
[84]   *Ibid* at p 82.
[85]   *Ibid* at p 83. The report referred to the Royal College of Physicians and the Royal College of General Practitioners as holding this view.
[86]   *Report on the Assisted Dying for the Terminally Ill Bill* at p 41.

doctors conscientiously objecting should not be forced to refer applicants to another physician. On the subject of how the Bill would affect medical ethics, or indeed of medical ethics itself, the committee was silent.

V. Conclusion

In all of the reports considered here, there has been a wide range of opinions and sources of discourse in evidence. It is perhaps not surprising, then, to find that within each report there are differing conceptions of what medical ethics is and what it is there to do. They also demonstrate distinct approaches on the part of each committee. In Warnock, the committee was prepared to be more directive than in the other two. Indeed, the starting point in that report was the law and what society would consider to be acceptable. The ethics were expected to follow suit. Indeed, even if one might disagree with the amount of discretion for ethical matters given to medical practitioners, it is the framework conceived by that committee that is to be applauded. The law and medical ethics were conjoined and envisioned as working together, thus defragmenting the different sources of discourse.

In the 1994 House of Lords Select Committee Report, on the other hand, the most pronounced aspect was the abrogation of responsibility to the medical profession. This was recognised by the committee itself, as can be seen by the fact that in its conclusion it defended itself against anticipated criticism on this point. In that report, medical ethics were seen as an effective regulatory tool that the law should not be seen to be interfering with – an approach that reflects the attitude of many of the judges in Chapters 4–7. It is difficult to conceive of a more total capitulation than that of that Select Committee. Medical ethics were trusted totally, and the views of medical professionals that *they* were best placed to make decisions at the end of life were accepted without qualification. This is almost the polar opposite to Warnock, in the sense that once the ethical issue was identified, the law was seen as most appropriately withdrawing and not interfering. Given the lack of ethical guidance from the GMC and BMA on this topic in 1994, as we saw in Chapter 7, this abrogation is even more surprising and even less justified. Ethical decisions were seen as best left to *individual doctors* due to the absence of formal and semi-formal guidance, an incredible occurrence that ignores the lessons of Plato and Nuremburg, not to mention Szasz and Kennedy.

The report of the committee considering Lord Joffe's bill, meanwhile, did not really come to any conclusions regarding medical ethics at all. Despite two schools of thought regarding it being present and identifiable, the report did not really engage with the issue. Nor did it comment on the notion that medical practitioners were still seeking responsibility for matters that were not medical in nature. In this respect, the attitude of many of the witnesses was similar to that to be found in the 1994 Select Committee Report. The warnings given by Szasz and Kennedy again come to mind. This is particularly the case when one considers the fact that the GMC and BMA both argued for approaches that would allow the medical profession to keep control of issues at the end of life. When this is combined with the GMC's attitude in *Burke*, it can be seen that even today 'cultural flaws' exist in the medical profession, corroborating the view Bristol Inquiry Report. Also evident is a desire on the part of the profession to maintain its (excessive) professional autonomy. If we also accept that there has been a fragmentation of discourse and regulation, then all three elements of the process identified at Bristol can be seen to be present, just as in Chapters 5–7.

9

Conclusion

I. Medical Law and Medical Ethics – A Symbiotic Relationship

The relationship between medical law and medical ethics is clearly a symbiotic one. Both organisms must coexist, and each must rely on the other. We have seen throughout this book that medical ethics and ethical principles have had to be dealt with by the courts and committees, while legal rules have had to be considered by medical ethics. Moreover, the law has frequently seen medicalisation and the abrogation of responsibility to medical ethics as a panacea, and the latter has therefore had to shoulder this burden, albeit willingly. But can this relationship be said to be mutually beneficial? I would have to say no. In this book I have argued that, rather than acting in concert, medical law and medical ethics have, at times, effectively cancelled each other out, leaving a regulatory vacuum to be filled by the conscience of individual medical practitioners. That is not to say that the relationship always fails to work – as risk disclosure in Chapter 4, and the Warnock Committee's report in Chapter 8 demonstrate.

Nevertheless, there have also been times that the relationship has failed to work, as we saw in Chapter 5, where the law gave responsibility to medical ethics on the misplaced *presumption* that it would regulate medical behaviour. This was also evident in Chapter 6, where the approach of both the law and medical ethics was to leave decisions to the discretion of *individual* doctors, thus ignoring the lessons of Kennedy, Szasz, Plato and Nuremburg that this book has highlighted. However, perhaps the most concerning examples of the relationship can be seen in issues at the end of life, discussed in Chapter 7, and then in Chapter 8 with reference to the House of Lords Select Committees in 1994 and 2005. In all of these examples, the clearly ethical issues were openly medicalised, the medical profession sought and received decision-making authority, and the role of patients in making decisions about their own lives (and deaths) was marginalised. Again, medical law and ethics can be seen to have combined to have allowed more, rather than less, discretion for the conscience of individual medical practitioners.

Yet the problem lies not just in how medical law and ethics *have* combined, but in what the perceived model of this ethico-legal relationship has the *potential* to do. Indeed, what this book has shown is that the process identified by the Bristol Inquiry Report – cultural flaws, excessive autonomy and fragmentation – is replicated within the relationship between medical law and ethics. Indeed, as argued above, this has led to instances where the relationship has not worked, and that a regulatory vacuum has ensued. However, given the fact that the process has not been identified, it cannot be rectified. In this sense, an effective relationship between law and ethics, such as that regarding risk disclosure, can only be seen as fortuitous in the way that it has developed, and the exception rather than the rule. As I demonstrate below, the process almost inevitably results in decision-making responsibility being given to medical professionals.

II.   Cultural Flaws within the Medical Profession

That such flaws exist within the medical profession is undeniable. Indeed, the Bristol Inquiry Report itself identified that this was the case only five years ago. Thus, it will be remembered that the report found that patients were 'discourage[d] from asking questions', and were given 'only limited access to information'.[1] Moreover, it further warned that this attitude was not limited to the BRI, but rather all pervasive in the NHS.[2] This led to the creation of boundaries, silos and a lack of willingness to allow 'outsiders' to become involved in debates. Yet examples of such paternalistic behaviour by medical professionals pervade this book. In Chapter 3, we saw that the medical ethics renaissance's appropriation of medical ethics was not welcomed by the medical profession. Indeed, non-doctors were warned that their involvement in medical ethics discourse risked it being seen as a 'pedantic irrelevance' by the medical profession.[3] While it is easy to see their point, as the increased academisation of medical ethics and the subject-specific and 'critical' nature of debate can alienate rather than include doctors, it must be remembered that the renaissance was borne out of the horrors of what the Nazi doctors did in the name of medicine. Given this, the involvement of non-doctors in debate was as inevitable as it was, and continues to be, justified.

However, this book has also shown that the medical profession remains, in general terms, committed to keeping control over those ethical issues that it currently has decision-making power over. Indeed, as I have demonstrated in Chapters 2 and 3, the medical profession has willingly accepted responsibility for matters that are intrinsically ethical rather than medical. This can be seen to continue in both the case law examined in Chapter 4–7, and also the committee reports in Chapter 8. In every case, the medical professionals have argued for the continued power over non-technical issues. In Chapter 4 the issue was how much

---

[1]   *Learning From Bristol: The Report of the Public Inquiry into Children's Heart Surgery at the Bristol Royal Infirmary 1984–1995* (Cm 5207, 2001) at 268.

[2]   *Bristol Inquiry Report.*

[3]   C B Chapman, *Physicians, Law, and Ethics* (New York, New York University Press, 1984) at 133.

information to provide patients, in Chapter 5 they sought the right to treat minors without the involvement of their parents, in Chapter 6 it was the right to determine a patient's best interests, and in Chapter 7, most obviously, the GMC argued for the right to decide when and how a man such as Mr Burke should die. Chapter 8 contained similar arguments about the end of life, and also the right to decide who should receive assisted reproduction services. Whether they have received the responsibility or not, it has still been, and continues to be, sought by the medical profession, and when it is given power it has taken it willingly.

III. Excessive Professional Autonomy

In most cases, however, the responsibility has indeed been granted. The exception to this is Chapter 4, where the law has gradually wrested responsibility away from the medical profession, and even appears to be on the verge of rejecting *Bolam*. Nevertheless, this has been achieved within the context of formal and semi-formal medical ethics that have, again exceptionally in this book, sought to maximise the autonomy of the patient. This approach has not been replicated. Thus in Chapter 5 each and every case, whether supportive or not of adolescent autonomy, abrogated decision-making responsibility for the ethical question of whether to treat them to the medical profession and its ethics. In Chapter 6, with respect to best interests, the courts embarked on a process of de-*Bolam*isation similar to that in Chapter 4, only for Parliament to produce legislation that potentially leaves more discretion in the hands of the ultimate decision-maker. As I argued there, although it is less likely than before, in many cases it will still be *doctors* who make such decisions.

Chapter 7 is also unique in its approach, but for the opposite reason. Here, the process of de-*Bolam*isation was begun but then *reversed* by the Court of Appeal in *Burke*. The (clearly) ethical question of when a patient's life stopped being worth living was re-medicalised, and the patient's argument that *he* should make that decision was rejected. Indeed, *Burke* represents an almost total capitulation to the medical profession and its ethics in an area that, more than any other, it might be expected to demure from doing so. The pattern continues in Chapter 8. Thus the Warnock Committee report, despite envisioning a model for medical law and ethics that took account of the differences between the two, still gave doctors a significant degree of discretion regarding the ethical matter of who would receive treatment. The 1994 Select Committee's report was a total and conscious abrogation of responsibility towards the medical profession, and it may even be seen as the precursor of the view of the Court of Appeal in *Burke*. The 2005 Select Committee did not make too many recommendations but, as I argued, it demonstrated the fact that even now the medical profession resists any attempt to remove decision-making responsibility from it. In this way, it can be seen that the medical profession still enjoys a significant amount of autonomy regarding virtually every issue discussed in this book.

IV. Fragmentation

The Bristol Inquiry Report noted that there was a fragmentation of responsibility at the BRI, and that this led to various different bodies potentially regulating the staff there. This abundance of guidance, however, did not regulate *more* but instead cancelled itself out, leaving a regulatory vacuum. Thus:

> The SRSAG [Supra Regional Services Advisory Group] thought that the health authorities or the Royal College of Surgeons were doing it; the Royal College of Surgeons thought that the SRSAG or the trust were doing it, and so it went on. No one was doing it. We cannot say that the external system for assuring and monitoring the quality of care was inadequate. There was, in truth, no such system.[4]

The same is true in contemporary medical ethics. As Chapters 2 and 3 demonstrated, the medical profession has traditionally regulated itself and, in general, its ethics have been created by doctors and for doctors. This changed with the renaissance which, ironically, has done more than anything else to help fragment ethical discourse. As I have argued, one of the catalysts for the medical ethics renaissance was a desire by non-doctors to get involved in ethical issues after the horrors exposed at Nuremburg. This led to more discourse on medical ethics, from a great variety of sources, with different and often totally incompatible viewpoints. Indeed, if we include all ethical discourse under the umbrella term 'medical ethics', then it must be possible to 'ethically' justify any opinion that one cares to hold. However, this increase in volume of writing, without categorisation or hierarchy, has by its very nature created an ethical black hole through which regulatory vacuums may be born. Thus if it is possible to find ethical justification both to transfuse or not to transfuse a Jehovah's Witness, or both to proceed with an abortion on a 17-year-old who refuses consent to it or not to do so, then something *other* than medical ethics will have to make the ultimate decision, because after applying the ethics all avenues remain open. Yet this is exactly how medical ethics, due to the lack of hierarchy and categorisation, operates today. Indeed the three sectors of ethical discourse, formal, semi-formal and unofficial, have all been cited by the courts in support of their decisions on ethical matters. Furthermore, as I argued in Chapter 3, the formal and semi-formal sectors have become more like the unofficial sector, thus perpetuating the idea of a more analytical approach to ethical reasoning.

This fragmentation could be reversed by the law, which could send a message to doctors concerning the prioritisation of the different sources of discourse. However, the courts are instead complicit in the fragmentation. Thus in Chapter 4 the House of Lords in *Chester* considered unofficial medical ethics and that from the semi-formal sectors (though not the BMA) despite comprehensive and authoritative guidance being available from the GMC. This was even more

---

[4] *Bristol Inquiry Report* 192.

pronounced in Chapter 7, where the House of Lords in *Bland* found a BMA discussion document to represent medical ethics and the court in *Re G* was similarly subservient towards the BMA. In *Burke* at first instance, BMA guidance was praised while the GMC version was found to be incompatible with the law – and yet the judge did not comment on the undesirability of this state of affairs. The Court of Appeal in *Burke* was to reverse this finding, but the general impression in that chapter is that the BMA is more influential than the GMC in issues at the end of life. This suspicion is strengthened by Chapter 8, where at the 1994 House of Lords Select Committee the BMA was represented while the GMC was absent. Again, while this was to change by the time of the 2005 version, the BMA appears to be ever-present while the involvement of the GMC s more sporadic.

Thus, if the law should be what Sheila McLean called the 'buffer between medicalisation and human rights', then it can only be said to have failed.[5] Indeed, as I have mentioned above, only in Chapter 4 has the law actually demedicalised the ethical issues before them. In Chapter 6 the *courts* began the process, but the Mental Capacity Act 2005 will perhaps be a step backwards in that respect, in the sense that it gives more discretion to the decision-maker. In Chapters 5 and 7 on the other hand, the abrogation of ethical matters to medical ethics is total, conscious and explicit. Whether one agrees with the effect of the law or not, it is surely inappropriate to medicalise such matters when the law could itself maintain control through the courts or legislation. Indeed, the confidence expressed in medical ethics as a regulatory tool, and the conscience of individual medical practitioners, is almost complete.

Yet more concerning than all of this, however, is the automatic acceptance of the assertion by the doctors, in the case of *Re B* in Chapter 7, that to respect the wishes of Ms B would be 'unethical' despite the explicit view to the contrary in BMA guidance. The lack of recognition by the court that this constituted a problem indicates an acceptance on the part of the judge that what is or is not ethical is to be determined by the individual doctor. In the absence of a hierarchy or categorisation of ethical discourse, the law is essentially complicit in the fragmentation, and indeed its general abrogation of responsibility means that it has at times become little more than just another fragment of discourse.

V. The Dangers of Fragmentation

At Bristol, the Inquiry identified the fact that the fragmentation of responsibility and regulation led to the individual silos being able to effectively do as they pleased. The vast array of standards paradoxically combined to create *no* standards, and it was the discretion of individuals that filled the gap. In three of the

---

[5] S McLean, *Old Law, New Medicine: Medical Ethics and Human Rights* (London, Pandora 1999) 2.

four issues in Chapters 4–7, and in two of the three legal frameworks recommended by the committees in Chapter 8, this is also evident. Thus, as the law abrogates responsibility to medical ethics, thinking that it is an effective regulatory tool, it does so based on a false premiss, as the formal and semi-formal medical ethics considered in this book leave much to the discretion of individual doctors. Indeed, in those chapters law and ethics cannot be said to complement each other, but rather to leave decisions to the discretion of medical practitioners.

Chapter 5 provides the most obvious and extreme example of this. It will be remembered that in *Re W* Lord Donaldson felt such confidence in medical ethics as a regulatory tool that he left a legal loophole, safe in the knowledge that it would not be able to be exploited:

> Hair-raising possibilities were canvassed of abortions being carried out by doctors in reliance upon the consent of parents and despite the refusal of consent by 16- and 17-year-olds. Whilst this may be possible as a matter of law, *I do not see any likelihood taking account of medical ethics*, unless the abortion was truly in the best interests of the child. This is not to say that it could not happen.[6]

I also demonstrated, however, that no such medical ethics existed at the time that would do as his Lordship presumed that it would. Moreover, since the case was decided, the GMC and BMA medical ethics have developed in such a way that they *still* do not do as he presumed.[7] Rather, both equivocate and advise the reader of the legal position. Thus, the GMC advises that 'where a competent child refuses treatment, a person with parental responsibility or the court may authorise investigation or treatment which is in the child's best interests'.[8] The BMA is even more explicit, stating that doctors 'must act within the law and balance the harm caused by violating a young person's choice against the harm caused by failing to treat. *In cases of doubt, legal advice should be sought*'.[9]

Two points emerge from this situation. First, that the regulatory vacuum identified at Bristol can be seen to have developed. In this area, the law abrogated responsibility to medical ethics, presuming that it would be willing and able to perform a regulatory function. However, this was a misplaced assumption, and indeed medical ethics does not do so, instead deferring to the inconsistent legal position. Thus, both the law and medical ethics presume that the other is regulating behaviour, and do not see the need to do so themselves, and thus just as at Bristol *no* regulation occurs. The second point of note is that the law in this situation becomes little more than another fragment of discourse. Indeed, by stating its disapproval of the behaviour in the example but neglecting to threaten legal sanctions, Lord Donaldson was telling doctors what he thought that they

---

[6]   *Re W (A Minor)(Medical Treatment: Court's Jurisdiction)* [1992] 4 All ER 627 at 635. Emphasis added.

[7]   For a more detailed discussion of this point see J Miola, 'Medical Law and Medical Ethics: Complementary or Corrosive' (2004) 6 *Medical Law International* 251.

[8]   GMC, *Seeking Patients' Consent: The Ethical Considerations* (GMC, 1998) para 23.

[9]   BMA, *Medical Ethics Today* (BMA, 2004) 131. Emphasis added.

ought to do rather than what they *must* do. The consequence of all of this is that as neither the law nor medical ethics provide directive guidance, it is legal and ethical *both* to perform the abortion, and also not to do so. Whatever the basis of that decision might be, we know that it is not either medical law or medical ethics.

A somewhat similar state of affairs developed in Chapter 6, where both the new legislation and the ethical guidance potentially leave much to the discretion of the medical practitioner. In that chapter the ethical guidance was initially more onerous than the legal duty, but still defined the concept of best interests as essentially a clinical judgment. Furthermore, doctors were not required to do anything. Rather, the language used was permissive and equivocal. The GMC therefore provides a checklist of factors that the doctor has to 'take into account'.[10] The BMA guidance contains a similar checklist of factors that doctors should 'consider'.[11] Yet the common law caught up with the guidance, and even overtook it in the cases of *Re A* and *Re SL*, and a potential problem loomed as the law was becoming more sensitive to the rights of patients then medical ethics. This wholly undesirable state of affairs has been averted due to the passing of the Mental Capacity Act 2005.

The legislation, however, brings with it its own problems. Chief among them is the fact that the wording of the Act resembles that of the guidance in its equivocal nature. Thus we again see factors that the doctor 'must consider', others that she must 'take into account' and yet others for which 'regard will be had'. In the context of a proposed sterilisation, therefore, two doctors 'considering' the same facts can conceivably come to different conclusions regarding the ethical justification for carrying out the procedure. On a literal reading of the guidance, to proceed could be *both* ethical and unethical. The law would state the same and, as we saw in the case of *Re G*, albeit in a different context and before *Bolitho*, there is precedent for the courts accepting that an ethical imperative to 'consider' only obliges the doctor to consult, and not also to act on the results of that consultation. Just as in the Chapter 5, then, the relationship between the law and ethics ensures that something other than law or ethics is making the decision.

In Chapter 7 the situation is somewhat different, because the discretion of doctors occurs due to a deliberate and conscious medicalisation of issues at the end of life. Thus, the GMC sought, and the Court of Appeal in *Burke* granted it, decision-making powers regarding when Mr Burke's life stopped being worth living. Clearly, in seeking such responsibility regarding a non-technical issue, the GMC was displaying what the Bristol Inquiry would term a 'cultural flaw', and the courts have granted it excessive professional autonomy. All that is left to complete the Bristol process here too is fragmentation, and again the law encourages rather than prevents it. In Chapter 7, it does this by seeming to favour the BMA over the

---

[10]   GMC, *Seeking Patients' Consent: The Ethical Considerations* n 8 at para 25.
[11]   BMA, *Medical Ethics Today* (2004) n 9 at 108.

GMC, as the cases of *Bland, Re G, Ms B* and even *Burke* at first instance indicate. This is unproblematic in practice as long as the guidance from the two groups is substantially the same. Yet *Burke* and its aftermath have shown that cracks are beginning to appear. As we have seen, the BMA has declared that a competent advance request for ANH not to be withdrawn must be respected, while the GMC went to the Court of Appeal to argue that this should not automatically be the case. Yet again, depending on which body a doctor prefers, it can be ethical *both* to respect the request, and also not to do so.

The two House of Lords Select Committees indicate that the problems in the courts are unlikely to go away. The 1994 committee totally abrogated responsibility, as I demonstrated, not just to the medical profession but also to individual medical practitioners. It is worth remembering that, barely more than ten years ago, the committee noted that 'by virtue of their vocation, training and professional integrity ... [doctors] may be expected to act with rectitude and compassion', and that this was a part of its justification for its capitulation.[12] The 2005 committee examining Lord Joffe's Bill did not engage with medical ethics per se, but what is noticeable is the confirmation of the fact that both the GMC and BMA were resistant to any removal of responsibility from them regarding an ethical matter. Given the potential conflict in Chapter 7, it is imperative that the courts and Parliament identify what they would be abrogating responsibility to, and consequently resist the temptation to do so.

VI. Rectifying the Problem – A Proposal for the Future

Thus, the courts and committees can be seen to have given a significant amount of discretion to medical ethics and, as I have shown above, medical ethics does not justify the confidence expressed in it. Rather its amorphous, fragmented state ensures that the delegated issues are often being abrogated to the conscience and personal morality of individual medical practitioners. But before a solution can be found to the issues identified in this book, it is first imperative that future courts and committees actually recognise the problem that exists. In short, they must identify the fact that their confidence in medical ethics is misplaced.

Indeed, in virtually every case (the 1994 Select Committee excepted), the *intended* abrogation has been to medical ethics rather than individual medical practitioners. Thus, to take some examples from the House of Lords, Lord Templeman in *Sidaway* referred to doctors as having to be 'obedient to the high standards set by the medical profession'.[13] In *Gillick*, Lord Fraser stated of doctors who acted badly that he would 'expect him to be disciplined by his own professional body accordingly'.[14] In *F v West Berkshire*, Lord Goff referred to

¹² *Report of the Select Committee on Medical Ethics* (HL Paper 21-I, 1994) at para 272.
¹³ *Sidaway v Board of Governors of Bethlem Royal Hospital* [1985] 1 All ER 643 at 665.
¹⁴ *Gillick v West Norfolk and Wisbech Area Health Authority* [1985] 3 All ER 402 at 413.

doctors acting under 'no greater duty than that imposed by his own Hippocratic Oath', implying a mixture of good conscience and a professional code.[15] Finally, in *Bland* Lord Goff emphasised that the courts should regard doctors' 'professional standards with respect'.[16] This list, indeed, does not even include Lord Donaldson's hypothetical example in *Re W*, or any other of the occasions that pepper Chapters 4–7. Once again, this is replicated in Chapter 8, where the 1994 Select Committee rejected calls for legal regulation, instead recommending that the various colleges and faculties of the medical profession 'should jointly develop a code of practice'.[17]

Yet the courts do not seem to have learned that what they *think* they are delegating to is not what they *are* giving responsibility to. Perhaps they think that, because there is so much medical ethics discourse, then there must be more regulation. As this book has demonstrated, this is of course not the case. The ultimate irony is that the non-doctors who constitute the medical ethics renaissance involved themselves in ethical debate precisely in order to prevent the consciences of individual doctors from making such decisions, only to cause a fragmentation that has encouraged exactly what they sought to eradicate.

After this, there must be a further recognition that the discretion given to individual medical practitioners rather than medical ethics is a consequence of this fragmentation of discourse. As I have shown, the courts in particular have at some points actually become complicit in this. The prioritisation given to the BMA in Chapter 7 is an example of this, as is the use of semi-formal ethics by the House of Lords in *Chester* in Chapter 4. Indeed, the lack of categorisation of ethical discourse has *actually* resulted in instances where it can be considered 'ethical' to act in contradictory ways, as shown above. Until this is identified it cannot be rectified. The key to this is the absence of a hierarchy of discourse, which means that different bodies and groups actually compete with each other rather than 'knowing their place'. To this end, the GMC must accept much of the blame. Traditionally, it has been slow to publish ethical advice – certainly slower than the BMA – and much of what it has published is somewhat vague in nature. Indeed, a simple comparison between the latest version of the GMC's *Good Medical Practice* and the BMA's 800-page new edition of *Medical Ethics Today* illustrates the point more than adequately. If the GMC wants to fulfil its statutory role as the guardian of ethical guidance to the medical profession, then its documents must reflect that and be authoritative. It might well be more than a coincidence that the one area where the GMC has led, informed consent, is the one issue in this book where medical law and ethics work very well together, as Chapter 4 shows.

This is unlikely to occur in the near future, however. Indeed, the GMC has recently received more criticism than praise. In 2006 the Chief Medical Officer

---

[15]   *F v West Berkshire Health Authority* [1990] 2 AC 1 at 77–8.
[16]   *Airedale NHS Trust v Bland* [1993] 1 All ER 821 at 872.
[17]   *House of Lords Select Committee on Medical Ethics* n 12 at para 265.

(CMO), Sir Liam Donaldson, published a report that examined medical regulation and the maintenance of standards.[18] The CMO recognised that in the 1970s, 1980s and 1990s the GMC had faced mounting criticism of its ability to regulate the medical profession in the light of a number of 'highly publicised medical scandals', with the events at BRI seen as a 'major turning point'.[19] Mainly concerned with revalidation and clinical fitness to practice, the report nevertheless accepted criticism of the GMC on the basis that it had failed to adequately regulate medical behaviour. It noted bluntly that this had always been the case and that 'at no point during its long history has it been able to command the respect of all its constituencies – public, doctors and politicians – simultaneously'.[20]

This has been exacerbated by the fact that there is still confusion as to what the GMC is actually there to do. Indeed, some doctors still think that the GMC's role is to 'represent' them.[21] Such confusion cannot be good for medicine, for patients, or for medical ethics. It is certainly arguable that the confusion regarding the role of the GMC is a consequence of fragmentation, and that it points to the regulatory vacuum identified by the Bristol Inquiry Report. Moreover, the recommendations made by the CMO, that the GMC should license affiliates within the NHS to investigate complaints, miss the point of Bristol. Contracting out regulation only serves to add other potential fragments to an already overcrowded arena, and I would argue that there is more chance of *more* fragmentation rather than less unless it is identified soon, as others step in to fill the perceived regulatory hole.

Indeed, perhaps it is the case that the GMC can no longer justify its role as the regulator of the medical profession. Dame Janet Smith's report into Harold Shipman has recommended this, and the Bristol Inquiry report also favoured the creation of a new body that would set standards.[22] In both cases this was done in a clinical context, and Margot Brazier has argued that there is no distinction between clinical and ethical issues in this regard, and that consequently a Commission for Health Care, Law and Ethics should be established. She views the remit of this commission as being wider than the development of the law, and including ethical standards, 'and when it is appropriate for the ethical standard to be set higher than the law'.[23] I would agree. However, Brazier envisions this body working with the Law Commission regarding the law, and the GMC with regard

[18]   The Chief Medical Officer, *Good Doctors, Safer Patients: Proposals to strengthen the System to Assure and Improve the Performance of Doctors and to Protect the Safety of Patients* (Department of Health, 2006).

[19]   *Ibid* (vii).

[20]   *Ibid* 170.

[21]   *Ibid* 69.

[22]   *The Shipman Inquiry: Fifth Report; Safeguarding Patients: Lessons from the Past – Proposals for the Future* (The Stationary Office, Cmnd 6394, 2004). *Bristol Inquiry Report.*

[23]   M Brazier, *Medicine, Patients and the Law* (3rd edn, London, Penguin, 2003) 485. See generally pp 481–7.

to ethics. This is where I would part company with her, and instead prefer that a new body be set up that would seek to ensure that the law and ethics complemented each other on its own, rather than as an intermediary between others.

Only in this way can the antidote be found for fragmentation. A new body with *sole* power to determine ethical standards and ensure that they are consistent with the law is the only way to ensure that there is no competition between categories of discourse. In the interim, judges and committee members must realise that when they abrogate responsibility for ethical matters, they are mistaken with regard to the real recipients of their *largesse*. The cultural flaws in the medical profession and the excessive professional autonomy can wait. Indeed, the key to heeding the lessons of Plato, Nuremburg, Kennedy and Szasz, and in finally achieving the aims of the medical ethics renaissance, lies in defragmenting medical ethics. A whole is far easier to fix than a vast and varied collection of disparate parts. For the moment, however, the law is a part of the problem rather than the solution, and its relationship with medical ethics can only be described as mutually detrimental, and the result is a total contradiction to what it sets out to achieve.

Bibliography

ABRAMS, N and BUCKNER, D (eds), *Medical Ethics: A Clinical Textbook and Reference for the Health Care Professions* (Cambridge, Mass, MIT Press, 1983)

ATKINS, K, 'Autonomy and the Subjective Character of Experience' (2000) 17 *Journal of Applied Philosophy* 71

BAINHAM, A, 'The Judge and the Competent Minor' (1992) 108 *LQR* 194

BARRY, V, *Moral Aspects of Health Care* (Belmont, California, Wadsworth, 1982)

BEAUCHAMP, T and CHILDRESS, J, *Principles of Biomedical Ethics* (4th edn, New York, Oxford University Press, 1994)

BIGGS, H, Euthanasia, *Death With Dignity and the Law* (Oxford, Hart, 2001)

BMA, *Consent, Rights and Choices in Health Care for Children and Young People* (BMJ Books, 2000)

BMA, *Discussion Paper on Treatment of Patients in Persistent Vegetative State* (BMA, 1992)

BMA, *Ethics and Members of the Medical Profession* (BMA, 1949)

BMA, *Guidelines for the Treatment of Patients in a Persistent Vegetative State* (BMA, 1993)

BMA, *Medical Ethics Today, Its Practice and Philosophy* (BMA, 1993)

BMA, *Medical Ethics Today: The BMA's Handbook of Ethics and Law* (2nd edn, BMA, 2004)

BMA, *Philosophy and Practice of Medical Ethics* (BMA, 1988)

BMA, *Report of the Consent Working Party: Incorporating Consent Toolkit* (BMA, 2001)

BMA, *The Handbook of Medical Ethics* (BMA, 1980)

BMA, *Withholding and Withdrawing Life-Prolonging Medical Treatment: Guidance for Decision Making* (BMA, 1999)

BMA, *Withholding and Withdrawing Life-Prolonging Medical Treatment: Guidance for Decision Making* (2nd edn, BMA, 2001)

BRAZIER, M and MIOLA, J, 'Bye-Bye Bolam: A Medical Litigation Revolution?' (2000) 8 *Medical Law Review* 85

BRAZIER, M, 'Patient Autonomy and Consent to Treatment: The Role of the Law' (1987) 7 *Legal Studies* 169

BRAZIER, M, *Medicine, Patients and the Law* (3rd edn, London, Penguin, 2003)

BRAZIER, M, *Medicine, Patients and the Law* (2nd edn, Harmondsworth, Penguin, 1992)

BRIDGE, C, 'Religious Beliefs and Teenage Refusal of Medical Treatment' (1999) 62 *MLR* 585

CALLAHAN, D, 'Bioethics as a Discipline' in Humber, JM and Almeder, RF, *Biomedical Ethics and the Law* (New York, Plenum, 1976)

CANE, P, 'A Warning about Causation' (1999) 115 *LQR* 21

CAPLAN, A (ed), *When Medicine Went Mad: Bioethics and the Holocaust* (Totowa, New Jersey, Humana Press, 1992)

CARREL, A, *Man, The Unknown* (New York, Harper and Row, 1939)

CHAPMAN, CB, *Physicians, Law, and Ethics* (New York, New York University Press, 1984)

CHIEF MEDICAL OFFICER, *Good Doctors, Safer Patients: Proposals to strengthen the System to Assure and Improve the Performance of Doctors and to Protect the Safety of Patients* (Department of Health, 2006)

COMMITTEE OF INQUIRY INTO HUMAN FERTILISATION and EMBRYOLOGY, *Report of the Committee of Inquiry into Human Fertilisation and Embryology* (Cmnd 9314, 1984)

CONRAD, LI, NEVE, M, NUTTON, V, PORTER, R, WEAR, A, *The Western Medical Tradition 800 BC to AD 1800* (Cambridge, Cambridge University Press, 1995)

CORNFORD, FM (trans), *The Republic of Plato* (New York and London, Oxford University Press, 1945)

DAVIES, M, 'The New Bolam' Another False Dawn for Medical Negligence?' (1996) 12 *Professional Negligence* 10

DEPARTMENT OF CONSTITUTIONAL AFFAIRS, *The Government's Response to the Scrutiny Committee's Report on the Draft Mental Incapacity Bill* (Cm 6121, 2004)

DEPARTMENT OF HEALTH, *Best Practice Guidance for Doctors and Other Health Professionals on the Provision of Advice and Treatment to Young People under Sixteen on Contraception, Sexual and Reproductive Health* (Department of Health, 2004)

DODDS-SMITH, I, 'Clinical Research' in Dyer, C (ed), *Doctors, Patients and the Law* (Oxford, Blackwell, 1992)

DWORKIN, R, *Life's Dominion* (New York, Vintage Books, 1994)

DYER, C (ed), *Doctors, Patients and the Law* (Oxford, Blackwell, 1992)

EMANUEL, E, *The Ends of Human Life- Medical Ethics in a Liberal Polity* (Cambridge Mass, Harvard University Press, 1991)

EBERT, RH, 'A Twentieth Century Retrospective', in Ginzberg, E (ed), *Medicine and Society- Clinical Decisions and Societal Values* (Boulder and London, Westview Press, 1987)

ENDELSTEIN, L, 'The Hippocratic Oath: Text, Translation and Interpretation', in Temkin, O and Temkin, CL (eds), *Ancient Medicine: Selected Papers of Ludwig Endelstein* (Baltimore, John Hopkins Press, 1967)

FENG, TK, 'Failure of Medical Advice: Trespass or Negligence?' (1987) 7 *Legal Studies* 149

GAYLIN, W, 'Foreword', in Gorovitz, S, Jameton, AL, Macklin, R, O'Connor, JM, Perrin, EV, St Clair, BP, Sherwin, S, *Moral Problems in Medicine* (London, Prentice Hall Inc, 1976)

GELFAND, M, *The Philosophy and Ethics of Medicine* (Edinburgh, E&S Livingstone Ltd, 1968)

GILLON, R, *Philosophical Medical Ethics* (Chichester, John Wiley & Sons, 1986)

GINZBERG, E (ed), *Medicine and Society- Clinical Decisions and Societal Values* (Boulder and London, Westview Press, 1987)

GLANNON, W, *Biomedical Ethics* (Oxford, Oxford University Press, 2004)

GLOVER, J, *Causing Death and Saving Lives* (Harmondsworth, Penguin, 1990)

GMC, *Good Medical Practice* (GMC, 1995)

GMC, *Good Medical Practice* (GMC, 1998)

GMC, *Good Medical Practice* (GMC, 2001)

GMC, *Good Medical Practice* (GMC, 2006)

GMC, *Professional Conduct and Discipline – Fitness to Practice* (GMC, 1993)

GMC, *Seeking Patients' Consent: The Ethical Considerations* (GMC, 1998)

GMC, *Withholding and Withdrawing Life-prolonging Treatments: Good Practice in Decision-Making* (GMC, 2002)

GOROVITZ, S, JAMETON, AL, MACKLIN, R, O'CONNOR, JM, PERRIN, EV, ST CLAIR, BP, SHERWIN, S, *Moral Problems in Medicine* (London, Prentice Hall Inc, 1976)

GOSTIN, L, 'Consent to Treatment: The Incapable Person' in Dyer, C (ed), *Doctors, Patients and the Law* (Oxford, Blackwell, 1992)

GRUBB, A, 'Clinical Negligence: Informed Consent and Causation' (2002) 10 *Medical Law Review* 322

GURNHAM, D, 'Losing the Wood For the Trees: Burke and the Court of Appeal' (2006) 14(2) *Medical Law Review* 253

HARRIS, J, *The Value of Life: An Introduction to Medical Ethics* (London, Routledge, 1994)

HERRING, J, *Medical Law and Ethics* (Oxford, Oxford University Press, 2006)

HILTON, B et al (eds), *Ethical Issues in Human Genetics: Genetic Counselling and the Use of Genetic Knowledge* (New York, Plenum, 1973)

HONORÉ, T, 'Medical non-disclosure, causation and risk: Chappel v Hart' (1999) 7 *Torts Law Journal* 1

HOUSE OF LORDS, HOUSE OF COMMONS, *Report of the Joint Committee on the Draft Mental Incapacity Bill* (HL Paper 189–1, 2003)

HOUSE OF LORDS, *Report of the Select Committee on Medical Ethics* (HL Paper 21-I, 1994)

HOUSE OF LORDS, *Report of the Select Committee on the Assisted Dying for the Terminally Ill Bill* (HL Paper 86-I, 2005)

HUMBER, JM and ALMEDER, RF, *Biomedical Ethics and the Law* (New York, Plenum, 1976)

JACKSON, E, *Medical Law: Text, Cases and Materials* (Oxford, Oxford University Press, 2006)

JOHNSON, A, *Pathways in Medical Ethics* (London, Edward Arnold, 1990)

JONES, M, 'But for' causation in actions for non-disclosure of risk' (2002) 18 *Professional Negligence* 192

JONES, M, 'Informed Consent and Other Fairy Stories' (1999) 7 *Medical Law Review* 103

JONES, WHS, *Hippocrates*, Volume II (Cambridge, Mass., Harvard University Press, 1923)

JONSEN, A, *The Birth of Bioethics* (New York, Oxford University Press, 1998)

KATZ, J, 'Abuse of Human Beings for the Sake of Science', in Caplan, A (ed), *When Medicine Went Mad: Bioethics and the Holocaust* (Totowa, New Jersey, Humana Press, 1992)

KENNEDY, I and GRUBB, A, *Medical Law* (3rd edn, London, Butterworths, 2000)

KENNEDY, I, 'Consent to Treatment: The Capable Person' in Dyer, C (ed), *Doctors, Patients and the Law* (Oxford, Blackwell, 1992)

KENNEDY, I, 'Patients, Doctors and Human Rights', in *Treat Me Right: Essays in Medical Law and Ethics* (Oxford, Clarendon Press, 1988)

KENNEDY, I, *The Unmasking of Medicine* (London, George Allen & Unwin, 1981)

KENNEDY, I, *Treat Me Right: Essays in Medical Law and Ethics* (Oxford, Clarendon Press, 1988)

KEOWN, J, *Euthanasia, Ethics and Public Policy* (Cambridge, Cambridge University Press, 2002)

LAW COMMISSION, *Mental Incapacity* (Law Com 231, 1995)

LEAKE, CD (ed), *Percival's Medical Ethics* (Baltimore, Williams and Wilkins, 1927 (reprint))

Learning From Bristol: The Report of the Public Inquiry into Children's Heart Surgery at the Bristol Royal Infirmary 1984–1995 (Cm 5207, 2001)

LORD CHANCELLOR'S DEPARTMENT, *Making Decisions* (Cm 4465, 1999)

LORD CHANCELLOR'S DEPARTMENT, *Who Decides? Making Decisions on Behalf of Mentally Incapacitated Adults* (Cm 3803, 1997)

LORD WOOLF, 'Are the Courts Excessively Deferential to the Medical Profession?' (2001) 9 *Medical Law Review* 1

MACINTYRE, A, 'Patients as Agents', in Spicker, S and Englehardt, HT (eds), *Philosophical Medical Ethics: Its Nature and Significance* (Dordrecht, D Reidel Publishing Co, 1977)

MACLEAN, A, 'Beyond Bolam and Bolitho' (2002) 5 *Medical Law International* 205

MACLEAN, S and MASON, JK, *Legal and Ethical Aspects of Healthcare* (Cambridge, Cambridge University Press, 2003)

MACLEAN, S, A *Patient's Right to Know: Information Disclosure, the Doctor and the Law* (Aldershot, Ashgate, 1989)

MASON, JK and Laurie, GT, *Mason and McCall Smith's Law and Medical Ethics* (7th edn, Oxford, Oxford University Press, 2006)

MASON, JK, and MCCALL SMITH, RA, *Law and Medical Ethics* (5th edn, London, Butterworths, 1998)

MCLEAN, S, *Old Law, New Medicine: Medical Ethics and Human Rights* (London, Pandora 1999)

MIOLA, J, 'Medical Law and Medical Ethics: Complementary or Corrosive' (2004) 6 *Medical Law International* 251

MONTGOMERY, J, 'Medical Law in the Shadow of Hippocrates' (1989) 52 *MLR* 566

MORISON, RS, 'Implications of Prenatal Diagnosis for the Quality of, and Right to, Human Life: Society as a Standard' in Hilton B, et al (eds), *Ethical Issues in Human Genetics: Genetic Counselling and the Use of Genetic Knowledge* (New York, Plenum, 1973)

NEWDICK, C, *Who Should We Treat?* (2nd edn, Oxford, Oxford University Press, 2005)

NORRIE, K, 'Common Practice and the Standard of Care in Medical Negligence' (1985) *Judicial Review* 145

PELLEGRINO, E, 'Toward an Expanded Medical Ethics: The Hippocratic Ethic Revisited' in Veatch, R (ed), *Cross Cultural Perspectives in Medical Ethics* (Boston, Jones and Bartlett, 1989)

PELLEGRINO, ED and THOMASMA, DC, *A Philosophical Basis of Medical Practice-Toward a Philosophy and Ethic of the Healing Professions* (New York, Oxford University Press, 1981)

PRABST BATTIN, M, *Ending Life: Ethics and the Way We Die* (Oxford, Oxford University Press, 2005)

RAMSEY, P, *The Patient as Person* (Yale University Press, New Haven, 1970)

ROSEN, G, 'Cameralism and the Concept of Medical Police' (1953) *27 Bulletin of the History of Medicine* 42

ROSEN, G, *A History of Public Health* (New York, MD Publications, 1958)

SCORER, G and WING, A (eds), *Decision Making in Medicine* (London, Edward Arnold Publishers Ltd, 1979)

SCORER, G, 'Moral Values, Law and Religion', in Scorer, G and Wing, A (eds), *Decision Making in Medicine* (London, Edward Arnold Publishers Ltd, 1979)

SCOTT, R, *Rights, Duties and the Body: Law and Ethics of the Maternal-Foetal Conflict* (Oxford, Hart, 2002)

SMITH, J, *The Shipman Inquiry: Fifth Report; Safeguarding Patients: Lessons from the Past – Proposals for the Future* (The Stationary Office, Cmnd 6394, 2004)

SMITH, WD, *The Hippocratic Tradition* (New York, Cornell University Press, 1979)

SPICKER, S and ENGLEHARDT, HT (eds), *Philosophical Medical Ethics: Its Nature and Significance* (Dordrecht, D Reidel Publishing Co, 1977)

STAPLETON, J, 'Cause-in-Fact and the Scope of Liability for Consequences' (2003) 119 *LQR* 388

STAUCH, M, 'Taking the Consequences for Failure to Warn of Medical Risks' (2000) 63 *MLR* 261

STRONG, PM, 'Collegial Authority', in Abrams, N and Buckner, D (eds), *Medical Ethics: A Clinical Textbook and Reference for the Health Care Professions* (Cambridge, Mass, MIT Press, 1983)

SZASZ, T, *The Theology of Medicine* (New York, Oxford University Press, 1979)

TEMKIN, O and TEMKIN, CL (eds), *Ancient Medicine: Selected Papers of Ludwig Endelstein* (Baltimore, John Hopkins Press, 1967)

THORNTON, R, 'Multiple Keyholders – Wardship and Consent to Medical Treatment' [1992] *CLJ* 34

VAUX, K, *Biomedical Ethics – Morality for the New Medicine* (New York, Harper and Row, 1968)

VEATCH, R (ed), *Cross Cultural Perspectives in Medical Ethics* (Boston, Jones and Bartlett, 1989)

VEATCH, R, *A Theory of Medical Ethics* (New York, Basic Books Inc, 1981)

VEATCH, R, *Medical Ethics* (Boston, Jones and Bartlett, 1989)

WEBB-PEPLOE, M, 'The Medical Profession', in Scorer G and Wing A (eds), *Decision Making in Medicine* (London, Edward Arnold Publishers Ltd, 1979)

WILLIAMS, G, *Textbook of Criminal Law* (2nd edn, London, Stevens, 1983)

Index